A History
of Childhood
and Disability

Philip L. Safford &
Elizabeth J. Safford

FOREWORD BY
Seymour Sarason

Teachers College
Columbia University
New York and London

Published by Teachers College Press, 1234 Amsterdam Avenue, New York, NY 10027

Library of Congress Cataloging-in-Publication Data
Safford, Philip L.
    A history of childhood and disability / Philip L. Safford &
Elizabeth J. Safford : foreword by Seymour Sarason.
        p.   cm.
    Includes bibliographical references and index.
    ISBN 0-8077-3485-3 (cloth : acid-free paper)
    1. Handicapped children—History. 2. Handicapped children—
Education—History. 3. Special education—History. I. Safford,
Elizabeth J., 1958– . II. Title.
    HV888.S23 1995
    362.4'083—dc20   95-36258

ISBN 0-8077-3485-3 (cloth)
Printed on acid-free paper
Manufactured in the United States of America
03 02 01 00 99 98 97 96   8 7 6 5 4 3 2 1

Contents

Foreword, by Seymour B. Sarason   v

Preface   vii

1   Childhood and Disability: A Legacy of Neglect   1
Historical Significance of Childhood   1
Persistence of Past Themes   3
The Middle Ages to the Renaissance   12

2   Enlightenment and Revolution   26
Foundations for a Pedagogy of Experience   26
"Curing" the Deaf   28
Natural Language   35
Thinkers and Healers   43

3   Childhood, Education, and Social Reform   55
Social Policy and Child-rearing   55
Schooling for All   63
Common Schools, Diverse Pupils   77

4   Deafness, Communication, and Identity   90
Experiences of Children   90
The American School   92
Conflicting Ideologies and Traditions   95
Alexander Graham Bell and the Oral Revival   100
A Family Affair   106
Conflicting Ideologies   109
Transmission: Genetic and Cultural   113

5   Blindness: Charity to Independence   122
Experiences of Children   122
Schools in Europe   124
Schools in the United States   127
The Chevalier and His "Brothers-in-Arms"   132
Helen and Teacher   137
Literacy   138
Day Classes   143

6 **Mental Retardation, Educability, and Worth**   **153**
  Vicissitudes of Progress   153
  Experiences of Children   154
  Extension of Reform: Howe and Seguin   155
  Institutional Models   158
  Interpretations of Mental Retardation   164
  Educability and Limits of Improvement   170
  Measuring Intelligence   175
  Day Classes   179

7 **Body, Mind, and Spirit: Children's Physical
  and Health Impairments**   **188**
  Cultural Imagery and Social Forces   188
  Experiences of Children   189
  Four Overviews   191
  Mortality and Risk in Childhood   200
  Settlement Workers and Volunteers   207
  War, Disability, and the Allied Health Professions   211
  School Health Services   216
  Agencies, Schools, and Special Classes   219

8 **Feared Victims: Dependent, Neglected, Disturbed,
  and Delinquent Youth**   **223**
  Innocent Victims and Willful Burdens   224
  Asylums for Orphans   229
  Management of Delinquents   232
  Child Guidance, Juvenile Justice, and Mental Health   242

9 **Children with Communication and
  Processing Disabilities**   **257**
  Evolution of a Knowledge Base for Special Education   257
  Communication Disorders   262
  Language Impairment   267
  Parent Advocacy and the Learning Disabilities "Movement"   277
  Redefinitions, Rediscoveries, and New Understandings   280

10 **Dimensions of a "New History"**   **286**
  "The Century of the Child"   286
  Diversity: The Context of Childhood Exceptionality   287
  Early Intervention and the "New Environmentalism"   295
  Coda   299

References   301
Index   327
About the Authors   342

Foreword

The literature in special education, as in so many other fields, tends to be narrow and specialized. That is not meant in criticism. The problems we study are complex, our resources are limited, and we have to be content with studying parts of a problem, in the hope that over time we will see matters more whole. That is all the more reason we should be grateful when individuals, like the authors of this book, take on the task of painting a scholarly canvas that permits us to see our particular field or interest in a broad, historical framework. In this instance the authors took on the truly Herculean task of tracing over the ages how conceptions of the diverse handicaps arose as a function of time, place, culture, religion, and more. There have been similar books, but they concerned one or two types of handicap (e.g., blindness, epilepsy). But the authors of this book wisely saw that what we needed was a comprehensive historical account that would begin to fill an intellectual-conceptual-social-professional void in the literature. They have done their job admirably, giving us the guts of those histories in a concise way and allowing the reader to see the larger picture both in the past and present.

One message comes through loud and clear in this book: people in each historical era had no doubt that they understood not only the origins and nature of the different handicaps but also what was the best way of responding to the afflicted. It is true that in many of the eras there were differences of opinion, but each camp had no doubt that they had a monoply on the "truth." They were wrong, of course, in whole or part, and that is what adds to the instruction and fascination of the story this book tells. It also should cause the reader to ponder this question: Granted that we have come far from those earlier eras, but is it not possible, indeed likely, that much about which we are not in doubt today will be brought into doubt in the future, that our theories and educational practices will be seen as antique, quaint, museum pieces? Have we reached the point where what we think we know and how we implement that knowledge are independent of our time, place, culture, and morality?

This book deserves a wide professional audience that needs stimulation to go beyond the parochial boundaries that parochial training reinforces. I need not tell the reader that this is an era of specialization, which is quite a mixed blessing. Candor requires that I say that I consider it a semi-disaster. There is a larger picture about which we should be informed and this book can help the reader see that larger picture.

This book should be of interest to the general reader, if only because it tells that reader that in all eras "experts" were not without their feet of clay. That is no criticism of experts; it is a truism this book well documents. What the experts tell us informs social policy, as it should, but that is no warrant for not taking seriously that the verdicts of history are not all that kind to the experts of the past, as they will not be to most experts of the present. History, as this book demonstrates, is the cruelest of critics. It is also a most instructive one.

Seymour B. Sarason
Yale University

Preface

There are diverse reasons for reading, and for writing, history—to learn from past errors so as to avoid repeating them; to grasp great themes and forces that continue to impinge on individuals, groups, and nations; to understand and appreciate one's own heritage, or that of others; to be better informed in the conduct of one's work, perhaps of one's life. This book, motivated by all those objectives, was undertaken at a time of crisis for children with special needs or "at-risk," and of seemingly unprecedented societal change affecting them. Possibly lessons of the past can provide a compass for the adults—parents, professionals, and policymakers—who inevitably determine the fate of children, and thus of society, indeed of humanity.

In recent years, the history of childhood has burgeoned as a field of scholarship but, with the notable exception of Deaf studies at Gallaudet University, that of exceptionality has been more a history of service providers than of persons served. While the historical record concerning persons considered exceptional is a rich and, we believe, a fascinating one, it is thus not without significant gaps. One's ability to know what it was like, or is like, to be, or to be considered, "different" is constrained by one's own life experiences, a limitation only beginning to be breached through efforts to present the perspectives of exceptional persons themselves. Among history's most eloquent spokespersons have been persons who themselves experienced sensory or other physical disabilities or mental illness. Yet, much of the record concerning exceptional *children*, virtually all in the case of retardation, concerns the beliefs, goals, and achievements of their benefactors.

The late Burton Blatt wrote that no professional enterprise has so ignored its history—to its great detriment—as has special education. But of course the history of a profession (and various professions, or professional specializations, exist precisely because of human exceptionality) is not the same as the history of its "clients," as they, in their own voices, might recount it. Only within the past two decades have scholars systematically endeavored to obtain what Robert Bogdan calls "insiders' versions," but where the historical record yields such accounts, as indeed it does, they are in every case those of adults. This book is intended as a history of *children*, specifically of those children who have been considered exceptional, and therefore it can only be a part of the history of exceptional individuals.

This choice of focus compounds the problem of perspective, for even autobiographical or other literary depictions of childhood experience are filtered through a reconstructive lens of maturity. It is also perilous, for "child orientations" have highly negative connotations for adults with disabilities, especially those with societal labels signifying cognitive impairment, who have been infantilized in many ways, spoken of as children, and kept in a childlike state of dependency. And yet, the very fact of children's dependence on adults, to tell their stories as well as to protect, nurture, and advocate for them, seemed itself reason to undertake this history. Until late in the 19th century, special schooling, if provided at all, often did not begin until adolescence, long assumed to be the "formative period." That fact, with all its implications concerning beliefs about childhood, suggested the value of a contextual approach. Accordingly, we consulted studies by a wide range of social historians, as well as literary sources, biographies, newspaper articles, and various official documents, in seeking understanding of the historical context in which exceptional children have lived and services for them have been provided.

While "categories" of exceptionality are socially constructed and arbitrary, just as are other categorizations of humanity, such as race, each seems to have its own themes, which guide the organization of this book. The first three chapters are explicitly contextual, although Chapter 2, placing the origins of specialized education in the context of rationalist philosophy and humanistic movements, specifically concerns deafness, blindness, the beginnings of moral treatment, and the classic story of Itard and Victor. Chapters 4, 5, and 6 consider, respectively, deafness, blindness, and retardation, the "conditions" traditionally associated with specialized approaches. Chapter 7, on physical and health impairment, and 8, on emotional and behavioral impairment, tell quite different stories, each influenced by its own facets of social history, such as wars, epidemics, scientific developments, and demographic changes, which also, in combination with advocacy (especially by parents), gave rise to the further differentiation of childhood exceptionality, considered in Chapter 9. Chapter 10 is intended as at once a brief synthesis of themes, an epilogue, and a prospective for a "new history," now emerging and yet to be written, of children considered exceptional.

In attempting to synthesize different "histories," we are unapologetically indebted to such scholars as Berthold Lowenfeld, Richard Scheerenberger, Harlan Lane, Ruth Bender, and others for their ground-breaking and comprehensive treatments of manifestations of exceptionality. We did not attempt to do again what they have already done, but sought in this book to bring together and synthesize information (and interpretation) already avail-

able on the history of blindness, mental retardation, and deafness with accounts of areas less studied: children's physical and health impairments,
emotional and behavioral problems, and language and learning disorders.
Rather than eschewing a "history-of-the-reformers" approach, we found it
both unavoidable and useful to look closely, through biographies, letters,
and assessments by their contemporaries, at the lives and work of a parade
of figures who have influenced the course of history for exceptional children—
unavoidable because of their extraordinary influence, useful because we, and
our anticipated readers, are their heirs. Can we learn from their wisdom,
find inspiration in their conviction, learn from their mistakes? This book itself
represents acknowledgment of debt to past leaders, reformers, visionaries,
and innovators, though, like them, we recognize our greater debt to children and their families—those of the past and those we would empower today
and in the future.

On a more concrete level, we gratefully acknowledge the assistance many
persons provided in helping us access archival collections, particularly those
of the American Foundation for the Blind; Elwyn Institute; Berea Children's
Home and Family Services; Teachers College, Columbia University; and
Allen Memorial Medical Library of Case Western Reserve University, as well
as a host of children's service agencies and advocacy and professional organizations who provided us with helpful materials. The substantive assistance
of many others is also gratefully acknowledged, particularly that of Louise
Bates Ames, Vincent Arduin, John Caddey, Thomas Fagan, Catherine
LeForme, Caven Mclouglin, William Morse, and Marjorie Ward, as is assistance with research provided by Elizabeth Brennan, Ronna Davis, Kriselle
Fox, Harriet Frey, Robert Steele, and Roberta Thoryk. We are particularly
grateful for the wise, patient, supportive, and extraordinarily knowledgeable
help of our editor at Teachers College Press, Brian Ellerbeck.

Philip L. Safford
Elizabeth J. Safford

CHAPTER 1

Childhood and Disability: A Legacy of Neglect

HISTORICAL SIGNIFICANCE OF CHILDHOOD

"The progress of child-saving work appears very slow," Amos W. Butler of Indiana told the 1901 Conference on Charities and Correction (1901, p. 210), though this chairman of the Committee on Destitute and Neglected Children anticipated "the children's century . . . [when] the most important work will be the elevation of all childhood" (p. 213). While the Century of the Child has seen "whole industries . . . devoted to making children happy, healthy, and wise" (Greenleaf, 1978, p. xiii), a national commission warned in 1990 that "never before has one generation of American children been less healthy, less cared for, or less prepared for life than their parents were at the same age" (National Commission on the Role . . . , 1990, p. 3). Child malnutrition, abuse, and exploitation, like poverty, have always been with us, though many perils for children cross socioeconomic boundaries. The "long-forgotten child" (Despert, 1965, p. 16) is by no means at last safe, secure, and understood.

Defined negatively, childhood is the absence of adulthood; children are incomplete, unfinished, in process, "minors," until recently, as Margaret Mead (1955, p. 3) noted, even "newcomers" as objects of study. Just as most children's lives do not reflect the enormous importance we accord childhood today, the child of history stands paradoxically at the center of human society and at its margin. While enculturation of the young is a universal priority, valuing progeny in the abstract does not necessarily imply feeling for a particular child, nor does parental love depend on awareness of *childhood* (Aries, 1962). We have a double paradox: children can be valued yet not recognized as individuals, while genuine fondness may coexist with ignorance of the nature of childhood itself.

1

Conditional Nurture

Maria Piers (1978) wrote that in the 18th century "nobody was as badly off as a young, poor servant woman . . . except for her out-of-wedlock child" (p. 62). For many children things got worse, as industrialists discovered that "children, especially poor ones, constituted the world's most inexpensive labor force" (p. 80). The consequence of that discovery was portrayed vividly by Dickens and in Zola's images, in *Germinal*, of small, naked children working long hours in cramped, airless mine tunnels. But such conditions, and worse, exist today, attested daily by accounts of virtual industrial enslavement, starvation and trauma, systematic murder of street children as a social control measure in other lands, and numbing statistics on malnutrition, prenatal drug exposure, violence, and child suicide in the United States. For persons with disabilities, self-advocacy and technology have brought great progress. But social conditions, and even social policy, continue to place many children at risk, and when norm-violating behavior results, children are more likely to be blamed than helped. Mistreatment and neglect have never been the fate of all. Decisions to nurture or abandon were, and are, predicated on the perceived needs of the group; thus, children's fate has always been outside their own control, a matter of chance or custom. But appreciation of the uniqueness of childhood fosters awareness of each child's uniqueness, and recognition of special needs *among* children has been linked to awareness of the special needs *of* children.

When "the devil was everywhere, and the earth was his empire" (Zilboorg, 1941, p. 163), a "child was nurtured on condition . . . that it was of the proper sex, that economic conditions were good, that it had no mark of the devil on it, and that it was not the product of an illicit union" (Greenleaf, 1978, p. 1). The "mark of the devil" might have been a blemish, a cleft palate, a clubfoot, more or less than the usual number of fingers or toes. Many newborns with anomalies were considered changelings, offspring of fairies substituted for a stolen child. If not satanic or elfin mischief, "giving birth to a monster that cannot be a legitimate child of her husband" might represent punishment for a wife's presumptive infidelity, prompting "'the frantic search for the father'" (Shahar, 1990, p. 336). Since the church forbade infanticide, a child who in other societies might have been exposed was likely in this world to be abandoned, if fortunate entrusted to the care of others. While demonism waned, fear of deviance persisted, as did the need to ascribe blame; as the 20th century dawned, children with retardation were cared for, yet considered a menace from which society must be protected. Such conditional nurture has always been the lot of children; the "conditions" might change, but a child's inability to choose the circumstances of birth and upbringing has not.

PERSISTENCE OF PAST THEMES

Exceptional Risk

Various factors have influenced attitudes of groups toward their deviant members. What is considered deviant, and the salience of certain forms of deviance, has always been culture-specific, depending on the priority accorded certain abilities. The very notion of *specific learning disability*, the largest classification of exceptional children in American schools, is not meaningful in some societies. Yet the implied cultural-utilitarian formula does not explain, assuming the importance primitive peoples must have ascribed to strength, stamina, and sensory acuity, archaeological and anthropological evidences of protection and inclusion of members with physical and sensory impairments (Scheerenberger, 1983, pp. 5–6). Nor is the idea of inexorable progress in treatment of people with disabilities or of children entirely valid. The broad "eras" often identified do not represent discrete periods or stages through which human society has passed, abandoning practices of one era as the next is born. Vestiges of older beliefs remain, even today. No one would assert that humanity has left behind cruelty, apathy, ignorance, and fear, and that is surely true of attitudes toward persons with disabilities.

Successive eras of extermination, ridicule, asylum, and education are usually identified, but while the era of education is commonly said to have begun with Itard and Victor, the "wild boy of Aveyron," extermination, ridicule, and asylum have not disappeared. The horrors of systematic extermination under the Nazi regime continue to be revealed and infanticide, considered a sin in the Middle Ages, continues, even in industrialized nations (Powell, Aiken, & Smylie, 1982), as when surgical correction of gastrointestinal complications, otherwise routinely provided, has been withheld from newborns with Down syndrome. Although denial of medical treatment constitutes unlawful discrimination, debate continues over Baby Doe issues of "who shall survive."

While in some societies persons with disabilities had been accorded dignity, a shift in Western culture from extermination to *ridicule* came with the beginning of the Christian era, when Romans could purchase a human being with physical deformities for amusement (Durant, 1944). Dwarfs, venerated in antiquity, were kept by emperors as jesters (Wood, 1868), and "fools" provided entertainment for the wealthy and powerful. Exploitation through exhibition, which survives today in sideshows and tabloids, was common in the 18th century (Bogdan, 1988). As late as 1815, parents could, for a penny, take their children for a Sunday outing to view the inmates of London's Bethlehem Hospital, known as "Bedl'm," displayed for public amusement (Foucault, 1965, p. 68). Despite moral treatment reforms, this practice continued, even in the hospital Benjamin Franklin helped found in Pennsylvania. Ridicule in the form of jokes associated with physical or cognitive impairment has been commonly viewed as socially acceptable; it is yet expressed in colloquialisms, cartoon characterizations, and even such aberrant practices as "dwarf tossing."

Laws have established society's responsibility to educate all children with disabilities, not just to provide custodial care, but deinstitutionalization, the presumptive end of the era of asylum, has not realized the vision of 19th-century reformers. While few endorse "putting away" their fellow humans, family-style group homes are accepted only if "not in my back yard." This account describes the era of education of children considered exceptional, but the phrase does not denote a discrete period of time so much as a long, uneven process of change. It suggests a perspective that continues to evolve, that exceptional children are able to benefit from adult advocacy and contribute to society as unique individuals. This odyssey must begin with what has always been the most basic concern of humankind.

Survival

In *The Republic*, Plato (trans. 1928) offers this counsel: "The proper officers will take the offspring of the good parents to the pen or fold, and there they will deposit them with certain nurses who dwell in a separate quarter; but the offspring of the inferior, or the better when they chance to be deformed, will be put away in some mysterious, unknown place, as they should be" (p. 413). Three recurring themes are captured in this terse formula: eugenic assumptions, consignment of children to the care of others, and disposal of those who are rejected. We are not told what is to be the fate of those who are "put away," or the nature of the "mysterious, unknown place," but plainly they are to be disposed of. Plato was not the first to recommend this course of action, nor would he be the last. Aristotle, in the *Politics*, advocated "a law that no *deformed* child shall live" (p. 315). But the implied importance of immediate disposal suggests another theme associated with infanticide in the past and as "a current social reality appearing in comparatively 'normal' circumstances" (Piers, 1978, p. 14): the phenomenon of *attachment*. While throughout history child-killing, especially by a parent, has been regarded with horror, "the murder of newborn infants . . . can be an accepted norm" (Shahar, 1990, p. 126).

In Sparta and Athens, child-rearing was explicitly in the service of the state, in the former to prepare for war, in the latter for peace. Under the laws of Lycurgus, each newborn was brought to a panel of elders and if judged strong was entrusted to the state for military training, which began in infancy; those found unfit were exposed. In Athens, cultural rather than military training was the focus, a newborn's fate determined by the father, to live or to be disposed of "in clay vessels . . . left by the wayside" (French, 1932, p. 33), actually a form of abandonment, with the implied hope that some "stranger" might care for the baby (Boswell, 1988). The Roman Law of the Twelve Tables made children property of the father, who as *paterfamilias* could command a slave to set an unwanted infant adrift in the Tiber, in a basket designed for that purpose, or invoke the right of *abdicatio* to expel a difficult child from the household or sell a child into slavery (Durant, 1944).

The decision to abandon a newborn had to be made during the first eight days, and since some impairments would not have been apparent, we can assume that many exceptional children survived. Moreover, rejecting a newborn, as Boswell (1988) notes, was not the same as killing it outright: "Although Roman law and custom apparently allowed parents to kill deformed children . . . there is virtually no evidence about what families under the empire did with such offspring" (p. 106). As the empire expanded, however, infanticide as a general practice increased, until Augustus, through his wife's urging, instituted measures to restore family life and alleviate the lot of increasing numbers of poor people—key factors bearing on infanticide. But infants continued to be abandoned. In the first century, this often took the form of leaving infants at the base of the Columna Lactaria, to be picked up by state-supplied wet nurses—dubious rescue, for many were mutilated to enhance their appeal as beggars, though Seneca opined that they were fortunate "inasmuch as their parents had cast them out" (Boswell, 1988, p. 106). Many survived for a life of mendicancy, but many more could not endure the hardships of such a childhood.

Boswell (1988) argues that, while historians have conflated child abandonment and infanticide, the former was often the alternative to the latter. Even "exposure" (*exposito*) of newborns does not necessarily imply an intent to destroy: "The overwhelming belief in the ancient world was that abandoned children were picked up and reared by someone else" (p. 131). Indeed, the legend of Rome's origins involves abandoned infant twins, Romulus and Remus. A more compelling motive to destroy rather than abandon, he suggests, was fear of inadvertent incest, a pervasive theme in classic literature and myth. In antiquity and in even earlier societies we see a range—from acceptance and care to rejection and abandonment—of children, elderly persons, and persons with disabilities who, while certainly at risk, were by no means uniformly destroyed. Archaeological evidence reveals instances of relatively long life, group inclusion of members with physical impairments, and even attempts at surgical correction (Lowenfeld, 1975).

Shaman and Physician

Surgical treatments were practiced in prehistory, such as *trephination* to expel the presumed source of such conditions as hydrocephaly and epilepsy through an opening in the skull, evidenced by necklaces made from circular pieces of cranial bone ("rondelles"), probably worn as amulets. The spirit world was invoked both in accounting for and attempting to cure illness and impairment. Though this theme of attribution to supernatural forces recurs throughout history, systematization of medical knowledge in the great early civilizations fostered understanding of exceptionality in the context of nature. Precisely when disease began to be viewed as a natural phenomenon, rather than visited on humans from the spirit world, is uncertain, though scriptural evidence reveals that the Hebrews recognized contagion (Abt, 1965, p. 27). A papyrus with the first known reference to the brain suggests that Egyptian physicians understood it as the seat of control of the lower limbs and associated speech abnormalities with head injuries, millennia before aphasia was described (Breasted, 1954). Egyptian medicine was especially notable in identifying many of the drugs in use even today and in delineating vision problems; the Ebers Papyrus, written between 1553 and 1550 BCE, discovered in the Necropolis of Thebes in 1872, listed 20 distinct eye diseases (French, 1932, p. 31). That there is little evidence of application of this sophisticated medical knowledge to children with disabilities does not imply lack of concern for children or for exceptionality; belief in the soul's immortality was incompatible with infanticide, and persons with disabilities were provided a place, sometimes privileged status, in society.

Greek physicians advanced in classifying maladies and differentiating treatments on the basis of presumed cause. Moreover, while in mythology the gods might take away a person's mind, and oracular powers were attributed to one experiencing mental illness, physicians began to consider behavioral deviance within their purview, linking spiritual phenomena to the physical by a kind of vital force, by which the soul regulated the body. Heraclitus (535–475 BCE) noted that individuals might perceive the same reality differently, and Hippocrates (460–370 BCE), who described phobias and such states as postpartum depression, believed that mental and physical complaints revealed imbalance among the basic substances of blood, phlegm, yellow bile, and black bile, located respectively in the heart, liver, spleen, and brain (Zilboorg, 1941). Ascribing madness to black bile rather than "possession" clearly represented an effort to establish a basis in nature for understanding human behavior.

Considering empiricism the prime index of medical progress, the eminent medical historian Zilboorg (1941) called Plato's (427–347 BCE) "mysticism . . . a step backward" (p. 45), but Aristotle (384–322 BCE) again attempted to address the problem of differential human behavior, and the link between spiritual and physical, in terms of natural phenomena. Early attempts to establish the location of the soul had placed it in the diaphragm, but Aristotle thought its locus was the heart. To explain how people interpreted information, then translated it into speech and action, he posited a *sensorium commune*, a concept with profound ramifications for beliefs about deafness, for it ascribed to hearing, speech, and reason a common source. This notion did not account for the propensity of deaf persons to communicate through manual signing, which had been observed throughout recorded history. Even as inquiry flourished in Greek civilization, the dogma prevailed that deaf persons, being incapable of speech, are therefore incapable of reason.

Aristotle's (trans. 1910) actual pronouncement in "History of Animals" (355 BCE) was that "men that are deaf are in all cases dumb; that is, they can make vocal sounds, but they cannot speak." That the words he employed—*kophi* (deaf) and *eneos* (speechless)—acquired connotations of "stupidity" was more than an unfortunate coincidence, given his notion of the sensorium commune, but his statement was often taken out of context to legitimate what common sense seemed to make obvious: It was "ridiculous to try to teach language where it did not exist naturally" (Bender, 1970, p. 20). One might suppose that casual observation revealed enough exceptions to call into question the invariant coexistence of deafness and lack of speech. In fact, although dogma effectively precluded education for centuries, the Code of Laws formulated in 530 CE by Justinian required that a guardian be appointed for a deaf individual *unless the person were literate,* having been postlingually deafened.

Although the assumption that a person born deaf was physically incapable of speech remained unquestioned, Claudius Galen (138–201 CE), the greatest of the Roman physicians, advanced a more sophisticated explanation. Recognizing the linkage of mental phenomena with brain structure and function, Galen posited a center in the brain as the common origin of both speech and hearing, injury to which would affect both. His analysis, though wrong, was remarkably advanced for its time and, like his other theories, based on neuroanatomical research. Attributing differences in what he termed *temperament* to degrees of softness or dryness of nerve tissue, he related soft and hard portions of tissue to differences in observed behavior, anticipating by centuries the discovery of afferent and efferent nerve functions (Boring, 1950, p. 27). Positing varying degrees of moistness of tissue, Galen, as had Hippocrates, attributed a role to climate in both etiology and treatment, another notion revisited centuries later in connection with cretinism, as well as tuberculosis.

Also in the Hippocratic tradition, Roman medicine delineated such conditions as mania, melancholia, hallucinatory behavior, and hysteria, the last believed a condition peculiar to women, anticipating 19th-century theories. Notwithstanding their nosological sophistication, physicians often prescribed primitive treatments intended to expel an offending substance from the body of the sufferer. Sometimes the means of exorcising the presumed cause was relatively innocuous, if ineffective, but other "cures," such as castration of epileptics, could not, from our perspective, meet the cardinal standard—first of all, do no harm. Yet recommendations for humane treatment of insane persons of Galen's predecessor, Soranus of Ephesus (98–138 CE), foreshadowed the *moral treatment* introduced late in the 18th century.

Characterized as "the falling sickness" and "the sacred disease," epilepsy has throughout history been misunderstood and attributed to emotional disturbance, moral defect, and demonic possession. Until early in the 20th century, "epileptics and paralytics" were assumed to have intractable forms of "idiocy." The pairing suggests that the conditions continued to be seen as linked, as they had been in antiquity (Temkin, 1945, p. 48). Since seizuring may occur with cerebral palsy (*symptomatic epilepsy*), and both reflect neurological involvement, that is perhaps not surprising. (Later, the term *idiopathic epilepsy* was used to denote seizure disorder where cause is unknown.) Seizure disorder, among other conditions, has inspired all manner of intrusive measures to vacuate "pernicious humours"; allowing a presumptive invader to leave via trephination, driving it out through exorcism, bleeding, leeches, and purging suggest a common thread. A 13th-century text recommended opening the skulls of "melancholics, epileptics, and others" to allow the humours to escape (p. 74).

Though seizure disorder was known to the ancient Egyptians and Hebrews, and is referenced in the Code of Hammurabi, the origin of the word *epilepsy* is Greek, from the word meaning "seizure," a person with epilepsy being "one seized." In his treatise "On the Sacred Disease," written about 400 BCE, Hippocrates attacked magical explanations and charlatans' claims of cures. Scriptural allusions suggest possession and associations with mental aberration, as in the case of a boy whose condition is described to Jesus, who drives out the demon, as "lunacy" (Mark 9:14–29; Matt. 17:14–20; Luke 9:37–43). Long after Charcot distinguished epilepsy from hysteria, the former biogenic, the latter psychogenic, and Jackson formulated a systematic neurological theory, an authority (Temkin, 1945) owned that "the nature of the disease is as yet obscure" (p. vii). Even subsequent medical advances did not end prejudice, as many persons today could attest.

Convulsions, so frequently observed in infancy that epilepsy was sometimes known as the "children's disease," were not differentiated from chronic seizure disorder until late in the 15th century, although there had long been conjecture that they might have different causes. Galen thought that when seizures appeared in adolescence, bad diet, poor health regimen, or drunkenness were implicated; in childhood, sudden fright might be responsible. A later Germanic belief was that nocturnal visitation by an evil spirit would so frighten a small child as to induce convulsions; thus, nurses were cautioned not to frighten children with folktales. As for other maladies, hereditary transmission was also blamed, though merely witnessing a seizure could cause one to seize. Esquirol ordered separation of epileptics from insane persons in the Bicetre to avoid "contagion"—a concern that no doubt prompted later separation in institutions for persons with retardation—but until 1838 children experiencing seizures and adult "incurables" were treated alike (Temkin, 1945, p. 245).

That development occurred in a milieu congenial to interest both in children and in exceptionality that emerged gradually following a "great decline . . . in man's attitude toward himself" (Zilboorg, 1941, p. 95) from the time of Galen to the Renaissance, with superstition and talisman embedded in Christianity. Throughout the Middle Ages, while scholars pursued theological interests, among the people at large a superstitious religiosity prevailed. But faith inspired many parents, rich and poor, to make supplication to saints for a child's cure. An arduous pilgrimage to a shrine offered a less fearsome prospect than surgery, and often in fact a more hopeful one: The "cure rate" for pilgrims was probably at least as good as that for patients (Shahar, 1990, p. 149). Religious traditions have always greatly influenced the treatment of persons with disabilities and children in general.

The Least of These

The historical relationship of religion and exceptionality has been paradoxical; beliefs might benefit persons with disabilities or place them in greater jeopardy. In prehistory, physical and behavioral deviance were attributed to spirits animating the natural world, their powers invoked for protection and cure, their mischief counteracted by exorcism and trephination. Necrophagia was practiced to internalize powers of feared enemies, attributes of revered members of one's own group, or spirits responsible for an affliction, though not the affliction itself.

Children today are sometimes placed at risk by their elders' religious beliefs, but nowhere has that occurred in more horrifying manner than in the practice of human sacrifice. The prophet Jeremiah (7:30) decried as an abomination that "they have built the high places of Tophet, which is in the valley of the son of Hinnom, to burn their sons and their daughters in the fire; which I commanded them not, neither came it into my heart." Child sacrifice may never have been widespread, but that it has occurred at all says much about the precariousness of children's lives in societies of true believers, like the advanced civilization of ancient Carthage, where "thousands upon thousands of infants were slaughtered to appease the gods Ba'al Hammon and Tamit. The charred ashes of the victims were swept up into ceramic urns and buried in pits capped with funerary markings" (Soren, Ben Khader, & Slima, 1990, p. 124). Of a tophet discovered in 1921 in Tunisia, Plutarch had recounted that persons with no child of their own to offer would buy a child of desperately poor parents, to be slain before their eyes. A mother's tears or cry would invalidate the sacrifice, and the purchase sum had to be returned. Whether a child with an impairment was more or less likely to meet this fate is a matter of speculation, but for a child of the poor life was, as it has always been, most tenuous.

The association of deviance and spiritual visitation has a long history. Many scriptural passages allude to persons voluntarily or involuntarily hosting an evil force from the spirit world; Leviticus contains the injunction that a "wizard" or person with a "familiar spirit" should be stoned. This connection, invoked in literature, such as Alice Walker's *The Temple of My Familiar*, antedated the medical advances in Egypt, Greece, and the Orient, but reemerged with new virulence in medieval Europe when "familiars," usually animals, were believed elements of the witch's satanic arsenal. In some traditions, newborns with impairments had special significance as messengers of the gods. While the "message" was often one of retribution for parental sin, it sometimes involved attribution of spiritual powers, as to a blind person or one with epilepsy or dwarfism. In Mesopotamia, birth of a malformed child was thought a sign presaging events for the parents or for the entire group (Oppenheim, 1977, p. 221). Naturally, such events had to be interpreted by one wearing the mantle of religious authority. But the teachings of the major world religions and ethical systems are marked by injunctions to care for and protect persons with impairments or who were otherwise in need. Its eye-for-an-eye provisions notwithstanding, the Code of Hammurabi (1948–1905 BCE), sixth in the line of Amorite kings of Babylon, mandated protection of children, especially if orphaned, widows, and the poor.

Among precepts in the Torah involving exceptionality are the injunctions "Thou shalt not curse the deaf, nor put a stumbling block before the blind" (Lev. 14:14) and "Cursed be he that maketh the blind to wander out of the way" (Deut. 27:18; "who misleads a blind man on the road" in the Revised Standard Version). While the literal meaning suggests refraining from cruelty, an intent to counsel helpfulness can be inferred. Reference to retardation is found in the Koran's injunction to be kind to "those without reason" (Kanner, 1964, p. 3). Such accounts of Jesus' healing as that in Mark 7:32–37 imply attribution of deviant speech to deafness, but other references suggest it was sometimes considered a primary disability viewed in much the same way as impaired vision or hearing; Moses, protesting his inadequacy to the task the Lord had assigned him, described himself as "slow of speech, and of a slow tongue" (Exod. 4:10). Biblical accounts suggest that deviant speech, while experienced as handicapping, elicited neither pity nor scorn, though we might infer a belief that it could be overcome through faith, talent, or determination. Though not in the context of religion, other striking instances in antiquity suggest the latter, notably Aesop, the composer of fables, Aristotle himself, reputedly a stutterer, and Demosthenes (382–322 BCE), who tradition has it overcame his impairment to become a great orator. What are now considered language impairments were viewed differently; *glossolalia,* or "speaking in tongues," suggested spirituality.

There are also negative references, however, suggesting taint and unworthiness. In Leviticus 21:16–20 we read of proscriptions concerning priestly privilege:

> And the Lord said to Moses, "Say to Aaron, None of your descendants throughout their generations who has a blemish may approach to offer the bread of his God. For no one who has a blemish shall draw near, a man blind or lame, or one who has a mutilated face or a limb too long, or a man who has an injured foot or an injured hand, or a hunchback, or a dwarf, or a man with a defect in his sight or an itching disease or scabs or crushed testicles."

That, incidentally, is the only biblical reference to dwarfs, although Zaccheus, "little in stature," sought a better vantage point to see Jesus, and various historical figures such as Aesop, even rulers such as Attila, were unverifiably rumored to have been dwarfs (Ablon, 1984). Biblical proscriptions did not mean that persons with impairments were to be shunned. Rather, a compassionate impulse was expressed, as in codified stipulations that responsibility for the care of persons with disabilities was to be entrusted to a guardian. Implicit in such provisions, of course, was an assumption that these persons could not manage their own affairs, own property, or marry, excepting deaf persons able to use signing to contract marriage (Bender, 1970).

Monotheistic systems advanced a strongly positive view of children as "an heritage of the Lord" (Ps. 127:3), and Judaic tradition also reflects awareness of differences in children's abilities and learning styles. Citing analogies to "sponge, funnel, strainer, and sieve," Despert (1965) describes four classifications: "pupils swift to hear and swift to lose . . . , pupils slow to hear and slow to lose, pupils swift to hear and slow to lose ('a happy lot'), pupils slow to hear and swift to lose ('an evil lot')" (p. 3). It would be tempting to see in such recognition of individual differences the birth of the "era of education" of exceptional students, especially since teachers were enjoined not to abandon the more challenging ones but to provide extra help. However, it is not likely that even the pupils considered "slow to hear and swift to lose," or like "sieves," included those whose impairments markedly set them apart. We can be fairly certain they were not considered candidates for education at all, nor would they be for centuries. But a period of history during which *asylum* was, at least nominally, the norm clearly was inspired by religious tradition.

Christianizing of the empire brought steps to halt abuses of children, as Constantine I issued edicts forbidding infanticide, selling children into slavery, and maiming them as beggars, while initiating measures to assist parents too poor to support their children and mechanisms for formal adoption. In 325 the Council of Nicaea decreed that hostelries for the sick and poor be established in each village, some becoming mainly asylums for children. With infanticide proscribed, mothers were urged to leave unwanted infants at a church rather than abandon them where they might die. The Council of Vaison, in 442, provided for a period of sanctuary while efforts were made to locate parents (Scheerenberger, 1983). After the destruction of the empire, efforts to provide asylum for unwanted children continued; the first of the foundling homes that eventually proliferated throughout Europe was established in 786 by Daltheus, Archbishop of Milan. Although these were intended to provide not only asylum but basic nurturance, it appears that most of the children died. What had been known since antiquity about children's physical needs may have been forgotten, for contagion clearly contributed to these appalling death rates. But lack of understanding of children's emotional needs and consequences of maternal deprivation must also be considered; throughout history, infants taken in for prolonged institutional care have been likely to deteriorate and die, victims of "infanticide by incidental neglect" (Piers, 1978, p. 18).

THE MIDDLE AGES TO THE RENAISSANCE

The period known as the Middle Ages is generally described as beginning with the destruction of the empire in 476 and ending, over some two centuries, with the dawning of the Renaissance, but the dominant child-rearing and educational conventions had earlier origins, notably in *The Confessions* of St. Augustine (356–430). Reflecting on his own memories of childhood, Augustine attributed to children, themselves the result of sin, inherent propensities for evil; children had to be redeemed from the sinful state into which they were born, saved from their own nature. Yet New Testament images of children, familiarly reassuring to modern Christians, were cited throughout the Middle Ages; even Augustine thought that, compared with adult sinfulness, that of a child is less reprehensible because committed with more innocence (Shahar, 1990). Nonetheless, the new doctrine of original sin had profound implications for children with disabilities, and for their parents;

no longer considered holy innocents, these children represented punishment for parental sin or the workings of Satan. But they were by no means unique in maintaining a tenuous existence. During this period great cathedrals were built, universities founded, and enduring literature created, but for most people this was a time of famine and disease, ignorance and superstition, and grinding struggle for subsistence.

Children as Pawns

Children generally had a precarious existence throughout this period, but as always experiences varied subject to "conditions." Well into the Christian era boys, as well as girls, were commonly sold into prostitution or it was imposed on them subsequent to abandonment, but reforms instituted by Justinian in 529 included measures to curb this. As in antiquity, abandonment was motivated by "prophecy, adultery, incest, illegitimacy, and jealousy," but it was also an alternative to infanticide (Boswell, 1988, p. 213).

A "Christian innovation [constituting] . . . the most humane form of abandonment ever devised in the West" (Boswell, 1988, p. 239) was oblation (*oblatio*, meaning "offering"), though it was neither uniquely Western nor Christian; similar practices have been followed in Eastern cultures. At 7 or even younger, children could be offered as oblates by their parents with the assurance that a child would be cared for, rather than hoping that some kind stranger would take it in, though this meant separation and binding vows on pain of excommunication. There were status distinctions, with children of better families able to take vows, those of lower classes likely to become laborers. Training was rigorous with threat of severe punishment, and while it provided opportunities to learn not otherwise available to girls, a convent education prepared a girl for life as a nun, rather than for worldly life. While children themselves had little to say in the matter, whether they could be forced to remain became a major controversy in the ninth century. Some who decided it was not for them were withdrawn, their parents having in effect used the convent as a nursery. But oblation was apparently a major source of recruitment; records of one English monastery show that between about 1030 and 1070 85% of the monks had been oblates (Boswell, 1988, p. 297).

How likely were children with disabilities to be destined for the religious life? This was a controversial matter, Boswell (1988) suggests, noting Jerome's complaint "that parents dedicate to virginity those daughters who are deformed or defective in some way" (pp. 240–241). Ulrich of Cluny, an 11th-century church leader, was more explicit, complaining of "parents who . . . commit to monasteries any hump-backed, deformed, dull or unpromising children they have" (p. 298). "In prosperous families, they were the first

to be put out to nurse and then sent to monasteries" (Shahar, 1990, p. 148).
An incentive to accept what another described as "'the lame, the malformed,
the one-eyed, the squinting, the blind, the crippled'" was the obligatory
offering of money or land accompanying the child (Boswell, 1988, p. 299).
As oblation became less common, the fate of abandoned children continued to be influenced by religious convention. A major determinant of whether
an infant, even one with severe impairment, would be cared for was evidence,
signified by salt, of baptism.

During the period traditionally called infancy, the first seven years, a
child's care was entirely provided by women, and medieval literature contains extensive evidence of affection, as in a mother's unwillingness to turn
over her baby's nursing to another (Régnier-Bohler, 1988, p. 338). There is
also evidence that many with birth defects—impairments *a navitate*—were
not rejected (Shahar, 1990, p. 148). Accidents as causes of head injury and
orthopedic or vision impairment seem to have been common, but whether
more or less so than today is difficult to establish. Most parents took measures to protect their small children; well before the wide publication of
printed "manuals" for child-rearing there was no dearth of advice to parents and wet-nurses about guarding children from injury or illness. A child's
accidental death was more often attributed to negligence than to divine
punishment and almost certainly was not interpreted as "disguised murder"
(p. 143). Should a child's drowning or other calamity be judged the result
of a mother's poor supervision or neglect, penance was imposed, but her
own grief was thought sufficient punishment.

However, since death in childbirth was very common, many children
were orphaned or placed in the care of a stepmother, a central figure in the
fairy tales that originated during this period. The fear or actual experience
of loss, abandonment, and cruel treatment by a surrogate must have had
enormous psychological consequences. In the absence of a love bond for a
stepchild, we might speculate that burdens of care placed a child with special
needs at greatest risk for ill treatment. While economic considerations often
determined a child's fate, well into the Renaissance many children of the
more affluent were remanded to the care of a *nourrice*. A child of privilege
fortunate enough to be cared for within a family environment during the
early years was likely, at 7, to be "turned over to the lord of some castle or
to some high churchman" to be trained as a page (Despert, 1965, pp. 62–63).
The lot of many of these children was nevertheless relatively fortunate, and
we shall see that a few deaf (male) children would be among those thus
privileged.

How could parents so readily consign a child to the care of others? Aries
(1962) ascribed the apparent absence of emotional involvement to likelihood of loss; one could have little confidence that a child would live to

maturity and, while having many children increased the likelihood that some would survive, attachment would have been weak. Willingness to offer a child as an oblate was encouraged by church doctrine, for duty to God was primary among loyalties, but we might only reflect on the force of custom; this is what was done. Still, the opportunity to enable a child to attain learning and a more secure future in perilous times was perhaps thought worth whatever pain came with separation. Devereux (1956, pp. 33–34) has suggested that the practice of turning children over to others to educate and train—to slaves in antiquity or a nobleman's court or religious enclave in medieval times—may have reflected parental desires to retain a child's affection, since parents expected that the training the child would receive would be rigorous, if not brutal. Boswell (1988) argues that in medieval times "'fostering' . . . relationships were idealized as great and ennobling rather than makeshift or second-rate" (p. 360), and childhood was defined differently than today: "Sending a nine-year-old daughter to be married . . . or apprenticing an eight-year-old son to a knight in another country . . . could have been a normal, responsible parental gesture—'childhood' being over at this point" (p. 27).

By the time children reached age 7 it appeared more likely that they would live to adulthood, so measures to prepare them were considered worthwhile. Since crowded living conditions permitted little privacy, and since they saw their parents at work in the home or the fields, the line of division was not actually so sharp. Nevertheless, "with the exception of those who were placed in monasteries at a very early age, children up to the age of 7 generally enjoyed freedom" (Shahar, 1990, pp. 101–102). Small children were expected to play among themselves, gradually beginning to share such work responsibilities as errands, tending animals, and the like as part of their socialization experiences as parents deemed appropriate and custom dictated. Shahar (1990) points out that stage theories of development like Piaget's and Erikson's in fact had medieval predecessors, with demarcations of *infantia* (to age 7), *pueritia* (7 to 12 for girls, to 14 for boys), *adolescentia*, and *juventus* (p. 22). As would be the case for centuries, "The poorer the family, the sooner the carefree days of childhood came to an end. Many children began working at an early age, with little girls hired out as maids as young as age six" (La Ronciére, 1988, p. 224). However, in descriptions of medieval childhood we find nothing to compare to Industrial Age exploitation in mills and mines.

The fact that medieval children were separated from their homes at young ages prompted deMause (1974) to characterize the period from the 4th to the 13th century with the phrase "abandonment mode," preceding the "ambivalent mode" of the 14th to the 17th century. But as we have seen, abandonment did not necessarily reflect lack of parental concern. Moreover, as in our own time, official records of child abandonment, as well as abuse or infanticide, can suggest a distorted picture of relationships of parents and children. One wonders how future historians will interpret statistics concerning poverty, homelessness, and lack of immunization among American children in the 1990s.

The most extreme instance of children leaving their homes at a young age in medieval times has no modern counterpart, since many did so voluntarily. The first Children's Crusade began with a shepherd boy's vision in 1212 and involved some 30,000 children, some of nobles but most of peasants. Most who did not die en route or drown in the Mediterranean were captured, tortured, and slain, or made slaves. Though a reflection of the piety of the age, which children presumably internalized, this sad event was an aberration, without ecclesiastical sanction, "born out of anarchic fervor and apocalyptic tension" (Shahar, 1990, p. 250).

Wards and Unfortunates

As we saw, the network of foundling homes begun when Constantine I unified church and state under what we know as the Byzantine Empire was intended as an alternative to infanticide, but the result was most often the same. By the 14th century, more specialized hospices, such as San Gallo in Florence, were established, followed by Innocenti, in 1445, and others in French and German cities. The actual number of children left at foundling homes, convents, and monasteries is not known, but it grew during the Renaissance and even more in the 16th century (Shahar, 1990, p. 1250). While abandonment was not limited to the poor, its prevalence increased proportionally to that of poverty, the wealthy using foundling homes mainly for their illegitimate children, poor families turning to them from economic necessity (La Roncière, 1988). As the Age of Reason dawned in Paris, 5,000 to 6,000 children each year—32,000 from 1771 to 1777—were brought to the hospice in Paris founded by Vincent de Paul (1577–1660) (Hewett & Forness, 1974). The increased number of hospices no doubt reflected increased demand, but their very availability probably also encouraged abandonment. Figures documenting abandonment in 18th-century France, from 10 to over 25% of births, and in Italy—from 14 to 43% in Florence and from 16 to 25% in Milan—are underestimations since they are based on admissions to facilities with birth and baptism records (Boswell, 1988).

And again, most died, mainly from exposure to communicable disease: "The paradox of the foundling hospital—neatly organized, modern, civic, discreet, and deadly—was exquisitely calibrated to the times" (Boswell, 1988, p. 426). Estimates of the number in Paris and London foundling homes in the 17th and 18th centuries who died in their first year of life range from a highly optimistic 33% to as many as 90% (Shahar, 1990). For perspective, we must recognize that all children were at risk; in 18th-century London, nearly 60% died before age 5, and only about one-third survived beyond age 10 (Hewett & Forness, 1974).

The single group of persons with disabilities referenced in the context of specialized charitable aid throughout the Middle Ages is those who were blind. Hospices specifically for blind persons originated with a community established for blind beggars in Syria by St. Lymnaeus, but the most influential of these "hospital brotherhoods of the blind" was the Congregation and House of the Three Hundred, or *Quinze-Vingts*, established by St. Louis in Paris in 1254 (French, 1932, p. 46). The residents—never to exceed or be less than 300—comprised a lay congregation, distinctive for their common dress, which was a long blue gown adorned with a lily. Although comprised of mixed sex, whose members could marry, this was very like a religious community. Their children could remain with them in the community, but only to a certain age. The concept was tried in other settings, although apparently not as successfully; to be blind was, most often, to be a beggar or a ward (Lowenfeld, 1975).

There had been little medical progress since Galen. The "role of Byzantium in the history of medicine was that of an embalming medium or cold storage plant for the accumulated knowledge of the past" (Abt, 1965, p. 47). Such medical care as was provided was typically dispensed by monks who, within their limited capability, "kept alive medical, as indeed every other form of knowledge, during the centuries of barbarism that succeeded the fall of Rome" (Rowling, 1968, p. 175). Hippocrates had catalogued maladies specific to childhood, and one who did build on his tradition, and who described retardation, was Avicenna, whose actual name was Abu Ali al-Husayn ibn Sina (980–1037). His prolific writing, not only on medical but also philosophical topics, as well as poetry, would long inspire and influence scholars and physicians. But very few people were treated by physicians. Hospitals were sometimes enormous multipurpose facilities, like one that "included 7,000 beds, providing a military hospital, an orphanage and a home for the blind" (Scheerenberger, 1983, p. 26). A child was not likely to receive good care, as Despert (1965) describes,

> where the sick, the old, the young and very young, the blind, the leprous, passing pilgrims, and unfortunates of all kinds were thrown together, five or six to a bed. . . . When a woman came to the hospital . . . , her young progeny came along to be distributed among places which happened to be available in the beds. Children who had been abandoned or were admitted because of illness were completely assimilated to the adults, bedded with them, and given the same treatment. (p. 64)

Laws Against the Poor

The juxtaposition of disability and poverty has been a constant theme, seen in the collective designation of "unfortunates" and in the fact that, while some impairments do not respect social status, poverty and its correlates contribute mightily both to reproductive casualty and that of nurture. There has also always been inequity, as today, in access to preventive and ameliorative care. As we consider the long period before such services were provided, it is important to have a sense of the grim conditions under which many people lived.

By 1000, Western Europe's population was nearly twice its low point in the 7th century, and relative prosperity and calm over the next three centuries, with a beginning shift to urban economies, brought another fourfold increase. But with the Black Death of 1348–1350 Europe's population reached "lows from which it would not fully recover for centuries" (Boswell, 1988, p. 270). Braudel (1979) provides a powerful picture of the struggle for survival well into and beyond the Renaissance, recounting, based on national records, the unremitting, successive general famines—26 in the 11th century—in addition to local ones, from the 10th through the 17th century. The Black Death was preceded by "devastation caused by food shortages between 1308 and 1318 . . . [that] spread throughout Europe" (p. 74), while in Asia and India "famines . . . seemed like the end of the world" (p. 76). One need not be reminded of the implications of malnutrition for children's physical and mental development and susceptibility to disease. Common infant illnesses included high fever due to influenza or other causes; bronchial diseases and breathing difficulty; measles, smallpox, or other "rashes or poxes"; dehydration; tuberculosis; bowel and urinary tract problems; bodily swelling, tumors, hernias; "ulcers, carbuncles, and sores which did not heal" (Shahar, 1990, p. 146). We should consider, too, the impact of such hardship on family life and children's emotional development.

While all were affected, infant mortality during the "period of plagues (1348–1430)" was especially high among peasants and working classes (Duby, 1988, p. 223). And while dwellers of the increasingly populous towns suffered greatly from famines, their effect on peasants in the countryside was even more disastrous: "Positive armies of the poor" came into the towns in the desperate quest for food, "begging in the streets and often dying in public squares" (Braudel, 1979, p. 75). Some relief measures were taken, but mainly ordinances were enacted "to place the poor in a position where they could do no harm" (p. 76):

> In Paris the sick and invalid [were] directed to the hospitals, and the fit, chained together in pairs, were employed at the hard, exacting and interminable task of

cleaning the drains of the town. In England the Poor Laws . . . were in fact laws *against* the poor. . . . Houses for the poor and undesirable gradually appeared throughout the West, condemning their occupants to forced labour in workhouses, *Züchthauser* or Maisons de Force for example, that body of semi-prisons, united under the administration of the Grand Hospital de Paris, founded in 1656. This "great enclosure" of the poor, mad, and delinquent, as sons of good family placed under supervision by their parents, was one psychological aspect of seventeenth-century society, relentless in its rationality. (pp. 76–77)

Altruistic motives were not altogether absent from the English Poor Laws enacted between 1563 and 1601, which required almshouses and workhouses supported by local taxes. With the Reformation, according to a historian of blindness (French, 1932), "policing of poverty was displaced by a genuine poor relief" (p. 53), while in France the Catholic Church regulated local charities. Still, conditions worsened to the extent that "the 18th century must really be called the 'beggars' century'" (p. 55). It would be France, in its Revolutionary constitution, that would dramatically affirm the duty of the state to provide for those who could not work.

Exorcists and Alienists

Just as the church's prohibition of excessive mourning for a child's death could not force parents to bear the event with equanimity (Shahar, 1990), its prohibition of pagan practices like incantations in treating ailments failed to halt their use. Treatment involved a peculiar blend of knowledge preserved from antiquity with faith healing, astrology, and prescriptions of substances ranging from all manner of herbs to powdered earthworms and excrement. For aberrant behavior, *stigmata diaboli* were studied to determine how to exorcise evil forces responsible. Interestingly, while explanations were predicated on demonology, the behaviors themselves were often those that psychiatrists would later identify, but one who was "possessed" inspired fear or awe, rather than helping impulse; it was "taken for granted that medicine had no power, even no right, over the mentally sick" (Zilboorg, 1941, p. 23).

Even as the Renaissance spread, persecution of women accused of witchcraft or of practicing birth control or having had abortions, as well as heretics, was legally codified. In 1487, *Malleus Maleficarum* (The Witches' Hammer) was published by Johann Sprenger and Heinrich Kraemer, Dominican monks appointed by Pope Innocent VIII as "Inquisitors of Heretical Depravities." This "textbook of the Inquisition," the authoritative reference on witchcraft for more than two centuries, laid out procedures for identification, prosecution, and punishment of suspected practitioners. "Not all accused of being witches and sorcerors were mentally sick, but almost all mentally sick were considered witches or sorcerors, or bewitched" (Zilboorg, 1941, p. 153). Any anomaly that did not yield to the primitive treatments available was thought the work of the devil; to be different aroused suspicion of being possessed or actively in league with Satan. For most children with seizures, cognitive delay, or unusual behavior the former was assumed, but even in a child as young as 9 differentness could result in trial and execution, as Murray's (1921) chronicle of the *Witch-Cult in Western Europe* recounts. We can only guess how many children were victimized in the course of this protracted war with the devil and his emissaries.

Nor was witch-hunting confined to the Inquisition; it was an entirely ecumenical phenomenon. The Reformation was anything but that with regard to attitudes concerning mental deviance; both Luther and Calvin thought children with retardation "filled with Satan" and objects of revulsion (Barr, 1910). This obsessive association of deviance with the occult proved extraordinarily durable and resistant to reform. Even the humane Felix Platter (1536–1614), one of the first specialists in "mental alienation," having exposed himself to confinement to experience the suffering associated with mental illness, concluded that madness was indeed "the handiwork of the devil" (Zilboorg, 1941, p. 24). Despite the ascendance of science in the 16th century, epidemic belief in witchcraft persisted, peaking in the 17th. Yet interest in nature had found expression in 14th-century Italy, then France, then England in the scientific method. While persons with disabilities have often been victims rather than beneficiaries of scientific "progress," this aspect of the Renaissance brought important medical discoveries. Childhood diseases such as chicken pox, smallpox, whooping cough, and scarlet fever were identified and the first pediatric texts published, although such advances had little effect on the treatment most people received, which often entailed esoteric potions to purge humors, both for physical ailments and "idiocy and folly."

But physicians were joined by poets, playwrights, and essayists in advocating for those who were shunned and persecuted. Thomas More's *Utopia*, which H. G. Wells credited with inspiring the Poor Laws, argued for human dignity and equality for women. Anticipating Montaigne's rational exposure of occult phenomena, Reginald Scot offered natural explanations in *Discovery of Witchcraft* (1584), which England's James I ordered seized and burned. A physician, Johann Weyer (1515–1588), led this "first psychiatric revolution" (Zilboorg, 1941, p. 175), arguing that mental illness could make one susceptible to hallucinations, and that those who thought themselves bewitched were delusional or very vulnerable to suggestion, but his theories met with derision. Equally outspoken but just as unsuccessful were another physician, John Schenck (1530–1598), and Frederick Von

Spree (1591–1635), a Jesuit. Juan Luis Vives (1492–1540) of Valencia, one of the first to attempt interpretration of the bizarre mental associations reported by mentally ill persons, advocated humane treatment on religious grounds, but his pious nature seems to have restrained him from public criticism of practices he thought ignorant and cruel. That could not be said of Paracelsus, whom we shall shortly meet, who though equally pious challenged all received wisdom, and who, like Vives, was particularly indignant concerning the degradation of women inherent in witchhunting.

Changing Status of Children

Just as it did not end superstition, the Renaissance by no means ended neglect and mistreatment of children, although these sometimes took more subtle forms. In 14th-century Tuscany, children of some wealthy families were treated with great affection, provided many playthings, and handsomely outfitted (La Ronciére, 1988, p. 224), though this was certainly not true among the less affluent. Infants of most bourgeoisie families were wet-nursed, but since only about 25% of the wet-nurses lived in the family's home, most nursing infants were separated from parents and 53% were not "reclaimed" until about 15 months of age (p. 220). Live-in arrangements pose another issue that "did not concern the authors of medical and didactic works" (Shahar, 1990, p. 88). As Piers (1978) commented, "throughout the history of wet-nursing, the question of the nurse's own child is hardly ever raised. It is not an enjoyable question to contemplate" (p. 47). Neither a mother who remanded her infant to a wet-nurse nor the mother who at best neglected her own child to take on the work seems to have been considered "a bad woman"; people then, as now, tended to accept the prevailing customs (Shahar, 1990, p. 75).

In France, it was long customary among the more privileged to hand over an infant to a *nourrice* to raise, irrespective of that person's character or competence. It was not at all uncommon for a child, even of privileged family, to die from neglect under this system, and Montaigne's (trans. 1958) was nearly a lone voice, in *Les Essais* (1725), in protesting that even children whose physical needs were met were given but "spurious affection." He also decried the use of physical punishment, as well as milder forms of exploitation of children as sources of adult entertainment rather than persons in their own right.

Nor, as we saw, had life become easy during the period of great intellectual and artistic flowering. Even as Europe rediscovered humanistic values, human life itself was tenuous. In 1348, as the Black Death hit Italy, three-fifths of Florence's population died "in the midst of . . . scenes of inhumanity and desperate dissipation" portrayed in Boccacio's *Decameron* (Cleugh,

1975). But this collection of often warring states from which Italy was eventually formed encouraged learning and the arts to flourish. Knowledge was both cultivated and synthesized, rather than compartmentalized in the hierarchical system of medieval thought. And a growing awareness of, and genuine interest in, childhood can be discerned. Lorenzo di Piero de' Medici, the great patron of artists, writers, and scholars known as Lorenzo the Magnificent, who reputedly adored his own children, founded a school for humanistic education (Hilbert, 1975). As Greenleaf (1978) observed, Italian Renaissance art itself reveals a new phenomenon, as in the 12th and 13th centuries the image of Jesus portrayed in paintings became recognizable as a child, a development she considers "the single most important factor in improving the status of children" (p. 41). While motherhood had been idealized in medieval art, the supreme example of Mary used to encourage mothers to nurse their infants (Shahar, 1990), children appeared in family portraits and by the end of the 16th century as sole subjects.

In Western culture this appreciation of children may have been novel, but it it is well to remember that the walls of ancient Egyptian tombs depict what one scholar (Breasted, 1954) called "charming family scenes," with clearly identifiable children happily playing. In Europe, the awareness of children began with the Renaissance to be reflected in distinctive apparel and forms of amusement, but Aries (1962) has maintained that not until the 17th century did common attitudes express a "psychological interest and moral solicitude" in children as individuals (p. 131). This view has been challenged by Shahar (1990), who avers that "the educational theories of the Middle Ages were . . . closer to those accepted by modern psychologists and educators" (p. 3). Before age 7 medieval children were not generally expected to exercise self-control or assume demanding responsibilities, nor were medieval parents, unlike 19th century parents, enjoined to break the child's will in the interests of training for responsibility and morality. In any case, appreciation of children as individual persons in the process of development did have significance for the understanding of childhood disability within at least one context: the situation of a male heir who was deaf.

Although there had been child-care advice throughout the Middle Ages, greater awareness of children led to better understanding of problems to which they were uniquely vulnerable. A 1495 treatise by Bartholomeus Metlinger of Augsburg provided advice on infant care, endorsing breast feeding and considering weaning, teething, proper cradles (to prevent tipping or smothering), and health, nutritional, and developmental milestones such as the child's first steps (Braunstein, 1988, p. 593). A popular source of child-rearing advice in France was Scévole de Sainte-Marthe, whose Latin verses endorsed such practices as breast feeding on demand (Greenleaf, 1978). In the 16th century, in rapid succession, the first actual pediatric texts were published, in England (*The Boke on Children*, by Thomas Phayre, 1545), in Spain (*Libro del Regimento de la Saludy de las Infermadades de los Niños*, by Lobero de Avila, 1551), and in France (*De la Manière de Gouverner les Enfants des Leur Nassiance*, by Simon de Vallambert, 1565). Phayre's book, the full title of which was *The Regiment of Life, whereunto is added a treatise of pestilence, with the boke of children*, widely used for over a century, was basically a compilation of ancient beliefs and traditions made accessible to literate Britons. Movable type made possible dissemination of manuals on child care and a growing body of information on prevention and treatment of childhood maladies.

And exceptionality in children began to receive some attention in the medical literature. In 1573, in a book titled *Monstres et Prodiges*, Ambroise Paré (1510–1590), a French surgeon, delineated 13 causes of birth defects, some reflecting the superstitions that have continued to underlie certain beliefs of what an expectant mother should or should not do. But others, like maternal injury during pregnancy, we would certainly recognize as valid. Generally, however, the work did not reveal great changes from long-held folk beliefs about presumed causes of birth defects officially codified, under ecclesiastic auspices, early in the Middle Ages. "Christian couples could not engage in conjugal relations during menstruation, lactation, Lent, or on Sundays" (Boswell, 1988, pp. 259–260), for such could result in lameness, leprosy, deformity, seizures, or infant death. In the 14th century, parents were warned that, in addition to violation of rules concerning when, and how, intercourse was permissible, eating the wrong food could result in defective offspring (p. 338).

The iconoclastic Theophrastus Bombastus von Hohenheim (1493–1541), known as Paracelsus, was not an alienist or a specialist in childhood problems but an alchemist, yet some of his scientific endeavors are quite germane to our focus. His interest in the health problems of mine workers led to investigations of the role of chemical agents in cause and treatment of disease, and even a grand philosophical system linking elements in the body with cosmic forces in the universe. With such interests it was natural for him to become interested in cretinism, prevalent in the valley regions of Switzerland, and he was the first to associate the condition with retardation. Also, unlike most contemporaries, he recognized the great variability among persons with retardation. While no systematic classifications had been proposed, such terms as *imbecillus* (suggesting a general weakness) and *idios* ("a private person") dated, respectively, from Roman and Greek usage and, as we saw, Hippocrates and later Galen had differentiated various manifestations and presumed causes. Felix Platter (1536–1614), the son of self-educated humanistic scholar and educational reformer Thomas Platter, while practicing in Basel, was also struck by the high prevalence of cretinism, leading him to propose a classification of "mental alienation" anticipating Esquirol's by two centuries.

Although until the 20th century "there was not—and there could not be—anything that might in any sense be regarded as child psychiatry" (Kanner, 1944, p. 139), philosophers and poets were increasingly aware of the emotional lives of children. Moreover, since received wisdom could be questioned, the possibility of educating those previously presumed "incapable of reason" could be entertained. Among the humanistic scholars of the 15th century was one Roelof Huysman (1443 or 1444–1485) who, having changed his name after study in Italy to Rodolphus Agricola, had considerable influence on pedagogy in the Netherlands and Germany. Among the Renaissance ideas he promulgated were those of individual freedom and the role of education in cultivating all facets, physical as well as intellectual and cultural (ideas considered highly innovative when proposed by Herbert Spencer some four centuries later). His text, *De Formando Studio*, contains a description of a person apparently deaf from birth who had acquired the ability to read and write expertly—a direct refutation of conventional wisdom and dogma. As we shall see, Girolamo Cardano (1501–1576), a Paduan physician, would cite this account in proposing the revolutionary view that deaf persons are educable.

Persons of Merit

A collateral development of patronization of the arts directly involved certain highly gifted persons whose achievements clearly demonstrated that talent can coexist with disability. But this refers not to preternatural powers, like that attributed to blind persons to "see" the future. Instead, it was recognized that these individuals, demonstrating abilities of the same sort that other people have, sometimes do so to an extraordinary degree. One such was Juan Fernandez Ximenes de Navarette, known as El Mudo (the mute), who had lost his hearing at age 3. Born, according to varying accounts, between 1526 and 1532, he attained great fame as a painter with the patronage of Philip II of Spain, before his death in 1579. Whether early educators of the deaf were inspired by his example is unknown, but this was indeed a period when such efforts were being begun in Spain.

A French contemporary, Pierre de Ronsard (1524–1585), having been a page in the court of Charles I, aspired to a military or diplomatic career, but illness contracted at age 16 left him with a severe hearing loss. Determined not to abandon his ambition for significant achievement, he turned to literature, earning great prestige as a poet and also great affection, for his work expressed a particularly positive vision of life and of humanity. Known as the "prince of poets and poet of princes," with Rabelais and Montaigne a towering figure in 16th-century French literature, Ronsard was the most famous of a group of poets known as the *Pléiade*, who sought to elevate the literary status of the French language. Another member, Joachim Du Bellay (1522–1560), though less positive about his partial hearing loss resulting from childhood ear infection, was inspired by Ronsard. (Hippocrates had discussed *otitis media*, but the preventative implications have not been pursued until quite recently.) It was Du Bellay who, in 1549, wrote what was considered the group's manifesto, *Défense et illustration de la langue français* (Bender, 1970). That two individuals with impaired hearing were not only eminent poets but also champions of their nation's language is interesting indeed.

Most blind persons continued to live in poverty, although there had been enough exceptions to challenge the collective image of "ward" or "mendicant" (Lowenfeld, 1975). Innovators in music of the Italian Renaissance included a blind Florentine organist, Francesco Landini (c. 1335–1397), and clearly the role of titans like Homer and Milton has been critical in creating awareness of the potential of blind persons to be major contributors to society and culture. The spirit of the Enlightenment would be far more congenial to the notion that a means might be found to permit widespread education of persons without sight. The works of Locke, Condillac, and Rousseau established an intellectual foundation for compensatory pedagogy through the sense of touch, but accomplishments of blind persons themselves contributed profoundly to these developments. In his *Letter on the Blind for the Use of Those Who See*, Denis Diderot (1713–1784), perhaps the greatest philosopher of the Enlightenment, "brought to the attention of his contemporaries the fact that blind persons can be highly competent intellectually as well as physically; that they can lead normal lives and need not be beggars; and that in order to know more about them they can be asked themselves for answers" (Lowenfeld, 1975, p. 67). Valentin Haüy, as we shall see, did precisely that. "Blind emancipators," in Lowenfeld's phrase, were prominent in the intellectual community of 18th-century England and were influential in establishing that nation's first schools for blind pupils.

By then, philosophical traditions had been introduced that would have profound impact on all areas of human affairs, and their impact was felt most particularly in France, climaxing in the 1789 Revolution. Education of children generally, as well as those who were exceptional, was but one facet of this impact but an important one. With the Enlightenment, education came to be seen no longer as indoctrination, but rather as a freeing of the capacity of reason from the bondage of ignorance, tradition, and superstition that had been imposed, not by God or by nature, but by human beings on themselves (Devereux, 1956, p. 41).

CHAPTER 2

Enlightenment and Revolution

FOUNDATIONS FOR A PEDAGOGY OF EXPERIENCE

Philanthropy, education, and psychology were consecutive sources of progress in the understanding of retardation (Kanner, 1964), and of exceptionality in general. Philanthropy (as distinguished from the organized charity that developed later) encompasses influences from philosophy, literature, and medicine, as evidenced in the work of individual thinkers, poets, and healers who had expressed concern for persons with disabilities since antiquity. The second source, education, largely the product of physician-turned-educator innovators, complemented by clergy, was begun by 17th-century philosophers and scientists. In this extraordinarily productive time of Kepler, Galileo, and Newton, what began in England as an informal network became in 1660 the Royal Society, chartered in 1662. In France, the *Académie des Sciences*, which would serve as the arbiter of methodologies for teaching deaf persons, was established and recognized by Louis XIV in 1666. Soon, "France led all other nations, and the *Académie des Sciences* and Paris formed the scientific center of the world" (Boring, 1950, p. 19), with French the language of scientific discourse.

Philosophers' musings about human reason became foundations for modern pedagogy, and for teaching persons with disabilities. While Francis Bacon's *Novum Organum* (1620/1900) challenged the Aristotelian deductive mode, Thomas Hobbes's description of associations of sense experience revisited Aristotle's empiricism. The role of *associationism* as the foundation for experimental psychology is apparent in David Hume's delineation of the fundamental types of associations in *A Treatise of Human Nature* (1739), involving *resemblance*, temporal or spatial *contiguity*, and *cause-effect* relationships. John Locke was also interested in how ideas were combined, and in fact coined the phrase "association of ideas" in *An Essay Concerning Human Understanding* (1690/1894), but more in their source in sensory experience. While associationism broadly influenced 19th-century educators, Locke's concept of *tabula rasa*, or blank slate, on which experience writes, formed the very basis for stressing the role of instruction, particularly for persons with disabilities.

The "sense-realist" school was popularized in France by Voltaire, and its pedagogical implications were explored by Charles Rollin and Etienne Bonnet de Condillac, who thought the recitation, rote memorization, and repressive discipline prevalent in schools denied the key role of activity in learning. Condillac's (1715–1780) influence was important in the history of psychology in considering the differential and interactive functions of the senses. Both urged teachers to recognize variations among individual learners and addressed the importance of motivation, anticipating Thorndike and Freud with respect to the role of pleasure and pain. Rollin's (1661–1741) endorsement of kind yet firm discipline, emulation of models, specific objectives, ensuring that the pupil recognizes the value of what is taught, and approval contingent on appropriate behavior greatly influenced Edouard Seguin. These ideas were developed further by Jean-Jacques Rousseau (1715–1780), who, having been engaged to tutor Condillac's nephews, maintained a lasting relationship with him.

The philosophical flowering was inextricably associated with sociopolitical unrest, and publication of Rousseau's *The Social Contract* in 1762 was a link in the chain of events leading to the Revolution. His *Emile* (1762/ 1963), published the same year, seemed to glorify a "noble savage" ideal of children's inherent goodness but had little impact on practice; with the *hôpitaux* "overflowing" with abandoned infants, and infanticide "of unprecedented magnitude" (Piers, 1978, p. 56), life itself was in jeopardy for children of the poor, while those of the privileged were remanded to others to rear. Rousseau himself had abandoned his own five children to foundling homes, justifying the action on the basis of career exigencies, a justification he later disavowed.

No less than his antimonarchic views, Rousseau's insistence on children's rights to be happy and develop their own natural gifts was truly revolutionary. "All things are good as they come out of the hands of their Creator," begins *Emile*, "but everything degenerates in the hands of man." Branded a threat to public morals, this *Treatise of Education*, as it was subtitled, was condemned by the Sorbonne and the Paris Parliament as subversive, forcing its author to flee to his native Switzerland to avoid arrest for sedition (Cranston, 1991). On the question of nature versus nurture, that is, the relative importance of innate and environmental influences on development, Rousseau stressed sensory experience but was a "nativist," in contrast to Locke, in describing successive developmental periods as predetermined, anticipating stage theories and the notion of critical periods for certain kinds of learning, and in describing children as imbued with the desire to learn through discovery rather than formal tutelage. Most fundamentally, he invoked the "wisdom of nature" in asserting the child's inherent goodness, which, while widely misinterpreted as advocating permissiveness, meant that "nature intends that children shall be children before they are men. Let the over-strict teacher and the over-indulgent parent both learn the lesson of Nature itself. . . . The surest way to make a child unhappy is to accustom him to obtain everything he wants to have" (1762/1963, p. 32).

These ideas were not entirely original; a century earlier similar notions had been proposed by a Moravian bishop, Johann Amos Comenius (1592–1670). In 1654, when Comenius published his first picture book for children, Germany was recovering from loss of half its population following the Plague. Earlier, in *A Reformation of Schools* (1642), he set forth his *pansophic* philosophy, involving reforms to make schooling more generally available and to promote mutual understanding in order to end religious factionalism and bring about peace among nations. His own contributions to sharing of knowledge, basic to his reform agenda, included graded texts for Latin instruction, in vernacular translation and illustrated to enhance their meaningfulness. Anticipating Condillac's insight that children's understanding of things precedes words, he recommended that direct experiences should precede symbolic ones. While his nearly 200 published works were widely discussed, his ideas were far ahead of his time and would be better received when revisited by Pestalozzi.

By the time schools for deaf and for blind students were established in Paris, a legacy of specialized instruction already existed. But it was a legacy of individuals, self-educated or protégés of tutors who had come to the enterprise by chance, that had accumulated gradually and sporadically. Pre-revolutionary Paris marked the watershed, for here the idea of *public* instruction for pupils with disabilities was instituted. Here as literal chains were removed from people considered insane, figurative ones were removed from those who were deaf or blind, and here Jean-Marc-Gaspard Itard would demonstrate with Victor, perhaps the most famous of all exceptional pupils, methods considered even today to reflect "best practice."

"CURING" THE DEAF

Deaf people have considered such a concept deeply offensive, for it has historically meant rejection of sign language and cultural traditions. To be "cured" meant learning to use speech to communicate, an issue that has involved two centuries of controversy—"war," some would say—between hearing educators who think it essential for deaf persons to use speech in order to participate in the majority culture, and deaf persons themselves who have upheld their right to their own language and culture. These disparate views have in fact yielded different versions of history, epitomized by the titles of Ruth Bender's (1970) and Harlan Lane's (1984a) accounts, respectively, *The Conquest of Deafness* and *When the Mind Hears*, much of the latter told through Laurent Clerc, a great educator who was himself deaf. The controversy is analyzed in detail in Chapter 4, but here we explore its roots.

Spanish Beginnings

There are other fragmentary references, such as the Venerable Bede's account of a "dumb" youth whom St. John of Beverly, Bishop of Hagulstad, taught to speak about 685, but "it is Peter of Ponce . . . who created the art of teaching those deaf-mute from birth." So wrote Joseph-Marie de Gérando (1827, p. 307) in the first comprehensive chronicle of deaf education. The systematic instruction of deaf pupils, made famous in France, Germany, Britain, and eventually America, was first initiated in 1578 by a monk, Pedro Ponce de León (1520–1584), who, born into nobility himself, established his school to enable deaf scions to attain both salvation and eligibility as heirs of their family estates at the Benedictine monastery at San Salvador in northern Spain. While there are no extant records, various accounts refer to his great success in teaching "children of great nobles . . . to speak, to read, to write, and to keep accounts, to repeat prayers, to serve the Mass, to know the doctrines of the Christian religion, and to confess themselves with the living voice" (De Carlo, 1964, p. 12).

His method, which would have died with him had it not been for fortuitous circumstance, involved first teaching a pupil to write the names of objects, then drilling him (all his pupils were male) in producing the appropriate sounds for the words written. This seems straightforward enough but, as we know, it is no easy achievement; precisely *what* he did to accomplish this, and to move beyond it to speech and literacy, remained a mystery; the "secret" of teaching a prelingually deaf child to speak has involved one of the most controversial issues in the annals of special education. Peter of Ponce would no doubt have been willing to share *his* secret, but the same could not be said of some who followed in this tradition. Although the project was not continued after his death, stories of his successes had significant, though indirect, influence as the "schools" of oral education evolved.

Others may have been engaged in tutoring male children of families of means, but if so they worked in isolation and certainly did not comprise a professional community. Nor, unlike a next generation of pioneers, did they consider themselves founders of a discipline. Girolamo Cardano, an Italian physician who made oblique reference to Agricola's account mentioned in Chapter 1, proposed a similar method, based on association of written symbols with objects and pictures of objects. A physician, Pietro de Castro, referred in a text on children's diseases to instances of cure of deafness accomplished by Spaniards, meaning of course not restoration of hearing but learning to speak, specifically citing Emmanuel Ramirez de Carrión. Somehow he managed to take credit himself, rather than ascribing it to Ramirez (or Ponce de León), but in any case provided little information as to how he or Ramirez may have accomplished this.

Another Benedictine, Juan Martin Pablo Bonet, who did provide a description of oral methodology (*Reduccion de las letras y arte para enseñar a hablar a los mudos*, 1620), was fortuitously inspired by Ponce de León and inadvertently instructed by Ramirez, but credited neither. He determined to help a widowed duchess by finding a way to instruct her son, Luis, who had lost his hearing at age 2. By coincidence, the boy's grandfather had two brothers who had been pupils of Ponce de León, and the story of their learning to speak was part of family lore, though how it was accomplished was not. Bonet's search led him to Ramirez, who agreed in 1615 to come to Madrid to undertake Luis's instruction. His success was apparently noteworthy, for Luis went on to great accomplishment and, by chance, inspired the beginnings of oral instruction in Britain. When Ramirez felt compelled to return to the responsibilities he had reluctantly left, Bonet, having carefully observed his methods, continued the project.

Bonet used a visual system, based on a one-handed manual alphabet (a technique that would recur in various forms), which, when learned, was translated from the visual modality to vocalization. His approach provides the first written reference to lip reading, a skill critical for that transition but one he believed could not be taught but was accomplished by deaf persons due to their extraordinary attention to visual information. Later, Itard would make a similar observation to account for his own need to augment Sicard's methods in working with Victor, who he concluded lacked this habit of attention that appeared to be strong in deaf children. Bonet's strategy (or should it be attributed to Ramirez? to Ponce de León?) was to begin the transition to speech with vowels, move next to syllables, then one-syllable two-letter words and labels of familiar objects, ultimately undertaking syntactic constructions of phrases, clauses, and sentences (Bender, 1970). Luis was apparently a most responsive pupil if we are to judge from the impression he made on Sir Kenelm Digby.

The British Oral Tradition

Digby, the ancestor of the scholar of the same name, is credited with bringing education of deaf pupils to Britain, but perhaps the credit should go to Luis. The British tradition originated with a diplomatic visit to the court of Philip IV of Spain, in the course of which Digby became fascinated with a young lord, none other than Bonet's protégé, now ensconced in court. Learning of Luis's deafness, Digby was much impressed with his abilities, including that of speech. His account provided the first description in English of the outcome, if not the process (save whatever recollections Luis shared) of the education of a deaf child. It appears to have impressed John Bulwer, a physician engaged avocationally in speculative investigation of the possibility that, in "the language of the hand," a universal phenomenon might be found. This notion, set forth in his *Chirologia, or The Natural Language of the Hand* (1644), led him to consider manual signing used by deaf persons, although that was of only peripheral interest. A later book, *Philocophus or The Deafe and Dumbe Man's Friend* (1648), which refers to the account of Luis, asserts the necessity of a hearing teacher and analyzes the components of the speech act that must be systematically taught. Probably based more on introspection than on Digby's report, Bulwer noted that speech is the product of *movement*, not just position, of mouth and tongue, an important principle in oral rehabilitation (Bender, 1970).

While in Spain the church's influence was strong, though indirect, in the creation of a pedagogy out of highly pragmatic concern, in Britain the motive was philosophical. In both, the "case studies" were drawn entirely from well-to-do families. Another speculative philosopher interested in the universality of communication was George Dalgarno (1626?–1687), headmaster of a school in Aberdeen, Scotland, who devised a system he called *dactylology*, involving a manual alphabet in which letters were placed on the palm of the hand, each associated with a specific location. The system did not gain immediate application, though many future educators would cite it. Interest in communication as a philosophical problem certainly extended beyond the British Isles; thus, although he was neither a Briton nor concerned specifically with deafness, parenthetical mention is warranted of Franciscus Mercurius, the Baron van Helmont (1614?–1699). This Belgian chemist, perceiving an isomorphic relationship between the shape of printed letters and that formed by the mouth in pronouncing them, theorized that the "natural language" of mankind was Hebrew. While nothing seems to have come of this idiosyncratic notion, it may in some way have influenced the technique called Visible Speech invented by Alexander Melville Bell, whose son, Alexander Graham Bell, applied that system of teaching speech through imitation of visually displayed oral formations with deaf pupils.

Most famous of these early British educators was John Wallis (1616–1703), but this renowned mathematician would be denounced by Laurent Clerc, who was himself deaf, as a plagiarist who actually abandoned the attempt to teach his pupils to speak yet claimed credit for inventing that pedagogy (Lane, 1984a). Wallis's interest also evolved from other interests. In a book presenting methods for instructing foreigners in English grammar, he claimed that his system was also applicable for deaf persons, the goal for both being use of English. The attention it attracted served to bring to his personal tutelage a deaf youth, 16–year-old Daniel Whaley, and his apparent success, though described only in correspondence, attracted further attention and involved him in competition with a countryman. William Holder (1616–1698), a rector whose main interests were musical, also chanced to acquire a deaf pupil, the son of eminent parents, and also reported success, though neither seems to have been disposed to subject his methods to scientific scrutiny. To resolve their acrimonious debate as to who should be recognized as the first successful educator of the deaf in the English-speaking world, the Royal Academy accorded them jointly the recognition each coveted for himself. Holder's approach involved analysis of the position of the organs used in speech production, combined with the still novel idea (though used by Ponce de León and recommended by Cardano) of preceding spoken language with writing. Wallis's was informed, despite his claim to originality, by Dalgarno's manual alphabet, which surely owed some debt to Bonet (Bender, 1970).

This peculiar secretiveness was a major impediment to progress, for if methods were unavailable for scrutiny they could not be evaluated or, if effective, made generally available. Henry Baker (1698–1774) was the first to impose on pupils an actual "bond of secrecy." He was also apparently selective in choosing pupils, working only with those whose prognosis for speech was especially good (Bender, 1970). In such self-serving behavior, one begins to see the justice in Clerc's indictment (Lane, 1984a) of "hearing benefactors" who served only the privileged, exaggerated their successes and masked their failures, took credit for the innovations of others, and refused to share their methods in the interests of the deaf community. A different interpretation, taken by Seguin (1880), has it that, whatever their failings, their work was vital in contributing to integration of deaf persons in hearing society.

That Thomas Braidwood (1715–1806) was a most influential figure cannot be doubted, but he too came to guard his secrets, establishing a "family bond of secrecy" that would inadvertently shape the direction of deaf education in North America in the next century. But in this instance the cause was apparently frustration and pique, rather than fear of public scrutiny or proprietary right. In competition with numerous other reform-related petitions, his appeal to Parliament for support was unsuccessful. That deaf education in Britain took the form of a dual system—private, tuition-based instruction for the privileged, a "charity and asylum basis" for others, cannot therefore be laid at Braidwood's door (Bender, 1970, p. 117); the charity model, advocated by reformers like the Reverend John Townshend, was intended to ensure that benefits would not be denied children of the poor. This approach, also seen in British provisions for blind persons, repellent to

certain American reformers, stood in marked contrast to the public support
that would be introduced in France and later in Germany and America.

The German School

By the later 19th century the "German method," which emphasized speech
training without use of auxiliary aids, would be world famous. Its originator
was a physician, Jan Conrad Amman (1669–1724), who was in fact a Swiss
who lived most of his adult life in Amsterdam, where he saw his pupils.
Amman also took on cases of hearing clients with articulation problems,
stuttering, and apparently aphasia, as well. Thus, though the field of speech
therapy would not emerge for another two centuries, he is often considered
its founder.

Unlike his British counterparts, Amman contributed published accounts,
known to have been read by Wallis and by the French rivals Pereire and Epée,
whom we shall soon meet, but like most of the gradually accumulating literature in this field, these said more about outcome than method. (We consider in Chapter 3 whether the "secrets" of great teachers can be adequately
conveyed in the printed word.) His aim was expressed in the title of his most
famous book, *Surdus Loquens* (The Speaking Deaf), but successors had to
reconstruct the methods for themselves; as Seguin (1880) summarized,
Amman let it be known that he had been successful in teaching deaf children to speak but provided only broad descriptions of how this was accomplished. Seguin deduced that the main feature in his approach, and thus the
German school, was imitation, an aspect that greatly influenced Pereire,
whose work in turn inspired Seguin's techniques. We shall turn presently to
what Seguin termed the Spanish-French school, which through Pereire was
indebted to Amman. A Frenchman who supported Pereire's methods during a period of controversy, the abbé Deschamps had learned under Amman
himself, and he emphasized lipreading. Pereire employed a form of
dactylology that was, like Dalgarno's, borrowed from Bonet; neither Amman
nor his German successors used such devices.

One of those successors, L. W. Kerger, established a school in Silesia.
Another, Georg Raphael (1673–1740), learned of Amman's methods in
order to instruct his own deaf children and, in describing his experiences in
a book for parents, began a tradition of involvement of parents in working
with deaf children. Most notable was Samuel Heinicke (1727–1790), who,
born three years after Amman's death, had to rely on the printed sources.
His interest in the area was formed early when, in the course of private
tutoring, he chanced to have a pupil who was deaf. Referring to Amman's
accounts (as would Epée under similar circumstances), he seems to have
been very successful in improving the boy's speech, although neither the

degree nor the age of onset of the hearing loss is known. Military duties forced him to defer his new career goals, but in his late forties he was appointed headmaster of a school in which some deaf children were enrolled. Based on reports of their improved speech, Heinicke was able to secure governmental support for a school for deaf students, established in 1778 in Leipzig.

His innovations may have involved lipreading and a whole-word method in teaching reading, as advocated by Horace Mann, but whatever techniques he devised, he seems to have experienced conflict about disseminating them. Although he sought affiliation with the University of Leipzig for training for teachers, he was strangely reluctant to build a following. Nonetheless, he attacked the system gaining fame in France when it threatened to make inroads in the person of one abbé Storck, who opened a school in Austria using Epée's manual methods. Heinicke indignantly went to the source, precipitating a "friendly challenge" from Epée for the two to exchange demonstrations, but Heinicke did not accept, insisting only that speech was essential for "precision of thought" (Bender, 1970, p. 8). While his proprietary interest made him bristle at this French incursion, it would not allow him to place his system in the public domain. Had it not been for his widow, who urged a son-in-law, Adolph Eshke, to seek government support for a school in Berlin, it would not have survived. His great "secret," Lane (1984a) wryly suggests, may simply have been to enlist the sense of taste to complement sight, for apparently much was done with food. But as he jealously guarded it, so did his heirs, or such was their intent; Ludwig Grosshof, who taught under Eshke, had to be ordered by the government in 1812 to train Ferdinand Neumann (Bender, 1970).

Through Moritz Hill (1805–1874), who received visitors such as Edward Miner Gallaudet and other American educators, the German methods gained fame. According to Gallaudet, Hill freely shared that, contrary to general belief, signing was accorded a role in the German approach, but it had been so convincingly presented as free of French "contamination" that visitors (notably Mann and Charles Sumner) saw what they expected to see: speech, instead of sign language (Boatner, 1959). Through Hill, oral instruction shed much of its mystique and became more congruent with practices increasingly advocated for all children, emphasizing spontaneous activity rather than mechanical imitation and direct experience rather than rote memorization, ideas attracting attention, especially in Germany, through Pestalozzi's writing and demonstrations, as we discuss in Chapter 3. Seguin (1880) traced the lineage of German oralism from Amman, through Heinicke, then Hill in Weissenfels, as well as Saegert in Berlin, Janke in Dresden, and Hirsch in Rotterdam to a "Broadway, New York" branch: the Lexington School for the Deaf, nearly unique among American schools in its strictly oral orientation.

The Spanish-French School

While Seguin designated the third stream the "Spanish-French School," its major figure (after the Spanish originators), though born in Spain, was Portuguese and, moreover, employed a "combination" method. This was Giacobbo (Jacob) Rodriguez Pereire (sometimes spelled Pereira, 1715–1780). Pereire apparently succeeded in teaching his deaf sister to speak, but when anti-Semitism in Portugal became more virulent, he left for France where his reported successes in teaching deaf pupils soon brought him fame and recognition by Louis XV. He was thus enabled to open a school, in 1753, and effectively to obtain a sinecure for life. His method, based on the sense-realist notion that touch underlies all other senses, involved substituting it for hearing in the learning process. The emphasis on use of the tactile sense greatly impressed Seguin (1866, p. 54), who adduced that Periere taught speech by imitiation

> with vision as a guide to the internal positions in the mouth and the external muscles of the face and neck; and . . . with touch the conductor and monitor of the innermost positions and of the organic vibrations that together produce the emission of articulated sounds. By this method, the deaf-mute of ordinary capacity could learn to speak in twelve to fifteen months.

Seguin seems to have been more successful than others in learning what methods Pereire used, probably due mainly to a pupil of clearly more than "ordinary capacity," a young man named Saboureux de Fontenay. Intending that his son Isaac would carry on the work, Pereire, like Baker, had sworn his pupils to secrecy, but after his death Isaac and his son, Eugene, tried for years to discover the "secret," Pereire's widow locating another former star pupil, a woman by then aged, ill, and destitute. The efforts came to naught. Was the secret simply his manual alphabet, which was not his original invention? Of this we do have a fairly detailed description. Clerc alleged (Lane, 1984a) that there is reason to doubt that even his best pupils learned to speak well. That we shall never know, but the legacy of Pereire includes a highly articulate account by a pupil who felt compelled to break his vow of secrecy through a published "letter." At all events, he indeed had his detractors.

NATURAL LANGUAGE

If Laurent Clerc would derogate Pereire's work, as Lane (1984a) suggests, we must ask whether he spoke for deaf persons or only for his own rival "school." Clerc brought to North America not only sign language as a means of instruction but a culture-based view of deafness that had taken form in Paris. While Clerc was arguably its leader, that development was fostered too by hearing educators who honored signing as a "natural" language and rejected the view that successful instruction depended on the ability to use speech to communicate. "Hearing benefactors" have debated this matter ever since. As Diderot suggested concerning blindness, let us see what deaf individuals themselves have said.

Deaf Authors

While Pereire enjoyed considerable prestige in the Parisian scientific community, he had acquired a rival. The competition between Epée and Pereire involved public approbation and, importantly as a practical matter, recognition by the Academy of Sciences, which Pereire had achieved, but Epée posed a threat by publicly questioning the foundation of his approach. Thus, Pereire considered the young Saboureux de Fontenay "the most splendid gift of my life" (in Lane, 1984b, p. 14), whose "letter" may represent the first published account written by a deaf person. It provides most interesting insights concerning both the teacher's (Pereire's) artistry and the motivation required on the part of the pupil:

> Eventually overcoming with patience and persistence the tedium and difficulty of the study which at first set me trembling, I began to understand and repeat French, and by grasping the intellectual, abstract, and general ideas designated by words, sentences, and turns of phrase, I gave up the idea that it was impossible for the congenitally deaf to become as knowledgable, educated, capable of reasoning and thinking as others. . . . It is a wise teacher . . . who can adroitly and continually give the most needed words without bothering us with the less common ones which, nevertheless, he gradually and painlessly teaches through experience with things or through their connection with words that are already familiar. (In Lane, 1984b, p. 22)

Saboureux stresses the importance of the teacher's shrewdness and patience and the pupil's "memory, intelligence, and determination to meet the challenges posed by the genius of the language . . . and his motivation to hear, read, speak, write, and repeat the language." Teacher and pupil must "guess what is happening in each other's mind" (p. 23). An important element of the method was what Pereire termed *dactylology* (coined earlier by Dalgarno), a refinement of Bonet's Spanish manual alphabet, which

> consists of twenty-five signs for the letters of the alphabet . . . , and of the signs invented by M. Pereire to make it conform to the rules of French pronunciation and spelling. Hence, there are as many speech sounds . . . and as many

clusters in normal writing . . . as there are signs in the manual alphabet. . . . It is true that some letters and clusters vary in sound depending on the words in which they occur. In dactylology, all these different sounds are expressed with a single letter or with a cluster of letters; altogether, the system includes more than eighty signs. The hand is used like a pen for making drawings in the air of the periods and accent marks and to indicate the capitals and small letters and abbreviations. The finger movements mark the long, medium, short, and very short pauses observed in speech. [It] includes the signs for numbers and arithmetical operations. . . . Other signs can be added . . . to accommodate the rules of prosody, music, poetry. (p. 26)

That the pupil shared the method its inventor jealously guarded is interesting, but even more interesting is that he found this *manual* technique "as rapid and convenient as speech itself, and as expressive as good writing" (p. 26). But while this was a combination approach, its goal was speech, dactylology constituting an "artificial" rather than a "natural" communication system in that it had to be learned and that it was an instrumental process, not the end product.

The distinction of having been the first deaf author belongs to Pierre Desloges, whose *Observations d'un sourd et muet sur "Un Cours elementaire d'education des sourds et muets,"* published in 1779, was the first defense of sign language used by the deaf community written by one of its members. It was occasioned by a critique by a champion of Pereire's methods, Claude-François Deschamps, who, unlike others in this tradition (if this is not a canard), took poor pupils at no charge, drawing on his own resources. While praising Epée, with whom he had worked briefly, the abbé Deschamps was committed to the method he had learned under Amman. Then, "Pereire's most famous pupil . . . in turn criticized Desloges's book and thus the manualist-oralist battle was joined" (Lane, 1984b, p. 28).

First describing his own experiences as a deaf person, Desloges extols Epée's work, tellingly noting that "the worthy teacher gives public lessons; this way a crowd of onlookers could appreciate the excellence of his method" (in Lane, 1984b, p. 32). He then proceeds to analyze Deschamps's critique, exposing what he alleges are its inconsistencies, errors, and even inadvertent endorsements of signing. So each had his supporters, among both deaf *literati* and educators of the deaf. Epée's reputation was enhanced by Desloges's book and Condillac's endorsement (Sacks, 1989), but could not the field accommodate both? Pereire seems to have been inordinately proud, hostile even to "imitators" like a contemporary named Ernaud, whose reported success precipitated a charge of plagiarism, "difficult to substantiate . . . since he refused to divulge his method for comparison" (Bender, 1970, p. 95). Ernaud's technique may have been not only different but historically significant, for it involved stimulating residual hearing, a concept implying auditory training and anticipating the aural augmentation possible with hearing aids many professionals now consider critical. But for Pereire this was merely a sideshow; the basic principles underlying Epée's techniques represented a greater threat. As Epée gained recognition, Pereire seems to have become increasingly embittered.

The Beginning of "Manualism"

Charles Michel, l'abbé de l'Epée (1700–1789), believing himself "commanded by Providence to render the unfortunate deaf every service within my power for the benefit of current and future generations" (in Lane, 1984b, p. 52), founded the first public school for pupils with disabilities, one of two French schools, Seguin (1843) wrote, "which bring the greatest honor to our country" (p. 2). The Institution Nationale des Jeunes Aveugles, opened by Haüy in 1784 with Epée's inspiration, established for all time the educability of blind persons, as did the Institution Nationale des Sourds-Muets, which opened in 1760, in the case of deaf persons. Like that of others, Epée's involvement began by chance. A Jansenist, he had experienced difficulty in obtaining ordination, but—finally assigned a small parish—he found in one of the homes twin sisters, both deaf, whom he determined to teach to read. At first he used methods of his own invention, but his search led to the writings of Bonet (for which he had to learn Spanish) and Amman. As in other instances we have seen, this success led to more pupils, and Epée, believing his mission was to save as many souls as possible, adopted an approach in striking contrast to the guarded secrecy of others. His vision that the greatest number could be most effectively educated through publicly supported structures was consonant with both Enlightenment thought and sociopolitical developments.

In Epée and Pereire we have a most interesting rivalry. While Pereire, like his British and German counterparts, sought recognition for his accomplishments but would not share his techniques, Epée was a committed proselytizer, eager to demonstrate his methods. Nor did he have qualms about doing battle; since Pereire's criticism of his ideas had appeared in the newspapers, he felt compelled to respond, averring "that although M. Pereire's system of teaching—called dactylology or fingerspelling—could lead the deaf to speak, it was nevertheless utterly worthless for teaching them to think" (in Lane, 1984b, p. 52). Pereire had stated his intent to engage in public debate, he notes, but had failed to do so. We may wonder why Pereire did not join the contest to which he was challenged. (One may wonder even more why, intending that his secret be kept within his family, he failed to ensure even that.) In his increasingly discouraged state of mind, he may simply have chosen not to rise to the challenge. In the style of skilled debate,

Epée (in Lane, 1984b) acknowledges his rival's accomplishments, but left-handedly:

> He had acquired some reputation . . . , and his method for enabling the deaf to speak was considered a justly praiseworthy resource. This person [thus far unnamed] was not the originator of this method, however. It had been practiced about a hundred years before by Wallis in England, Bonet in Spain, and Conrad Amman, a Swiss physician in Holland, who had all published excellent treatises on the subject. He had, however, profited from their work, and his skill in this endeavor merits the approbation he obtained. (p. 52)

Thus, with this faint praise Pereire is damned as little more than a clever imitator. More basically, for Epée, "enabling the deaf to speak" might be a worthy enterprise, but it was neither the fundamental issue nor even of instrumental significance to what was: that deaf persons might realize their inherent potential to use *reason* to acquire academic learning. He thus dismisses his rival: "But I had other, more formidable adversaries to combat, namely those theologians, rationalistic philosophers, and academicians . . . who held that metaphysical ideas were inexpressible by signs and hence necessarily beyond the understanding of the deaf" (p. 53).

While, as today, we can assume that many people experienced progressive hearing loss associated with aging (*presbycusis*), deafness as an educational challenge surely involved then, as now, a relatively small number; thus, we might wonder how newsworthy was this debate. We can assume, given the zeitgeist, that it had a rather high social profile. As Epée implies, the ability of deaf persons to reason was a crucial philosophical issue involved in understanding the nature of reason itself. Moreover, scientific advance had become a matter of "official enthusiasm" (Schama, 1989, p. 185) and intense national pride. And finally, the ideals that would soon be articulated as liberty, equality, and fraternity made the rights of each individual and of every group important to uphold. Pereire had gained the approbation of the Academy of Sciences, but Epée took education of deaf persons to a level of more general significance.

As Louis Braille would transcend the assumption that literacy for blind persons must be based on the symbol system seeing persons use, Epée was the first educator to recognize the linguistic integrity of a manual alternative for deaf persons. The core of his approach was the idea that "the natural language of the Deaf and Dumb is the language of signs, nature and their different wants are their only tutors in it: and they have no other language as long as they have no other instructors" (in Lane, 1984b, p. 85). Since "they are strangers to all languages equally," signs had to be associated with words and grammatical constructions particular to the language to be learned. He assumed that students must commit to memory, through rig-

orous practice, an expanding repertoire of words and of the intricate combinations expressing tense and mood, number and case, and shades and
nuances of meaning. Thus, while instruction began with concrete experiences, transition to formal lessons, paralleling what was taught in regular
French schools, was made as soon as possible.

Predicated on the idea that for his pupils signing was a "mother tongue"
(Bender, 1970, p. 81), Epée's approach was to build on their "home signs,"
modeling French syntax. At first, he also tried to teach his pupils to speak,
using methods based on those of Bonet and Amman, with vowel and consonant sounds introduced in rapid succession, requiring students to practice each phoneme through drill and, as with vocabulary and grammar, learn
by rote. While lip reading and articulation were part of the curriculum he
set forth in a guide for teachers, he later concluded that these were not worth
the tremendous effort required to learn. That opinion seems to have been
shared by students, if one can generalize from Laurent Clerc's recollections
of his own exposure to speech training as odious in the extreme (Lane,
1984a). Epée also understood that deaf persons think not through internalized speech, but through the language of sign. For them, speech was an
"artificial language" (Bender, 1970, p. 85), a view totally alien to the conviction A. G. Bell would assert a century later: "*Speech is everything!*" Epée
was generous to and respectful of his pupils, sharing his own food and fuel
to the extent of jeopardizing his own health, and combativeness notwithstanding, he was more typically self-effacing than apparently was his successor, Roch-Ambroise Cucurron Sicard (1742–1822).

Sicard and His Deaf "Teachers"

Sicard, as head of a school in Bordeaux, was one among many disciples,
and his succession to the directorship was not a *fait accompli*. Being named
to lead the world-famous National Institute required some politicking, which
Sicard glossed over in characterizing himself as heir apparent. In any case,
as his contributions attest, he proved worthy of the mantle, but his tenure
was very nearly quite short. In the Terror in the wake of the Revolution,
priests were rounded up to be summarily tried and executed. Sicard's har-
rowing experience, legendary in the annals of Deaf culture, enters into
Schama's (1989) chronicle, *Citizens*:

> At some point the arrests became absurdly indiscriminant. The Abbé Sicard,
> who was a popular hero among the artisans of Paris as the pere-instituteur of
> deaf-mute children, was picked up and imprisoned in the Abbaye along with a
> large number of priests. On the thirtieth a deputation from the school came to
> the Assembly to plead for the release of their "instructor, provider, father, shut

up as if he were a criminal. He is good, just and pure," they went on, "and it is he who has taught us what we know; without him we would be like animals. Since he has been taken from us we are sad and sorrowful. Give him back to us and you will make us happy."

Moved by this demonstration, a deputy offered to take Sicard's place, but invoking the indivisibility of revolutionary justice, another member, Lequinio, insisted that there be no special exemptions, and the sad little delegation was sent away. The rejection very nearly cost Sicard his life. (p. 625)

When in the general confusion the abbé finally did gain his freedom, he would have been well advised to slip away, but instead returned to present himself to the Assembly and take his leave with dignity. The episode reveals courage, and a flair for high theatre, sustained in his dramatic return to his jubilant pupils and the distraught Jean Massieu, who had led the delegation (Sacks, 1989).

Sicard had enabled Jean Massieu (1772–1846), one of six deaf siblings, to realize his dream of attaining an education at the school at Bordeaux, where he so excelled in his studies that Sicard brought him to the Institution Nationale as an instructor. Through Massieu, Sicard came to a full appreciation of the richness of sign language, and together they refined a system, paralleling French, that would greatly influence American Sign Language (ASL). As a teacher of the deaf who was himself deaf, Massieu began a tradition that, through Clerc, dominated the field in North America for more than six decades. Massieu had a brilliant mind, but also apparently a certain naiveté. He would probably have succeeded Sicard had allegations of improprieties involving two young girls not forced his resignation. Clerc attributed the ouster to the "forces of oralism" led by de Gérando and Itard, as well as Massieu's "guileless" nature. In any case, he was not permanently disgraced. After a brief retirement in the rural countryside he had left to seek his education, he obtained a post at another school, becoming headmaster, and later headed a school at Lille, the first north of Paris (Lane, 1984a).

Clerc seems to regard Sicard's public renunciation of royalism (to which he privately remained committed) as hypocritical, though his negotiable virtue in these times, and also Haüy's as we shall see, might have been the better part of valor. The characterization serves mainly to contrast, for Clerc, Massieu's sincerity. Also, Sicard's contributions owed much to his protegé, for as important as his inspiring example was what he taught his own teacher; thus, in the annals of deaf education it is perhaps Massieu who should be revered, even more than Sicard: "Every great teacher of the deaf," avers Clerc, "is standing in front of a deaf man" (Lane, 1984a, p. 138). Laurent Clerc (1785–1869) surely knew that he too embodied this principle, but while critical of other hearing leaders in the field, his relationship with Thomas Hopkins Gallaudet seems to have been built on mutual respect and affection.

Although Clerc had lost his hearing in infancy, his education did not begin until he entered the Institution at age 12. Like Massieu, he progressed rapidly in his studies to become an assistant, then a teacher. Sicard saw the wisdom in having his two brilliant instructors accompany him on speaking engagements to show what might be accomplished if deaf students had opportunities commensurate with their native gifts; it was such a trip that occasioned their fateful meeting with a very frustrated Gallaudet. Clerc was already an important force in the formation of a deaf community, with the school at its center. As recounted in Chapter 4, this role for schools, the practice of deaf students being taught by deaf teachers, and the shared language and traditions that identify Deaf culture all owe much to him. Clerc, with justification, sees in Sicard's Preamble to his *Course of Instruction for a Congenitally Deaf Person* (in Lane, 1984b) some disingenuousness, in extolling his predecessor as "that sainted priest" and "creator of the art that has produced such an astonishing marvel," while subtly criticizing his methods:

> As for me, I who have the honor to be Epée's direct successor . . . and whom the dying priest charged with propogating his work, if I have made it into a complete system . . . , I must claim to have worked only for the glory of a justly celebrated teacher who gets credit for everything useful in this book. Here is the spirit of those lessons that I received from his lips in friendship. In publishing them, I am merely discharging my sacred debt as his sole heir. Enough for me is the magnificent title of disciple of that prodigious genius who had no guide or model, whose first masterpieces amazed both the city of their birth and the scholars of Europe who proclaimed their glory. (p. 91)

Following these disclaimers, the humble disciple proceeds to ascribe shortcomings to Epée's need for well-deserved "repose at this happy point in his journey" (p. 94): insufficient attention to syntactic analysis and composition of original sentences. The criticisms were well-founded, for Epée sought to replicate the formalism of traditional pedagogy, and Sicard recognized the limitations in this approach in fostering reason and in enabling the student to generate language, rather than merely parrot. To affirm that his work was seminal is to drastically understate the case, for with the insights he gained from Massieu he developed a comprehensive pedagogy. Eager as his predecessor to disseminate the school's philosophy and practices, he traveled widely in Europe, usually accompanied by Massieu and Clerc. After suffering the rebuffs and temporizing of the British educators, Gallaudet found in Sicard welcome assistance, extending even to the "loan" of the invaluable Laurent Clerc.

THINKERS AND HEALERS

In its linking of rationalist philosophy and social reform, the milieu of pre-revolutionary Paris had no precedent. Here, as the centuries-old "problem of the unfortunates" began to be seen in terms of state responsibility and individual rights, the concept of public education introduced for the deaf was extended to blind persons. While more humane care was introduced in reponse to mental aberration, however, "the great confinement" (Foucault, 1965) of insane persons together with criminals instituted in the previous century actually continued. They may have been treated better, but they remained, though unshackled, nevertheless confined. We next describe the first school for blind students, institutional reforms described by the term *moral treatment*, and, finally, the attempt to educate "the wild boy of Aveyron."

Blindness, Education, and a Great Breakthrough

"In three millennia of recorded history no blind child that received education is named until St. Didymus, who lived in the fourth century A.D." (Chevigny & Braverman, 1950, p. 72). More than another millennium passed before the next steps toward literacy beyond these primitive block letters were taken. Early in the 16th century, a Spaniard, Francesco Lucas, devised a means of engraving letters on wood blocks. In 1651, a German named Harsdorffer developed wax tablets so that a blind person could write. Later, Jacob Bernoulli, the great Swiss mathematician, developed a frame to guide Elizabeth Waldkirch's tracing of letters on wooden blocks. But neither block letters nor wax tablets addressed the problem of *what* blind persons could read or that of making literacy available to more blind people. Over the centuries-long "era of speculation" (Rodenberg, 1938, p. 158) many devices were created, with letters of wood, lead, cast metal, and other materials, and some individuals did indeed achieve a degree of literacy, but no feasible, accessible instructional system was discovered.

Then, inspired by a philosopher, an educator of the deaf, and two blind persons—a gifted musician and an impoverished youth—Valentin Haüy founded a school that would influence others and invented a practical method for teaching blind persons to read and write. But it would remain for a product of that school to recognize the need for an alternative to the code used by persons with sight, a departure too radical to gain ready acceptance. "For fifty years," lamented a British scholar, "the genius of Louis Braille was ignored in England" (Rodenberg, 1938, p. 158). In 1932, 80 years after Braille's death, a resolution to adopt a uniform braille system in English-speaking countries was approved, though conflicts continued. Controversies concerning blind literacy have in many respects paralleled those in the education of deaf students, most basically entailing the legitimacy of difference in communication mode, but that issue has in each case entailed others: *where, when* (at what age), *to what purpose,* and *how* instruction should be provided. As with deafness, while this history has involved major contributions of seeing persons, it is ultimately a history culminating in self-advocacy.

To Enlightenment philosophers, blindness was a problem of speculative importance, bearing on the role of sensory experience in reason. Locke (1690/1984) (in *Essay Concerning Human Understanding*) and Berkeley (in *Essay Toward a New Theory of Vision*) had posed theoretical problems involving tactile learning in compensation for vision and whether restoration of sight would effectively cancel the need for such compensation. Diderot pursued these ideas further in *Letter on the Blind* (1749/1965), which, though concerned primarily with religious orthodoxy, played a key role in the beginning of education for blind persons, even anticipating instructional practices. With prescience, he averred that a blind person's compensatory use of other sensory functions was learned, not innate. He also addressed the educability of persons who experienced both deafness and blindness, through systematic association of tactile signs with objects. As with Locke, Diderot's primary interest was in the origin of ideas. Blindness provided a natural circumstance for addressing that basic philosophical problem, rather than a social cause.

But for Valentin Haüy (1745–1822), blindness came to represent a personal commitment. The ideas of Diderot, combined with his admiration for Epée's work and his general sympathies for the poor and unfortunate, influenced the direction of his career. He had taken a minor government post in Paris while completing his education, but having intense interests, especially in language, he took advantage of access as younger brother of a respected mineralogist to a circle of intellectuals. Through these contacts, he met the famous Austrian organist, pianist, and composer Maria Theresia von Paradis, who shared accounts of her own educational experiences and those of an accomplished acquaintance, also blind, named Weissenburg. Haüy was both guided by this information and convinced that music should have an important role.

Individual exceptions notwithstanding, the general status of blind persons in society had always been that of shunned outcast, burden, or beggar, epitomized by the garishly costumed, untrained street performers Haüy observed to contrast so profoundly with Mme Paradis, and the boy who became his pupil he found begging for food for his seven brothers and sisters. Convinced that such things could be changed through training for productive work, he was determined to find practical ways to promote literacy and independence (Lowenfeld, 1975). The zeitgeist of Haüy's Paris, like that of Howe's Boston, was congenial to a young, practical idealist with a sense of mission. Because he was determined to emulate Epée, his choice of blindness was multidetermined; heeding Diderot's words and seeking von Paradis's counsel, he was eager to put that counsel into practice, but he needed a laboratory.

In François Lesueur, Haüy gained his first pupil and subject of experimentation with the devices described in accounts he had read. But he found the various types of apparatus devised to give a blind person access to the printed word impractical for widespread use due to their unwieldiness or the difficulties they would present for manufacture. He nevertheless achieved enough success with François to gain the support of the Société Philanthropique, which turned over to him the education of 12 blind children. Thus, in 1784, the Institution Nationale des Jeunes Aveugles was established. This first special class, though lacking a proper school, met regularly, enabling Haüy to extend his experimentation. It led to a chance discovery, the "greatest single step in the improvement of the condition of the blind" (French, 1932, p. 83), opening the door to literacy and independence.

It was in fact François who made the discovery, for Haüy observed the youth's interest in tactually exploring the letter images that emerged in relief while sorting papers on his teacher's desk. François further demonstrated his ability to decipher other signs and Haüy, noting that the relief effect was enhanced on the wet sheet used in printing, conceived the simple expedient of having type set in inverted form. He then saw the need to enlarge the letters, using a form of italics, to enhance their discriminability. This system of raised print earned the endorsement of the Academy of Sciences. Although later supplanted by the far more efficient dot code, it would die hard because of the merit Haüy identified: its legibility to persons with sight as well as those using touch. But the assumption that blind persons had to be fitted to "the conventions and traditions of sight" was also the fundamental limitation in his thinking (French, 1932, p. 90). As discussed in Chapter 6, Haüy's assumption that literacy must involve the printed word continued to be held by most sighted educators, long delaying widespread use of braille and availability of braille reading materials.

It is ironic that the same sociopolitical forces that created a milieu cordial to education of deaf and blind persons led to events that greatly jeopardized these very efforts. The two national schools created, in large measure, through royal endorsement, noble patronage, and, in the case of deafness, clerical dedication came during the Terror to be seen as "infamous relics of absolutist charity and clerical superstition"; the dominant sentiment was that the pupils should be returned "to the goodwill of the citizenry at large (in other words, to beggary and persecution)" (Schama, 1989, p. 189). Haüy's exhibition of his pupils' musical accomplishments had particularly impressed Louis XVI, and this royal favor alone might have been enough to seal the school's fate. But Haüy's "accommodating nature led him to present himself and his pupils to the Constituent Assembly as 'thoroughgoing Revolutionists,' [and] 'this body, carrying out a Revolution in the name of justice, could not refuse its aid to the weak and the needy'" (French, 1932, p. 91). His expedient stance was, like Sicard's, probably well advised.

Since both schools needed more space, they were temporarily combined in much larger quarters, sharing for three years the facilities of the Convent of the Célestines, under the jurisdiction of the Minister of the Interior, until it was requisitioned for military use. Haüy was named First Instituteur of the Institution for Those Born Blind, heading a staff hierarchy that provided for 18 minor official roles for blind persons, including Leseuer, the first blind teacher of the blind. Though nominally in charge during those turbulent times, Haüy actually had little authority. A year after its relocation to its own site, the school's function had changed significantly, again by decree, to that of "an industrial school and asylum combined" (French, 1932, p. 92), renamed the Institution of Blind Workers. Its 420 residents comprised the "Blind of the First Class," the Quinze-Vingts—the select "fraternity" that had enjoyed royal protection since the 13th century, and the "Blind of the Second Class," inclusion of which reflected presumably egalitarian intent.

By Napoleon's edict, Haüy was responsible solely for the children's education program, an eight-year course that could be begun at age 7. But it was accorded low priority and, in 1802, having incurred Napoleon's displeasure through his continued philanthropic ties, Haüy was dismissed. He next attempted to operate a small, private day school, but it closed in 1805 because of a mismanaged "manufacturing venture" (French, 1932, p. 94), and other sporadic attempts amounted to little. Although Haüy's work had been acclaimed, sociopolitical events kept him from being duly honored during his lifetime. Despite misfortunes of circumstance possibly compounded by indiscretions as an administrator, his contributions, as Lowenfeld (1975) wrote, were monumental: "the founding of the first school for the blind, the purpose of which was well-described as 'to open for them the entreé to the society of other men' . . . , as well as use of embossed print and vocational training" (p. 73). For advancement of education of blind persons, the scene shifted to Germany and England, and in time to America.

Pseudoscience of Mind and Moral Treatment

The Enlightenment's intellectual flowering notwithstanding, most literate Parisians probably found rationalist inquiry less intriguing than reports of sensational phenomena that transpired in the séances Friedrich Anton

Mesmer (1734–1815) conducted in the 1770s. As Pinel ministered to society's outcasts, drawing-room conversation concerned Mesmer's ability to cause wondrous occurrences, even spontaneous cures, as dressed like a magician he moved about a circle of participants around a *bacquet* containing various chemicals and lengths of iron. Unable to offer another explanation, he attributed his powers to animal magnetism based on the principle of magnetic force permeating the universe, a notion derived from astrology that Paracelsus had considered, but the Academy of Sciences interpreted this as evasiveness and branded him a fraud. Mesmerism was a stage in discovering potential therapeutic applications of hypnosis, but until James Braid associated the "trance" with visual fixation it seemed to indicate transport to the spirit world. Ultimately recognized as evidence of the power of suggestion, hypnotism came into widespread use in the late 19th century, most famously in Charcot's demonstrations with female patients experiencing hysteria (Corbin, 1990).

Throughout the 19th century, two distinct streams with respect to the understanding of the mind and mental illness can be traced, one concerned with humane treatment for the disenfranchised, but sanctioned in the interests of social control, the other with more esoteric issues involving the puzzling problem of mental infirmity among the more privileged and the nature of mind itself. From the latter would spring psychoanalysis, "mental health's second revolution" (Hobbs, 1964); the first occurred in the European houses of confinement.

The concept of *moral treatment* has had various and sometimes ambiguous meanings, but its professed intent was in every case to provide some measure of humane care for those who had been objects of both ridicule and fear. Reforms instituted in late 18th century asylums were foreshadowed in antiquity by Soranus, in the 16th by Johann Weyer's crusade against persecution of those accused of witchcraft, and by the work of Vincent de Paul and the Sisters of Charity in the 17th. But those reforms were not nearly as "radical" as another important antecedent. The colony at Gheel, Belgium, from its origin as a haven in the 7th century, represents one of the most striking departures in the annals of treatment of mental illness. Persons were not confined but able to come and go, not incarcerated but "hosted" by families. Kindness was required and cruelty not tolerated; to strike an insane person would disqualify one from being a host. Dorothea Dix was among the many visitors to be inspired by what she saw in Gheel, and other programs built along similar lines emerged, though most 19th-century alienists thought this *family care* approach too "open" for most clients.

While others had advocated humane care before Pinel, Chiarugi, Tuke, and Rush, their efforts had not appreciably improved conditions of institutional confinement. These conditions had, in fact, deteriorated in the lazar houses, the function of which had been converted from confinement of lepers to "formulas of exclusion . . . of vagabonds, criminals, and 'deranged minds'" (Foucault, 1965, p. 7). In a climate more receptive than ever before to humanitarian reforms affecting these and others at the margins, moral treatment was a major advance in society's response to exceptionality, though the unique needs of children would not be addressed for more than a century. Philippe Pinel (1745–1826), the most eminent physician in Paris, mentor to Esquirol and Itard, was the individual most generally identified with "removing the chains," which he gained approval of the Revolutionary government to do on assuming leadership of the Bicetre in 1793 and three years later of the Salpêtrière (Barton, 1987). As Scheerenberger (1983) summarized, his approach anticipated occupational therapy, involving "a calm retreat; a system of humane vigilance; the elimination of physical abuse and chains; freedom from indignities by staff; gentle treatment on a regular, schematic basis; and the provision of entertaining books and conversation, music, and employment in various agricultural pursuits" (p. 46).

"Moral" in the context of these reforms had reference to the emotional realm, but in addition to providing humane care it actually entailed teaching good habits, as would an adult to a child (Barton, 1987). It was, as Foucault (1965) observed, an essentially "*moral*" view of madness (p. 197), a concept Tuke would elaborate. Pinel himself addressed the forms of mental deviance, building on Locke's distinction: "Madmen . . . put wrong ideas together and reason from them; but idiots make very few or no propositions and reason scarce at all." In *A Treatise on Insanity* (1806/1962), Pinel identified five classifications: (1) melancholia, or delirium; (2) mania without delirium; (3) mania with delirium; (4) dementia, or the abolition of the thinking facility; and (5) ideotism, or obliteration of the intellectual faculties and affections. Of the last type he wrote, "The greatest number of ideots [*sic*] are destitute of speech or are confined to the utterance of some inarticulate sounds. Their looks are without animation; their senses stupified; and their motions heavy and mechanical" (p. 165). For them, he assumed, "education would not be appropriate owing to the natural indolence and stupidity of ideots" (p. 203), an assumption that guided him in advising Itard against undertaking Victor's tutelage. It was a view with which Itard concurred; he differed with his mentor concerning Victor's diagnosis, not the prognosis for "ideotism."

Vincenzo Chiarugi (1759–1820) must be ranked among the pioneers of humane treatment. Under his leadership, mechanical restraints of patients in the St. Boniface Hospital of Florence were abandoned in 1774, two decades before Pinel did this at the Bicetre. He also introduced vast improvements in conditions of patient care, especially sanitation, and ended abusive treatment, insisting the patient must be respected as a person (Lewis, 1941). But it was an English Quaker, William Tuke (1732–1822), who had the most pervasive and continuing influence with respect to moral treatment. Tuke was appalled by the degradation and horror of the conditions that prevailed in London's Bethlehem Hospital, founded in 1247, second only to one in Granada as the oldest in Europe. Chained and deprived of privacy and contact with family or friends, patients were "treated" by being bled or purged. The unexplained death of a Quaker woman in the York Asylum in 1792 prompted him to petition the Society of Friends to establish a facility at York along very different lines, with patients admitted irrespective of religious affiliation. The famous Retreat he opened in 1796 bore no resemblance to the usual "madhouse"; in contrast to "Bedlam," a calm, tranquil environment was created to which patients responded positively.

His work was carried on by his son, Henry, a grandson, Samuel, and a great-grandson, Daniel Hack Tuke (1827–1895), famous as both a healer and chronicler of healing. Samuel Tuke's *Description of the Retreat* (1813) suggests the influence of religion in the version practiced, combining benevolence with authoritarianism. The author draws parallels with techniques used to socialize children in guiding patients toward self-control through reward and punishment, "the patient's freedom . . . ceaselessly threatened by the recognition of guilt" (Foucault, 1965, p. 250). Still, treatment seems to have been characterized by an underlying kindness. In a paper, reproduced under the rubric "Psychiatric Romanticism" in a collection titled *Madness and Morals* (Skultans, 1974), S. Tuke described the fundamental principles of moral management: to promote the patient's general comfort, to strengthen patients' own efforts to help themselves and gain control of their problem, and to be cautious in the use of coercion, replacing physical restraint with self-restraint.

The first American mental hospitals, like the Friends Asylum founded in Philadelphia in 1813, were established by Quakers or drew heavily on Tuke's attempt to "reconstruct around madness a milieu as much as possible like that of the Community of Quakers" (Foucault, 1965, p. 243). The first mental asylum in the colonies appeared, in Williamsburg, Virginia, in 1773, even before the first free school, but the Pennsylvania Hospital, founded in 1751 through Franklin's leadership, established a separate section for patients with mental deviance. It was located in a cellar, however, and as in London's Bethl'm, patients were exhibited for a fee, as public entertainment. It was in this setting that Benjamin Rush (1746–1813), a signer of the Declaration of Independence, whose likeness is represented on the seal of the American Psychiatric Association, instituted reforms paralleling those in Europe. Already a respected physician, Professor of Chemistry at the College of Philadelphia, and charter member of Franklin's American Philosophical Society, he accepted a post at the Pennsylvania Hospital in 1787. Beginning in 1789, when he was Professor of Theory and Practice of Medicine, his responsibilities included supervision of the section for patients with mental deviance. His personal interest and philosophy were no doubt influenced by the fact that both a brother and a "favorite" son experienced extended hospitalization for mental problems (Hawke, 1971).

That philosophy was reflected both in the reforms he introduced and in a classic text, *Medical Inquiries and Observations Upon the Diseases of the Mind* (Rush, 1812/1962), published the year before his death. Rush shared the general spirit of optimism and belief in people's ability to control their own lives characteristic of the time. He insisted on humane treatment, with no form of cruelty tolerated, emphasizing pleasant living conditions and general cleanliness. He also advocated fresh air and exercise, which he thought desirable for everyone, anticipating an early 19th century "wellness" movement when vigorous outdoor activity became fashionable and endorsed by physicians.

In his text, which remained the authoritative source for decades, Rush proposed four categories of mental disorders: intellectual derangement (mania, manicula, manalgia, as in catatonic schizophrenia); partial intellectual derangement (hypochondriases, amenomania, as in paranoid schizophrenia); demence or dissociation; and fatuity (congenital, postfebrile, senile, postmanalgic) (Barton, 1987). Concerning the last, he shared the prevalent beliefs as expressed by Pinel, and thus, while insisting on moral management, did not recommend education or therapeutic *treatment* for such patients. Though he observed variability among cases of "fatuity," his understanding of retardation was rather superficial even by the standards of his time. It was not where his primary interest lay. Further, as a physician, Rush employed a curious blend of traditional and enlightened methods; while pioneering revolutionary approaches in treating mental illness, and establishing the first free clinic in North America, he continued to recommend bleeding for all manner of physical symptoms (Barton, 1987). But his concept of an individually tailored intervention plan would become the hallmark of special education. It clearly characterized the approach Itard used with the "wild boy of Aveyron," whom he named Victor.

"A Purely Medical Case"

If any single event could be identified as the watershed in the development of habilitation, it is surely the work of a French physician, Jean-Marc-Gaspard Itard (1774–1836), with a single pupil, a boy believed 12 or 13 years of age. Undertaking this project against expert advice, Itard, who had become a physician almost by chance, considered his effort a failure. At the time their association began, just after Itard had completed his medical training, the boy was already well known through reports of an apparently wild boy foraging for food in the forest near Lacaune. He had been twice captured and had twice escaped, the second time to the region of Aveyron. Again captured by hunters, he was sent to an orphanage, from which he repeatedly tried to escape. This was a newsworthy story arousing the interest of scholars, among them the Abbé Pierre-Joseph Bonaterre, a professor of natural history with a particular interest in the phenomenon of feral children, thought to exist "in a state of nature," isolated from human contact. Bonaterre's description of Victor concurred with the impression of some others that, lacking speech, he appeared to be deaf (Lane, 1976). Thus it was that Victor was sent to the National Institute for Deaf-Mutes, where he was assigned to the care of Itard, newly appointed to an especially created post.

The Revolution had changed Itard's career goals. Although without medical training, he had become an assistant surgeon in the military to avoid conscription, eventually completing his training in 1800. Rush had first contemplated a career in law; of Itard, Scheerenberger (1983) comments, "If it were not for the French Revolution, he undoubtedly would have become a banker" (p. 74). The abbé Sicard, apparently among his first patients, was sufficiently impressed with this young specialist in otology to create a post for him and to assign him what was surely a most challenging case, which Itard accepted eagerly. He concurred with Pinel that the boy's "whole life was a completely animal existence" (Itard, 1806, p. 6), but disagreed with his mentor's conclusion that this was due to "ideocy," seeing instead what could be the result of deprivation of experience. If Pinel were correct, Itard would have agreed that intervention would be a fruitless enterprise, but descriptions of behaviors conceivably adaptive to living in the wild, together with evidence of selective responsiveness to sensory stimuli, convinced him otherwise. Bonaterre had not "detected any clear sign of idiocy," and Itard saw "a child who would have the disadvantage of antisocial habits, a stubborn inattention, organs lacking in flexibility and a sensibility accidentally dulled [and thus] . . . his situation became a purely medical case, . . . the treatment of which belonged to medical science" (p. 10).

The France of Citizen Itard was marked by belief in the rights of the individual and the responsibility—of capable men, of the state, and of science—to honor those rights. Pinel, who advised him not to undertake the attempt to civilize the "wild boy," had effected dramatic humanitarian reforms in the care of unfortunates who languished, incarcerated, under conditions that had degenerated appallingly since Vincent de Paul. Pinel had unchained the mentally ill, founded modern psychiatry, and presaged occupational therapy; yet he believed "idiocy" beyond the scope of treatment or teaching. Itard's project was undertaken not only from humanitarian motives, however, but as an experiment addressing a problem posed by Locke, Condillac, and Rousseau. The notion of subjecting a theoretical proposition to empirical test was itself innovative, certainly in pedagogy. Itard (1804) declared his purpose to be "to determine what might be the degree of intelligence and the nature of the ideas of an adolescent, who, deprived from his childhood of any education, had lived completely cut off from individuals of his own species" (pp. 81–82). But this was more than an inquiry into the effects of early deprivation; it became a naturalistic experiment in application of systematic instruction.

Itard (1806), who proved to be a keen observer and a scrupulous documentor, described a "disgustingly dirty child affected with spasmodic movements and often convulsions who swayed back and forth ceaselessly like certain animals in the menagerie, who bit and scratched those who opposed him, who showed no sort of affection for those who attended him; and who was in short, indifferent to everything and attentive to nothing" (p. 4). We might note that this was, after all, a boy who had been "captured," confined against his will. Of course we cannot know more of his affective state than what observers described, but we surely can assume that he was frightened, perhaps desperately so. The animal imagery and notation of apparently primitive behaviors are certainly congruent with one's notion of how a feral child might behave. But no doubt some readers have observed reactions not unlike Victor's in a young adolescent just brought to a detention or treatment facility. Itard's (1806) theory that Victor had "a sensibility accidentally dulled" was not simply an assumption in line with Condillac's; he himself had seen the boy exposed to cold and dampness without adverse reaction, pick up and replace hot embers that had rolled from a hearth with bare hands, and remove potatoes, familiar from his foraging days, from a pot of boiling water (pp. 14–15). Thus, guided by Condillac's concept that "to think is to sense," he designed a program to stimulate the senses, then enlist them in the service of cognitive and language learning.

His first reports reflected that Victor (as Itard named him, observing an apparent response to the *o* sound) had learned to conform appreciably with requirements in civilization through activities to train the senses of touch, taste, and smell. The full instructional plan, set forth in the second report, involved activities designed to develop (1) sensory functions, (2) intellectual functions, and (3) emotional functions. Although these were designed as a sequence, in practice Itard observed that they were necessarily interactive and reciprocal. His approach (Itard, 1804) was predicated on five "aims":

> To interest him in social life by rendering it more pleasant to him than the one he was then leading, and above all more like the life he had just left. To awaken his nervous sensibility by the most energetic stimulation, and occasionally by

intense emotion. To extend the range of his ideas by giving him new needs and by increasing his social contacts. To lead him to the use of speech by inducing the exercise of imitation through the imperious law of necessity. To make him exercise the simplest mental operations upon the objects of his physical needs over a period of time, afterwards inducing the application of these mental processes to the objects of instruction. (pp. 10–11)

Today's special educator, steeped in principles of applied behavior analysis, cannot fail to be struck by their explicit role in Itard's discrimination training techniques through use of prompts and cues and exploiting of the "imperious law of necessity" in making reinforcing consequences contingent on specific behavior. His accounts of Victor's progress reveal that objectives were to be attained through successive approximations, with the goal of transferring learned behaviors to new, more complex, situations. Not surprisingly given the setting, he worked first on auditory stimulation, followed by visual training, focusing on the senses he considered to be "intellectual," stressing imitation and repetition, of phonemic and graphemic content respectively. Though he did not share Condillac's notion of the primacy of the tactile sense, he reported that soon after beginning instruction Victor's touch "showed itself sensitive to the impression of hot or cold substances, smooth or rough, yielding or resistant" (p. 18). Likewise, his sense of smell had become more sensitive, which he attributed to experiences of thermal and tactile sensitization. Describing the sense of touch, taste, and smell as "only a modification of the organ of the skin" (p. 20), he believed such generalized enhancement, or cross-sensory transfer, provided the foundations for more complex learning (Ball, 1971).

Thinking sensations the components of ideas, Itard then focused on cognitive tasks requiring visual attention and visual memory. In introducing basic imitative writing tasks prior to reading, he anticipated Seguin and Montessori, as well as today's whole-language methods, though in all areas he was flexible, ready to revise and regroup when indicated. For example, borrowing from Sicard's methods, he tried to teach Victor to match objects with their figural representations, outline drawings of the objects on a blackboard. When Victor did not cooperate, he devised an alternative strategy; having observed the boy's "most decided taste for order," he decided to enlist this preference: "By means of a nail, I suspended each of the objects below its drawing and left them there for some time. When afterwards I came to give them to Victor they were immediately replaced in their proper order. I repeated this several times and always with the same result" (Itard, 1804, p. 39). He then varied the order of the drawings, gradually adding more; Victor each time correctly replaced them, indicating that he had learned to discriminate and match based on visual information. After this departure, he

hoped to return to Sicard's sequence of training activities involving matching objects with their names, but this too proved problematic, and Itard
believed he knew why:

> After having been made to feel by repeated comparisons the connection of
> the thing with its drawing, the letters which form the name of the objects are
> placed on the drawing. That done, the drawing is effaced and only the alpha-
> betical signs remain. The deaf mute sees in this second procedure only a change
> of drawing which continues to be for him the sign of the object. It was not so
> with Victor . . . [but] it was easy for me to understand why it was insurmount-
> able. From the picture of an object to its alphabetical representation, the dis-
> tance is immense . . . for the pupil because he is faced with it during the first
> stages of his instruction. If deaf mutes are not held back at this point the rea-
> son is that, of all children, they are the most attentive and the most observing.
> Accustomed from their earliest childhood to hear and speak with their eyes,
> they have more practice than anyone else in the recognition of relations between
> visible objects. (p. 25)

"Itard was *never* content to accept Victor's performance at face value,"
wrote Ball (1971), in his study of Itard, Seguin, and Newell Kephart, a 20th-
century pioneer in sensory methods. "This essential procedure of evaluating the process involved is . . . at the very core of Itard's greatness and depth
as a teacher and a scientist" (p. 23). Itard's place in the history of specialized instruction is assured, his name familiar to every student of an intro-
ductory college course and indeed, through Truffaut's film *The Wild Child*,
to many more people. He went on to pioneer otology and otolaryngology
through his *Treatise on Disease of Ear and Hearing*, classify types of hearing
loss and their implications for children's language development, and work
in the areas of auditory training and speech instruction with deaf children.
Like other great special educators, he has been revered for both his willingness to accept a daunting challenge and for the outcome, reflected in a pupil's
achievement (far short of his goals). Most importantly, Itard created a
method that has influenced practice to this day. As Lane (1976) observed,
the idea of adapting instructional objectives and strategies to the developing needs and strengths of the individual pupil is such a commonplace today,
though imperfectly realized, that one must be reminded of how totally innovative it actually was (p. 5). Itard's far-reaching influence affected most
immediately a young, idealistic physician named Edouard Seguin, whose
innovative contributions to instructional method are described in Chapter 6.

CHAPTER 3

Childhood, Education, and Social Reform

Curiously, we have encountered few children. Even Victor and François Leseuer, young adolescents, were rarities among exceptional pupils, most of whom were adults. Training the young to serve the state, enhance family interests, or comply with divine purpose was as old as human history, but *education* was the prerogative of privileged adult males. That European pattern continued in the New World, with Harvard College founded before the new English convention of local schools was adopted. While the 19th century brought new awareness, the uniqueness of childhood was rarely considered in determining how or what they should be taught. "To educate children for themselves," wrote Seguin (1880) in his capacity as education commissioner, "is rare in Europe, and it is considered rather Quixotic" (p. 3). But the "Quixotic" notion had European roots. Johann Friedrich Oberlin (1740–1826), an Alsatian Lutheran pastor for whom Oberlin College and Oberlinhaus, a home for deaf and blind children, were named, related activities in schools he set up in the isolated villages of his parish to children's daily life experiences, providing care so that parents of very young children could work and obtain training. Seguin himself applied the Rousseauistic belief in educating children for themselves, and Pestalozzi's influence was more evident in classes for deaf youngsters proliferating in Germany than in American common schools. Such developments affecting children with disabilities depended on understanding not only, or even mainly, of disability, but of childhood.

SOCIAL POLICY AND CHILD-REARING

Responsibilities of and for Children

As in the Old World, children of the American colonies were viewed, and dressed, as miniature adults, "the boy . . . a little model of his father, likewise the girl of her mother" (Demos, 1970, p. 58). Mothers bore eight chil-

dren on average, due in part to the high rate of infant mortality and continuing risk to survival (Greenleaf, 1978). For a child who did survive, "reared
in fear of damnation and in morbid preoccupation with the salvation of his
soul" (Despert, 1965, p. 80), life was a serious affair. The state of sin in which
a child was born was evidenced in the very childlike qualities of playfulness,
willfulness, and pleasure-seeking, propensities it was the parents' duty to
curb, monitored by preacher and neighbors (Wishy, 1968). Though less
"puritanical" with respect to "married joys" than usually portrayed (Gay,
1984, p. 49), parents were serious about their child-rearing responsibilities,
imposing demands incommensurate with children's capabilities "to accept
the understandings and conventions that held the community together,
persuading them by precept or force to obey the laws of God and man"
(Handlin & Handlin, 1971, p. 14).

The Puritans, considering the laws of God and man pretty much the
same, attempted "to demonstrate the coincidence between what the Scrip-
tures required and what English law had already provided" (Boorstin, 1958,
p. 24); where major scriptural injunctions like filial obedience were not sufficiently addressed, amendments were added. By 1648, along with idolatry
and blasphemy, cursing a parent and filial rebelliousness were among the
capital crimes, the dire penalty probably never carried out but the offender
required to confess his misdeed publically (p. 28). The colonial, patriarchal
family unit was the mythic image to which reformers like S. G. Howe wist-
fully turned for the care of children with disabilities or without families of
their own. In fact, households often included, as well as extended family
members, "unfortunates" placed there (Demos, 1970). Responsibility for
unfortunates was a local matter, each town responsible to support its own
dependent residents if the family could not (Deutsch, 1949). That this convention persisted is illustrated by the experiences, after her mother's death,
of the young Anne Sullivan, who would become Helen Keller's teacher. But
in Lash's (1980) account we also see the shift, as communities became more
populous, from local responsibility to large, state-operated institutions:

> Even the run-down shack on her uncle's place was too much for her father to
> maintain. He gave it up, and she went to live in the house of her uncle and aunt
> who had taken Jimmie and Mary. Her uncle . . . , unable to get any help from
> her father toward the children's support, . . . appealed to the town. Mary was
> taken by another aunt. On February 22, 1876, Annie and Jimmie, who was on
> a crutch because of his diseased hip, were delivered in a Black Maria to the
> state poorhouse in Tewksbury. (p. 7)

In 1823, J. V. N. Yates, New York's secretary of state, having investigated the status of the poor in that state, reported a total of 22,111 "pau-
pers," 8,753 of whom were children under 14. He differentiated two classes,

6,896 "permanent poor" and 15,215 "temporary poor" but, since all were needy, proposed almshouse legislation. A Senate committee's inspection of the almshouses 30 years later revealed 1,307 children and 3,629 adults living in conditions so horrible that 770 deaths had been reported the previous year. Overcrowding and lack of ventilation, heat, and medical treatment were the norm, with children provided neither education nor "moral training" (Thurston, 1930, pp. 21–28). In 1874, William Pryor Letchworth, a wealthy private citizen (who later founded Letchworth Village, a colony for persons with retardation, in Thielles, New York) undertook an inspection of New York's almshouses. In one, he found 15 children, 6 under age 2 and 4 "defective," all unschooled but cared for by "lunatic and idiot women" (Thurston, 1930, p. 28). With Charles Hoyt, State Board of Charities secretary, he successfully urged legislation prohibiting such placement.

The first English-style workhouse and poorhouse were established in 1771 and 1773, respectively, in Philadelphia (Rothman, 1971), but townspeople developed their own ways of addressing the problem of persons unable to support themselves. Their services could be auctioned ("bidding out"). "Warning out" meant informing someone that the town would no longer assume responsibility for his or her support; unwanted persons, including those with retardation or mental illness, would be loaded into a cart and taken to another town ("passing on,") where the same was likely to be repeated. There were no safeguards against exploitation or assurance that a child would be well cared for (Deutsch, 1949).

The Family Metaphor and "Care of Unfortunates"

By the time Anne Sullivan was taken to Tewksbury, many states had adopted policies to regulate local provisions. Kentucky had since 1793 provided support to towns for placing out "idiots and lunatics," an ostensibly progressive system Dorothea Dix nonetheless thought impossible to monitor to prevent abusive treatment. Thus, while Howe argued for *dispersion* of dependent persons to surrogate families, Dix (1843) thought centralized arrangements essential. The issue especially involved children, for by midcentury there were more than 50 orphan asylums in the United States, inexorably increasing in both size and number (Rothman, 1971). Management was strict, regimentation to build character often crossing the line of abuse; as criticism grew, foster care and adoption alternatives gained support and, in 1909, endorsement of the First White House Conference on Children.

Moral management implied kindness, but it also implied obedience, compliance, and subordination to authority; its implicit "family metaphor," while humane, was at its heart a system of control. Moreover, increasingly crowded conditions in asylums of all kinds made repressive measures and militaristic regimentation inevitable. Sometimes such measures were adopted reluctantly, as means justified by worthy ends. Dr. Samuel Wolfenstein, superintendent of the Cleveland Jewish Orphan Asylum from 1878 to 1913, felt compelled by increasing numbers of newly arrived immigrant children to abandon his plan to run that institution on a family model, yet saw himself as a beneficient father figure, a perception shared by the trustees and even some children (Polster, 1990).

Quaker tradition emphasized service and beliefs congruent with American democracy in its essence: equality of all, rejection of superficial formalism, and tolerance of beliefs of others (Boorstin, 1958). While the new nation was established at "one of the lowest points in the influence of religion in its history" (Miller, 1987, p. 250), Quakers were joined by other denominations in service, if not in tolerance. The Second Great Awakening during the Republic's first four decades was, like the First, which occurred in the colonies in the 1730s and 1740s, essentially evangelical and concerned with personal salvation. But along with such reforms of morals as abstinence from drink, dancing, lotteries, and swearing, it stimulated "humanitarian associations: for aiding the poor, the deaf and dumb, the mentally ill, and, above all, for the ending of slavery" (pp. 252–253). From evangelicals to Unitarians, the image of a loving Deity inspired a social gospel and unprecedented philanthropy. By 1873, with establishment of the National Conference of Charities and Corrections, Boards of Charities were formed in most states and many large cities had Charity Organization Societies (Deutsch, 1949). Yet, charity is inherently patronizing, and the structures created by affluent and respectable society were also more elaborate systems of protection from the dangerous classes; while originally intended to bring people together, across social classes, in a harmonious community, philanthropy became by midcentury a "principal means of maintaining these divisions" (Dalzell, 1987, p. 161).

The fate of children of the poor, including the probable disproportionate number with disabilities, was as always subject to considerations other than their own well-being, but for others the situation was changing. Many feared that loosening of constraints and parental authority, essential to family and community integrity, meant a decline in morality; where colonial laws prescribed severe punishment, even death, for an insubordinate child, 19th-century statutes gave a son treated too severely by his father recourse to appeal to a justice of the peace. Child mistreatment had been proscribed by statute in Massachusetts in 1735, with intent to provide for neglected children a "good family life and a decent and Christian education" (Costin, 1979, p. 188), but abuse of course continued. Cases involving both British and American children long had advocacy only through societies formed to protect animals from cruelty (illegal in England since an 1822 Act of Parliament acknowledging the "rights of animals" to humane care [American Humane Association, 1992]). For many, economic value meant liberation. Another element, a core facet of Romanticism, was the "cult of childhood," which glorified this stage of life. We shall return to this growing sentimentality that coexisted with continued exploitation of children of the poor. Industrialization harbored little sentiment concerning "unfortunates," even children.

Child Labor

That children were exploited in 19th-century mines and mills is generally known; less well known is that many viewed such employment as a boon, alleviating the burden of slums and poorhouses. While the situation epitomized industrialization's paradox of deprivation in the midst of plenty, poverty resulting from progress, Edward Macauley maintained that the poor were "better fed, better lodged, better clothed, and better attended in sickness . . . owing to that increase of national wealth which the manufacturing system has produced" (in Roe, 1947, p. 90). Ridiculing Romantics like Robert Southey for thinking, in his "wildest paroxysms of democratic enthusiasm," that governments should be more concerned with "rose-bushes and poor rates" than steam engines, Macauley believed progress inevitable under a system of laissez-faire, with no restriction on the "industry of individuals" (p. 93). Even a child with retardation was a beneficiary in this "natural progress of society," for the factory owner was required to employ one "idiot child" from an asylum for every 20 poorhouse inmates. But in both England and America, children's 12– 15-hour workdays, in chains and under an overseer's whip, belied altruistic intent; "if there was a job in a factory that could be done by a five-year-old, one should be hired to do it" (Felt, 1971, p. 41), and more than half those so employed, some as young as 4, died or were crippled as a result (Todd & Curti, 1966). Since their lot would have been bleak in any case, industrialists were not greatly concerned.

The view that government should not interfere was prevalent in England, but while Southey, Elizabeth Barrett Browning, and other literati spoke out against exploitation of children, some took action. Most familiar is the name of Anthony Ashley-Cooper, seventh Earl of Shaftsbury (1801–1885), who sought reform in care of persons with mental illness, sanitation, and other causes involving the unfortunates of English society, including children exploited in mills and mines. His efforts to bring to public attention the many deaths from tuberculosis among child workers led him to be called the "Champion of the Factory Children" (Battiscombe, 1975, p. 77). Another was Richard Oestler, a land-agent whose friends included mill owners, one of whom invited him to see "reforms." Appalled by the grim conditions under which children worked, he began a crusade that earned him the sobriquet "Factory King," urging voters to reject any politician who would not pledge to support a reduced workday for children. The Factory Act of 1819, passed mainly as a result of his agitation, prohibited hiring of children younger than 9 and limited the workday to 12 hours for those under 16. His efforts to extend and ensure enforcement of these reforms resulted in accusations of betraying his class, loss of employment, and three years in the Fleet Prison for debtors until friends could raise a sufficient sum for his release. But his continued campaign led to further legislation (McCarthy, 1915).

Significant American reform in child labor did not occur until 1933, with Roosevelt's National Recovery Administration. In colonial times, the single right of women and children was the right to protection, but as industrialization gained momentum, conditions and wages deteriorated; a major factor was massive immigration, 500,000 in the 1840s and 1,500,000 in the 1850s. Labor, especially child labor, was cheap. For a child of 10, workdays that began at four in the morning and lasted until seven or eight at night were common. But although "hardly any institution . . . escaped scrutiny of some group determined to change it" (Frazier, 1971, p. 205), exploitation of children and degradation of women were not major preoccupations of reformers. Enslavement of African Americans was, of course, the crucible on which the nation's very existence would be tested, and "Bostoners" like S. G. Howe, whose causes were many, was a committed abolitionist. But abolitionists seemed to say little specifically about the impact of the institution on children. While encompassing them, most campaigns were not directed at children qua children, yet they paralleled a growing Romantic idealization of childhood against which the daily lives of children experiencing bondage, poverty, disease, and grueling, crippling labor stood in stark contrast.

Child-saving in a Philanthropic Era

While parents and children surely had bonds of affection, as well as duty, at a societal level an almost pedaphobic, pious hostility can be discerned (Wishy, 1968). Children could be an economic asset, but they could also be a liability. Large numbers of children in families, and of children without parents or with parents unable to provide supervision or suitable upbringing, concerned respectable folk. The social gospel preached the church's duty to the "perishing" and "dangerous" classes, a dual theme reflected in reforms involving children, particularly in cities and more particularly children of immigrants. Growing numbers of unsupervised young posed a menace, the most ambitious response to which was the Children's Aid Society, the beginning of American foster care.

Charles Loring Brace (1826–1900), having completed studies at Union Theological Seminary, was asked to head "a mission to children" in New York in 1853. Sharing Howe's belief that sending them to live with farm families represented their best hope, Brace devised a placing-out system to relocate the thousands of vagrant, mostly immigrant children, roaming the streets of New York and other Eastern cities. Over the 37 years he led the agency, Brace earned an international reputation as an authority on services for children. In his own account, *The Dangerous Classes of New York, and Twenty Years' Work Among Them,* Brace warned, "This dangerous class has not yet begun to show itself as it will in eight or ten years, when these boys and girls are mature. . . . They will have the same rights as ourselves. . . . They will poison society" (in Wishy, 1968, pp. 16–17).

Like the Poor Laws, many philanthropic enterprises seem to have been predicated more on the need to protect society than on concern for unfortunates themselves, even children. Perhaps this was the most effective way to enlist support. Brace's appeal to fears notwithstanding, the organization clearly benefited many children. From 1854 to 1874, about 20,000 were rounded up in New York and sent by train to live with midwestern and southern foster families; by 1929, the agency had placed out more than 100,000, and many more benefited indirectly from Brace's social ministry (Costin, 1979). The system was not without problems. Since the older ones were expected to earn their keep, there were concerns for exploitation, and while most were Catholic, placement was mostly with Protestant families, which drew church criticism, but increasingly Catholic and Jewish agencies worked for adoptive and foster placement in preference to asylum care.

Whatever other motives were operating, such efforts were surely driven in some measure by genuine concern for children, deriving from religious awakening, belief in rights of the individual, and a growing appreciation of childhood itself. Physicians were among the leaders of early 19th-century welfare efforts, including those affecting persons with disabilities, but their involvement reflected the general humanitarian movement, rather than medical or scientific interests (Bremner, 1970). The language of health and sickness was often used with reference to disability; "cure" in connection with deafness had in the oral tradition meant acquiring speech, the roots of the "medicalization of deafness" (Lane, 1992), and the issue of cure of retardation would also prove most problematic. But except in a metaphoric sense, disability was being viewed more in educational than in medical terms. In his "Sermon Delivered at the Opening of the Connecticut Asylum for the Education and Instruction of Deaf and Dumb Persons," in 1817, T. H. Gallaudet interwove such medical imagery with images of imprisonment and release:

But there is a sickness more dreadful than that of the body; there are *chains* more galling than those of the dungeon—*the immortal mind preying upon itself*, and so imprisoned as not to be able to unfold its intellectual and moral powers, and to attain to the comprehension and enjoyment of those objects, which the Creator has designated as the sources of its highest expectations and hopes. Such must often be the condition of the uninstructed deaf and dumb! (p. 1)

Physicians like Howe joined clergymen like Gallaudet in seeing instruction as the bridge for one reaching out for release from isolation. With neither sight nor hearing, Laura Bridgman was "alone and helpless in a deep, dark, still pit, and . . . I was letting down a cord and dangling it about, in hopes she might find it; and that finally she would seize it by chance and, clinging to it, be drawn up by it into the light of day, and into human society. And it did so happen; and thus she, instinctively and unconsciously, aided in her happy deliverance" (Howe, 1875, p. 73). Since many marveled at what had been thought impossible, reports of success were sometimes exaggerated. Caution may have played a role in the secrecy of oral educators of the deaf; hope that education might cure could, and in the case of retardation did, have disastrous consequences. But even less sensational reports could backfire, while some who marveled did so with a certain patronization. The fifth annual report, for 1841, of America's first state facilty for the blind, in Ohio, addressed both issues:

The ease with which most of the Blind learn to read, and the proficiency which some of them make in their general studies, have frequently led to reports concerning them highly exaggerated, and bordering on marvelous. These give rise to unreasonable expectations, which are unfavorable to them. No pretensions are made to extraordinary proficiency; nor do they invite the apology, so often made for them, that they do well *for blind persons*. They desire to be judged simply on their merits as scholars—not *as the blind*—and with no more indulgence than is awarded to seeing pupils. (Ohio Institution for the Instruction of the Blind, 1842, pp. 6–13)

Unrealized expectations threatened other reforms involving children, like the Infant School and the kindergarten. Many viewed child welfare as instrumental to other goals, but some, like Gallaudet, spoke for the child, nor was his concern restricted to those who were deaf. A guide for parents he published in 1831, blending religious values with empirical methods of instruction, was reflective of a genre coming into vogue that soon expanded markedly. While stressing the importance of Bible reading, Sabbath observance, and other orthodox conventions, he drew on new and unorthodox pedagogical ideas possibly suggested by experiences with deaf pupils. Mothers should capitalize on the child's "sense impressions of daily life," he advised, and lead their children gradually, building on what was familiar, to acceptance of God's guidance. They were cautioned not to overwhelm the child's mind or over-tax "tender emotions," but to capitalize on every indication of curiosity and be guided by the child's advancement through successive stages of development (Wishy, 1968, p. 30). The account of his youngest son and successor (Gallaudet, 1888) suggests that as a parent he practiced what he preached.

Building of character and inculcation of piety had lost none of their importance, but Gallaudet believed these goals better accomplished through gentle nurture than preachment and punishment. Later kindergarten pioneer Kate Douglas Wiggins, influenced by Rousseau, Pestalozzi, and Froebel, agreed that character need not be built at the expense of childhood pleasures; even as they were prepared for adult responsibilities, children had a right to their own world (Weber, 1969). But in the 1830s, the notion of children's rights was a "minor enthusiasm" (Wishy, 1968, p. 30) compared with other campaigns. More typically, articles in the *Mother's Magazine* enjoined mothers to impose discipline early, with the rod when necessary, to curb children's rebelliousness, cruelty to animals, and "teasing idiot or imbecile persons," which lead to criminality and family disgrace. Freud's claim that most beneficent adults were once little sadists would have seemed absurd to most people.

SCHOOLING FOR ALL

Developments that led to public responsibility for educating all American children began with a 1647 statute in the Massachusetts colony requiring townships of 50 or more households to appoint a teacher of reading and writing, "dame schools" that provided access, albeit crudely, to basic literacy. Towns of 100 households were required to establish an English-type Latin grammar school. Though couched in religious precept, instruction was aimed "to promote the welfare of the state by making citizens capable of self-government" (Tanner & Tanner, 1990, p. 31), consistent with the colonists' practical bent, combining piety with the business of building "a city on a hill" (Boorstin, 1958). With religious freedom considered "the first liberty" (Miller, 1987), and growing secularization of American life, preparing citizens for a democracy became the dominant concern, as it would be for Howe, Gallaudet, and Seguin with their exceptional pupils. The Revolution interrupted progress toward universal schooling, which had affected fewer than half the *white* children, but in 1789 Massachusetts authorized towns to form school districts, and in 1827 to empower school trustees to hire and fire teachers, a system of state-regulated local districts that has remained the fundamental structure of American public education.

The notion that education should be generally available was itself revolutionary, which contributed to the defeat in Virginia of Jefferson's proposal that all children have three years of elementary education at public expense, the "best boys" going on to grammar school (Pratte, 1973). The curriculum would be secular, religious instruction replaced by the study of history, and the grammar school curriculum of Latin, Greek, English, geography, and higher arithmetic serving as preparation for higher education. It met with ecclesiastical resistance, as had a plan conceived by Franklin, whose own formal education consisted of just one year in the Boston Latin Grammar School. Impressed by a visit in 1763 to the Negro School founded by Quakers in Philadelphia, he believed education should be available to African Americans and women, emphasizing preparation for practical and moral living. While unsuccessful, it gave impetus to the academy movement; an academy he himself founded in 1751, rechartered in 1755 as the College, Academy and Charitable School of Philadelphia, became the University of Pennsylvania (Blinderman, 1976).

"Public academies," which appeared after the Revolution, were not free but open to the public and, though unaffordable for most, by 1820 had virtually replaced publicly-supported grammar schools, which became basically schools for children of the poor. In cities like New York and Philadelphia, bequests and grants enabled incorporated school societies to provide rudimentary instruction, native-language schools for certain European immigrant groups constituting a third type. While academies featured a classical curriculum, they enterprisingly offered training in trades, responding to more utilitarian needs and thus attracting more tuition-paying students. They also introduced new equipment, such resources as libraries, and innovative methods. But their ascendance underscored class distinctions, which Mann's common-school concept opposed as counter to the democratic spirit and need for an informed electorate. Mann thought free schools for all could enable the poor to rise, but to avoid a two-tiered class structure, they must be of even better quality than private alternatives. Howe, Seguin, and Mann himself also advocated publicly supported education for children with disabilities so they too could become contributing citizens, a facet of a more general trend to extend schooling for the good of society.

Inclusion of girls is a striking instance. The "learned ladies" of history were all the more exceptional for the prejudices that long excluded females; European and hence American views of women and of schooling were that they were incompatible (Brickman, 1983). Philadelphia's Quaker Latin schools were pre-Revolutionary exceptions in enrolling girls (and poor children at no charge). Colonial statutes equated "children" with boys, but with extension of the philosophy of natural rights to women, girls attended schools in most communities. Waves of immigration between 1880 and 1914 would challenge the common school. In that same period, common schools would begin to provide for children with physical and mental disabilities, introduce services to ameliorate health problems, and deal with "unruly" pupils. These two sets of challenges were by no means unrelated.

How Do Children Learn?

While they continue to be debated, new perspectives on children's nature and nurture emerged with the Enlightenment. Children, once thought innately depraved, were innocent and malleable, and teaching, traditionally a process of abstract formalism and moralistic preachment, was viewed as nurturant care with provision for active experience. These changes did not occur at one dramatic historical moment but by degree. Pedagogy had long been based on memorization, and the idea of mental powers, made academically respectable by Scottish and German faculty psychologists, suggested a basis for recitation and drill. Thus, teaching of deaf pupils had relied heavily on mental training; for those with retardation, the question was whether they possessed certain faculties at all, for if not instruction was considered futile. (Later authorities reported absence of a "moral faculty" in a significant subgroup; old ideas, like old habits, die hard.) The issue of how children should be taught is inseparably related to that of what they should learn, and both depend on beliefs about the child's nature. In the southern colonies Anglicism influenced schooling; Calvinism influenced New England's dame schools, which, despite loose attendance and discipline, taught piety and precepts of righteous behavior under threat of damnation. The shift to a moral focus still implied that children needed to be controlled.

Rote instruction had its critics, notably Mann, who thought the alphabet method of teaching reading, reciting from *The New England Primer*, was meaningless memorization that destroyed pupils' motivation. He proposed instead a whole-word method as more consonant with the way children acquire language and more likely to engage them, an idea that found a more receptive audience in his friend Howe, influencing his work with blind pupils, than in the increasingly crowded schoolhouse where the concern was attaining some measure of efficiency in the face of a seemingly impossible situation. In many city schools a teacher attempted to instruct in one room as many as 80 pupils of all ages. Groups of pupils using the same book "said" their lessons, then, seated uncomfortably on chairs not appropriate for any age, awaited their next turn, a system both ineffective and inefficient. Since efficiency, a growing preoccupation in manufacture of goods, was assumed necessary in schooling, improved ways to monitor recitation were proposed.

Joseph Lancaster's model, which gained much attention in the 1820s, enabled a teacher to handle from 200 to as many as 1,000 pupils. Monitors selected from among the brightest scholars were instructed, then took their stations, each directing a row of about 10 youngsters, who moved rapidly from one lesson to the next with recitation almost continuous. As today, the economy of such a system, no matter its quality, appealed to policy-makers, but most schools that adopted the model abandoned it by the 1850s (Kaestle, 1973). As long as there was agreement that teaching was a matter of getting knowledge into the pupil's mind, that this was best done through reciting and memorizing, and that mass education required mass-production strategies, the only question remaining would seemingly be the classic one posed by Herbert Spencer (1860, p. 21): "What knowledge is of most worth?" But that question implies others about teaching and learning. A positive aspect of faculty psychology's influence was the view that the physi-cal, moral, and intellectual faculties were interdependent and should all be addressed. Though seldom put into practice, this principle implied a bal-anced curriculum to enhance the development of "the whole child" and "to prepare us for complete living" (p. 31). To some intellectuals, children and the process of their development were becoming subjects of great interest.

Pedagogical Innovators

Teachers of deaf pupils were not alone in their concern for method, nor were the social and intellectual forces influencing them distinct from forces influ-encing other pedagogues. The idea of natural rights underlay the American and French revolutions, and philosophical works that inspired them addressed not only the right to education but also how it might best be realized. Bacon urged teachers to lead pupils in thinking inductively about what they observed in nature, an approach Comenius systematized through "excursions" and use of pictures and objects as aids in the German *Realschulen*, anticipating Pestalozzi's "object lessons." Like Rousseau, Johann Heinrich Pestalozzi (1746–1827) believed the natural development of the child should guide in-struction. Since children learn through direct experience, self-initiated activ-ity, and "sense impressions," teachers should allow expression of natural impulses, encouraging play and observation of nature. He espoused the edu-cational psychology of his time that described the mind as comprising dis-crete faculties, but where others believed the faculty of memory, but not those of generalization and analysis, operative in young children, he considered young children's minds actively engaged in organizing experiences. Pestalozzi's credibility was greatly enhanced by demonstrations of his ideas in a school for poor children he opened at Yverdon in 1805 (Downs, 1975), and his influ-ence extended to German methods of teaching deaf children.

Nor was Mann the only American critic of prevailing practices. The notion that children needed nurture and liberation rather than taming and training found support among liberal religious leaders like William Russell, an emerging class of affluent women involved in reform, and Romantic transcendentalists like Bronson Alcott. Overseas, the Infant School movement began in 1816 when Robert Owens opened the "Institution for the Formation of Character" for young children of women employed in his factories in New Lanark, Scotland (Robson, 1989). The model, which stressed learning through play, observation, imagination, and active inquiry, eschewing moralistic lessons since children were innately good, gained an American following among educators like Elizabeth Peabody, who thought all schooling could be reshaped along such lines. But since many thought it a means to stabilize society through early training of poor children, what became translated into practice was a notion diametrically opposed to the spirit of the Infant School. As would prove true of a latter-day version, the so-called Integrated Day, its influence was short-lived, the failure in the 1830s as in the 1970s probably due to a gap between theory and practice. The notion of children as self-motivated learners was not reflected in these "American adaptations of Pestalozzian schools [which] . . . briefly flourished" but failed to take root (Hewes, 1990, p. 7).

By the century's end, the growing interest in the child was shared by social scientists, as well as reformers. In the proper nurture and education of the child lay the hope of humanity, and nurture and education were especially interwoven in Friedrich Froebel's kindergarten. Froebel, who had opened his first kindergarten in 1837 in Austria, believed that the young child's natural development should be fostered, toward an ideal of unity with God and nature, through certain materials ("gifts") and activities ("occupations") that symbolized such unity. His concepts represented a significant departure from traditional notions, as a government pamphlet (Harrison, 1914) suggested:

> For the teachers of the 18th century the child was . . . different from the adult only in size, strength, and knowledge. . . . Education consisted in training and instruction—not in development. It was artificial rather than natural. . . . For Rousseau and his disciples childhood was not manhood or womanhood in miniature, but something different, with interests, ideals, virtues, and activities of its own, a stage in the development of the individual, on the proper unfolding, strengthening and functioning of which depends the welfare of the future man or woman. . . . It remained for Froebel . . . to comprehend infancy— the first 6 or 7 years of life—as the most important period in the life of the individual and . . . most important problem in education. (p. 23)

The kindergarten posed a "problem" as the formative influence of early experience was increasingly recognized. Thus, "the fervent faith of the kindergarten enthusiasts led to the most extravagant claims. . . . [As] 'the one thing needful,' the kindergarten promised everything from the prevention of juvenile delinquency to the salvation of man and the regeneration of society" (Wishy, 1968, pp. 140–141). After Elizabeth Peabody (1804–1894), with her sister Mary Mann, opened the first English-speaking program in Boston in 1860, the number of kindergartens increased, from 10 to about 400 in the 1870s, the first public kindergarten appearing in 1873. Encouraged by social settlements and community associations of prosperous women, the number grew by 1894 to about 4,000 (Hewes, 1990). But the kindergarten had not been conceived as a compensatory program, as would be nursery schools in England.

While critical of European pedagogy, Seguin (1880) thought some practices superior to those of his adopted country: "The European children enter the school younger, are trained longer, and are advanced farther than the Americans" (p. 4). He was impressed by two developments in infant education: the Froebellian kindergarten and, for children of the poor, the Salle d'Asyl, organized by Madame Marie Pape-Carpentier, seeing Rousseau's (we would add Pestalozzi's) influence in both, with objects preferred to books and *joujoux* (playthings), "the intermediate means of experience between the great realities of life and the smallness of the child" (p. 40). Froebel's notions that children learn through play and that education should begin at age 3 or 4 were better received elsewhere than in Germany, for in 1851 the kindergarten was actually *banned* in Prussia. The experiential methods Seguin described were by then finding their way into some American elementary schools. In 1862, an educator named Adonijah S. Welch published a guide to train teachers in the normal schools in the use of object lessons. Both ideas, experiential learning and teacher training, reflected the influence of Pestalozzi, which began to be felt in America after the Civil War. Both had a strong advocate in Horace Mann, who envisioned education for all provided by skilled teachers, based on current and complete knowledge of the learning process.

Romanticism, Childhood, and Giftedness

The father of author Louisa May Alcott could, if we stretch a point, be seen as a pioneer in the facet of special education concerned with gifted children, but he was a central figure in the "cult of childhood" (Boas, 1966). Having learned of Philadelphia's and New York's Infant Schools, he was invited in 1816 to head such a school in Boston, where to enter grammar schools children had to be able to read and write. Infant Schools seemed a means to prepare children of poor immigrants, but Alcott, like Howe, reacted negatively to such charity mentality. Also, his agenda probably required rather different "material." Long before Hall used questionnaires to ascertain "the contents of children's minds," the baby biography was a child-study technique. While Hall's methods surely marked an advance in objectivity, the richness of a descriptive record of a single child's development over time argues for what we today call qualitative methods, and one could not fault the journals kept on the Alcott children for lack of detail. His goal was ambitious: Each journal, taken over by its subject and maintained throughout her life, would be a record of the "history of human nature" and the basis for a theory of education grounded in "scientific observation" (Bedell, 1980, pp. 57–58). Though his grandiose goal of a major philosophical work was not realized, the records of the early years of three of his four daughters constitute 2,500 pages, the most complete record of its kind to that time, and presaged the child study movement.

Guided more by personal inclination than by theory, he sought to instill in his children "a love of goodness, the spirit of self-sacrifice and a loving regard for each other, their parents, and the world" (Bedell, 1980, p. 78), mainly by inducing fear of loss of love. But accepting each as an individual, he eschewed pressure to achieve to the point of indulgence, valuing instead imagination, "the very core of holiness." Their drawings, stories, and make-believe revealed "the spiritual world from which they had come" (pp. 87–88), a Wordsworthian theme making teaching a process of drawing out wisdom rather than putting in knowledge. The highest level of knowledge was "spirit culture," a notion described by William Ellery Channing, the Unitarian minister who influenced Dorothea Dix (Albert, 1981), which he sought to evoke through conversation and journal-keeping. His "conversational method" of "tempting" or drawing out children's ideas greatly impressed Peabody, who thought the journals of his Philadelphia School of Human Culture pupils the work of "a cluster of Platos in miniature . . . as wise and solemn as their teacher himself, and like him steeped, from birth it seemed, in the philosophy of transcendentalism" (Bedell, 1980, pp. 90–91).

Temple School opened on the fourth floor of the Masonic Temple on Tremont Street in Boston on September 22, 1834, with 18 young pupils, including a "prize acquisition . . . a stuttering genius of five years of age, Josiah Phillips Quincy, whose grandfather was the president of Harvard and mayor of Boston" (p. 93). Imaginative self-expression was encouraged, and children's ideas were never to be criticized, even if they differed from their teacher's. In practice, however, his subtle control techniques of "rejection, abandonment, or threat of abandonment" (p. 96) made that unlikely. His control through guilt extended to having a disobedient pupil hit *him* with a ruler, with remarkable results; Peabody marveled that boys who would take punishment in stride were moved to tears when made to strike their teacher. That pupils' thoughts were astonishingly like their teacher's is not surprising, for "the thoughts [he] drew out . . . were his own . . . he thought that their Platonic utterances merely confirmed the divine rightness of his own ideas" (Bedell, 1980, p. 94). His belief in divine intuition may have been illusory, but the seriousness and enthusiasm of children of some of Boston's best-known families greatly impressed visitors.

The enterprise was short-lived. Though a depression had lessened tolerance for new ideas, Alcott characteristically would not temper his teaching, introducing instead what were rumored to be scandalous biblical discussions. As pupils were withdrawn, mounting debts forced him to locate the remnants of the school in his home. Abolitionist sentiments of these Bostoners notwithstanding, admission of a black child in June 1839 was the last straw; with no pupils, his career was destroyed. For all his foibles, Alcott's abundant gifts attracted intellectuals like Thoreau, who found him a receptive listener, and Emerson, whose melancholy temperament contrasted with Alcott's romantic optimism, his cares including a brother, Bulkeley, with retardation, as well as the tuberculosis that only he of several brothers survived. Alcott's conception of childhood found support in transcendentalism, but Emerson could share neither his romantic notions nor his optimism.

While "the transcendentalist Alcott was the messenger in a holy cause" based on neo-Platonic notions, discussions in the school the Reverend Joseph and Lucy Clark Ware Allen kept in their home in Northborough, Massachusetts, focused on everday problems rather than abstract ideas (Albert, 1981, p. 568). Sharing the transcendentalists' belief in children's inherent goodness but anticipating the progressivists' recognition of the often adverse role of the environment, the Allens created a "home school" that, from 1818 through 1852, served some 130 children, including their own seven. Many had family problems, often a father who was alcoholic or in jail, and Lucy Allen, whose father, Henry Ware, was an important figure in liberal Unitarianism, believed education for parenthood would be desirable if it were feasible. But she thought classical boarding schools and even the common schools, with their "long, tedious lessons . . . taught with the help of canes, and sullen children who reinforced a bad system with antisocial behavior," even worse influences than poor parenting (p. 576). The Allens believed children needed a degree of freedom in order to learn to make good personal choices, and that conflicts could best be resolved if the children themselves shared in formulating rules democratically.

"Special" Educators, "Special" Students

The Allens did not claim proprietorship of some "approach" for a certain "type" of child, and Alcott sought not to be a teacher of "gifted children" but to draw out the gifts in all children. To what extent he shaped the lives of his pupils we cannot know, though some, like Martha Ann Kuhn Clark, classical scholar and champion of higher education for women, achieved distinction. Should their achievements be ascribed to their visionary teacher, or might we infer that he had a select group of pupils? If the former, could not others—selectively—emulate his techniques? Instead, he is remembered as the father of Louisa May Alcott, whose strong will surely rebelled against his subtly manipulative means of control. Burton Blatt (1981) summarized the qualities of those who have developed "spectacular methods": "Each appears to have a dynamic quality . . . [and] a powerfully charismatic personality that brings droves of disciples into the fold" (pp. 20–21). The force of a powerful personality has been evident in pioneer special educators like Seguin, who shared Alcott's charisma, and also his difficulty in systematizing and communicating his methods. Seguin's legacy with regard to the instruction of "normal" children, was successfully passed on through Montessori, but his optimism concerning retardation paradoxically contributed to disillusionment when others could not replicate his success.

Despite attempts to test the merits of innovative methods objectively, belief has often outweighed evidence. Bender's (1970) reflections apply to many pedagogical innovations, though they concern the history of rival schools of deaf education, in which each promising new technique has become "so tinged with emotion that it frequently takes on almost the aspect of a cult . . . [making it] almost impossible to obtain an objective judgement on the results claimed" (p. 193). While 19th-century teachers likened teaching to a religious vocation, Alcott's possibly gifted pupils prompt questions about the *student's* contribution. Interestingly, some teachers attained fame because of, or in tandem with, a pupil, most famously Anne Sullivan Macy and Helen Keller, whose accomplishment Mark Twain saw as joint. Though "Teacher" was proud and confrontational, Harry Emerson Fosdick eulogized her for taking a background role in the very area where her genius was manifest: the achievements of her lifelong friend and only pupil (Lash, 1980, p. 658). Another famous, very different, linkage is that of Itard and Victor, but as Scheerenberger (1983) observed, Madame Guerin, Itard's housekeeper, was "the real heroine of this epic" (p. 77), having helped implement the project, then caring for Victor until his death.

Lane (1984a) states that the history of deaf education is one of teachers made famous by a single pupil, or at most a few. Luis illustrated the principle that a single success attested to a teacher's expertise and a method's viability, as did Saboureaux, who "continued his education on his own, becoming the most famous of Pereire's half-dozen pupils and securing for him reknown throughout Europe and an income for life" (p. 6). In continuing Epée's efforts to reach as many deaf pupils as possible, Sicard was aided by Jean Massieu, whom Laurent Clerc regarded, more than any hearing instructor, as his own true teacher. Clerc similarly supported Gallaudet, who displayed his prize pupils (a strategy Howe used to particularly good effect). Some whose innovations had worldwide impact generalized from experience with one pupil (Howe with Laura Bridgman) or a very few (in the case of Bell), but in other instances the name of one famous pupil is not forever linked to that of the teacher. By instructing many and guiding the instruction of countless others, Seguin established Epée's legacy that has dominated special education ever since. Blatt (1981) wrote that more important than any particular method have been the convictions of great teachers that "all people are equally valuable" and all people can learn (p. 27). Another who shared those convictions, like Itard, Seguin, and Howe a physician, created one of the most famous and durable of all pedagogical systems.

Maria Montessori

The first woman in Italy to earn a medical degree, in 1896, Montessori (1870–1952) was struck by her observations of children with retardation in asylums she visited through her work with the University of Rome Psychiatric Clinic, custodial arrangements typical in Italy, excepting a school run by the Sisters of Mercy in Aosta, an area of high prevalence of cretinism. Seeing even in their primitive behaviors indications of attention and curiosity, she thought their natural inclination to learn was not being encouraged, a belief supported by the reports of Itard and Seguin. Adopting the latter's view of retardation as a pedagogical rather than a medical problem, she extended his methods in the Orthophrenic School for the Care of the Feeble-minded she founded and for two years directed. When her pupils' examination performance compared favorably with that of "normal" peers, she thought her "more rational" approach could liberate the personality of all children and lead ultimately to a "complete human reorganization" in society (Kramer, 1976, p. 96).

Redirecting her efforts, Montessori established the first Casa dei Bambini in 1906 in Rome's San Lorenzo quarter, a slum. Reports of its success and publication of *The Method of Scientific Pedagogy as Applied to Infant Education and the Children's Houses* (1909), brought her world fame. "The 'Children's House,'" she explained, "is the *environment* which is offered to the child that he may be given the opportunity of developing his activities." It should be "a real house; . . . a set of rooms with a garden of which the children are the masters" (Montessori, 1914/1964, pp. 9–10). In

> an environment in which everything is constructed in proportion to himself, there will develop within the child that "active life" which has caused so many to marvel, because they see in it not only a simple exercise performed with pleasure, but the revelation of a spiritual life. In such harmonious surroundings the

young child is seen laying hold of the intellectual life like a seed which has thrown out a root into the soil, and then growing and developing by . . . long practice in each exercise. (Montessori, 1917/1965, pp. 19–20)

The quasi-mystical note is reminiscent of Alcott (and of Froebel's "gifts"), but Montessori's advocacy of liberation, like Rousseau's, did not imply total freedom. A biographer (Kramer, 1976) suggests that she "approached education with the attitude of a doctor treating patients. She knew best what was good for them. Like many rhetoricians of freedom, she was herself something of an autocrat" (p. 118). Along with the proper learning environment and materials, the style of the teacher was critical, her most innovative ideas involving the role of *directrice* and thus the entire conception of what constituted teaching. Her injunction, "Don't *tell*, *teach!*" meant that the teacher presented, modeled, and observed, as children learned through spontaneous activity, within defined limits. But "it is really the environment that is the best teacher. The child needs objects to act; they are like nourishment for his spirit" (Montessori, 1949/1972, p. 66). While content must become more complex, she advocated the same basic approach to foster natural physical, social, intellectual, moral, and spiritual development as pupils progressed.

As word of the Casas dei Bambini spread, Montessori was visited by such prominent American pedagogical authorities as Harvard's Arthur Norton, Princeton's Howard Warren, and William Heard Kilpatrick of Teachers College, Columbia University. Lightner Witmer and Arnold Gesell were attracted, as was G. Stanley Hall himself. Chicago's controversial school superintendent Ella Flagg and Jane Addams saw potential in her methods for work with immigrant children, while others saw implications for children with disabilities. A. G. Bell and his wife admired her ability to stimulate children's natural curiosity, as did Helen Keller, with whom she "communicated through a double process of interpretation, Montessori's words translated into English by Anne George for Anne Sullivan Macy . . . who then spelled them in the manual alphabet into Keller's hand" (Kramer, 1976, p. 195).

Her American visit came at a time of great interest in education among the middle class and affluent, who wanted enrichment for their own children, "Americanizing" for those of poor immigrants. Thus, numerous reports on her system soon appeared in the popular press, while it was also discussed at professional meetings, critiqued in journals, and described in bulletins issued by the U.S. Office of Education (e.g., Harrison, 1914). Yet, though world-famous, among American educationists she remained an outsider. Kilpatrick and Dewey thought her emphasis on personal freedom inconsistent with the progressivist vision, which stressed cooperative problem solving. To Kilpatrick's disciples, who advocated the group project method, "the individualistic, almost antisocial Montessori approach seemed heretical" (Simons, 1988, p. 341). The child's "inner feeling that personal power was being gained by learning" (p. 343) was not a priority concern of American progressive educators, whose criticisms effectively blocked acceptance. It remained outside the mainstream, by the 1950s paradoxically seen as desirable for more privileged children (probably since it was available only privately), until rediscovered in the 1960s in the context of the War on Poverty, and designated one of several alternative compensatory models.

Changing Demographics and Professionalization

The schoolmaster of history is a familiar figure, expressed in such archetypes as Ichabod Crane. Whatever the myths, this traditionally male occupation became rapidly feminized; in New England by 1840, women held between 30% and (in Massachusetts) 61% of all teaching positions (Preston, 1993). Mann, who opened the first normal school in Lexington, Massachusetts, in 1839, thought women better suited for instruction of young children; they accordingly comprised most of those trained in curricular subjects and pedagogical methods (Rury, 1989). Moreover, teaching was an acceptable alternative to marriage and a means of earning a livelihood or contributing to family support, although letters and diaries of female teachers reveal that many had scholarly and literary aspirations (Preston, 1993). As in all areas where women were employed, they were less expensive and, lacking other opportunities, more stable employees. Teaching was often a temporary role for men preparing for careers in law and medicine, and sometimes for women before marriage, incompatible with teaching (for a woman but not, of course, for a man). The Civil War radically shifted the gender balance; by 1870 about two-thirds of American teachers were women, the trend furthered by age-grading, which made discipline less problematic, until by 1900 women comprised 74% of the American teaching force (Rury, 1989).

Special educators had been even more likely to be male, but in the post–Civil War years women began to have important roles, especially in deaf education, a development Edward Gallaudet resisted. In addition to the Boston women who, with Bell, promoted speech, New York's Lexington School employed "two lady teachers, Miss Hubbard and Miss Stevens" in the 1870–1871 school year, as well as the wife of Principal Franklin Rising as matron (Connor, 1992). Widows of European educators of the deaf had attempted to see their husbands' work continued, but only one herself carried on that work. We learn indirectly of female teachers employed by Howe at Perkins. Male dominance in the field of retardation followed from male dominance in that of medicine, Montessori being the clear exception.

Dorothea Dix was an exception on both counts, but her memorials to the Massachusetts legislature had to be presented by a man, Howe. Only in Sweden were there institutions headed by women; and while the American superintendents' wives were "included" in the leadership group (Rosen, Clark, & Kivitz, 1976), only Catherine Brown and Seguin's widow were accorded status in their own right. Seguin (1880), whose wife continued his school in New York, advocated female teachers for pupils with retardation, supervised by "a competent physician" (p. 111).

Women had long had important though often unappreciated roles with children with disabilities, as individuals, like Madame Guerin, and collectively through such religious orders as the Sisters of Charity. But after the Civil War, their involvement began to be both formalized and formally recognized; as women found roles in common schools, they began also to shape special education as a profession. These constituted two distinct streams for, while the number of public and private normal schools increased from 18 in 1860 to 331 by 1898, the principal locus of training of special educators was the residential school (Connor, 1976). As in most other professions, but unlike regular educators, they were trained on the job through a mentoring or preceptor model. In both areas, however, training of what was becoming a predominantly female group was usually overseen by males, "pure oralism" in deaf education emerging—notwithstanding Bell's titular leadership—as a notable exception. Another exception, which proved important in recruiting special educators, was "child gardening," a field stimulated by women's volunteerism and involvement in reform.

At an abolition meeting in 1859, Margarethe Meyer Schurz, wife of abolitionist Carl Schurz, described the German-speaking kindergarten she had founded in 1856 in Watertown, Wisconsin, to Peabody, who opened the first English-speaking program and whose journal, the *Kindergarten Messenger*, and teachers' manual maintained Froebellian dominance of the movement for two decades (Weber, 1969). "Kindergartners" saw their mission as distinct from both common schools and protective care of poor and orphaned children. It was nurturant teaching, which Peabody thought a realization of woman's unique role (a belief about teaching shared by male leaders like Mann, Henry Barnard, and Edward Sheldon, but not necessarily female teachers themselves [Preston, 1993]) and a means of guiding mothers in such nurture. As programs proliferated, Froebellian orthodoxy was increasingly perceived to be inappropriate to the needs of American children, especially those of immigrants, and incompatible with Dewey's functionalism: "The rigidity of Froebel's discipline seemed out of harmony with a primary concern for the interests and needs of the child" (Cremin, Shannon, & Townsend, 1954, p. 49). Most influential of those championing a different approach was Patty Smith Hill who, before joining the Teachers College faculty, had studied with Parker at the Cook County Normal Schools, Dewey at Chicago, and Hall and William Burnham at Clark.

Although uncertain as to what competencies teachers of ungraded classes being formed should have, officials assumed expertise could be found in the institutions, and based on the presumed developmental levels of the pupils in the classes, candidates trained in kindergarten methods were sought. Once trained further by institutional leaders, they were given little supervision, until Elizabeth Farrell established an "inspector" model in New York. The *Journal of Psycho-Asthenics*, in its first issue to address day classes, included a report (Lincoln, 1903) of Boston's selection of "the best possible teachers"—

> women of experience in their profession, acquainted with kindergarten methods, some of whom had been trained . . . at Barre [the institution in Massachusetts] and Mrs. Seguin's school, while others had been sent by the Board to spend three months in residence at Elwyn [in Pennsylvania]. . . . The teachers thus chosen were practically allowed to act as their own judgment dictated. There was no requirement, scarcely even a suggestion, as to the results to be sought, or the methods to be used; the work to be done is very much the same as in state schools for the feeble-minded. (p. 84)

University involvement began in 1896 with Lightner Witmer's three-week summer course, Methods and Results of Child Psychology, at the University of Pennsylvania, expanded in 1897 to three courses. Soon, adequate preparation was assumed to require at least two summers (Wallin, 1914). Practical experience with children was recognized as essential, and beginning in 1903 the Vineland Training School in New Jersey provided summer programs under Goddard. They proved so popular that by 1914 enrollment had to be limited to 60 participants (Sarason & Doris, 1969).

New York University began the course Education of Defectives in 1906 and in 1908 Teachers College offered The Psychology and Education of Exceptional Children (Connor, 1976). Elizabeth Farrell, whose role in professionalizing the field is noted in Chapter 6, had long affiliations with both, lecturing at the latter from 1915 to 1922. By 1929, "37 teachers' colleges and eight normal schools in 22 states and an additional 54 colleges and universities in 38 states and the District of Columbia offered from 1 to 12 courses (p. 369)"; yet the New York Board of Regents (1935) reported an "insufficient supply" of teachers for New York's classes, a situation likely to become critical. Until federal initiatives provided support for preservice training in retardation in 1958 through P.L. 85-926, amended in 1963 as P.L. 88-164 to address other areas, a "summer soldier" approach was the norm. With postwar proliferation of special classes, assignment of teachers with no special training was common, though a baccalaureate and some certification were required. Even as degree programs were established and states developed licensure standards, shortages persisted, exacerbated by P.L. 94-142 and its 1986 amendment, which extended services to preschool children.

As normal schools became less uniquely suited to teacher training, their function was assumed by colleges and universities. European models, however, distinguished teacher preparation from academic programs. As in America, the focus in preparing special educators was at the elementary level, based on the assumption that pupils had limited capabilities, and any able to advance no longer required specialized education. Legislation enacted in the 1950s required teachers of deaf and of blind students in England and Wales to demonstrate competence by passing a national examination or a one-year course at designated institutions. By 1960, most Western European nations required the same level of preparation for special educators as for elementary teachers: at least four years' study in a teacher training institute (Taylor & Taylor, 1960).

After World War II, the Eastern Block countries established different patterns; consistent with an organic pathology orientation, as discussed in Chapter 9, training of special educators and other "defectologists" emphasized medical aspects. In Yugoslavia, divisions of the "High Pedagogic Schools" provided specialized training in *tiflopedagogy, surdopedagogy*, and *oligofrenopedagogy*, referring to instruction of visually impaired pupils; hearing- and speech-impaired pupils; and those with mental or physical impairments, or who were considered "maladjusted" (Taylor & Taylor, 1960). In Poland, Maria Grzegorsewska founded the Institute of Special Pedagogy in 1921, later affiliated with the University of Warsaw, which provided a two-year specialization course for experienced elementary teachers. By the 1970s, trained specialists staffed diverse facilities, but Polish educators were moving toward integrated, community-based services (Holowinsky, 1981).

COMMON SCHOOLS, DIVERSE PUPILS

Work specialization generally follows specialization in knowledge, commodities, technology, or all in combination. In the case of human services, a critical force has been awareness of diversity in the needs of clients, patients, and pupils, as is apparent in the service structure for exceptional children that emerged in the 20th century.

Homogenize Pupils or Diversify Programs?

Before the 1880s, "schooling was, as it had been for centuries, available only to a wealthy minority and to a pitifully small number on a charity basis"

(Pratte, 1973, p. 44), a distinction most pronounced in the South where private schooling and tutoring traditions were strong. Philanthropic societies ran pauper schools, but "masses of children were ignored" (p. 57), African-American children as a matter of policy. What progress had been made was set back by the Civil War. By 1865, about half the nation's children received some schooling, but very little: 50 to 60 days per year in the North, about one-fifth that many in the South. In 1876, the "common" schools enrolled less than 5% of American children 5 through 17 years old (Cremin et al., 1954); their expansion seemed to bear out Mann's conviction that they were essential for all in a democracy.

Many concerned about juvenile idleness and crime in the cities thought children of the poor especially in need of moral training. We noted that an emphasis on moral education reflected secularization and constitutional separation of church and state. But during a period when the spirit of nationalism was moving across Europe, it was also a response to growing religious and ethnic diversity, an effort to "conserve 'American' ideals and ensure a stabilized populace" (Pratte, 1973, p. 47) through a common language and common principles of morality. The first need, and to some degree the second, was addressed by a former teacher, Noah Webster, through a succession of spellers, readers, grammars, and ultimately a dictionary, specifically for American society. But waves of immigration exacerbated the dual challenge of sheer numbers and diversity. From 1860 to 1914, Philadelphia's population increased from 560,000 to 1½ million, New York's from 850,000 to 4 million, mainly attributable to massive immigration: some 10 million Italians, Poles, Russians, Slovaks, Hungarians, Greeks, and Rumanians (Pratte, 1973). Cubberly (1909) considered it essential to "amalgamate these people as a part of our American race" (p. 15), a view that, compared with others, was relatively benign.

Religious bias also fired protectionism. German Jews who had emigrated in the 1830s and 1840s to escape anti-Semitism feared the new Jewish arrivals would prompt resurgence of latent bigotry (Polster, 1990). With addition of new southern and eastern Europeans to the earlier Irish immigrants, the number of American Catholics increased to nine million by 1890, and in the next 30 years nearly doubled again (Blee, 1991). The Know-Nothing Party, begun by Charles B. Allen about 1850 as a secret society, the Order of the Star Spangled Banner (which paradoxically opposed slavery), was a powerful anti-immigrant, anti-Catholic organization. In 1884, the Reverend Samuel D. Burchard labeled the Democrats the party of "Rum, Romanism, and Rebellion," as Julia Ward Howe's (1891) plea to "save the country from being engulfed by this sea of pauperism and superstition from abroad" (p. 5) expressed widespread fears. Revitalized by the 1919 Red Scare, the Ku Klux Klan became a major force in the 1920s with membership of between 3 and 5 million and considerable governmental influence (Tucker, 1991). The Women of the Klan, who used strategies more subtle than cross-burnings (like boycotts), had chapters in 36 states; in Indiana, where the Klan was strongest, nearly a third of the white Protestant adult females were members (Blee, 1991). As Allen wrote in *Only Yesterday* (1931), super-patriotism

> took the form of an ugly flare-up of feeling against the Negro, the Jew, and the Roman Catholic. The emotions of group loyalty and of hatred, expanded during wartime and then suddenly denied their intended expression, found a perverted release in the persecution not only of supposed radicals, but also of other elements which to the dominant American group—the white Protestants— seemed alien or "un-American." (p. 52)

Laws restricting immigration were enacted in 1921 and 1924, the latter citing the inferiority of Mediterranean and Slavic "racial" groups; racial origin quotas remained on the books until 1965 (Pratte, 1973, pp. 62–63). Such campaigns were preceded by those of the strongly anti-Catholic American Protective Association, which flourished briefly in the 1890s, mainly in the Midwest. The Immigration Restriction League, founded in 1894 in Massachusetts, was both more influential and more respectable, including many prominent citizens. Fueled by eugenic sentiments and mental testing, concerns about immigration reached a nearly hysterical level of xenophobia; the growing nativism hardened prejudices that now drew support from "scientific" evidence.

Immigrant children already present posed a major challenge, priority concerns being rudimentary hygiene, nutrition, and skills needed for survival, especially use of English, which together with getting children to depart from the "uncouthness" of their parents (Polster, 1990), was deemed essential to amalgamation. But it was clear that standard methods were insufficient. Irving Howe (1976) described the system of 250 "Steamer" classes set up in 1905 in New York for immigrant pupils, which by 1912 enrolled 31,000 in classes of 30–35 pupils, smaller than the typical group of 45–50: "Given the poor conditions—overcrowding in the schools, fear and suspicion among the immigrants, impatience and hostility among some teachers, and an invariably skimped budget . . . [the] school system did rather well in helping immigrant children who wanted help, fairly well in helping those who needed help, and quite badly in helping those who resisted help" (p. 274).

Schools were being pressed both to educate all children and to keep them in school longer, to prevent their exploitation and keep them off the streets. However, as the pupil clientele became rapidly more diverse, educators had not even responded to the diversity among "native American" children (not to mention those properly so identified or African-American children). In 1860, there were slightly more than 300 high schools, many established to symbolize a city's importance and quality of life (Katz, 1968), but the number was increasing. The 11% of the nation's 14– 17-year-olds enrolled in high schools in 1900 represented a doubling within a mere decade, but with a curriculum geared entirely to the 15% who were bound for college, fewer than 12% graduated (Tanner & Tanner, 1990).

A movement to provide "essential and useful" vocational training inspired a number of schools, many sponsored by businessmen, modeled after the Manual Training School Calvin M. Woodward founded at Washington University in 1879 (Cremin, 1961). However, while such training was certainly not viewed as second rate, the movement again raised the specter of class. Noting that America was a composite of diversity, Dewey called for fundamental curricular restructuring to integrate preparation for work and for citizenship. Formal recognition of the need for high schools to accommodate students with diverse interests and goals came in 1918 with recommendations of the Commission on Reorganization of the Secondary School. Although all states by then had compulsory education laws, schooling was far from universal and few youngsters went beyond eighth grade. Educators influenced by Hall's research on early adolescence thought young people needed opportunities to explore alternatives before committing themselves to life decisions through tracking in academic or vocational curricula. Thus, pilot programs having been initiated in Berkeley in 1909 and Columbus, Ohio, in 1910, the junior high, first called the intermediate school, was born. By 1930 there were about 4,000 across the country (Tanner & Tanner, 1990).

These school reforms, like those of the 1980s, made no explicit reference to pupils with disabilities; special education essentially constituted a separate system. Yet the concepts of functional learning and vocational preparation integrated in the curriculum parallelled practices in schools for deaf and for blind pupils, and in some programs for those with orthopedic impairments. Another parallel can be seen in classes for pupils with retardation, a point noted by Arnold Gesell (1924), a prominent supporter. Along with their prevocational value, he hailed these concepts for the "strengthening effect . . . of drawing, handicraft, modeling, weaving, sewing, basketry, woodwork, and dancing, plays, games, and physical education [on] . . . the morale and the personality sense" of the pupil, noting that such activities "have had a beneficent, liberalizing effect upon the education of normal children," as well (p. 272). Assuming that special classes could never be provided in all communities, he seems to have accepted the practical necessity of mainstreaming, suggesting that "it is always possible to institute some special adjustments" whereby such a child could "share in the regular school work when he is able to do so," but otherwise kept "busy and content" (p. 273). In fact, of those pupils with retardation enrolled in school, few were in special classes.

Progressivism, Nativism, and Social Control

The progressive vision entailed a more fundamental agenda than such reactive modifications as tracking, or the charge to clean up and amalgamate immigrant children and keep them off the streets. It was "a many-sided effort to use the schools to improve the lives of individuals, . . . to apply the promise of American life . . . to the puzzling new urban-industrial civilization" (Cremin, 1961, p. viii). Equally manifest in social settlements and social sciences—sociology and the nascent field of child psychology—was its philosophical basis in Pragmatism, a uniquely American expression of the liberal tradition, articulated principally by Charles Sanders Peirce, William James, and Dewey. "Progressivism," wrote Cremin (1961), "implied the radical faith that culture could be democratized without being vulgarized, the faith that everyone could share not only in the benefits of the new sciences but in the pursuit of the arts as well" (p. ix).

While Dewey's is the name most commonly linked with educational progressivism, he himself considered Colonel Francis Parker its originator. Exposure to the ideas of Froebel and Pestalozzi through study in Germany convinced Parker that teaching should be based on children's natural modes of learning. Thus he, like Mann, favored a word method in teaching reading, using conversation to integrate reading, writing, spelling, and thinking. The "New Education" he inaugurated in the late 1870s in Quincy, Massachusetts, was soon a topic of widespread interest, suggesting applications ranging from learning through play in kindergarten to the value of elective courses in higher education. Among Parker's (1894) key progressive themes were an individualized approach, direct experience, fostering intrinsic motivation, and integration of content. Believing teachers should build on a child's natural propensities to initiate learning in all subject areas, he identified nine *physical modes of expression* (gesture, voice, music, speech, making, modeling, painting, drawing, and writing) that, when integrated with the *mental modes of attention* (observation, hearing language, and reading), yield unity of thought and action (Campbell, 1967).

Particularly germane to the spirit of progressivism was Parker's view of the school as a democracy in microcosm. Asserting that children of diverse backgrounds can learn from each other, he stressed mutual responsibility, as well as "learning by doing," anticipating Dewey's dictum that education is not just preparation for but should actually *be* life in a democracy. Another who considered schools laboratories for citizenship was Lester F. Ward, who has been called "the architect of environmentalism" in American education (Tanner & Tanner, 1990, p. 109). Ward saw discrepancies between social classes not as natural but as due to inequalities of opportunities to gain knowledge. In *Dynamic Sociology* (1883), he proposed that a better society could be made through *telesis*, conscious shaping of the environment beginning with systematic education of the young, rather than social control through eugenic policies.

The profound impact of the eugenics movement on exceptional persons is noted in subsequent chapters on retardation and deafness, as American leaders insisted that procreative regulation was essential to prevent the increase of disability and a host of associated societal ills. While British eugenicists, after Galton, were mainly concerned with "positive" eugenics, their American counterparts, influenced by Bell and Goddard, stressed "negative" eugenics. And while "race" (encompassing ethnicity) dominated American pronouncements (including anti-Semitic, white supremacist, and various ethnocentric views), the issue in Britain was class. Galton shared the "standard views of 'inferior races,'" but for him, "the professional classes were the prime repository of ability and civic virtue, and his eugenics made them the keystone of a biological program designed to maintain a conservative meritocracy" (Kevles, 1984, p. 56), the theme of his influential *Hereditary Genius* (1869). Plato had expressed ideas of social stratification, but the concept of class as implying permanence of societal status, which became important in British life, emerged in the late 18th and early 19th centuries. From the work of his cousin Charles Darwin, Galton inferred that evolutionary progress could be accelerated; it was the *duty* of the better classes to procreate.

While Galton was concerned that the wrong people heeded the Malthusian warning and were limiting procreation, his successor, Karl Pearson, asserted that "natural selection . . . had been suspended, and replaced by 'reproductive selection,'" whereby the *less* fit produced the most progeny (Kevles, 1984, p. 86). He argued that educational expansion and reforms to benefit "unemployables, degenerates, and physical and mental weaklings" were based on the mistaken notion that intelligence could be taught and encouraged the least productive to increase in number. (Bertrand Russell went further, endorsing in *Marriage and Morals* [1929/1970] the American approach of sterilization of feeble-minded women.) Pearson's view, which found a receptive audience among certain American leaders, was an aspect of nativism clearly at odds with Ward's environmentalism. But the new field of child psychology entailed another facet of Darwinism that, while advocating educational change, was equally inimical to progressive concepts of Parker and Ward.

Child Study, Maturationism, and Laissez-faire

While many at first thought it a fad and oversentimentalized, the child study movement begun in the 1880s by G. Stanley Hall soon gained academic respectability. Unlike Witmer's approach, Hall's was normative and emphasized the role of natural maturation. He saw the study of children as the route by which educational reforms could be made, believing that schools should adapt to the characteristics of children. Accordingly, with questionnaires and using teachers as observers and interviewers, he accumulated normative information that implied such curricular changes as emphasizing large muscle activity in kindergarten, rather than activities requiring precise fine motor coordination. But he did not think such reforms instrumental to changing either the child or, in the immediate future, the society. He was an evolutionist, and evolutionary change is by its nature gradual. The "child-centered" curriculum he advocated was thus a laissez-faire curriculum and, although both laissez-faire and the name of Hall himself were later linked with progressivism, his ideas were antithetical to the spirit of progressivism.

A man of many enthusiasms, Hall was revered by his famous students, such as Gesell, who credited him with making the developing child the center of a new science of "genetic psychology" and pioneering child study as a means of linking the social sciences with pedagogy (Gesell & Gesell, 1912). Having received the first American Ph.D. in Psychology, under James, he pursued further study with Wundt, Helmholtz, and Fechner, and in the biological sciences, which left him a committed Darwinian. Before he accepted the presidency of Clark University, which opened in 1889, his students at Johns Hopkins included Woodrow Wilson and John Dewey (Ross, 1972). His continuing leadership in American psychology was evidenced by important texts, the historic sponsorship of Freud and Jung at Clark in September 1909, and his holding the presidency, twice, of the American Psychological Association.

Eager to apply genetic psychology, Hall, like Spencer, maintained that education should cultivate all facets of the person as preparation for complete living. His evolutionism was in the tradition of Recapitulation, or Culture-Epoch, Theory, which while dating back to Aristotle, was revived by the German zoologist Ernst Haeckel and found impetus with Darwin's *Origin of Species* (1859) and *The Descent of Man* (1871). Haeckel's "fundamental biogenetic law," that ontogeny (development of the individual) recapitulates phylogeny (development of the species), implied a biologically programmed, maturational determinism with a limited role for experience. Some bizarre inferences were drawn from the theory, inspiring such school practices as sequencing units of study according to cultural evolutionary sequence, from primary through the secondary grades. Like Dewey, Edward Thorndike (1914) was critical both of biological determinism and the scientific shortcomings of Hall's child study (though his opposition to the former was to maturationism, not geneticism, as his later enthusiasm for ability testing and eugenics revealed). With barely concealed scorn, he summed up "the doctrine of nature's infallibility":

> By the "Nature is Right" doctrine, the actual terminus of evolution is the moral end of human action. What is going to be, is right. Our duty is to abstain from interfering with nature, supposing such interference to be possible. . . . The *summum bonum* for the race is to live out its own evolution with interest and freedom. No stage to which nature impels, should by human artifice be either hastened or prolonged, lest the magic order be disturbed. The ideal for humanity is to be sought in its natural outcome, in what it of itself tends to be, irrespective of training. Human effort should be to let the inner forces of development do their perfect work. (pp. 116–117)

Thorndike then proceeds to counter this view, on the basis of both common sense and his own empirical studies of learning. The nature versus nurture debate would continue as the fields of child psychology and educational psychology took shape, but in the case of exceptionality, especially retardation, it was already an old issue. The emergence of mental testing added new dimensions, as we consider in Chapter 6.

Educational laissez-faire had another face. Whether to recreate society or to accommodate to the nature of children, the American educational leadership was not unanimous about need for change. William T. Harris, commissioner of education from 1889 to 1906, opposed the manual training school idea, but also virtually all proposals to modify the curriculum (Cremin, 1961). Like J. F. Herbart, Hall enjoined educators to study individual learners to determine "where they are" and teach them accordingly in order to enhance interest and motivation. But Harris, who vigorously opposed Herbart's ideas of "unity" and linking new content with each child's previous experience, maintained that natural sorting would result from the free action of the individual learner. Pupils should be free to move ahead by virtue of their own efforts, thus serving their own needs and those of the society, the school a force for social stability rather than for change. This staunch defender of the status quo no doubt reflected the views of a great many Americans in his belief in getting ahead by dint of one's own efforts, his laissez-faire view of the learning process as a form of free enterprise, and his wish to keep things as they were (Curti, 1964).

While they differed about need for change in schools, Harris and Hall shared a view of individual freedom that did not imply external intervention. To progressivists, the very individualism that Harris exalted was responsible for many social ills, problems Hall did not believe relevant to how and what children were taught. Nor did they think progress, albeit slow, was inevitable, instead urging planned change. Ward's thesis was that persons should take control of their destiny, setting goals, then taking the actions necessary to achieve them. Based on the conviction that one's destiny is neither fixed nor outside one's control, nor is that of the society, progressivists aspired to improve the quality of life for all. Freedom in a democracy meant freedom to *act*, and forces that limited such freedom were also susceptible to change. Limits were set not by the "wisdom of nature," but only by the will of citizens and by the institutions they created. Human nature, wrote Thorndike (1914), "progresses not by laissez faire, but by changing the environment in which it operates. Only one thing in it, indeed, is unreservedly good, the power to make it better" (p. 124).

While all institutions could be changed, progressivists considered education fundamental to social reform, and while criticism of traditional pedagogy found support in Thorndike's studies on transfer of training, it arose more from recognition of new demands of industrial society, reflected in Harvard president Charles W. Eliot's (1893) proposal for curricular restructuring. Rather than memorize facts, pupils should study such current issues as housing conditions for the urban poor. Education in a democracy, wrote Dewey (1916), should encourage the "freeing of individual capacity in a progressive growth directed to social aims" (p. 115). Unthinking obedience and suppression of independent inquiry could not produce responsible citizens, and the freedom Dewey espoused did not imply anarchy but orderly participation in goal-directed experiences. This belief in power to bring about change was more compatible with traditions of liberty, optimism, and egalitarianism than with deterministic doctrines; inequities were not simply immutable facts of life but could be rectified.

Provisions for Gifted Pupils

In the 18th century the word *genius*, the original meaning of which had suggested an inner-dwelling homunculus, became associated with superlative accomplishment, and Galton revived it in 1869 in his study of men of eminence. The successive movements of the late 19th and early 20th centuries—eugenics, child study, and mental testing—gave impetus to differential arrangements based on the assumption that some pupils were inherently more capable. From 1867, when Harris, then St. Louis School Superintendent, introduced flexible promotion through 1899, similar schemes enabling students whose parents wished them to advance rapidly were piloted in Elizabeth, New Jersey (1886), Cambridge, Massachusetts (1891), and other districts (Sumption & Luecking, 1960). The influence of child study, specifically that of Hall, was evident in schemes initiated between 1900 and 1919, with accelerated progress of individual pupils based on reported differential maturity. Ability tests seemed to offer a more scientific basis for such decisions, and in the 1920s group tests began to be used to identify students eligible for placement in separate tracks, as well.

As with disabilities, definitions for educational purposes have been problematic; how "clever," to use a British designation, must a child be to be considered gifted? Cleveland's Major Work Program, begun in 1920, established an IQ of 125 as a required criterion, together with evidence of superior achievement and good citizenship. Multidimensional conceptions implied a more flexible and inclusive construct. While the plan proposed by Commissioner of Education Marland (1972) identified several forms of giftedness in addition to general intellectual ability—specific academic aptitude, creative or productive thinking, leadership ability, visual and performing arts—group ability tests continued to be virtually universally used as a principal, sometimes the sole, means of identifying eligible pupils. Exceptions are specialized schools for pupils demonstrating special talents and advanced placement classes in high schools, eligibility for which is based strongly on performance.

As ability testing came into use in schools concerns were expressed that, while attention had been focused on children with problems, very capable youngsters were more "handicapped," since they "do not force themselves as a problem on the consciousness of the teacher and the school administrator" (Horn, 1924, p. 24). But society neglected them at its peril (a warning repeated at later times of perceived national crisis—the Russian Sputnik launch in the 1950s and in the 1980s reforms spurred by invidious comparisons of American with Japanese students). Cubberly (1922) protested, "One child of superior intellectual capacity, educated so as to use his talents, may confer greater benefits upon mankind, and be educationally far more important, than a thousand of the feeble-minded children upon whom we have recently come to put so much educational effort and expense" (p. 45).

Leta S. Hollingworth (1924) attributed the neglect to the "current social philosophy . . . [which] denies the existence of innate, permanent, hereditary superiority" (p. 299). To the "objection . . . that special education for the bright is not suitable in a democracy, where all are equal," she responded, "The biological truth is that all are unequal. Schools cannot equalize children; schools can only equalize opportunity" (p. 298). Citing the "new knowledge gained from mental tests" and reports of programs in Germany for *Hofnungskinder* (children of promise), she predicted that "we shall soon have as much accumulated knowledge about the gifted as we have about the deficient, and shall be in a position to do justice to the competent as well as to the incompetent" (p. 299). Two "myths" cited concerning gifted children are that they are odd, unstable, and physically and socially inept; and that, since "the cream always rises," special considerations are unnecessary for they will flourish under any circumstances. Early reports of Terman's (1925) longitudinal study of 1,528 children with a mean IQ of 150 seemed to expose the first, and subsequent reports (Terman & Oden, 1959) to demolish it. The second was paradoxically strengthened by his findings that gifted children seemed *more* robust, adjusted, and successful in life than their average peers.

Hollingworth (1924) elaborated a "democratic myth": that giftedness is often found among "the offspring of the humble." On the contrary, she averred, IQ studies confirmed "that the great majority of these children originate in families where the father is a professional man, an owner or executive in business, or a clerical worker . . . it has been proved again and again that ability 'runs in families'" (p. 290). Since in America "the social-economic competition is relatively free for all," the small number of children of "manual workers" with high IQs can be attributed to the fact "that the very intelligent are those who rise in the world by competition, and who are also able to produce children like themselves" (p. 290). The IQ test, "proof" of differential genetic endowment, was hailed as an efficient method for assigning children on this unquestionably level playing field to the stream that would best prepare them for their predetermined niche. (The persisting "elitism" canard with respect to special provisions for gifted pupils is perhaps understandable.)

Spring's (1972) phrase "the sorting machine" portrays schooling as a societal sorting mechanism, enabling children of the privileged to enhance their status and keeping the poor in their place. By 1880, American education, wrote Katz (1971), was "universal, tax-supported, compulsory, bureaucratic, racist, and class-biased" (pp. xix–xx), and while progressivist ideology stressed child-centeredness and social reform, in reality schooling was "something the better part of the community did to the others to make them orderly, moral, and tractable" (pp. ix–x). Even the emphasis on cooperation had a sinister intent in the service of the corporate state, in Spring's (1972) view, in valuing compliance and devaluing individual liberty, but most insidious were vocational guidance and testing to determine future roles: "The rhetoric of opportunity masks the failure to provide it," wrote Lazerson (1971), for "vocationalism and testing . . . create an educational meritocracy based on race and class. The schools are thus primarily concerned with selecting out rather than educating in" (p. 281). Greer (1972) contended that, contrary to common belief, schools did little to further immigrants' upward mobility, but African Americans have been uniquely victimized by intentionally inferior schooling. Such "radical" critiques were heard at a time of "crisis in the classroom" (Silberman, 1970), but at a later time of crisis, Kozol's (1991) documentation of systematic fiscal inequity—of "savage inequalities"—gives credence to charges that schooling perpetuates injustice rather than equalizing opportunity.

Regrettably, from the standpoint of pupils with superior and those with impaired cognitive ability, equity and "excellence" have often been seen as incompatible. More common than separate programs for highly capable pupils, if often less satisfying, have been attempts to provide for them by enriching the curriculum, reflecting progressivism's legacy. By 1940, though scattered reports of their benefits continued to appear in the literature, there were fewer than 100 "special opportunity" classes in American schools; the next great push would await Sputnik. Advocacy for differentiation, most commonly today through "pull-out" programs, continues to be predicated on both societal and individual pupil arguments. In some states, provisions affecting children with disabilities are applied to gifted children, though some maintain that the concept of Least Restrictive Environment "takes on an inverse connotation when applied to the gifted exceptional student" (Hershey, 1981, p. 27). Advocates of Full Inclusion (e.g., Sapon-Shevin, 1994) counter that identification processes are biased (evidenced by underrepresentation of children of color or with disabilities), that such special opportunities serve to increase class-based inequities, and that all children benefit when classroom diversity is maintained and valued. "A gifted child," however, "is a child with special needs" (Silverman, 1995, p. 381).

Ideology and Expectancy

Educational programs for children with disabilities were congruent with both positive and negative aspects of progressive ideology. On the positive side, as Blatt (1981) wrote, they have been based on the core beliefs that all people are worthy and that all people can change. Thus, although pupils are not all alike, they are all equally entitled to opportunities to learn, and these are made available through *different* forms of instruction. Nor is difference destiny, for, while special education cannot cure disability, it can offer different futures for pupils with disabilities than they would otherwise have. But disability has also been a basis for schools to differentially educate, a sorting explained as in the interests of the pupil, although separate streams of schooling have also provided outlets for students who "don't fit," as did the early classes for "unrulies." Moreover, like persons with disabilities themselves, special education has been marginalized in various ways, such as locating a special class "next to the boiler room." Most crucially, special placement may, for some pupils, limit opportunities, rather than extend them, through restrictive curricula, lowered expectancies, and social stigma (Hobbs, 1975).

In the United States, the Education of All Handicapped Children Act of 1975 (renamed in 1990 the Individuals with Disabilities Education Act) sought to correct these problems, as well as discriminatory practices.

At all events, children had become a focus of study and advocacy, and awareness of differences among children inspired efforts to provide differentially for them in schooling. Such differentiation would be greatly extended with the later discovery of specific learning disabilities, learning problems not attributable to other impairment. Increasingly, differential educational diagnosis of pupils, leading to presumptively appropriate school placement, would involve collective professional judgment supported by inferences based on assessment. But the first provisions addressed pupils whose differences were assumed to impair learning. Accordingly, we return now to deafness, the oldest special education challenge.

CHAPTER 4

Deafness, Communication, and Identity

In the whole history of education of the deaf, wrote earlier chroniclers (Frampton & Powell, 1938), "the stupidity and cupidity of man stands out" (p. 5), a harsh assessment based, in part, on the fact that skills deaf persons learned without instruction, long ignored by hearing educators, once discovered were placed in opposition as mutually exclusive. While it is easy to judge our forebears, it would be a mistake to discount the contribution of pioneers like Pereire because of some failing, especially since, from another perspective, the apparent flaw is at least understandable; Seguin (1880) dismissed the secretiveness of early oral educators as simply "the dress of science in former times" (p. 45). The cupidity charge, though not groundless, is surely excessive; more often, desire for recognition was involved. The history of educators of the deaf has indeed had its heroes, persons of courage and dedication. But it is a different history than the one recounted by deaf persons themselves, in the drama and storytelling important in Deaf culture (Padden & Humphries, 1988).

While it may seem that inordinate attention is accorded communication mode, the conflict is not simply a difference about teaching method; it is "a matter of culture, politics, and history" (Lane, 1992, p. 134), involving fundamental issues of identity. Deaf persons themselves have much to say about methods used to teach deaf children, their views often at odds with those of the children's parents—nearly all of whom are not deaf. Who should speak for the child? In the United States, two children with impaired hearing, Alice Cogswell and Mabel Hubbard, powerfully influenced two 19th-century pioneers, both hearing, who took divergent paths, Thomas Hopkins Gallaudet and Alexander Graham Bell.

EXPERIENCES OF CHILDREN

At the school he was thought very intelligent. He learned the lessons before the rest of the pupils. But he could never become used to speaking with his lips. It was not natural to him, and his tongue felt like a whale in his mouth. From the blank expression on people's faces to whom he talked in this way he felt that his voice must be like the sound of some animal or that there was something disgusting in his speech. It was painful for him to try to talk with his mouth, but his hands were always ready to shape the words he wished to say. When he was twenty-two he had come South to this town from Chicago and he met Antonapoulos immediately. Since that time he had never spoken with his mouth again, because with his friend there was no need for this. (McCullers, 1940, p. 8)

While an "infirmity model" (Lane, 1992) is inadequate, deafness is at one level a physical condition involving interference with the transmission or processing of information via sound, of several kinds, in various degrees, resulting from various causes. In the 1960s an epidemic of rubella, maternal German measles in the first trimester of pregnancy, caused impairment of hearing and vision, as well as retardation, in many newborns. Other prenatal and perinatal factors may cause hearing impairment, and young children's susceptibility to upper respiratory infections imposes particular risk. In the 19th century, childhood diseases like scarlet fever were frequent causes of hearing loss. Thus, many children whose language and speech development had been proceeding in typical fashion experienced *postlingual* deafness. A child who is "born deaf" is, of course, more likely to reflect a hereditary pattern than one who incurs hearing loss later, but since very few deaf children have a deaf parent, a congenital loss is seldom expected, and thus often not discovered until parents become concerned about delayed speech. This means that, during a crucial time for language development, the child is not receiving auditory information and, in the absence of other communication modes, is acutely disadvantaged. Moreover, young children, unlike adults who experience lessened acuity with aging, do not know when they are missing important elements in an oral message.

While deafness respects no class boundaries, for centuries a child's opportunities for education were greatly influenced by family circumstances, true for all children but especially true for a deaf child. As we saw, in Europe, a very few male children who were deaf, of privileged families, received the benefits of instruction. In the new American republic, some deaf children, thought "idiots," were given asylum of sorts in almshouses. More fortunate children had families who could at least protect them, give them love, and no doubt often establish a means of communicating with them. But in the school Epée founded in Paris, a new and democratic tradition began, potentially capable of erasing class distinctions and binding together persons who shared a language, a history, and a culture. In the 19th century such a culture took root in North America.

THE AMERICAN SCHOOL

Now called the American School for the Deaf, the Connecticut Asylum for the Education of Deaf and Dumb Persons was opened on April 15, 1817, founded by the father of a deaf daughter, a minister, and a deaf teacher brought from the famous school in Paris, who became "the leading figure in the development of the signing community and its language in the United States" (Lane, 1984a). Recounting this history through the persona of Laurent Clerc, Lane adds that "the leading figure in its undoing was Alexander Graham Bell [who] sought to banish the sign language; to disperse the deaf and discourage their socializing, organizing, publishing, and marriage; to have deaf children educated in and use exclusively the majority language" (p. 340). It is impossible to review the development of educational programs for children with impaired hearing without continued reference to this conflict. Even though sign languages—in North America, the American Sign Language (ASL)—are recognized as viable *languages*, pedagogical arguments continue. There yet seem to be, among professionals at any rate, two irreconcilable positions, one seeking to augment and enhance the hearing of many children, the other supporting the right of a linguistic minority to be who they are. We believe history demonstrates the validity of both—for different groups and under different circumstances—and thus offers more fundamental lessons about pluralism and justice.

Gallaudet and the Cogswells

In 1814, when Thomas Hopkins Gallaudet graduated from Andover Theological Seminary, 9–year-old Alice Cogswell, who had lost her hearing at age 2 as a result of spinal meningitis, was being tutored by Lydia Huntley Sigourney, herself an innovative educator and a well-known poet. The girl's father, Dr. Mason Fitch Cogswell of Hartford, was determined that more systematic provisions should be instituted but, as Lane (1984a) comments, "He saw at once that the great challenge was not to make Alice speak but to find a way to educate all the Alices of the new nation" (p. 182). Accordingly, he convened in his home a group of 10 friends, like himself men of affluence and influence, to discuss how such an ambitious project might be undertaken. He invited also a neighbor, the young minister who had shown some success in communicating with Alice using methods described in Sicard's book, which Dr. Cogswell had secured (Boatner, 1959). Plagued by frail health, as he would be throughout his life, Gallaudet had turned to the ministry as an avenue that might prove both less physically taxing and more spiritually fulfilling than the commercial ventures he had contemplated. As would Howe, Gallaudet leaped at a fortuitous opportunity presented at a critical juncture in his life and, like Howe, he saw the need to learn first-hand from models already in existence, especially in Britain, that were reportedly successful in teaching deaf pupils to understand and use speech.

Cogswell was not the first American parent of a deaf child to advocate for education. Major Thomas Bolling of Cobbs, Virginia, whose family had a history of congenital deafness, was determined that his three deaf children would be educated. Learning of the British system through a book by Francis Green (1783), an American tory, he arranged for them to sail for England to enroll. The family seems to have been so gratified by the successes achieved with the children that, on learning that John Braidwood, brother of the school's director, was in America, their hearing brother engaged him to start a private program. But Braidwood's mismanagement, duplicity, and carousing suggest that Bolling placed confidence in the wrong person. A school was established in Virginia in 1830, under public auspices (Boatner, 1959). Gallaudet was determined to bring the English methods to America himself.

Innocent Abroad

"And you see what this report is," a palpably frustrated 28–year-old Thomas Gallaudet wrote to Cogswell in an 1815 letter explaining the proposal Joseph Watson had engineered.

> If I comply with it I must *bind* myself to *labor for Dr. Watson* three whole years, be subject to his complete disposal of me during that time, have no hope of freedom unless he please (and all his feelings of interest would lead him to detain me in order to make his art appear as difficult and important as possible), and what is worse than all be continually retarded and cramped in my progress of the pupils whom I might instruct. Besides, when am I to avail myself of the Abbé Sicard's kindness? During these three years? No; Dr. Watson would not consent to this. Afterwards? Then four or five years must elapse from the time when I left you to my return. This is too monstrous a sacrifice of time and patience and money. . . . The more I think of this proposed arrangement the more I dislike it, and I already begin to look for some other way in which Providence may guide me to the accomplishment of my wishes. (in E. Gallaudet, 1888, pp. 67–68)

According to Edward Gallaudet (1888), his father resolutely refrained from public complaint of the ill treatment he received. If so it is curious that the newspapers took sides in the dispute, supporting the "obligations of gratitude and truth" expressed in the Braidwood family bond and accusing Gallaudet, who questioned its legal authority, with "obtuseness of understanding." In any case, once all principals were deceased, Edward thought it not a betrayal of his father's wishes to publish letters revealing his indignation, and also that he did not give up easily in his quest to learn the "English mode of instruction" (p. 69). He hoped to find a more gracious reception in Edinburgh, but Robert Kinniburgh, bound to secrecy by the founder's grandson, Thomas Braidwood, felt he could not release his methods without the latter's consent, which he would not grant, suggesting instead that the work in America be initiated by his brother, a suggestion that Gallaudet was disinclined to consider.

Gallaudet, as his youngest son described him, was extraordinarily conscientious, a single, inadvertent overindulgence in wine precipitating a lifetime of abstinence, and a single lapse in truthfulness—to spare young ladies at a social the sad news of a friend's drowning—an abhorrence of dancing. He would not have seen in John Braidwood one to whom such an important mission ought to be entrusted. As he wrote Cogswell, "The truth is, he left this place . . . in disgrace. He was solicited to undertake the superintendence of a public school for the deaf and dumb. He conducted so badly and contracted so many debts that he was obliged to abscond. What dependence can be placed on such a character!" (pp. 77–78). Despite his frustration, Gallaudet did not blame the "worthy and able" Kinniburgh: "I have not the smallest doubt, that had it been possible, I should have received from the institution, gratuitously and cordially, every assistance which it could afford me" (p. 82). It happened that, as he was being held at arm's length, Sicard, accompanied by Massieu and Clerc, was lecturing in London. He was predictably enthusiastic on hearing of Gallaudet's project for, like that of his predecessor, his attitude and that of the oral educators could not have contrasted more. But eager as he was to accept Sicard's warm invitation, Gallaudet felt compelled to persevere. Eventually, he must have perceived the guiding hand of Providence to be offering "some other way."

A Historic Partnership

In Paris with Sicard, now nearing 80, Gallaudet found a more hospitable environment. He was given full access to all pupils, classes, and staff, most significantly—in addition to private lessons from the gifted Massieu—a teacher of about his own age, Laurent Clerc. Eager to set about his work but concerned that he lacked sufficient expertise, Gallaudet suggested that, if accompanied and assisted by "some deaf-mute," he could proceed to establish a school. Clerc was quick to volunteer, Sicard, no doubt with some reluctance, agreeing to this plan. With a contractual appointment for the period of three years, Clerc became "the first educated deaf man to walk the streets of this country, and his presence encouraged the establishment of the French method of signs and finger spelling that became the basis for the democratic

Combined System . . . practiced by the residential schools for the deaf in the United States" (Boatner, 1959, p. 6). The assignment extended to a lifetime.

CONFLICTING IDEOLOGIES AND TRADITIONS

Deaf Persons and Their "Hearing Benefactors"

Later in the century the oralism-manualism debate, reopened, would again rage—that is, among hearing parents and educators. Until that occurred, American deaf education was dominated by the approach introduced by Clerc and Gallaudet; though opposing views were expressed and to a limited extent applied, it was long an unequal contest. In 1880, a fateful year with regard to this issue, Seguin, a consistent partisan of Pereire's work, summarized his view of the state of the art: "The contending parties are the schools of mutism, large, numerous, and supported by states or rich corporations; and the schools of speech, which have fewer pupils, smaller endowments, and a staff whose support is principally the intelligent knowledge of their subject and the heroism of their object" (p. 45). The *method de signes*, Seguin avers, was a "fatal present" to deaf persons, for in legitimizing the *language naturel des signes* their educators had consigned them to mutism. He allows that to teach a congenitally deaf child to speak is not easy, but he insists that the assertion that, to elicit speech, an individual teacher is required for each pupil is a calumny spread by "mutists." Tarred with this brush, too, are those like the Gallaudets who professed to use a combined method but, Seguin charges, abandoned speech by accepting gesture. Like advocates of Total Communication today, Edward Gallaudet denied the allegation, but it was not then nor is it now without foundation.

History is recounted quite differently by Seguin and by his countryman Clerc, the latter as interpreted by Harlan Lane (1984a). Both describe the three "schools" of oralism, but differ in emphasis. Pereire's major innovation, in the view of Seguin (who found this an extremely important one), was systematic use of the sense of touch, but Clerc avers Periere wanted to sell his method and, failing that, to retain its secret for his son's use, which as we saw was also unsuccessful. Seguin claims that in the "Anglo-American" school, speech had been the original goal; that it was all but abandoned he considers a direct result of the congregation of large numbers of deaf persons in communities centered around the "schools of mutism." In such communities, by virtue of strength of numbers, the value of speech was minimized and common use of signing legitimized. From a different perspective, it is in the very community of people experiencing deafness that culture is found and transmitted. And the historic role of schools for the deaf has been, from such a perspective, invaluable in creating "a structure that has provided a sense of continuity to the community for over two hundred years. Each new generation of children entering any one of the schools . . . inherited a history, passed down in the school and in the community organized around the school" (Padden & Humphries, 1988, p. 31).

Thus are framed two very different conceptions of the meaning of deafness and the identity of deaf persons, two different models: the infirmity and the cultural (Lane, 1992), the pathological and the social (Padden & Humphries, 1988, p. 3). From their own perspective, deaf persons are not persons with defects, but members of a sign language–using community, users of a language different from that of the majority, like Spanish-speaking persons in the United States and speakers of the Basque language in Spain; that is their distinction (Lane, 1984a). In contrast, the "metaphor of affliction" (Padden & Humphries, 1988, p. 17) suggests deviance from what is accepted. In the context of Deaf (capitalized in this usage) *culture*, signing does not imply affliction, nor is it a "prosthesis" or accommodation, but a wholly legitimate mode that satisfies the definition of a language as a shared system of symbols and rules. For Lane, and presumably for the Deaf community, oral rehabilitation, auditory training, and the ever more frequent use of cochlear implants are predicated on a pathological model that denies the viability of an indigenous language and the rights of a linguistic minority.

Thus, with exquisite irony, Lane (1984a) sketches a version of history, as seen through Clerc's eyes, tracing the origins of the speech model to Ponce de León in the 16th century, who reputedly "taught the deaf scions of a noble family to speak, read, and write—to the astonishment of scholars in Spain, and as word spread, throughout Europe" (p. 5). Through various indirect means three later pioneers were guided by his approach in founding the three streams of oral education: "Jacob Pereire in the Romance-speaking countries, John Wallis in the British Isles, and Jan Conrad Amman in the German-speaking nations . . . [who] labored under conditions similar to Ponce, as did their many disciples well into the nineteenth century" (p. 5).

> A wealthy family has a deaf son (deaf daughters were commonly sequestered at home or in convents). The family hires a tutor, often a man of letters, who works to maintain, perhaps restore, the boy's speech and to expand his knowledge of arts and sciences. The boy makes progress; a philosopher notes it; the tutor publishes letters announcing his achievement, but withholding his method. The tutor goes on to other things; the boy, generally, does not. (p. 5)

Who should speak for deaf persons? To Lane, no one, surely no hearing person, is better qualified than Laurent Clerc. Thus, in *When the Mind*

Hears, the first and longer part of which is written as a first-person account by an octogenarian Clerc, the centuries-old attempt at "demutizing" the deaf is recounted as "a false history." Clerc challenges all those whose feats were noted by Baron Joseph-Marie de Gérando, Napoleon's appointee to direct the Paris school, in his two-volume history, *The Education of the Congenitally Deaf*, to "step down" if they have not actually taught a congenitally deaf person to speak. One by one, he eliminates most, challenging those who remain to present their data. What we have, he alleges, is a strange secretiveness. Ponce de León appears to be an exception, but precisely what he did cannot be established. Nor can we know the extent or age of onset of deafness of those even he taught, critical information with respect to speech learning. Moreover, he asserts, oralism reveals a history of catering to a few privileged males: "The history of oralism is aglitter with bejewelled aristocracy" (Lane, 1984a, p. 69). What of the multitudes not thus privileged?

Role of the Residential Schools

Until the successful challenge of Bell and his collaborators, the residential school model was the dominant system of schooling for deaf pupils, in America as in other nations. The first school in Italy was founded, coincidentally, in Milan, site of the fateful International Congress, in 1780, exactly a century before that event. Carl Oscar Malm, a deaf man trained at a school in Sweden, founded the first in Finland, in 1846, which like Norway's Trondheim School (1825) and another in Oslo (1848) later became state-operated. However, in Denmark, which in 1817 mandated education for deaf children, the Royal Institute for the Deaf and Dumb in Copenhagen began as a state facility in 1807. The Netherlands' three "institutes" for the deaf were founded as private facilities, one nonsectarian (1790), the second Roman Catholic (1840), the third Protestant (Taylor & Taylor, 1960).

That these schools, and schools for the blind, were residential was based on pragmatic considerations: A single facility might be the only resource to serve a vast region, even an entire nation. Some, like the Grimley Institute in Capetown, South Africa, were missionary enterprises (Behr, 1978), and the strong religious tradition tended to be carried on when they became governmental-supported Institutions. In the United States, Benjamin Rush advocated clerical involvement in all schools, and in those for deaf pupils, even if nonsectarian, that tradition had deep European roots. Although the school at Hartford established a precedent of publicly supported instruction at a time of secularization of general education, religious goals were unapologetically linked to the instructional mission; educators sought to rescue deaf persons from "intellectual darkness" and to bring them "to a knowledge of the truth as it is in Jesus" (Van Cleve & Crouch, 1989, p. 46).

Separation of church and state had yet to be reflected in policy or curriculum in schools for the deaf, and efforts on behalf of persons with disabilities
were associated in the public mind with Christian benevolence.

Even Howe, of a Unitarian family and one who avoided church attendance himself (Schwartz, 1956), frequently invoked religious notions in
addressing cause (parental disobedience of the "natural laws" ordained by
God) and prevention of disability, as well as in advocating and practicing
what he himself considered a "social gospel." His correspondence (in
Richards, 1909) reveals, however, that while recognizing the need to show
that the spiritual development of his famous deaf-blind pupil, Laura
Bridgman, was being addressed, Howe's greater concerns were her intellectual and social development. It is likely that support to pursue the latter
was enhanced if assurance of the former was provided, implying a form of
paternalism that was at least an improvement over the "charity mentality"
he deplored.

The Virginia School, which opened in 1830, was the first state institution to adopt the practice, first used in England then briefly in Paris, of serving
both deaf and blind pupils. Correspondence of the family of young Thomas
Tellinhast with Joseph D. Tyler, the principal, suggests that speech was not
an expected outcome; their main concern was that their son acquire practical skills involved in a "mechanical art" (Van Cleve & Crouch, 1989, p. 53).
For his part, the Reverend Mr. Tyler's sense of his work as a calling is
expressed rather paternalistically. "Be assured," he responded to Tellinhast
in November 1842, "that your dear little boy will want for no attention in
my power to bestow. My feelings toward all my pupils are, I think, warmer
and more endearing than usual between teacher and pupils in ordinary
schools, simply because my pupils are more helpless and more entirely
dependent upon me" (p. 53). This perception of helplessness seems at odds
with parental expectation, as well as with the advocacy of Clerc, who clearly
did not see himself, or Massieu, as helpless and dependent, but such a view
underlay the asylum concept Howe opposed. Though this concept characterized institutions that proliferated in the late 19th century, it was much
less apparent in schools for the deaf (Van Cleve & Crouch, 1989, p. 53),
however; moreover, a historian at Gallaudet University (Crouch, 1986)
found little evidence of a "missionary posture" in the numerous letters from
Tyler, who was in fact the first deaf principal in America, to the Bolling family
(p. 323).

By mid-century evidence of the ability of deaf pupils to benefit from
education was accumulating; without schooling, one deaf leader (Camp,
1848, in Lane, 1984b) averred in 1848, deaf persons would live in a "de-
graded condition, but little superior to that of the brute creation" (in Lane,
1984b, p. 214). In fact, most who had been provided schooling succeeded

in acquiring basic preparation at the elementary level, frequently the secondary level; some had graduated from college, and a few had acquired graduate and professional degrees (Van Cleve & Crouch, 1989, p. 169). Far from regarding deaf persons as unfortunates to be protected, the Connecticut School's leadership treated pupils with respect, particularly reflected in the attitude toward signing as the natural language of deaf persons and in no way inferior. Such an attitude stands in marked contrast to an account by a biographer of A. G. Bell (Mackenzie, 1928), which suggests that, to hearing parents and teachers, the very sight of signing was distasteful, even scarcely human.

Opposition to sign language was one of two inseparably related issues driving the attack that led to a shift to a day-class model; the other was advocacy of dispersion of persons with disabilities throughout society. It was the very concentration and segregation of large numbers of deaf pupils to which Bell objected and against which he warned. Like Howe, who advocated dispersion and integration for all exceptional groups, Bell thought it essential for deaf persons to be assimilated within hearing society in order to experience "normal life," which required the ability to communicate with hearing people. Another reason for his opposition to bringing deaf persons together, also shared by Howe, was based on concern about marriage and hereditary transmission. To what extent Bell advocated government regulation may be a matter of disagreement, but he indisputably was a leading figure in the American eugenics movement.

Emergence of Deaf Culture in North America

Two parallel and closely related developments accounted for the emergence of self-advocacy and a deaf intelligentsia, an intellectual vanguard. Gallaudet College, later Gallaudet University, was chartered through federal legislation enacted in 1864 and began operation as a college division of the Columbia Institution in Washington, under the leadership of Edward Gallaudet. This, the first institution of higher education in the world exclusively for deaf students, attracted the nation's most capable and ambitious deaf young people, and at a time when most Americans had little if any formal education, let alone higher education, some deaf citizens became the first members of their families to experience college. This vastly expanded vocational opportunities, and those who attended Gallaudet soon came to constitute an elite leadership group that has, for more than a century, dominated national organizations and publications for the Deaf community. It was also the principal supplier of deaf teachers during an era in which professional preparation of teachers for general education was still in its infancy. Thus, when in Britain appeals were still being made for charitable aid for deaf persons, their American counterparts already included college graduates and had established a national organization, the National Association of the Deaf, the self-advocacy of which is reflected in the words of its first president, Robert McGregor: "What heinous crime have the deaf been guilty of that their language should be proscribed?" (in Lane, 1984b, p. xvi).

American organizations were unique in being "of" rather than "for" deaf persons (Van Cleve & Crouch, 1989), and the views represented were those of deaf persons themselves, rather than those of hearing society. Based on their own experiences, they argued in favor of educational arrangements that permitted use of sign language and against those that sought to prohibit its use. Bell, on the other hand, with his consuming interest in sound transmission and, specifically, in human speech, expressed views welcomed by hearing parents and values shared by hearing teachers: Deaf children must, and can, be assimilated within society; therefore, they must—and can—be taught to speak. George Veditz, instructor at the Colorado School for the Deaf and Blind and twice president of the National Association of the Deaf, described Bell as "the most to be feared enemy of the American deaf" (in Van Cleve & Crouch, 1989, p. 114).

ALEXANDER GRAHAM BELL AND THE ORAL REVIVAL

A Familial Preoccupation

Although "oralism" is centuries old, the name most closely linked with its history is that of Alexander Graham Bell, an individual with a lifelong fascination with human speech, coupled with a passion for teaching; he came by both naturally. "Graham" (also familiarly known as "Aleck") was the third in a succession of Alexander Bells who formed careers focused on the human voice. His grandfather, a teacher of elocution and author of a text on the subject, was a promising actor who chose instead to become a "corrector of defective utterances" (Mackenzie, 1928, p. 15), assisted by his son, Alexander Melville, who later advertised his services as a "Professor of Elocution and the Art of Speech." Though in 1860 he published with his brother a widely read text, *Bell's Standard Elocutionist*, that Bell's most notable contribution, one that led to his son's involvement in deaf education, was *Visible Speech*, a system in which printed symbols represented the anatomical positions of the speech mechanism associated with certain sounds. It inspired Shaw's *Pygmalion*, as well as educators and students of language throughout the world; in fact, Mandarin Chinese was the first language to be translated in the form of Visible Speech. A popular lecturer, Melville also gave Shakespearean readings and was sufficiently avante garde to present works of contemporaries like Dickens (Bruce, 1973).

A. G. Bell was thus raised in a home in which speech was a family pre-occupation, but another key influence was his very musical, and hearing-impaired, mother, to whom he was devoted and who inspired his love of musical evenings and probably some of his imaginative teaching techniques. As a teacher, Bell was adept at dramatizing and introducing play formats, presumably to the delight of young George Sanders, his best-known pupil (whose father's patronage would be a critical factor in supporting his inventions). He would employ music and dancing, as well as nursery rhymes, in order for the pupil to gain a sense of the rhythm that is important in speech. In some fashion, his mother clearly influenced his attitudes about deafness: a combination of commitment and abhorrence. Bell viewed deafness as a "terrible curse" to the individual and, genetically, as a threat to society (Van Cleve & Crouch, 1989, p. 145).

Melville had spent some time in Canada's Maritime Provinces for health reasons, and concern for Aleck's health prompted a family move, first to Brantford, Ontario, and then to Baddeck, Nova Scotia. Working increasingly with his son's assistance, the elder Bell made that his base of operations, but finding himself unable to accept an invitation to lecture in Boston, he suggested his son as a substitute. Thus, in 1871, at the age of 23, A. G. Bell began what would be a lifetime commitment to two fields that were for him inseparable: teaching children with impaired hearing and transmission of human speech. The innovation of Bell's adaptations of his father's system was in making those who tried to teach articulation to deaf pupils aware of the positions of parts of the speech mechanism in producing certain sounds, the importance of which Sarah Fuller, who negotiated the lectures, quickly recognized.

Skeptical about lipreading, he continued to work on devices, like the *phonoautograph*, to enable a deaf individual to see language, a concept that ultimately did find realization in technology. While his telephone initially seemed to increase the isolation of deaf persons, later development of the teletypewriter (TTY) led to expanded and more generally available Tele-communication Devices for the Deaf (TDDs) and a wide variety of other electronic assistive devices (Breunig, 1990). While speech was the goal, Bell recognized the primacy in children's development of receptive language, that receptive repertoires always precede and exceed expressive repertoires. He therefore devised techniques enlisting the visual modality, notably a glove not unlike those used by early oralists, but while integrating a variety of visual experiences, he increasingly emphasized writing as a base. His Boston lectures extended beyond the intended two months, punctuated with lectures at the Clarke Institution and, interestingly, at the school in Hartford. (If E. M. Gallaudet [1888], who had succeeded his father, is to be believed, he was not only receptive to speech instruction but eager to welcome Bell to shared leadership status in the field.) Relocated in Boston, where he opened a "school of vocal physiology" for instruction in Visible Speech, Bell found a climate sufficiently receptive to his ideas to yield an invitation to lecture at a national conference for principals of schools for the deaf in Flint, Michigan. At 25, he was already attracting a following, and soon gained a faculty appointment at Boston University as Professor of Vocal Physiology.

At this time, while schooling for deaf students had become well established in the United States, only a few students—about 140 according to a Bell biographer (Mackenzie, 1928, p. 245)—were receiving speech instruction, mainly in the Clarke Institution, the Lexington School in New York, and the Boston Schools facility (later named the Horace Mann School) that had sponsored his lectureship. Excepting the last, all schooling was provided in residential facilities, to which pupils were typically admitted at about age 10. Within little more than two decades, that pattern would begin to change, as day classes and oral methodology gained ascendancy, and instruction began to be introduced earlier in the interest of fostering speech and language. While Bell soon arrived at its head, the "oral revival" had actually begun earlier with a parent's advocacy for public policy that would, in his view, provide more timely and more normalizing intervention.

Hearing Parents and Oral Educators

Mabel Hubbard's name may be unfamiliar to many (excepting old movie aficianados who remember who it was that Don Ameche's Bell courted), but her role in shaping the history of this field may have been pivotal. At age 5, the daughter of Gardiner Greene Hubbard of Cambridge, who in 1888 founded the National Geographic Society, had incurred middle-ear damage as a result of scarlet fever, leaving her functionally deaf. According to a Bell biographer (Waite, 1961), Hubbard learned that the professional wisdom of the day dictated that she would therefore lose the ability to speak, or at best her voice would be "worse than the screech of a steam locomotive" (p. 17). At 10, she could be placed in a residential school to learn the language of signs. He was further shocked, as a member of the state board of education, to learn that even these provisions were not available in Massachusetts. Not satisfied with these prospects, Hubbard sought out the famous educator Samuel Gridley Howe.

In promising support, Howe was reviving a campaign begun earlier by his colleague, Mann. The oral methods by then widely used in Germany, and in Italy, were virtually unknown in America, nor were teachers trained in such methods available. Impressed by what he had observed in the German programs, Mann, with Howe's help, succeeded in convincing officials of the American Asylum in Hartford to introduce articulation training, but after a short, disappointing trial it was abandoned. In his enthusiasm about outcomes, Mann should perhaps have been more attentive to process; had he studied the German methods closely he might have seen strategies anticipating Bell's later observation that "congenitally hearing impaired . . . children should be taught the [English] language in written form before being required to rely upon the mouth alone" (in Cornett, 1990, p. 146). Bell stressed the need for a language context in order for the child to interpret the partial oral information obtained, a concept congruent with both Pestalozzi's and Mann's beliefs about language and reading instruction for all children. Even more extravagant in his enthusiasm about the German schools was Howe's "alter ego," Charles Sumner, whose reports even Howe questioned. Clearly, Moritz Hill had not only refined the methods learned under Eshke, Heinicke's son-in-law, but introduced innovations to make instruction more congruent with best practice (from a Pestalozzian view) for hearing students, which his willingness to receive visitors and train educators were effectively disseminating.

A first attempt, in 1864, to introduce enabling legislation to fund speech instruction for deaf children in Massachusetts failed, apparently due largely to opposition of Lewis Dudley, father of a deaf daughter. In that instance, even Howe's forceful eloquence could not prevail, though his was joined by other important voices: Frank Sanborn, secretary of the State Board of Charities, endorsed the effort and Mary Lamson, one of Laura Bridgman's teachers at Perkins, described the methods she had observed while visiting the German schools. But Hubbard was not defeated. Largely with his own resources, he established a small, private school at Chelmsford in 1866, engaging Harriet Burbank Rogers (1834–1919), who, having taught in several country schools and at the academy at Westford, had—in the tradition of oral educators—been asked to work with a deaf child, Fanny Cushing. Interestingly, Ms. Rogers's sister, Eliza, was another of Laura Bridgman's teachers, and it is likely that it was through this connection that she was aware of the work in Germany. Gleaning the basic techniques from a newspaper article, she tried the techniques with Fanny, placing the girl's hand in front of her own mouth to feel the breath escape and then in front of Fanny's to elicit imitation. She followed a similar process for the child to feel vibration in the throat and chest. Her success convinced her that she had found her calling as an educator (Bruce, 1973).

Mabel Hubbard, who with the private tutelage of Mary True had apparently been progressing remarkably while attending a regular school, was not among Ms. Rogers's pupils, however. Using speech reading learned during a sojourn in Germany to great advantage, Mabel seems not to have experienced the predicted deterioration in quality of vocal production, and her mother preferred that she continue to interact with hearing children in school (Waite, 1961). Impetus for Hubbard to reintroduce the proposal for legislation came in the form of an unrelated event. Apparently unaware of Hubbard's efforts since there were no stipulations concerning pedagogical philosophy, one John Clarke, motivated by his own experience of presbycusis, offered to contribute $50,000 if the Commonwealth of Massachusetts would establish a school for deaf children in Boston. Among those called to testify in the course of hearings on the proposal, the "star witness," if we are to believe a Bell biographer (Waite, 1961), was the 15–year-old Mabel Hubbard, whose demonstrated ability to lipread and quality of speech reportedly won the day, convincing even Dudley. The former skill eventually influenced her future husband to consider more seriously the role of speechreading, but for children who were congenitally deaf Bell maintained the position that a language base must be established, for which written language provided the best avenue (Cornett, 1990, p. 146).

The resulting legislation comprised two parts, one providing for what would become the Clarke School, which opened on October 1, 1867, in Northampton, under Harriet Rogers's direction, the other for instruction of children beginning at age 5 and continuing through age 10 (the standard age for enrollment in schools for the deaf) in articulation and lipreading. The act provided that such instruction could occur at Clarke or at other schools, thus authorizing establishment of additional programs. Consequently, with a grant from the legislature, the Boston School for Deaf-Mutes opened on November 10, 1869, headed by Sarah Fuller, who would bring first Melville Bell and then his son to Boston in support of the oral revival. It was renamed the Horace Mann School for the Deaf in 1877, in recognition of Mann's continuing advocacy.

Sarah Fuller (1836–1927), like Harriet Rogers, had been a teacher for some years, in Boston and in Newton, Massachusetts. She would, together with Bell and Caroline A. Yale, Rogers's successor at Clarke, establish in 1890 the American Association to Promote the Teaching of Speech to the Deaf (AAPTSD), one of the most effective political forces in the history of special education. Fuller believed strongly in providing the earliest possible intervention in order to enable deaf children to participate, as speaking members, in hearing society. Thus, in 1888, a century before such services were mandated, she founded the first program for preschool-age children with disabilities, the Sarah Fuller Home for Little Children Who Cannot Hear (Fay, 1893), the beginning of a "Union of Kindergartens for the Deaf," organized in 1893 (Hudson, 1893–94). Fuller also made key contributions to teaching methods incorporated into formal teacher training programs, including a manual for the teaching of language, a set of speech exercises, and methods for working with infants with congenital deafness. She continued to be influential in oral education in America even after retirement from the Horace Mann School in 1910 (Adams, 1927).

The third co-founder of the organization that was eventually named for Alexander Graham Bell was Caroline Ardelia Yale (1848–1933), who succeeded Rogers as principal of the Clarke Institution in 1873, three years after joining its faculty, a role she held nearly a half-century until retiring in 1922. Like Fuller, she published materials for teachers, most notably speech charts for articulation training, developed in collaboration with Alice C. Worcester, a Clarke teacher. Under her leadership, a teacher training department was established at Clarke in 1889, subsequently recognized as the official training school of the AAPTSD. This formalization of teacher preparation, together with various publications, was of great importance in disseminating oral education (Taylor, 1933).

The "pure oralism" movement could have had no more committed leadership. Bell's own vigorous advocacy for the teaching of speech and for integration in hearing society was clearly motivated in some measure by personal experience, especially with his mother and his accomplished wife. Having encountered a number of persons with hearing loss yet enough residual hearing to enable them to learn orally, who had not developed oral communication skills, he was convinced that the presence of many teachers in the residential schools who were themselves deaf had effectively deprived such people of the opportunity to develop speech capabilities. These three factors—residential schools, deaf teachers, and sign language—were linked in his mind as forming a system by which deaf persons were segregated, though his views concerning the last were more complex and less categorical. In any case, the resolution adopted at the First International Congress, in Paris in 1878, stating the goal of "restoration of the deaf-mute to society," captured his own goal perfectly. That event, during the week of September 23, was in fact organized by members of the Pereire Society, and all 27 participants represented what were then termed "articulation schools." The Second Congress, in Milan in 1880, was only slightly more representative; of 164 members, only 21 were from countries other than Italy and France, prompting Brill (1984) to comment, "It is not improper to say that its pronunciamento in favor of the oral method was the expression of little more than local opinion" (p. 140). Despite Edward Gallaudet's efforts, the congress resolved to oppose instructional use of signing, recommending a seven- to eight-year course of study beginning at age 8–10.

Recognizing that language underlies all forms of communication, and that a child's early years are crucial in language development, Bell and his colleagues worked for policies to ensure that opportunities for oral instruction were provided in a timely fashion. Legislation enacted in many states as, or just before, the 20th century began was intended to address both issues. Ohio, where considerable political activism for oral instruction was undertaken, provided successively for: state reimbursement for special day classes in major cities, including transportation (1896); extension of reimbursement ($150 per child per year) to districts with at least five eligible children (1898); initiating instruction at age 3 with funding for boarding home placement if distance precluded daily travel, with a minimum of nine months trial with oral methods (1906); manual instruction for children unable to learn orally, but in a "separate school," and classes for children with mild hearing loss (1913) (Ohio Department of Education, 1985). The trial period was to ensure that every child had an opportunity to learn orally, with no use of signing—nor was signing permitted, thus the insistence on physical separation that continued to be maintained where "oral-only" methods were used.

A FAMILY AFFAIR

The Bell lineage, though in some respects unique, was by no means the only instance of "hereditary calling." Even today business enterprises pass from parent to child, and so it was with schools in times when many were entrepreneurial. In this convention can be understood the Heinicke pattern of transmission (through his wife's efforts) to a son-in-law and, in France, Pereire's wish (not realized, despite efforts of *his* widow) that the "secret" and thus the work would pass to the son Isaac and then the grandson Eugene. Other familial transmission patterns can be found, not only within the field of deaf education. The Tukes represented four successive generations of leadership. Howe's son-in-law, Michael Anagnos, took over the reigns of Perkins, though not without some struggle, following a tradition of sons-in-law where sons were absent (Howe had three daughters, his only son, Sam Howe, Jr., having died in 1862) or perhaps disinclined. Stepping into the breach on Howe's death, he bridled at the prospect of second fiddle, demonstrating that he was the leader the school needed. Subsequently, the spirit of the revered Dr. Howe was pervasive, kept very much alive through the continued presence of his widow (a source of conflict for Anne Sullivan), as it is in Anagnos's (1882) own chronicle. But he was his own man, casting out in such new directions as initiating a kindergarten.

As his situation illustrates, increasingly the mantle was not simply passed but had to be assumed, while previously starting a school, if private, was indeed like starting a business; more accurately, it *was* starting a business, but public auspice required a different mentality. In the case of the Braidwoods, a nephew inherited the "family business" and, with it, the family trust. At Perkins and at the American School at Hartford there was a tradition, but more generally a cause, to be sustained, a national not just a family trust. Like Howe, Gallaudet embodied a tradition not of entrepreneurialism, but of Epée's and Sicard's evangelicism. A comparison of the Gallaudets and the Braidwoods is instructive with respect to family tradition.

The Braidwood Dynasty

It will be recalled that the four schools from which Gallaudet had hoped to gain expertise, in London, Birmingham, and Edinburgh, whether or not a Braidwood relative was actually in charge, were all under the family's control. The family bond of secrecy was firm, ending only when the last Watson, believing himself released by the death of the last Braidwood, published *Instruction of the Deaf and Dumb*, in 1866. We have made many allusions to this peculiar convention, which, viewed in the present-day context of "networking," multiple professional conferences, and academics eager to publish, seems at best suspect or eccentric, at worst a serious impediment to progress. Although the expectation for a scientist's work to be subjected to scrutiny was firmly established by the various national academies, a school was often a business enterprise; defense against plagiarism was understandable since pirated methods could jeopardize both one's status and one's livelihood, or a child's inheritance. Inventors who failed to hold on to their secrets could incur substantial loss, and proprietary disputes, as Bell would discover in the case of his invention, could be quite messy.

The Braidwoods' entry into this field followed a familiar pattern. Thomas Braidwood, who ran a private school for the teaching of mathematics, in 1760 got as a pupil 9-year-old Thomas Shirrel, deaf since age 3 and son of a wealthy merchant. Thus began Mr. Braidwood's Academy for the Deaf and Dumb, the success of which enabled him in 1775 to take on an assistant, his nephew, John Braidwood. In 1783, the school moved to Hackney, near London, and a second assistant was appointed, another nephew, Joseph Watson, who headed the school, established in 1792 as the London Asylum for the Deaf, until his death in 1829. He was succeeded by his son, Thomas James Watson, who, on his death in 1857, was succeeded by *his* son, the Reverend James Watson. The bond of secrecy, and what has been gently termed a "nepotic tendency" (Bender, 1970), had lasted for 118 years. It was this last Watson who finally saw fit to make public the Braidwood techniques, which, interestingly, turned out to be strongly derivative of those of Wallis, notwithstanding the latter's lack of disposition to be forthcoming. But through that long period the Braidwood reputation had spread, first as a result of a visit by the great Dr. Johnson and his amanuensis, Boswell, in 1773, and then further with publication of Green's (1783) book a decade later. The experience of the Bolling children, three of the four American Braidwood pupils, inspired their hearing brother, Colonel William Bolling, to contact John Braidwood, which as we saw, was ill-advised, for the school he started in Baltimore during the War of 1812 was doomed from the start by the wastrel ways of its head.

There had been dissenting voices. During his fateful and frustrating visit, Gallaudet had spoken with Dugald Stewart, a philosopher in Edinburgh, who questioned why speech per se ought to be the main objective in teaching deaf pupils. From what Stewart could see of the approach carried out by Kinniburgh, pupils were merely taught to parrot. Sicard's emphasis on developing intellect, and effort to make instruction generally available rather than restricted to a privileged few, seemed to him a more significant mission (Boatner, 1959, p. 5). Gallaudet was beginning to agree. With that of the Braidwood family, oral education's hegemony in Britain grew, as well. Yet, beyond reports that he carried a spatula-like instrument, presumably to position the tongue, little was known of precisely how Braidwood and his assistants proceeded. With the Watson publication, the training of teachers came firmly under the control of the Association for the Oral Instruction of the Deaf and Dumb. Paralleling developments in Germany and the United States, what should occur next was opening of day classes. An influential figure in that transition was William Steiner, Superintendent of Instruction of the Deaf for the London School Board, who seems to have "converted" following the fateful International Conference in Milan in 1880 (Bender, 1970).

The Gallaudets

His frail health exhausted after 13 years as head of the American Asylum for the Deaf, Thomas Gallaudet requested "early retirement" to devote his remaining years to religious writing for children, with associated guides for parents. Having gained great respect among civic leaders and the public, he was offered, but declined, directorship of the planned New England Institute for the Blind and the Worcester Asylum for the Insane, though he did serve for eight years as chaplain of the Hartford County Prison, where he was "said to work miracles with the men" (Boatner, 1959, p. 9) and, from 1838 until his death in 1851, of the Hartford Retreat for the Insane, a private facility modeled after Tuke's Retreat. Edward Miner, a sensitive 14–year-old when his father died, was the youngest of eight children born to Gallaudet and Sophia Fowler, the daughter of Miner Fowler and one of his first students. Thus, Edward shared with Aleck Bell the experience of having a mother with impaired hearing, and his father, like Bell, had a wife who was deaf.

While study was a regular part of Gallaudet family life, the father's beliefs in the importance of the "whole being" and in education as a "continuing process," rather than a painful but time-limited experience, led him to limit formal study to three hours each day. Edward was raised with gentle strictness, his father eschewing physical punishment, favoring other means he thought "just as effective." Thinking novels frivolous, he imposed literary censorship, though allowing at least one exception: *David Copperfield*. As in the Bell household, music was important. The elder Gallaudet gently urged his son to consider college, perhaps to become a teacher of deaf children, but Edward was attracted to business although he seems to have experienced inner conflict between "higher and baser impulses."

As it happened, his introduction to the world of work occurred earlier than planned, and though family friends helped him secure a job as a bank clerk, his father's death made his "higher impulses" more insistent. With an older friend, Henry Clay Trumbull, he joined the church, volunteering with the Young Men's Mission Society his father had organized and gaining teaching experience at the Morgan Street Mission Sunday School, of which he became clerk and librarian when Trumbull was made superintendent. Now determined to pursue higher education as his father had wished, he attended Trinity College part-time, admitted as a junior. Gifted intellectually, drawn to learning and to service, and emerging from uncertainty as to what he should do with his life, the younger Gallaudet was retracing his father's steps. Thus, at first tentatively, he entered the field of deaf education, but was soon given responsibilities he had neither sought nor been bequeathed. These would soon take him to the nation's capital and involve him in higher education.

Amos Kendall (1789–1869), postmaster-general during the Jackson administration, had acquired considerable wealth as business manager for Samuel Morse, inventor of the telegraph. That his philanthropic impulses turned in the direction of education of deaf persons he attributed to the influence of Morse's wife, who was deaf (Stickney, 1872). As president of the board of trustees of a small school established on his own estate in 1857, Kendall engaged the young Edward Gallaudet as its director. President Lincoln signed enabling legislation in 1864 to establish a national college for the deaf, initially as a higher education department of Kendall's Columbia Institution. In 1894, two distinct entities, Gallaudet College and the Kendall School, were established, the former later becoming Gallaudet University.

CONFLICTING IDEOLOGIES

Bell had a scientific interest in sign language, even taking a year's instruction, but was convinced its instructional use interfered with learning. As Cornett (1990) interprets his view, "*The proper use of signs is to illustrate lan-*

guage, not to take its place" (p. 151; emphasis in original). Orin Cornett (1990) who in 1966 developed the Cued Speech method, suggests that her system made it possible to "secure the possible advantages of sign language without incurring the disadvantages which preoccupied Bell" (p. 153). Concerning speech, Edward Gallaudet also claimed a position somewhere between extremes, seeking to accommodate both. Unlike Mann and Sumner, he saw such an accommodation in the German approach, with signing instrumental to attaining speech, and he professed both to value and to practice instruction in speech. Seeing in their "Combined Method" a deception, if an inadvertent one, Seguin (1880) included the Gallaudets among the "mutists" who deprived deaf persons of speech. But Edward Gallaudet maintained his "great aim" was the same as Bell's: to teach *language*. Their similar backgrounds notwithstanding, as the latter's biographer (Boatner, 1959) wrote, "In temperament there could have been no two men more opposite than Alexander Graham Bell and Edward Miner Gallaudet [who] . . . reached out to share . . . but Bell always withdrew" (p. 122). Gallaudet

> honestly thought there existed something to be gained by an alliance that would be more beneficial to the deaf. . . . He hoped that Bell would eventually understand that he, too, wanted the deaf to be given the advantage of learning to speak. . . . But he also hoped Bell would come to see that the great mass of the deaf would never be financially able to secure enough individual attention to attain adequate speech, and that in any event, their individual differences would thwart such attainment. What, then, would become of those who preferred to live as deaf people . . . if they had their natural language of signs and spelling taken from them? . . . a more liberal way could also lead to a beautiful and full life, and a social adjustment far beyond the circumscribed manner . . . that Bell prescribed. (pp. 124–125)

Communication mode used in teaching epitomizes the conflict, but it involved other basic issues: the location of instruction, whether teachers themselves ought to be or could be deaf, social relationships, and very importantly to Bell (as to Howe) marriage and parenthood. It was also a conflict involving rights, power, identity, and disagreement as to whether deafness constitutes a disability or identifies a culture. More than sign language, Bell became preoccupied with "centralization," that is, congregating hearing-impaired students in residential schools. In these inseparably related campaigns his fight was with the Deaf community, to whom the schools and the language of sign represented cultural identity.

As in Europe, as schools for children with disabilities were formed in America it went unquestioned that these must be specialized enterprises and that pupils would necessarily have to leave their homes. The term used traditionally for such arrangements was *asylum*, a term that America's most vocal advocate for exceptional individuals found repellent. "The more I reflect upon the subject," wrote Howe, "the more I see objections in principle and practice to *asylums*. What right have we to pack off the poor, the old, the blind to asylums? They are us, our brothers, our sisters—they belong in families; they are deprived of the dearest relations in life in being put away in masses in asylums" (in Richards, 1909, p. 48).

Howe's involvement with deafness, as advocate of oralism and opponent of residential schools, was consistent with his general philosophy: The aim for all "defective" individuals was assimilation within society. Of blind pupils he said, "We educate them for the world, for citizens of a free country; and when their education is finished, we bid them go out into the world and take their place among men" (in Richards, 1909, p. 297). He had no doubt that for deaf persons the goal would be the same, and that being the case they must be taught to speak. Thus, Hubbard found in him a strong advocate, who had already been tentatively exploring the area of deafness. Exaggerating her father's role, his daughter (Richards, 1935) claimed that his "experiments" in articulation "led to the establishment of a small school in Chelmsford . . . for the teaching of articulation to deaf-mute children" (p. 153). He was at all events vigorous enough in his support of the enterprise as a preferred alternative to concern E. M. Gallaudet about possible losses in enrollment. Until 1880, when the tide was turned with endorsement of "pure oralism," while sign language was predominant, specific pedagogic methods varied, journals and congresses reflecting healthy debate. According to his biographer (Boatner, 1959), Gallaudet had attempted to use his own leadership role, first in Hartford, then in Washington and in the field at large, to urge inclusion of speech instruction. That was not enough for Bell.

In 1867, the same year that the Clarke School was opened, the "Broadway, New York" branch of German oralism was formally established with the organization of the Association for the Improved Instruction of Deaf Mutes. It had begun in 1864 with six children and a teacher, Bernard Englesmann, who had been trained at "a famous oral school in Vienna" (Connor, 1992, p. 13). Again, the impetus had come from parents, Hannah and Isaac Rosenfeld, concerned that their daughter, Carrie, would have appropriate educational opportunity. They not only provided financial backing and located a teacher, but Carrie reported later that, owing to "'the teacher's unfamiliarity with the English language, . . . my dear mother was obliged to act as interpreter'" (p. 15). The Lexington School for the Deaf, as it was renamed when relocated in 1885 in a new structure on Lexington Avenue, would epitomize pure oralism in a residential school, where instructional signing was strictly proscribed. It departed from tradition in other important ways: "Establishment of a school for handicapped students in the middle of Manhattan was a distinct departure from the national practice of isolating such children in rural settings" (p. 30), as was admission of girls and pupils as young as age 7.

The "benevolent gentlemen" who founded the New York Institution for the Deaf and Dumb in 1817 were less concerned with method than that some form of schooling be provided deaf children identified by the almshouse chaplain, the Reverend John Stamford (Letchworth, 1903/1974). We shall see that similar circumstances led to the founding of New York's first school for the blind. Samuel Akerly provided leadership as "physician, secretary, and superintendent" (p. 1) of the school, which, though private, received state aid (p. 1). As at Hartford, articulation training was briefly tried, but in 1831, under Harvey Peet, Sicard's methods were adopted. A Catholic facility, St. Mary's, was established in Buffalo, in 1853, offering a five-year academic and vocational curriculum for pupils beginning at age 6 (Connor, 1992). While St. Mary's introduced Bell's Visible Speech in 1873, two other private New York institutions that opened in 1875 used the Gallaudet Combined Method of sign language and finger spelling. St. Joseph's Institution for the Improved Instruction of Deaf Mutes enrolled girls, beginning at age 6, and the Central New York Institution for Deaf Mutes in Rome provided a five- to eight-year curriculum for both sexes, ages 5–19. A sixth private facility was opened in Rochester in 1876. A trend toward beginning instruction earlier is apparent, but with it the issue of separating children from their families became more troubling.

The shift to oral day classes, begun in Massachusetts, was heralded by a steady march in Wisconsin, which by 1900 had 15 day schools. Ohio, which would become a strongly oral state, had in fact enacted legislation in 1827, in response to the petition of parents of three deaf children, providing for reimbursement at the rate of $100 per child per year for the Village of Tallmadge to form a class taught by one Colonel Smith. But when the Asylum for the Education of Deaf and Dumb Persons was opened in Columbus in 1829, the class was transferred there. This facility would continue to have an important role in Ohio, as did its counterparts in other states. Day classes in all Ohio's "city districts of the first class," begun in Cincinnati in 1879, were mandated in 1898, motivated more by the need to relieve overcrowding in the residential school than by ideology, but as pure oralism reached its zenith, ideology and parent advocacy were dominant influences. By 1937, 18 Ohio communities had a total of 70 day classes, with 11 specifically for "hard-of-hearing" pupils (Ohio Department of Education, 1985).

Who Shall Teach Deaf Pupils?

If signing is the language of instruction, what better teachers could there be than well-educated native users of that language? Clerc had established this tradition in America, exemplified by Tyler's appointment to head the school in Virginia and Gallaudet College's key role in teacher preparation. But the rise of pure oralism brought a radical shift:

> In 1850, 36.6 percent of the teaching force . . .—excluding private and denominational schools—were deaf teachers. Eight years later, the ranks of deaf teachers peaked at 40.8 percent. . . . Within the next decade, the percentage fell to 30.9 percent, and the outlook was gloomy. By 1927—probably the height of pure oralism in this country—only 14.0 percent of the teachers were deaf. The prospects . . . were so bad that officials at Gallaudet College openly discouraged deaf students from considering a teaching career. (Gannon, 1981, p. 3).

Predictably, Gallaudet and Bell clashed concerning teacher training. Bell's opposition to Gallaudet's efforts to establish a normal school was based on his conviction that the proposed enterprise was intended for deaf teachers, which Gallaudet insisted was not so. When the matter was brought to the U.S. Congress in quest of enabling legislation, a split occurred in the ranks of educators whose support Gallaudet had enlisted. It seemed to him, his biographer (Boatner, 1959) states, that "Bell was like an octopus trying to get its tentacles around the whole profession of instructors of the deaf" (p. 137). Whether to seek compromise or a forum for debate, he anticipated an opportunity for them to share the Chautauqua platform in July 1894, but Bell, who had been among the many public figures to address that audience, chose not to participate. Lest we think their enmity a one-way affair, when Bell's multifarious involvements forced him to give up teaching, Gallaudet insisted he be denied membership in the American Convention of Instructors of the Deaf (Breunig, 1990). Even as universities assumed responsibility to prepare teachers, as well as speech therapists and audiologists, with oralist hegemony, American training was dominated by the organization first named the American Association to Promote the Teaching of Speech to the Deaf. Interestingly, in announcing its formation, in 1890, Bell averred that all committed to that purpose, irrespective of instructional approach, would be welcome in AAPTSD!

TRANSMISSION: GENETIC AND CULTURAL

With his success with the telephone (achieved with the backing of Hubbard and Thomas Sanders, his pupil's father), the ensuing court challenges, and his work in promoting its adoption, Bell's career as a teacher had ended in the 1870s, but he remained very much in the forefront of this now international movement. Having helped to establish a school in Greenock, Scotland, in 1878, he used it as a model for one he opened in Washington, D.C., in 1883. With the AAPTSD he was more than a figurehead and, with customary enthusiasm, he had committed himself to a program of research concerning the hereditary transmission of deafness. In this, he joined others at the forefront of another cause with more general ramifications.

Bell's Genealogical Research

To Galton's genealogical approach, Bell applied the new statistical methods of correlation and probability estimation that Pearson had introduced, widely used in agriculture. Armed with the tools of science, Bell, as would others, found confirmation for beliefs he already held. He was convinced that within his (New England) data pool the deaf population was increasing faster than the general population due to the incidence of deaf children born to deaf parents and thought the system of education directly implicated, in that it fostered restriction of acquaintance, friendship, and ultimately romantic relationships. Schools that brought deaf persons together segregated them from hearing society because of the specialized communication system used and the strong group identification fostered, leading to further spread of this "hereditary defect." Alternatively, day classes could permit children to remain in speech-using environments; establish friendships with hearing children (as Mabel's mother had insisted); and, should they marry, marry hearing partners. In effect, he urged social controls not only on how, where, and by whom deaf persons should be taught, but also on whom they should marry.

A biographer (Mackenzie, 1928), attributing the ensuing hostility in the deaf community to a misunderstanding, insists that Bell did not appeal to Congress for legislation proscribing endogamous marriage. It seems that a reporter, noticing a pamphlet that inexplicably happened to be in a congressman's office, drew unwarranted inferences, though she does allow that its title, "Memoir upon the Formation of a Deaf Variety of the Human Race," was "unfortunate." This was a paper Bell presented to the National Academy of Sciences in New Haven in 1883. But of his opposition to endogamous marriage there can be no doubt, and the "Memoir" presents statistical findings supporting his argument. We now know that, hereditary deafness being a recessive trait and deafness itself resulting from various causes, the matter is not so straightforward. But at that time traits were still thought to be transmitted directly, from generation to generation, as Galton had "shown"; one didn't need data to support this self-evident proposition. Howe prohibited reunions at Perkins in the belief that continued contact might lead to marriage, as did Anagnos (Van Cleve & Crouch, 1989, p. 148), whose sisters-in-law (Howe & Hall, 1903) wrote of their father, "Marriage between two blind persons he always denounced as against every law of morality. The justness of this view is too evident to need demonstration" (p. 24). In fact, statistical evidence suggested some *decrease* in prevalence of deafness (Best, 1914), probably due to progress in treating infectious disease in children.

Despite their advocacy for blind and deaf individuals, neither Howe nor Bell doubted that these conditions were afflictions. Bell regarded deafness as a "terrible curse" to the individual and a threat to society (Van Cleve & Crouch, 1989, p. 145). Whatever the views of deaf persons themselves, to late-19th-century hearing society, including "the deaf" among "defectives" in the census seemed entirely appropriate, although Bell was instrumental in separating deafness and blindness from the category that included other "defective, dependent, and delinquent classes." (Both Gallaudet and Bell can be credited with more appropriate census reporting, the former for eliminating the word "dumb" [Boatner, 1959], the latter for the change [as we might expect] from "deaf-mute" to deaf [Mackenzie, 1928].)

Naive as was the Victorian understanding of hereditary transmission, it was an improvement over past myths; though considered a curse, even a societal threat, deafness was rarely seen as divine retribution. Unlike leaders in the field of retardation, Bell did not use the word *menace*, but his warnings fed growing fears of deviance no less than did theirs. His prominence heightened the public sense of deafness as an aberration at a time when the Deaf community had gained visibility and a strong identity. There was growing concern about "different" groups, which would reach the level of alarm. For many, deafness and sign language—together with conversation in Italian, Yiddish, or other "non-native" tongue, Catholicism, and unfamiliar costume and custom—had taken on a particularly negative aspect.

Convinced that heredity was implicated, Bell urged measures against intramarriage, but instances of seemingly random occurrence, irrespective of hearing status of parents, puzzled him. His beliefs concerning both hereditary transmission and the need for deaf persons to use speech in order to interact with hearing persons were challenged by what he saw on Martha's Vineyard, where in the towns of West Tisbury and Chilmark for at least two centuries incidence of deafness had been extraordinarily high. That fact supported his beliefs and provided the basis for his carefully researched but inflammatory "Memoir", (1883), but what must have confounded him was the evident "adjustment" of deaf members of these communities, and of their hearing neighbors to them. They were generally economically successful and accepted socially, notwithstanding their use of sign language, and free to marry as they chose, hearing or deaf partners, without apparent fear on anyone's part. Their inclusion in all facets of community life reflected no humanitarian motive; it was simply an accepted fact of life. As reported in the *Boston Sunday Herald* in 1895, "every resident . . . learns to talk with fingers as early as with his tongue, for he will have to do with the deaf socially and in business every day and every hour of the day" (Groce, 1985, p. 75).

Puzzled by the seeming randomness with which a deaf child might be born to hearing parents, or a hearing child to deaf parents, Bell tried to identify other factors that might somehow influence transmission, even speculating about the possible role of a layer of clay beneath Chilmark. But he was in any case convinced, given the extraordinary prevalence, that here was clear evidence of what happens when many deaf persons are congregated together. In the Volta Laboratory he had established, now relocated to Washington, he continued his actuarial analyses, establishing a division, the Volta Bureau, to handle correspondence and dissemination of information about deafness. This was done at the suggestion of his assistant, John Hitz (whom Anagnos characterized as "the picturesque secretary"), a gentle intellectual whose Swedenborgian beliefs influenced Helen Keller's spiritual development (Lash, 1980). Having challenged Bell's conclusions, Dr. Edward Allen Fay, editor of the *American Annals of the Deaf*, was invited to access Volta Bureau resources for his own research; the result, Fay's (1898) *Marriage of the Deaf in America*, partially supported Bell's position. Also under Volta auspices, Fay (1893) edited the authoritative *Histories of American Schools for the Deaf.*

Bell continued to pursue his own investigations, using various forums to report his findings to a broad audience. These included prestigious scientific journals, as well as the annual meetings and publications of the American Breeders' Association. This organization was formed in 1903 to bring together biologists interested in the study of evolution and those seeking efficient ways to improve plant and animal strains, but the former focus attracted other intellectuals, social scientists, and progressive reformers like Charles B. Davenport, probably the most influential American eugenicist, who with Bell, Luther Burbank, and other important scientists served on its Committee on Eugenics. The committee's intent, according to its first chairperson (Jordan, 1908) was, "to investigate and report on heredity in the human race; to devise methods of recording the value of the blood of individuals, families, peoples and races; to emphasize the value of superior blood and the menace to society of inferior blood; and to suggest methods of improving the heredity of the family, the people, or the race" (p. 201).

As we noted in Chapter 3 and elaborate further in Chapter 6, American eugenicists were very much concerned about the future of "American stock." While some were also in the forefront of moves to restrict immigration, Bell's preoccupation was with hereditary transmission of defect, but his concerns extended beyond deafness. In an 1885 paper published in *Science*, titled "Is There a Correlation Between Defects of the Senses?" he reported that, based on his findings, there indeed was. Census data from 1880 revealed clearly, he concluded, that the incidence of hearing impairment in blind persons was much greater than in the general population, as was the incidence of visual impairment in deaf persons. Adding that both appeared to occur frequently in conjunction with retardation and mental illness, he concluded that all such impairments may often derive from a common cause, "perhaps arrested development of the nervous system" (Bell, 1885, p. 129). Thus, while working to separate deafness and blindness from the general class of "defectives," Bell paradoxically contributed to a growing dichotomization that distinguished collective abnormality from normality.

Unlike leaders in the area of retardation, Bell may have stopped short of calling for restrictions on the right to marry and procreate. But he believed that practices that promote endogamy should be discouraged, deaf persons should be warned of the risks of genetic transmission (anticipating today's genetic counseling), and all reasonable measures should be taken to prevent spread of this defect, reduce its prevalence, and ameliorate its impact on the society as well as the individual. Despite the assault on Deaf cultural institutions, however, Lane (1992) observes that a "striking feature of this culture is its high rate of endogamous marriage: An estimated nine out of ten members of the American deaf community marry other members of their cultural group" (p. 17). Interestingly, Edward Gallaudet shared with his rival both the understanding of deafness as a defect and the view that marriage to hearing partners would greatly reduce its prevalence. The latter proposition is presumably an empirical question; the former is a question of values. The auditory condition of deafness may be transmitted through heredity, but not in the majority of instances and not directly from parents to child. Hereditary deafness among children in school today is estimated to involve "somewhere between 11 and 30 percent" of the cases (Padden & Humphries, 1988, p. 4) and only about 10% of deaf children have a deaf parent (Reagan, 1985). Hearing parents can give birth to a deaf child, whether heredity is or is not involved, and deaf parents most often give birth to a hearing child. But, from a cultural perspective, "the fact of not hearing is not itself a determinant of group identity" (Padden & Humphries, 1988, p. 4).

The Deaf Culture Perspective

While language and culture are typically transmitted from parent to child, that is not the case with sign language and Deaf culture since few deaf children have deaf parents. Instead, the transmission of sign language has been from peers in residential schools, of culture from the Deaf community formed around the school through tradition and storytelling, theater (as with the renowned National Theatre of the Deaf), personal accounts, and discussion among members of the many clubs, churches, and athletic organizations. The *d* versus *D* distinction, first proposed by Woodward (1972), involves whether reference is made to a culture or to an audiological condition. Noting that communities of deaf people are found in many places in the world, and accordingly use different versions of sign language, Padden and Humphries (1988) define the Deaf culture of North America as

> a particular group of deaf people who share a language—American Sign Language (ASL)—and a culture. The members . . . reside in the United States and Canada, have inherited their sign language, use it as a primary means of communication among themselves, and hold a set of beliefs about themselves and their connection to the larger society. We distinguish them from . . . those who [lose] their hearing because of illness, trauma, or age; although these people share the condition of not hearing, they do not have access to the knowledge, beliefs, and practices that make up the culture of Deaf people. . . . this knowledge . . . is not simply a camaraderie with others who have a similar physical condition, but is, like many other cultures in the traditional sense of the term, historically created and actively transmitted across generations. (p. 2)

They describe a fascinating instance of mythic tradition in the form of a storytelling portrayal of Epée as "inventing" sign language. Of course, no shared language is invented by a single individual, but the dramatization represents Epée's great contribution in recognizing the viability of signing and building a pedagogy on it. American Sign Language represents an amalgamation of the French sign language, due to Laurent Clerc, with the signing of his American pupils. It is therefore, as Gallaudet claimed, a "democratic" system, developed in the same manner as had been the French form that was based on signing used by the Deaf community in Paris. While ASL is more "like" French than English, ASL (and other of the worlds' natural manual languages) is absolutely distinct from spoken languages, as Sacks (1989) noted, not because of "deficiencies," but in its use of a *visuospatial* dimension: "The single most remarkable feature of Sign—that which distinguishes it from all other languages and mental activities—is its unique linguistic use of space" (p. 88).

In addition to its shared language, a source of pride and a powerfully cohesive force conveyed in use of the sign DEAF to communicate the expression "my friends," and the high rate of endogamy, Deaf culture is characterized by a strong organizational network encompassing athletics, theater, and social and political organizations. As Lane (1992) notes, "the grouping of deaf children and adults has always been voluntary, while the segregation of children and adults with disabilities was generally involuntary" (p. 21). Is deafness a disability? Throughout the civil rights and self-advocacy movements, climaxing in the United States in the Americans with Disabilities Act of 1990, Deaf people have aligned with other groups in order to access benefits. But many use the term *disabled* only with a disclaimer, preferring "terms deeply related to their language, their past, and their community. Their enduring concerns have been the preservation of their language, policies for educating deaf children, and maintenance of their social and political organizations" (Padden & Humphries, 1988, p. 44).

Thus, while one set of issues concerns teaching method, the more basic issues are linguistic and cultural. In ASL, the sign ORAL conveys a meaning suggesting hostile ideologies, the "ever-present threat, the malevolent opposition" (Padden & Humphries, 1988, p. 51). It is not speaking that is feared but the proscription of signing, or effectively as harmful, the insistence of the "audist establishment," in Lane's (1992) phrase, on teaching *English* under the pretense of teaching language. In an authoritative dismissal reminiscent of Aristotle, Myklebust (1957) presented the then standard view that sign language is an ideographic system, and thus inferior, for ideographic systems "lack precision, subtlety, and flexibility. It is likely that Man cannot achieve his ultimate potential through an Ideographic language." (pp. 241–242). However, subsequent analysis (e.g., Stokoe, 1980) demonstrated that ASL satisfies "every linguistic criterion of a genuine language, in its lexicon and syntax, its capacity to generate an infinite number of propositions" (Sacks, 1989, p. 78). Moreover, "Sign's . . . unique, additional powers of a spatial and cinematic sort" (p. 90) exceeds the power of speech to express and communicate. But ignorance of the integrity of sign language has historically resulted in efforts to replace or improve on it:

> The mistaken belief that ASL is a set of simple gestures with no internal structure has led to the tragic misconception that the relationship of Deaf people to their sign language is a casual one that can be easily severed and replaced. This misconception more than any other has driven educational policy. Generations of school children have been forbidden to use signs and compelled to speak . . . [or] use artificially modified signs. (Padden & Humphries, 1988, p. 9)

Compromise and Counter Positions

"Artificially modified signs" comprise various adaptations based on English syntax (in the United States), developed for formal instruction, as Epée had done with French. Such systems of "methodological signs" had been abandoned in the 19th century, Lane (1992) writes, for linguistic and pedagogical reasons: "The structural principles of the two languages were so radically different that their bizarre superposition would not be transmitted from one generation to the next" (p. 112). From a cultural perspective, it is unnecessary, even oppressive, to attempt to "improve" one's language by making it like another; from an educational perspective, learning English is not enhanced by "scrambling" grammatical order of signs to parallel English syntax (Lane, 1992): "No deaf child has ever learned such a system as a native language, nor indeed could he, for it violates the principles of the manual-visual channel of communication" (p. 47).

A related debate is between "oral-alone" and "oral-plus" educators, who employ simultaneous speaking and signing (Moores, 1987), as in the Rochester Method, which adds fingerspelling. Some professionals agree with Bell's view that signing, however modified, does not enhance but impedes language learning, since having to attend to two sets of visual stimuli, both the face (for speechreading) and the hands of the speaker, is difficult, especially for a young child. Pointing out that very few are completely unable to hear human speech, they insist that children's ability to use residual hearing can be systematically enhanced, but that hearing potential is neglected when any visual means, signing or lipreading, is accorded primacy (Flexer, 1994). This *unisensory* approach, where it is feasible, is consistent with Bell's belief that neither signing nor lipreading can establish the basic language context hearing children build through hearing and imitating speech.

Many hailed Total Communication (TC), a system credited to Roy Holcomb, a deaf graduate of the Texas School for the Deaf and Gallaudet University, as the perfect compromise. In this approach, communication mode is individually determined and, through simultaneous signing and speaking, the goal is to maximize communication as well as comprehension. With greater acceptance of signing beginning in the late 1960s, and the spread of Total Communication in schools, it might appear that another "revolution" had occurred; by the later 1980s, nearly 80% of students with profound, 75% with severe, and 30% with mild-moderate hearing loss had been exposed to signing (Jordan & Karchmer, 1986). But proponents of both extreme positions are not so sanguine. Those who insist that aural (hearing) abilities can and should be exploited, and that speech is essential for full societal participation, complain that those skills are neglected in TC classrooms. At the other extreme are those Deaf persons who consider TC as simply legitimizing an added, and unnecessary, tool in teaching. The intent within the Deaf community was more far-reaching: *to legitimize Deafness itself* (Reagan, 1985). To those who identify themselves with Deaf culture, this remains essentially a debate among the hearing professionals. They *have* a language.

Other Dimensions

We shall return to the issue of acceptance of difference in Chapter 10, but must comment here that hearing persons have certainly become far more aware of sign language in recent years. It has gained acceptance in a growing number of schools and universities as an acceptable alternative for students to satisfy a language requirement. While in the past use of speech was considered essential for children to be integrated in mainstream classes, sign-language interpreting qualifies under American special education policies as a related service. Adult sign-language users are also provided interpreter services in courts of law, college classrooms, at public meetings, and in many houses of worship. While it had been assumed that deaf persons would have to accommodate to the hearing majority, many hearing persons, like the residents of the Martha's Vineyard communities, learn to use signing to communicate with a relative, friend, or classmate who is deaf. Further, signing has been found to be an effective tool in working with children with various disabilities involving language, such as autism. Additionally, technological innovations have made it possible for deaf persons to communicate over vast distances, access information and entertainment previously available only to hearing persons, and translate sound into print. Increasingly, albeit paternalistically, it *is* "all right to be deaf" in a society with a majority of hearing persons, to use a language other than that of the majority.

At the same time, educators have been made increasingly aware that impaired hearing, considered a low-incidence disability in children, is actually far more pervasive, and handicapping, than had been supposed. Otitis media, or middle-ear infection, increasingly common among young children in consequence of early, out-of-home child care, impedes a child's hearing during the time of infections, which may be chronic or intermittent, and often results in long-term problems, ranging from significantly reduced hearing acuity to distortions in perception associated with learning disabilities (Naremore, 1979). Thus, as children move into and through classroom environments that become increasingly *auditory*, when foundations and a "set" for learning are supposed to be established, a great many are not hearing. Young children, asked by the teacher, "Did you hear?" may affirm that they did—and indeed they may have "heard," but inaccurately or only in part; they do not know what they do *not* hear (Flexer, 1994). This suggests a number of interventions, most basically attention to treatment of ear infections and regular, thorough evaluation of hearing status, as well as modifying educational environments to enhance hearing efficiency, as through sound field amplification.

For children who use hearing, it is certainly important to optimize its use. But it is understandable that such intrusive procedures as cochlear implants to "correct" a child's deafness are viewed with alarm, certainly suspicion, within the Deaf community. As Lane (1992) notes, the actual benefits—and risks—have not yet been well established, and the decision for a deaf child to undergo the procedure is made *for* the child by hearing parents and professionals. Again, who speaks for the child? History reveals determined and persistent efforts by hearing persons—the "audist establishment"—through pedagogy, social controls, and surgery, to "cure" a difference that needs to be better understood from the perspective of those affected.

CHAPTER 5

Blindness: Charity to Independence

If over the centuries the most invidious phrase used with reference to deafness is "deaf and dumb," its counterpart for blindness must surely be "blind beggar." While the former was based on ignorance—of the nature of deafness, the relationship of hearing and speech, the distinction between speech and language, and the linguistic integrity of signed communication—the latter had some basis in reality. Blindness and poverty have been linked throughout history, and in the absence of other options, mendicancy was often an adaptive response. Yet since antiquity blindness has evoked responses other than pity. Fear, awe, even reverence, were founded on superstition, of course. But as we have seen, accomplished blind persons suggested yet other images, images of competence, independence, even sometimes special talent, and blind persons of unusual talent and erudition have had major roles in the development of services for blind children and adults.

EXPERIENCES OF CHILDREN

Just as Jean Massieu's experiences were not representative of what life was like for most deaf persons, we cannot think François Lesueur's life prototypic with respect to blindness. That the gifts of both, realized as teachers, were nurtured was due to some degree to accidents of fate. What would Lesueur's life have been like if he and Haüy had not found each other? Might he have enabled some other seeing benefactor to discover the possibilities in embossed systems? But in one respect, Lesueur was indeed representative of many blind European youth of his day: His family being very poor, he began early to contribute to the support of his brothers and sisters by begging on the streets.

While it has been oddly difficult to obtain accurate demographic data concerning prevalence, severe visual impairment in American children reportedly occurs twice as frequently in families with income below the poverty level (Barker & Barmatz, 1975). An explanation for this contemporary phenomenon would certainly have been applicable in the past: Visual impairment often is a concomitant of biological risk factors such as prematurity, often reflecting inequity in access to ameliorative and preventive measures. If an earlier estimate that "not more than 25 per cent of blindness is inevitable" (Berens, 1938, p. 17) is even nearly valid today, it is, compared with other disabilities, highly preventable. Reports of children in almshouses with inflammation of the conjunctiva, the result of opthalmia neonatorium, inspired intervention and, beginning in 1908, a "crusade" to prevent the condition by putting silver nitrate in the eyes of newborns (Scholl, Mulholland, & Lonergan, 1986). But while this coincided with more frequent delivery in hospitals, or at least medically attended delivery, a poor mother was unlikely to have access to either.

A related American phenomenon especially apparent in the case of blindness involves race and ethnicity. In 1913, the Society of American Indians warned that an estimated 1,700 of the 5,000 Native American children in boarding schools who were infected with trachoma were likely to become totally blind (Thomas, Miller, White, Nabokov, & Deloria, 1993, p. 372). Prevalence was also high among African-American children, for whom special schools evolved on a segregated basis, the first "for the colored blind" established in 1869 in North Carolina (Wallin, 1924). By 1931, there were 5 such schools in the United States and 10 separate sections for African-American pupils in other residential schools. While this historical fact certainly speaks to the issue of educational segregation based on race, does it also suggest that blindness was more prevalent in African-American children than other disabilities? Is visual impairment in the United States still more prevalent among minorities, particularly African Americans? That apparently is the case, although again data are unreliable (Kahn & Moorhead, 1973). Public images of blindness may be those suggested by Ray Charles and Stevie Wonder, while we know that musical talent is neither invariably found in persons who are blind nor in persons of color.

A child's visual impairment is less likely today to result from infectious disease and more likely, in the case of retinal damage, to result from risk factors associated with preterm delivery and low birthweight, which are related to maternal health and prenatal care, still differentially available in American society. Appallingly often, trauma resulting from accident or being shaken in infancy causes visual as well as other neurological impairment. In such instances as color discrimination problems, more prevalent in males and usually transmitted as a recessive trait from the mother, heredity is involved. Although cases had been reported as early as 1684, the first description of color blindness was published in 1794 by a Quaker chemist named Dalton (hence "Daltonism"), based on his own impairment, also experienced by Benjamin Franklin. But that condition seldom involves impaired acuity. Descriptions of Haüy's school or those that followed provide little information concerning type or severity of impairment, but it is probable that most pupils were, in today's terms, educationally blind, needing to use alternative sensory modes to read or write.

SCHOOLS IN EUROPE

Diderot's advice to those who sought to understand the nature of human reason to consider blindness and, in order to do this, to learn from persons without sight was based in large measure on his own acquaintance with two eminent blind persons, Maria Theresia von Paradis and Nicholas Saunderson (1682–1739), a Cambridge mathematician (Roberts, 1986). As we saw, Haüy heeded this counsel, also having the good fortune to benefit from acquaintance with von Paradis. Another who was inspired by this brilliant pianist and teacher of music was Johann Wilhelm Klein, who himself was blind. Probably with little initial knowledge of the specifics of Haüy's work, Klein began a school for blind pupils in Vienna in 1804. As had Haüy, he started with a single pupil, a youth named Jacob Braun, but unlike Haüy he apparently avoided dependence on appeals to philanthropy. He was instead convinced that, if all blind children were to benefit from education, as he believed they should, their instruction should be provided through the general system of schooling (Lowenfeld, 1975, p. 81). In any case, his "sound pedagogy" and competent management gained him royal endorsement and government support, enabling him to lead the school for a half-century (Farrell, 1956, p. 27).

His students were apparently particularly responsive and productive in the vocational aspects of the program, but music also had an important place. Moreover, with Klein's introduction of the system of embossed printing devised by Haüy, literacy was accorded priority status and the curriculum had a degree of balance and comprehensiveness beyond what Haüy had been able to achieve due to the political turmoil that prevailed during his tenure. This stability also permitted opportunity for growth and innovation. Many educators came to the school for training, and with publication of his *Teacher's Manual for the Education of the Blind* in 1819 Klein's influence spread, inspiring among others the first Dutch "institute" for the blind, a nondenominational facility established in 1808 (Taylor & Taylor, 1960). Among those who trained under him was Franz Muller, who then, with the advocacy of Carl Egan, Prince of Furstenberg, opened a school in Baden that he directed from 1826 to 1852. Muller was assisted in this enterprise by a young German educator named Julius Friedlander, who made good use of this experience; as we shall see, when determined to establish his own school, he emigrated to America (Freund, 1959).

St. Basil reportedly established the first hospice for blind persons in Caesarea in the fourth century and, as we noted in Chapter 2, St. Lymnaeus attempted to provide education, as well as asylum, in one he founded in Syria in the fifth century. England's long involvement in this area also began with a hospice, called Elsing Spittle, opened by a merchant in 1329. This facility provided asylum care for 100 blind men for some two centuries until, as Pritchard (1963) recounts in his history of services for blind persons in Britain, it was "confiscated by the Reformation" (p. 2), though it is not clear for what purpose. The English Renaissance inspired both renewed awareness of blindness and a more positive perspective than that associated with asylum care. As in other nations, the presence of blind individuals of talent throughout the British Isles was surely a factor. The blind minstrel was, of course, a mythic figure, and Homer is not the only one to figure in the world's literary history; the famous 15th-century poem *The Wallace*, recounting that Scots hero's military feats, was composed by one Henry the Minstrel, known as "Blind Harry." Two centuries later, John Milton, classically educated poet, political essayist, and historian, experienced progressive loss of his sight when at the height of his powers, becoming totally blind in his early forties. In lines that begin "When I consider how my light is spent,/E're half my days, in this dark world and wide," Milton reflected on his own loss of vision philosophically. Some philosophers were reflecting on the phenomenon of blindness as a key to the understanding of human reason.

Berkeley and Locke considered the role of the senses in learning and thought, while also suggesting their possible interplay and mutual compensatory potential. Such notions were posed as philosophical issues, however, not arguments for reform, and with respect to education of blind persons had more influence in prerevolutionary France than in Britain. Reform movements in Britain in the late 18th and early 19th century, like those initiated by Shaftesbury in prisons, mines, and asylums, resulted rather from a general humanitarian impulse propelled by such religious movements as Methodism and Evangelicism. These influences also gave momentum to efforts in Britain to establish educational provisions for persons with disabilities, including blindness (Pritchard, 1963).

In the early work in Britain, blind individuals themselves, not charitable agencies, played key roles in establishing schools; however, most pupils in these schools were adults. Nevertheless, despite this important element of self-advocacy, a charity theme emerged fairly early. Edward Rushton, a blind poet, and John Christie, a musician who was also blind, were influential in the development of a school in Liverpool. But this school of "music or the mechanical arts," in which Christie himself taught, could not have become a reality without major fund-raising efforts, led by Henry Donnet, a seeing person. Though first called the School of Instruction for the Indigent Blind, it was soon renamed the Asylum for the Indigent Blind. Both titles, Pritchard (1963) avers, were misnomers, the first since a full educational program was not provided, the second since pupils were in fact nonresidents. But it was in any case a charitable enterprise. The school's first pupils ranged in age from 9 to 68, but age ranges were soon stipulated to be 14 to 45 for men and 12 to 45 for women. A small number of younger pupils, between 8 and 16 years old, could also be admitted for a four-year program in music if they demonstrated "promising genius." This sole educational facet of the school program was quite limited in scope due to concerns of pupil-teacher ratio, as well as the stipulation concerning demonstrated talent. Otherwise, the focus of the school was providing training, for adolescents and adults, in a circumscribed number of trades.

Strong sentiment was beginning to be expressed in some quarters that sole emphasis on occupational training, whether in trades or in music, was far from adequate. Literacy and, with literacy, education in the sense that seeing persons were educated had not been addressed in Britain as it had by Klein. In 1838, the London Society for Teaching the Blind to Read was established, with the aim of extending education beyond vocational training. This marked a turning point, not only in Britain but in other nations, including America. The influence of British educators and advocates has subsequently been important in four areas of great significance in the education of blind persons worldwide: curriculum, alternative print systems, day classes, and higher education. While the last is outside the scope of this book, the Worcester College for the Blind—"The College for the Blind Sons of Gentleman," founded in 1866—bears mention as the world's first, for its revealing title, and for invention of the Taylor Arithmetic Frame, a numeracy counterpart of embossed print, by the Reverend William Taylor, co-founder (Thomas, 1920, p. 2).

The first of those areas, the instructional program, had actually been addressed in Britain earlier, and by another blind person. Thomas Blacklock had overcome the dual handicaps of his family's poverty and his own blindness since infancy to become a minister, poet, and scholar. His translation of Haüy's *Essai sur l'education des aveu'gles* did not appear until after his death, however. Nor would he live to see the opening, in 1791, of the school at Edinburgh he had labored to establish, the first public institution in the British Isles for blind and deaf children (Lowenfeld, 1975). The practice of combining school programs, adopted as a temporary, post-Revolutionary expedient in Paris and later instituted in the United States in Virginia, was again attempted with the Institution for the Blind and Deaf and Dumb, in Bath. Unlike all other British schools, this facility enrolled only children, but mutual resentments seem to have developed between the two groups and it closed in 1896 after "54 turbulent years" (Pritchard, 1963).

Pupils who were both deaf and blind may have particularly benefited from such arrangements, but that is a matter of conjecture; surprisingly, one finds virtually no early references to this dual impairment, which, though rare, poses extraordinary challenge to the individual and the teacher—thus the deserved fame of Howe's achievement with Laura Bridgman referred to in Chapter 3. Howe is considered the first educator to have taught a deaf-blind pupil successfully, though he seems to have drawn on an account by Sicard. We have also met Anne Sullivan, whose famous—and only—pupil, Helen Keller, inspired, and advocated for, others who were both deaf and blind, collectively and individually, as with a youngster named Tommy Stringer (Lash, 1980). Perkins continued to be the world's acknowledged center of excellence in the area of deaf-blindness, but as this dual impairment was seen increasingly in newborns, first with the rubella epidemic of the 1960s, more recently with survival of infants with very low birthweight and concommitant multiple-risk factors, the importance of early intervention was recognized. By the 1980s, federal funding initiatives in the United States made deaf-blindness a priority, stimulating research and demonstration projects to develop models for work with infants and young children.

Other schools that combined deaf and blind pupils included a private facility in Stockholm, Sweden, which continued the arrangement from its founding in 1808 until the two programs were separated in 1879. In Belgium, five schools for deaf and blind students were established between 1834 and 1840, all under church auspices (Taylor & Taylor, 1960). Church influence continued in North America as in Europe in the education of both deaf and blind persons. The young deaf-blind American in Joanne Greenberg's (1988) novel *Of Such Small Differences* "knew a great deal about religion. . . . Many of his deaf and deaf-blind group were very religious; they had been taught in religious schools" (p. 61).

SCHOOLS IN THE UNITED STATES

As we saw in Chapter 3, American social reform movements of the early 19th century, like those in England, were driven by religious reawakening. But as in France, the Revolution added a new dimension, an assertion of the rights of the individual. Moreover, with the need of the new nation to establish a common identity for its citizenry and prepare its diverse people for responsible citizenship in a democracy, what philanthropy began would increasingly be defined as public responsibility.

American reformers of the early 19th century typically worked on many fronts, no one more than the individual most closely identified with establishing education for blind persons in America. Samuel Gridley Howe entered the fray in the field of deaf education, pioneered instruction for children with retardation, and advocated Dorothea Dix's reforms for persons with mental illness. He spoke out on the subjects of juvenile delinquency, prison reform, and a host of other causes, including the one in which the nation was farthest from its avowed commitment to human rights: the enslavement of African Americans. Howe was among the most committed of New England's abolitionists. He vigorously supported the causes led by Dorothea Dix, Horace Mann, and Charles Sumner, his "alter ego," and they in turn endorsed and abetted his campaign to educate blind persons to become productive citizens. Like Epée and Sicard in France and Seguin, in Paris then in America, Howe became by virtue of actual accomplishment combined with force of personality a towering figure in the history of education of persons with disabilities, especially blindness. Thus, this chapter includes a section devoted to Samuel Gridley Howe, his causes, colleagues, contributions, and controversies. But as in Europe, education for blind children and youth in America was by no means the project, or the creation, of a single individual.

"The Great Triumvirate"

Incorporated in 1829, the New England Asylum for the Blind, later named the Perkins Institution and Massachusetts Asylum for the Blind, opened in 1832. Its opening was in fact preceded by several months by the New York Institution for the Blind, incorporated in 1831. The Pennsylvania Institution for the Instruction of the Blind, later called Overbrook, followed in 1833, in Philadelphia. In each case a small number of civic-minded citizens laid the foundation. While common forces led to the creation of all three, in Massachusetts a census played an especially critical role. In New York, the discovery of blind children in almshouses was the prime impetus. In Pennsylvania, it was the more general tradition of Quaker humanitarianism. The directors of all three, two of whom were physicians, the third an educator, looked to Europe for models.

While "defectives" were conglomerated in census records throughout the century, the census of 1830 did differentiate blind persons. Data for Massachusetts, sought by Dr. John D. Fisher, whose interests had taken him to Paris, revealed an estimated 400 blind persons, the number in New England about 1,500, probably including all those in almshouses (Best, 1919). On February 19, 1829, he convened a gathering of other reform-minded men at Boston's Exchange Coffee House to begin discussions that culminated in a successful appeal to the legislature. Beyond what Fisher had learned from his travels, the only direct experience represented in this group was that of William Hickling Prescott, the eminent historian, whose vision was impaired. Otherwise, though committed to the cause, their collective knowledge of this specialized field was minimal. As the reality of the venture became imminent, they needed to find someone to provide the necessary leadership.

The anecdote describing how this was resolved has an apocryphal ring, but is reported (variably) in various sources. Howe's daughter (Richards, 1935), among other sources (e.g, Meltzer, 1964; Schwartz, 1956), has it thus: One day in 1831, some members of the group were deeply engaged in discussing who that leader might be as they walked together down Boylston Street. Observing a "dashing young man" approaching them, Fisher exclaimed, "Here is Howe, the very man we have been looking for all this time!" The issue of site was resolved through Colonel Thomas H. Perkin's donation of property on Pearl Street. The facility that Howe would make world-famous moved in 1839 to more spacious surroundings in South Boston, later to Watertown.

Dr. John D. Russ had had reports since 1827 of blind children, most resulting from opthalmia, in the New York City almshouse, a not uncommon situation to which Dorothea Dix had brought attention elsewhere. He knew that with proper and timely intervention the condition could be corrected, but otherwise progressive loss of vision would result. For Anne Sullivan, surgeries finally provided in the almshouse at Tewksbury slowed the course of deterioration but were too late to prevent it. Russ was determined that appropriate intervention be provided for such children of poverty who, while under public care, were actually placed at even greater risk rather than cared for and nurtured. Under his superintendency, the New York school opened on March 15, 1832, its student body initially comprising three youths from the almshouse, soon joined by three more (Best, 1919). Before long its many students ranged in age from 12 to 25. The school's rapid growth created an almost immediate need for more space, a need met in 1837 through James Boorman's gift of a house and land (Farrell, 1956).

In Pennsylvania, the Society of Friends had expressed interest in schooling for blind children at least since 1824, when Roberts Vaux presented ideas along these lines to Joshua Francis Fisher, who made it a point to visit several schools for the blind in the course of an 1830–1832 European tour. His return to Philadelphia fortuitously coincided with the arrival of Julius Friedlander, who, inspired by his experiences with Muller and visits to the schools in Baden, Paris, and London, eagerly accepted the directorship. Under Friedlander's leadership, the new school addressed not only local and state needs but regional ones, through formal agreements with neighboring Delaware (1835), New Jersey (1836), and Maryland (1837) to serve blind children in those states. The school remained in Philadelphia until its relocation in 1899 in Overbrook, for which it was renamed. Friedlander's chronic ill health led to his death from pneumonia at age 35, after a tenure of only six years, but his influence was profound. His conversion from Judaism to Christianity during his student years was apparently motivated by genuine religious feeling, for he was considered a young man of deep conviction, whose sincerity, though unamplified by Howe's charisma, inspired confidence and commanded an equal measure of respect (Freund, 1959).

Like Howe, Friedlander accorded highest priority to promoting independence, through providing good general education complemented by specific preparation for productive work in the community. He nevertheless believed that many pupils, especially those without family or whose families were impoverished, would require continued support and oversight maintaining accordingly that it was essential to set up an affiliated and adjacent facility, where graduates needing such assistance could carry on trades (Freund, 1959). Despite superficial resemblance to later sheltered workshops or today's supported employment models, the need he perceived was not based on the clients' lack of mastery of work skills; it was rather a supported living notion, an extension of the family metaphor. After Friedlander's untimely death, the school continued to move forward in the course he had set, under the apparently very able leadership of Mr. A. W. Penniman, who, having been trained at Perkins, had in 1837 gone to Ohio to instruct the five pupils enrolled in the nation's first state-supported school for the blind (Ohio Department of Education, 1985).

The three schools' leaders worked together, sharing ideas and innovations—notably in the area of printing—and were apparently of a common mind with respect to the goals of literacy, independence, rights, and responsibilities of those they educated. They were also the major, indeed long the only, domestic sources of trained teachers for the many schools that would soon be established. But it was the leader of the enterprise in Massachusetts who would most energetically and effectively work to disseminate that philosophy and to convince legislators in other states of the need for, and promise of, schools for blind students.

State Schools: Establishing Public Responsibility

Before opening, in a rented cottage, the first publicly supported school for blind students in the United States, Ohio already had had some legislative history in this area. In 1811 and again in 1818 the legislature had authorized allowances for "relief," in the first instance to a father of five congenitally blind children, in the second to a father of nine, six of whom were blind (Ohio Department of Education, 1985). This recognition of unusual family burden associated with blindness, and linking blindness with indigence, continued in America as in Britain. Ohio, and other states, initially provided reimbursement for indigent pupils in the form of "relief." Extension of public support to all, irrespective of family resources, paralleled the emergence of the common school and reflected Mann's philosophy.

The director of the Massachusetts Institution, within the first years of its operation, was already exhorting legislatures of other states, complementing his own estimable eloquence with evidence of what education could accomplish in the form of star pupils. This was clever, for proposals to set up schools for the blind were often ridiculed as "wild" and "utopian" (Anagnos, 1882), and these exhibitions demonstrated their legitimacy. Moreover, despite his vaunted aversion to the notion of asylum and insistence that blind persons become fully contributing citizens, he was pragmatic; the appeal in America as in Britain, as Pritchard (1963) observed, was to the heart: "At the prospect of bringing light to the darkened minds of the blind, there were few who could not be moved" (p. 269). Just as this approach was effective in eliciting charitable contributions—and is still exploited today—it influenced legislators, ever mindful of their constituents' vulnerability to emotional appeals. The practice of "exhibition" of the accomplishments of blind students that Haüy instituted would later be severely criticized by a blind psychologist, himself a product of the system (Cutsforth, 1933), as preparing them for mendicancy, rather than independence. At this juncture, whatever the cost in principle, Howe's approach got results.

In being entirely state-supported, the Ohio Institution for the Instruction of the Blind departed significantly from the pattern of the eastern schools, and those that followed Ohio's lead either began on this basis or soon shifted to it. Two years after it opened, the facility moved from its original makeshift quarters into a newly constructed building. As would happen in other states, the site was located in the state's capital, where it has remained through a succession of replacement and expansion facilities, to the present day. Virginia's institution, established in 1839, provided for both deaf and blind pupils, as noted previously. Kentucky's (1842), like most that followed, began as a private operation, shifting to state funding after the first year. It was followed by schools in neighboring Tennessee (1843), in Indiana (1847), and in Illinois (1848). Just past mid-century, only two and a half decades after the founding of the first three eastern schools, 19 states had schools for the blind. Within another quarter-century, 10 more states established schools. As with deafness, the residential school model was well established in North America.

Howe had indeed been extraordinarily effective in initiating a national movement, as state after state enacted policy to provide blind children places in which they could be taught. The structure that emerged, however, was in fundamental respects incongruous with the philosophy Howe came increasingly to espouse, for institutions by their very nature bring together persons with a "common difference." Paradoxically, in view of his key role in bringing about establishment of centralized institutions, Howe would become the most vocal advocate of dispersion and assimilation of the 19th century.

THE CHEVALIER AND HIS "BROTHERS-IN-ARMS"

At the time Fisher and his colleagues determined him to be just the man to bring their vision to fruition, Samuel Gridley Howe was 30 and at loose ends. Having compiled an undistinguished record at Brown, he had pursued medical training at Harvard, taking his medical degree in 1824. But instead of opening a practice, Howe, like a number of his countrymen caught up in the fervor of the Greek Revolution, sailed for Greece, where the next six years saw him immersed totally in the cause, contributing his medical expertise and even actively participating in combat against the Turks. Intermittently, he returned to America to campaign for financial support for the revolution and, on its successful conclusion, contributed his managerial talents to efforts to establish social order. Among the revolutionaries expressing their gratitude with an honorific—the *Chevalier*—was Michael Anagnostopoulos (Anagnos), his future son-in-law and successor (Schwartz, 1956).

With no more revolution to serve but still restless, he set forth on a year's tour of Europe, which brought him to France at the height of the July Revolution, where he met Lafayette. The Marquis counseled him to find a way to channel his exuberant energy and manifest talents in the service of his own country. This he was determined to do, but until the chance encounter with Fisher and his group he had fallen into a depression, uncertain as to his future. "He brooded over his lost opportunities," his biographer, Harold Schwartz (1956) observed, "and looking about him, he realized he was falling behind. His schoolboy friends were men of affairs. . . . He alone was rootless" (p. 42). Accepting this new challenge with characteristic enthusiasm, Howe at once set off again for Europe, this time to visit schools for blind pupils, especially those in Paris, Berlin, and Edinburgh, and several in England. But his quest was not single-minded. In the course of his travels, he again became caught up in a revolutionary movement, this time agitating for aid for Polish insurgents, and managed to land in a Prussian prison, where he languished for five weeks. We do not know how Dr. Fisher and his colleagues received this news.

This diversion notwithstanding, Howe's visits proved instructive with respect to the expertise he sought. Mainly they provided the basis for convictions that would guide his whole approach, in educating blind children as in the many other reform efforts he would pursue. He did not like all that he saw. Particularly repellent, Anagnos (1882) reflected, was a pervasive attitude of charity and an "asylum touch," especially in British institutions, which seemed more "refuges" than schools, and not run by "scientific men." In these perceptions, as we have seen, he was largely correct. One might well expect such a reaction in one of Howe's temperament, but it also reflected a more general disposition evident in American reform efforts. As Farrell (1956) observed, "While an ardent spirit of benevolence abounded in America of the 1830s, there was a definite practicality about the processes and their application" (p. 158). The public-spirited civic leaders who had led the campaign for a school for the blind were imbued with that blend of benevolence and practicality. Samuel Gridley Howe embodied it.

He had become convinced that instruction of blind students should be guided by three basic principles. First, both the pupils' individual abilities and likely opportunities to put their training into use in their own communities should be considered. Second, the curriculum should be well-rounded and, except for greater emphasis on handicrafts and music, be as much as possible like that provided in the regular schools. Most important, the main objective must be to prepare the pupils to become contributing members of their communities, fully integrated within the social and economic life (Farrell, 1956, p. 45). That conviction, which would be reflected in his general approach as an educator and reformer, make understandable his instinctive opposition to the asylum concept. It was a principle born of personal belief rather than experience or evidence. One senses that firsthand acquaintance with blind persons would not have been necessary for Howe to reject the view of them as pitiable unfortunates and burdens. He seems never to have doubted that they were worthy of respect, capable of independence, and able to take their place as productive citizens. If by today's standards such notions would not be exceptional, by those of his own day they were revolutionary.

The new institution where he first translated these beliefs into practice "quickly surpassed all schools in existence to become the foremost educational agency of its type in the world, and he the foremost educator" (Schwartz, 1956, p. 49). He was clearly the right person, in the right role, at the right time, and not incidentally in the right place. As Lash (1980) observed, "Boston in the nineteenth century was America's Olympus . . . here beat the nation's philanthropic heart" (p. 15). What Paris had been in the late 18th century, Boston was becoming in the 19th. A core facet of the identity of each was its role as a center for humanitarian reform and innovation in the education of persons who had been throughout history at worst despised and oppressed, at best pitied, but most certainly excluded.

And why Howe? This impetuous, adventurous individual who had been given the honorary title "Chevalier" (his friends called him "Chev!" [Donald,

1960]) was described as "a truly Byronic figure" and "the Lafayette of Boston" (Schwartz, 1956). His father had been a prosperous rope manufacturer but had incurred severe losses during the War of 1812. Still, the Howes had firm New England roots and were well known and respected, even respectable, though in some respects nonconformist: Jeffersonian-Republicans in Federalist Boston, Unitarian in a city in which their class tended to be Congregationalist. Throughout his adult life, the pattern of Howe's behavior would continue as it had in Greece, with total, consuming involvement in a succession of causes—agitating, exhorting, organizing, and, in the classroom of the new school as in European revolutions, involving himself directly in "front-line" action. Laura Richards (1935) subtitled her biography of her father *Servant of Humanity*, and in a memorial poem written at Howe's death, in 1876, Oliver Wendell Holmes asked, "But what has heaven for thee to do/In realms of perfect bliss?"

He was also a formidable adversary, characterized by Laurent Clerc (in Lane, 1984a) as "committed to the struggle and well-nigh indifferent to the cause."

> He is combative by nature, his spirit rises in opposition, and he has found in reform a way of remaining contentious all his life. He is proud, cantankerous, quick to take offense. His voluminous publications on all manner of reforms are paternalistic and condescending, and in the face of opposition, vituperative and contemptuous. (p. 286)

One would not be eager to be on opposite sides of a debate with this man. Concerning his championing of oral instruction of deaf students, Clerc alleges that Howe was basically naive, but so given to enthusiasms and so convinced of the truth and generality of his core belief in dispersion that he would not hesitate to carry that banner onto the battlefield of deaf education or any other. To his credit, Howe apparently questioned Mann's glowing accounts of the successes of German oralism. In communicating what Howe surely wanted to hear Mann may have been overzealous, but correspondence of the day, like Howe's own impassioned pleas to lawmakers and his likening of the Abendberg to the "holy mount," tended toward the extravagant. Still, he challenged Mann's unqualified assertion that "mutism" simply did not exist among the German deaf, reminding his ally that his lack of proficiency in German could make it difficult to judge a pupil's speech proficiency. Notwithstanding these misgivings, Howe skillfully orchestrated and forcefully advocated an "incursion," Clerc charges, based on emotional appeal and empty rhetoric (Lane, 1984a). So successful was he that, with Hubbard, he had instigated a tradition in deaf education to which Boston would remain faithful, the base from which Bell launched his assault on the instructional use of signing and on the residential school model itself.

A person of uncertain piety, who though rumored a free thinker often invoked divine will, Howe referred to his work as "practical religion" (Richards, 1909, p. 218). Of the benevolent action performed in "houses of religious works" like Perkins, which he averred were as necessary as houses of religious worship, he wrote, "The disposition to act thus is innate . . . and as it is more or less developed, so are we more or less men" (p. 458). Or women? He was not at all supportive of the notoriety of his famous wife, the former Julia Ward, who, nearly 20 years his junior, had been known as one of the "three graces of Bond Street" (Clifford, 1979). In their tenuous marital relationship, a more general attitude toward the role of women is revealed. Though frequently absent, he insisted on controlling all details at home as he did at work, including such domestic matters as hiring and firing of servants, decisions to move, and handling the children's education. His daughters revered him, but the marriage was clearly strained; Howe adamantly (though unsuccessfully) opposed his wife's literary aspirations and speaking engagements, indeed any public role.

While believing woman's place to be in the home, he allowed an exception in the case of Dorothea Dix, for he admired her work and lent it full support. Since in Massachusetts a woman could not address the legislature, it was Howe who presented her memorials. (She could speak for herself in Pennsylvania [M. Rosen, 1993 personal communication].) And she, having often been shocked to find deaf and blind persons confined with "the idiotic," insane, or others of society's castoffs, enthusiastically supported his crusades.

The third famous woman in his life was Laura Dewey Bridgman (1829–1899). Left blind, deaf, and without the sense of smell as a result of scarlet fever at age 2, Laura first came to Howe's attention through an article written by a physician on Dartmouth's medical faculty. She entered Perkins in 1837. This girl, who retained only the tactile sense as a potential conduit for information from the outside world, had roused considerable medical interest. Determined that she could be taught once a communication bridge was built, Howe located a report of Sicard's attempts with a deaf-blind child and accordingly set out to establish communication through touch. Beginning with a spoon and a key, he led her to the realization, later dramatized so vividly in the water pump episode with the young Helen Keller, that *things have names*. From this base he evolved an educational program, relying initially on raised letters in the manner introduced by Haüy. Then, using labels in raised print, he engaged Laura in successively increasing the matching of labels to objects until the insight formed that she, too, could communicate her own thoughts. He next introduced a slate on which Laura could move type to form words. For conversational purposes, he shifted to finger spelling with the manual alphabet (Ross, 1951).

Howe's success with Laura Bridgman was an international sensation, beyond the fairly circumscribed world of education of persons with disabilities. Among the famous and influential who came to see this wonder of enlightened, creative tutelage, in the course of visiting Boston's institutions with Charles Sumner and Mayor Jonathan Chapman, was Charles Dickens. Dickens's 1842 account of his meeting with Miss Bridgman, later included in *American Notes and Pictures from Italy* (1907), was read by millions—including, as it happened, the mother of a young deaf and blind girl named Helen Keller. The young woman sent in response to the Kellers' request for a teacher had, as a pupil at Perkins, lived in the same house with Laura and had learned the manual alphabet in order to converse with her (Ross, 1951). It may in fact have been her interest in Laura Bridgman, nearly as much as their shared advocacy, that brought Dorothea Dix and S. G. Howe together. After their first meeting, Miss Dix and Miss Bridgman carried on a correspondence for several years, as a letter in a Dix biography (Wilson, 1975) suggests:

> My dear Miss Dix. How is your health now. I wish you a happy morning. It is a great while since I saw you. Miss Wright is my excellent teacher for almost nine years. . . . I should like to have you come to see me very much this summer, and receive a long letter from you. I rejoice that you are so willing to make sacrifices to do good to the poor. (p. 117)

Helen Keller's extraordinary achievements, actually those of her teacher, Anne Sullivan, would occasion resentment in Howe's widow and even in her own mentor, Michael Anagnos, in seeming to diminish Laura's (or rather Howe's) achievement (Lash, 1980). In his critique of institutional practices, written a half-century after Laura's death, Cutsforth (1933) commented that the standards had changed: "Howe received international recognition for educating Laura Bridgman to the upper level of feeble-mindedness. The twentieth century deaf-blind win fame only when they become bachelors of arts or deliver lectures" (p. 203). What Laura might have become we shall never know. A biography by Mary Swift Lamson (1881), Laura's teacher for three years from her second at Perkins, at 13, and thereafter a close friend, complemented recollections with Howe's log notes. One by two of Howe's daughters (Howe & Hall, 1903), titled *Laura Bridgman—Dr. Howe's Famous Pupil and What He Taught Her*, is hagiographical with respect to their father, who they said had long intended to write a full account of his work with Laura, an intent expressed in a letter shortly before his death. Laura herself, helped by a succession of teachers, kept a journal containing mainly poems and observations on religious themes.

Less is known of Oliver Caswell (1829–1889), left deaf and blind from scarlet fever at age 3. Though the same age, he was admitted to Perkins four years after Laura and they were taught together, Howe recalling him as "jollier" than Laura, though less bright and inquisitive (Schwartz, 1956). Laura, who outlived him by a decade, remained the rest of her life at Perkins where Anne Sullivan, much younger and of very different temperament, came to know well this "frail, wispy woman . . . in her fifties. Although able to communicate with the outside world, she had never learned to cope with it. . . . She moved from cottage to cottage, and Annie learned the manual alphabet in order to spell into her hand the gossip of the girls" (Lash, 1980, p. 38). Anne Sullivan, in a sense, herself had a deaf-blind teacher.

HELEN AND TEACHER

Analysis of the relationship, and joint accomplishment, of Anne Sullivan Macy and Helen Keller is clearly beyond the scope of this chapter. Both have been subjects of many biographies, and Keller herself left a rich legacy of written work about herself and her teacher (Keller, 1955, 1903/1976). At 18 months of age, Helen had experienced "brain fever" due to some still undetermined illness, possibly scarlet fever, that left her without sight or hearing. Her early development was probably important in her subsequent social-emotional and intellectual development, but as is well known her young teacher confronted a daunting challenge in this 6-year-old, not lessened by the family's disinclination to set limits.

Interestingly, Captain Keller's contact with Anagnos, who had succeeded his father-in-law, was mediated by Alexander Graham Bell, by then in Washington. Bell, who thereafter maintained both a friendship with and a professional interest in Helen and Anne, responded with alacrity to Captain Keller's request for counsel, inviting him to be his dinner guest and to bring the child. Also interestingly, in view of their rivalry, Edward Gallaudet was invited to "look in in the course of the evening," a gesture that, with the referral to Anagnos for a teacher, would seem to reveal much about Bell's attitude as a scientist and stature as a person. He could, after all, have regarded Helen as a "find" of his own, proprietarily claiming her for his own cause; instead, Helen Keller's worldwide advocacy would be aligned with the American Foundation for the Blind. Bell would also be quick to recognize that the genius of her teacher extended across, and beyond, exceptionality (Lash, 1980).

By his own account, Anagnos did not hesitate to recommend the just-graduated Anne Sullivan. Although she had been, to put it mildly, a challenging and even rebellious student, her gifts were apparent and her valedictory address had moved him. They would eventually come into conflict, but early on he was her staunch supporter, enthusiastic advocate, willing resource, and eager publicist. Her "bad eyes" were a concern—by age 5 she had trachoma—but her family's impoverished circumstances and ignorance concerning the cause left it untreated. Not long after her mother's death, when her embittered father was unable to provide financial support for her care by relatives, she and her younger brother, whose untreated tubercular hip would result in his death, were taken to the state poorhouse at Tewksbury. A kindly priest's intervention had enabled her to have surgery and obtain live-in work, but she was returned to Tewksbury when the surgeries failed; the family did not want her back, and her benefactor had been reassigned in the interim. As yet unschooled, and pleading for the opportunity, she learned of an impending investigation of conditions at the poorhouse by the State Board of Charities. Her importuning of Frank B. Sanborn, its chairman, succeeded and, suffering what she always considered the shaming experience of interviews with charity workers, she entered Perkins on October 7, 1880, at 14; born three months earlier, the child who would be her pupil and lifelong companion was then a healthy infant (Lash, 1980).

At 20, a new and honored graduate, Anne Sullivan had no thought of becoming a teacher and was taken by surprise by Anagnos's proposal. But after overcoming initial misgivings, she set off on the long train trip to Tuscumbria, Alabama, to begin what was arguably the most inspiring career in the annals of special education, certainly to teach history's most inspiring exceptional individual. The relationship that began with her arrival in March 1887 lasted until Anne Sullivan Macy's death in 1936. Helen Keller's fame as an adult did not rely alone on her educational attainments, of course, although the breadth of her learning, and the fact of her graduation from Radcliffe cum laude, represent truly impressive achievement. Nor was it only that she, a person both blind and deaf, was an accomplished author. She was an important intellectual force, as well as a spiritual one, an outspoken advocate not only for people with disabilities but also for more general causes—woman suffrage, socialism, world peace. But even for individuals of transcendent genius, a basic task must be to establish some means of receiving the wisdom of others and of expressing thoughts to be shared by others. For persons experiencing blindness, whether gifted greatly or modestly, reading and writing are core skills for independence.

LITERACY

In adapting embossed print for use by blind persons, Haüy had surmounted a major barrier; a blind person could now, in principle, access the printed information available to those with sight. Of course, their extent was extremely limited, but Haüy believed it important that such materials could be read also by seeing persons. Touch in lieu of vision could be accepted, but the printed word was the printed word. The assumption that a blind person must read like a person with sight constituted another barrier to learning and thus to independence. It would take a blind person to break it down.

Louis Braille

Without doubt, the most famous student to attend the Institution Nationale des Jeunes Aveugles was Louis Braille (1809–1852), blind since injuring himself at age 3 playing with an awl used by his father, a harness maker. There was at first little encouragement for the boy to develop his intellectual resources, but at 10 he was admitted to the famous school in Paris. So outstanding a student was he that, at 17, he was invited to remain at the school as a junior master and, at 19, he was made an instructor (Kugelmass, 1951). His interest in the potential of a nonprint code was first aroused when in 1821 Charles Barbier, an army artillery officer, demonstrated a system of embossed dots he had invented at the institute in 1808. With this tactile code, called *Ecriture Nocturne* (Night Writing), which involved various combinations of 12 dots, firing orders could be transmitted in the dark without risk of miscommunication or of revealing position to the enemy (Scholl et al., 1986). It had been suggested to Barbier that it might be of interest to educators of the blind, and while others seem not to have seen its potential, one young instructor sensed the possible advantages of an alternative to the embossed print he used.

Braille was just 15 when, through experimentation, he discovered that 12 dots would be confusing to a blind person and that the 63 permutations possible within a cell containing just six dots would be sufficient. Five years later, now having the status of instructor, he presented his system to the institute staff. Whatever its initial reception may have been, Louis continued to revise the system, finally presenting a "perfected version" in 1834. But its official use was not authorized, so he could try his dot code only with pupils he saw privately. After 17 years' illness with tuberculosis, Louis Braille died in 1852, two years before the institute finally adopted his code. Seven years later, a newly established school for the blind in St. Louis was the first in America to adopt the system bearing his name.

An accomplished church organist, Braille also extended the use of the code to musical notation. This capability, which no form of line printing had, was a key factor in its survival, in view of the important, sometimes central, role of music in schools for the blind. Nonetheless, despite the early emphasis on music in British schools, the first use of braille in those schools did not occur until 1872, and for another two decades line printing continued to predominate (Pritchard, 1963). It is possible that the growing emphasis in the British programs on literacy may have made nonprint alternatives suspect and at odds with the fundamental goals of the London Society for Teaching the Blind to Read. A nonprint system may have been identified with the second-class status to which exclusively vocational training programs had seemed to relegate blind persons. In any case, the focus of British efforts was for many years on alternative line print systems.

Competing Systems

Blacklock's translation of Haüy's work generated interest in possibilities for improvement, and within the decade 1832–1842 various schemes for teaching blind persons to read were put forward, encouraged by general "contests." Most entries, each (e.g., *Lucas*) named for its developer, were essentially stenographic variations. By 1838, Pritchard (1963) comments, "the era of arbitrary systems" had begun. The most durable of these proved to be a literal embossed form of Roman type and an adaptation of Roman type called "Moon," developed by William Moon in 1847 and propogated through the Moon Society, led by the inventor until his death in 1894. With the death of Moon's daughter, who succeeded him, the society was taken over by the National Institute for the Blind in 1914. By 1884, Moon was the official type used in 36 British institutions; a half-century later, Rodenberg (1938) reported that Moon "is read by only two or three percent of the reading blind and is all that remains of the long-lived letter era" (p. 160). Despite strong advocacy, neither Roman nor Moon achieved lasting acceptance; as educators warred for years among themselves over this divisive issue, blind persons derived little benefit (Pritchard, 1963, p. 49).

In the United States, the enterprising Howe, having built a printing press at Perkins in 1837, developed a form of Roman type called "Boston Line Type" that, by 1852, was standard in American schools and would predominate for a half-century. While printing became an important enterprise at all three of the eastern schools, and at others that followed, an old problem remained: The variety of reading materials available was quite limited. It was compounded since the same few books, most of a religious nature, were published in various line letter forms. (A recurring theme of solicitousness concerning the spiritual development of blind and deaf persons is striking to note.) Believing blind readers as entitled to amusement as any others, Howe approached Dickens with an appeal for one of his novels to be printed in Boston Line Type. Dickens not only agreed, selecting *The Old Curiosity Shop*, but contributed substantially toward the costs (Farrell, 1956). Although a greater variety of content gradually became available, its extent continued to be limited by both duplication in several type forms and the limitations inherent in line letter adaptations. The American Printing House for the Blind, incorporated in Kentucky in 1858, produced work in braille, and soon in a competing system called "New York Point," but continued line printing.

The problem of validation of alternative "models" of educating exceptional children has persisted. Today, structures for professional review exist to consider the merits of a system or method and whether its measured outcomes are consistent with its goals, but in the previous century, though scientific review bodies had been established, much depended on a system's receiving some form of endorsement, in an atmosphere often dominated by rhetoric. So it was that in the late 1870s the London School Board, the body that would establish another critical precedent for blind pupils—day classes within the regular system of schooling—determined to resolve the issue of literacy systems. The relative merits of Roman and Moon, the major contenders, were weighed, but consideration was also given to braille, which, though used in France and to some extent in America for some 20 years, had only just been introduced in Britain. That it was finally subjected to study, which demonstrated its advantages, and ultimately favored, was largely due to the advocacy of Thomas Rhodes Armitage (1824–1890). This physician, who had turned his efforts to educational issues affecting blind persons as his own vision progressively worsened, believed that the question must be resolved by blind persons themselves (Farrell, 1956).

In championing braille at the first Congress of Teachers of the Blind in Vienna in 1873, Armitage effectively spoke for the *minority* faction of the British and Foreign Blind Association he represented. While most professionals continued to favor line printing, this "Great Missionary of braille" claimed it was in use "everywhere," which was far from the case; as many as 10 forms of line printing were used in Britain. Even "in the '80s its triumph was by no means certain, for over half of the British institutions were using Moon type and all of the American schools New York Point, while line letter books were still being produced" (Rodenberg, 1938, p. 165). But among the schools to adopt braille was the famous Royal Blind School of Edinburgh, in 1876, formed through merger of the Royal Blind Asylum founded by the Reverend Dr. Johnston in 1793 and the Edinburgh School for Blind Children founded by James Gall. That move by so prestigious and venerable an institution was a critical event in bringing about the long-deferred "braille era" (p. 165).

In fact, due largely to Armitage's salesmanship, braille *was* being introduced, if not "everywhere," in various parts of the world, such as Japan in 1875 and China in 1876. In India, the multitude of regional dialects were ingeniously accommodated through different codes. Yet it continued to be difficult to convince European and American educators that a dot code was viable, indeed a preferred alternative. An additional strong advocacy for that position came in America, paradoxically, in the form of yet another rival system. While braille characters were coded based on a principle of *logical sequence*, William Wait, superintendent of the New York Institution for the Blind, invoked the principle of *frequency of occurrence*. According to this principle, those characters needed most often should be most simply formed, and thus easily learned, remembered, and encoded. It is uncertain to what extent the approach known as New York Point had been inspired by ideas of his predecessor, but Wait with justification claimed to be its inventor.

At all events, he must be considered a "great missionary for punctiform type" (Rodenberg, 1938, p. 163) and the first to provide systematic evidence of its merit. Through a series of careful experiments done between 1859 and 1866, Wait subjected the competing systems to study to ascertain their comparative legibility. The alternative point system he devised, like braille adaptable for musical notation, would admit more than braille's 63 characters. On this basis he was able to convince the American Printing House for the Blind to add New York Point to the systems in which materials were printed, while it also gained endorsement of the American Association of Instructors of the Blind at its 1871 meeting (Irwin, 1938). Another New York Institution, opened in Batavia in 1865, reported that about half its 150 students could read and write with Wait's system after it was introduced there (Letchworth, 1903/1974). New York Point soon gained widespread American adoption, while across the Atlantic, and throughout the world, braille was the point system of choice, its competitors mainly the lingering line printing methods.

Braille finally surpassed its "greatest foe" in America mainly through the advocacy of Frank H. Hall and Edward Allen. Hall, superintendent of the Illinois School for the Blind, has been hailed as second only to Braille himself in the pantheon of blind literacy (Rodenberg, 1938). His preference was based on braille's mechanical simplicity, which accounted for its legibility. In the early 1890s, Hall developed two key innovations that enhanced its accessibility: a new technique for book printing and, even more important, a braille typewriter, or braillewriter, developed with Sieber. Allen, of Perkins, would pioneer extension of specialized instruction to pupils with low vision, where print adaptation was feasible; for those unable to read print he stood strongly for braille.

Meanwhile, a growing blind literati was becoming impatient with these internecine wars and with the narrow scope of reading materials available. Howe had attempted to rectify the latter problem but it persisted; as Joanne Greenberg's character in *Of Such Small Differences* reflects, "The Braille libraries had lots of prayer books and religious works. Years ago, Martin [his friend] had said, such books were all there were in Braille" (1988, p. 61). While the problem had been much worse, persons using New York Point and those using braille were each effectively able to access half of what a uniform system could make available. To confuse matters further, the British system had by 1905 three grades of braille (fully spelled, moderately contracted, and highly contracted), and an adaptation called "American braille" had been introduced based on work at Perkins (Irwin, 1938). Helen Keller protested in 1907, three years after graduating from Radcliffe, that her reading needs required mastery of four embossed codes (Lowenfeld, 1975). Finally, in 1931, the American Foundation for the Blind convened in New York the World Conference on Work for the Blind, with 37 nations represented. A resolution, implemented the next year, to adopt a uniform braille system in English-speaking countries was passed, and the International Clearing House was established to avoid duplicated publication of books (Irwin, 1938).

Controversy concerning use of braille in residential schools for blind pupils paralleled to some degree the controversy involving use of sign language in schools for deaf pupils, especially as needs of children with low vision but able to read print came to be identified. But the situation was reversed; some blind individuals able to read print protested that general use of braille was restrictive, while in the Deaf community sign language (ASL in North America) is viewed as liberating. The issue of culture identification is not generally raised by blind persons and, in contrast to the area of deafness, residential schools and employment of blind teachers have seemingly been defended more by professionals than by blind persons themselves. Though based partly on the low incidence of blindness, the defense involved professionals' assumption of parental inadequacy to meet a child's needs. Changes in such attitudes were key to moving from a predominantly residential school model to one that permitted children to remain with their families.

DAY CLASSES

In his 43rd and last report to the Perkins trustees, Howe (in Richards, 1909) wrote, "The practice of training . . . a considerable proportion of blind and of mute children in the common schools . . . will hardly come in my day; but I see it plainly with the eye of faith, and rejoice in the prospect of its fulfillment" (p. 25). There had been early attempts in Edinburgh in the 1830s to integrate blind with seeing children, but these were abandoned. Again, in 1868, efforts were renewed, resulting in enactment in 1872 of legislation supporting the education of blind pupils with their seeing peers. Then, in 1888 (12 years after Howe's death), the London School Board acted to establish day classes in the form of "centres . . . attached to ordinary schools" (Pritchard, 1963, p. 79). In the 23 "centres" thus created, a total of 133 pupils were instructed by five teachers (suggesting a surprising ratio indeed). The shift signaled two emerging principles: Exceptional children may benefit from association with "typical" peers, and families have a potentially positive role to play in contributing to the child's development. It did not occur immediately in the United States, where until after midcentury, "the prevailing pattern for the schooling of nine-tenths of the blind children . . . has been to take them from their families" (Farrell, 1956, p. 67).

Social Cohesion and the Family Metaphor

While Howe had "decried this practice" (Farrell, 1956), he allowed that "if separation from the home is necessary there should be small intimate units simulating family life for all children handicapped physically, mentally, or emotionally" (p. 67). So he sought to arrange Perkins accordingly, initiating a "cottage-family plan" later adopted in some other institutions (Roberts, 1986). This was certainly a more qualified form of "dispersion" than that implied in Bell's advocacy for day classes, which must also have impacted on the thinking of some educators of blind students. Howe, like Bell, believed fervently that the aim of education of exceptional children and youth must be to prepare them to become independent, productive contributors to society, but the family model he embraced suggests an emphasis differing somewhat from Bell's. "In providing for the poor, the dependent, and the vicious," he wrote, "especially for the young, we must take the ordinary family as our model. . . . God . . . seems to have ordained that the natural institutions of the family . . . must be at the foundations of all permanent social institutions" (in Richards, 1909, p. 521).

As his words imply, this belief in social cohesion, founded on the institution of the family, guided Howe's thinking concerning all areas of deviance, including delinquents and criminals ("the vicious") as well as the poor and persons with disabilities. It was in fact a vision of an older society that he invoked, rather than the industrialized one of the 19th century, a society in which "the people" assumed responsibility for persons who were less fortunate. He envisioned a cohesive unity, with "deviants" of all types dispersed throughout the land, nourished by the proper morality of good families, and maintained as useful members of communities. To Howe, the state, where it should assume reponsibility, was but an extension of the community, the community an extension of the family (Katz, 1968). With such phrases as "all who are born to her" and "her motherly care," he characterized the state as essentially a surrogate mother (Schwartz, 1956).

For Howe, the blueprint for the future corresponded closely with a mythical, and idealized, communal, well-ordered past, rather than the hard realities of an industrialized state. The medical superintendents of the asylums for persons considered insane and those with retardation, while sharing his idealized vision of the past, may have understood the disparity of their age more clearly. As Rothman (1971) wrote, they "were certain that their society lacked all elements of a fixity and cohesion because they judged it by a nostalgic image of the eighteenth century . . . [and thus] designed their institutions with eighteenth century virtues in mind" (p. xviii). As Howe articulated his vision, in "Principles of Public Charities," in 1866, for the State of Massachusetts, the large, factory-like institution was already emerging. It was seen as an orderly alternative to disorderly society, an *asylum*. Yet Howe contended "that we should build up public institutions only in the last resort" (Richards, 1909, p. 516). As we shall see in the next chapter, the conviction growing among leaders in the field of retardation was that the last resort was at hand.

At all events, Howe himself had had an enormously important role in both the proliferation of those very "public institutions" for the blind and in the continued public support they received. They had become a source of pride, their accomplishments heralded not only by reformers but also civic and political leaders; President Grover Cleveland had, in fact, been a teacher in New York's first institution (Farrell, 1956). Since the American public had become convinced of their value, legislators showed little hesitation about increasing funding to permit expansion. Eventually, all but nine states had residential schools for the blind (Lowenfeld, 1975). While Howe saw the inherent conflict between segregation in institutions and his core belief in "separation and diffusion," his conception of mainstream alternatives remained romantic and anachronistic. He could not envision, except as distant possibilities, what we would today call community-based alternatives. And while invoking the metaphor of family, he feared that families per se were ill-equipped to raise a blind child to be an independent, self-reliant, productive citizen. He was especially concerned that parents would tend naturally toward overprotectiveness and oversolicitousness during the early years. In his "Counsels to Parents of Blind Children" (in Ross, 1951), he advised parents not to be "overanxious" about their young child:

> Do not watch him too closely. Do not smooth away all difficulties and carpet his walk of life. . . . Do not prevent your blind child from developing, as he grows up, courage, self-reliance, generosity, and manliness of character, by excessive indulgence, by sparing his thought and anxiety and hard work, and by giving him undesired preference over others. (p. 150)

Establishing a kindergarten at Perkins, nearly another "first"—one had been begun at the Pennsylvania institution in 1882 (Scholl et al., 1986)— was Anagnos's project after Howe's death; it was dedicated in 1887, with his widow among the luminaries attending the exercises. Even at that, early patterns would be established in the home, and Howe's experiences, or prejudices, must have suggested that these might not be in the best interests of the future pupil. Incorporated in his report for 1874, the "Counsels" would seem intended to convey a public position as well as sound advice. Though not altogether unwarranted, this assumption that parents would tend naturally to be overprotective and to work at cross-purposes with specialized educators became fixed as an attitude of near animosity. Lowenfeld (1975) quotes a society in New York in the early 1900s:

> Help from the untrained parent is not to be expected. A mother can no more save her blind baby from growing up feeble-minded if left solely to her care and instruction than she can, when it is older, give it a college education without specialized assistance. . . . A mother is the blind baby's worst enemy. Filled with the horror of the fact that her baby is blind, she devotes her life to waiting on it, doing anything to hush or quiet the peculiar wail of the little soul that has brains, but not sight. (p. 99)

The issue of residential versus day schools was not simply a matter of where classrooms should be located; it was at the core a question of whether total environments for children's socialization run by professionals were preferable to what one's own family and community could provide. The *First Biennial Report* of the Michigan School for the Blind, in 1882, pronounced it "undeniable that a blind child can be better cared for, better fitted for the future, when gathered into suitably conducted institutions for its education and care" (p. 7). The report also noted that, while some of its pupils had come to the institution from "unfit" families, many others had been in poorhouses, to which the officials were determined they must not return. Indeed, "suitably conducted institutions" would have been the much preferable alternative. As he predicted, Howe did not live to see day classes for blind children in the common schools. Two later staunch defenders of the residential school model (Frampton & Kerney, 1953) described the years 1892–1900 as a period of "incubation of the day-school movement proper in the United States, in line with opposition to 'institutions'" (p. 101). Occurring simultaneously were efforts to affirm and sustain the family as a preferred alternative to any form of outside-the-home placement of children. Presumably, Howe, had he lived, would have been in the vanguard of both these interrelated movements.

Much as he disdained the "asylum touch," however, there was an inherent conflict between Howe's stated convictions and his impulse to rescue and protect. He was driven to take up the cause of all those society had forgotten or, like African Americans, oppressed and deprived of the most basic human rights. Consistent with his principles, he favored minimal federal involvement following emancipation; "Give to Negroes," he counseled Sumner, "the ancient privilege of starving if they preferred not to work, and use no coercion. . . . The sooner they stand alone, the better" (in Schwartz, 1956, p. 266). But concerning persons with disabilities, was he, as Clerc alleged (Lane, 1984a), "paternalistic" and "condescending" in spite of himself? Lionized, Howe was the subject of tributes like John Chapman's, that "the sight of ['defectives'] . . . aroused in him such a passion of benevolence, such a whirlwind of pity, that he could do whatever was necessary. He lifted them in his arms and flew away with them like an angel" (in Richards, 1935, p. 103).

If a person with a disability would today find these flowery words more than a little patronizing, not to say offensive, it should be remembered that the attitudes and beliefs implicit in the tribute were reflective of the times, Chapman's as well as Howe's, as were the rhetorical flourishes. One would hope that Howe would have disavowed such praise. His annual reports consistently stressed the themes of competence and independence, with the implication that as long as blind people were unable to support themselves they would remain an economic burden. Thus, he counseled parents that even neglect was preferable to coddling. Also, his promotion of physical education in the curriculum was predicated on concern for a tendency toward passive inactivity in blind children that may indeed result from parental overprotectiveness, a concern today (Lowenfeld, 1975, p. 89).

Since Howe preached independence, why did he view integration as the desired outcome of segregated education instead of pressing for inclusion in the common schools? Some still maintain that children with disabilities must master the skills required in the educational, or societal, mainstream as a condition for entry, while others argue that those skills are most readily acquired in environments in which they are to be used than in contrived settings. In any case, the shift that began a quarter-century after Howe's death reflected the fundamental principles of his vision: a family model, dispersion rather than centralization, and a goal of societal integration. It was becoming increasingly apparent that simulated family environments could only be, at best, a "least-harmful" alternative if the child's own parents were truly inadequate. While some educators continued to assume that to be true of most families, many blind individuals themselves disagreed and increasingly questioned the belief that segregation, especially given conventions associated with life in institutions, constituted effective preparation for independence and integration into society. Could specialized instruction appropriate to the needs of blind children be provided, as Howe had prophesied, within the common school?

Moreover, as the important influence of early experience was recognized, the belief that children should be removed from their homes was dying; few endorsed separating small children from their families. The kindergartens established at the Pennsylvania institution and at Perkins were followed by others in Germany and Austria, but these were dispersed to permit children to live at home. By the 1930s, a few day nursery schools for blind children appeared in the eastern United States; these, like other early childhood educational models, involved a collaborative relationship between families and professionals (Irwin, 1938). Also, the assumption of parental overprotectiveness as a rationale for turning child-rearing over to professionals in residential schools had been challenged in a sociological analysis of blindness by the internationally respected Pierre Villey (1927), which suggested the desirability of alternative means of involving professionals that permitted children to remain with their families.

A full-scale attack began later, its signs clearly discernible when two officials of the New York School for the Blind (Frampton & Kerney, 1953) undertook a defense with *The Residential School: Its History, Continuation, and Future*. Their major antagonist, though they did not name him, was Thomas Cutsforth, a blind clinical psychologist, residential school graduate, and author of *The Blind in School and Society: A Psychological Study*. His book, first published in 1933, seems to have been perceived at the time as a radical attack, but until its republication, in 1951, his position had little support. Between these dates, a "maiming war" had intervened, changing public attitudes; most Americans had a neighbor, friend, or family member with a disability.

These two works framed the debate, in North America at any rate, as it stood at midcentury. Frampton and Kerney (1953) devote the longest section of their book to numerous and lengthy quotations from persons who had been involved in the education of blind individuals. They acknowledge that critics of institutions had extended their criticisms to schools for the blind, but maintain that such an extension was unwarranted, most critics being inadequately informed concerning the tradition begun by Haüy and continued by Howe. These pioneers shared the conviction, they insist (questionably, in Howe's case), that only residential schools could address the needs of blind persons comprehensively, providing not only specialized instruction but also training in a trade, attention to psychological needs, and the pleasures of shared experiences with others like themselves. Berthold Lowenfeld (1975) described the history of blindness as a progression toward full integration, but these authors even find in Lowenfeld's (1956) acknowledgement of the contributions of residential schools a suggestion that he had "recanted" his endorsement of day classes. He had not.

Cutsforth essayed, as had Villey and as would other social and behavioral scientists, notably Lowenfeld, a study of personality development in blind individuals, the results of which led him to criticize severely the prevalent service structure, dominated as it was by residential schools. He charged that the schools, rather than ameliorating the problems of psychosocial development for which blind persons may be at particular risk, contributed to those problems. Somewhat disingenuously, Cutsforth (1933) suggests that his criticisms are mild, nothing at which anyone could take offense. But he charges educators with being "so absorbed in the maintenance of the integrity of the institutions with their methodologies and mores that they have lost sight of the blind individuals, of the fact that each pupil represents a separate and individual social problem instead of another justification for the existence of an institution, which social practice and tradition have perpetuated" (p. 200). He ascribes the little progress since Howe to educators' preoccupation with the efficient operation of the schools—the priority in all institutions (p. 199). As for Howe's legacy, "They have imitated his material results solely by building bigger and better institutions" (p. 200). The size, overall structure, staff expectations and characteristics, and the milieu of the school itself continue to result, he charges, in *undereducating* blind students.

Worse, they promote stigmatizing behavior disparate from societal norms, a "differentness" far less acceptable in an age when conformity is valued. Moreover, requirements for education in the 20th century are far different from those of the 19th; training a blind person to work at one of a circumscribed number of trades is insufficient. Cutsforth (1933) condemns the practice of "exhibiting" students' achievements as demeaning and degrading, though "a splendid way in which to harden the student to the seeing public. No better method could be devised to render the blind students emotionally fit to become street beggars and applicants for state aid" (p. 220). Excoriating administrators whose "selfish egotism and unsympathetic ignorance" perpetuated this "barbaric practice," Cutsforth charges that "the questions that the stupid visitors ask are more often than not irrelevant and actually insulting" (p. 219). (His indignation may strike a familiar chord among today's professionals who have had to host visitors' days and public relations or fund-raising events, as well as persons with disabilities.) Thus, in this "mild criticism," he articulates the issue of *rights* in contrast to charity mentality, and the case for *normalization* instead of exploitation, patronization, and stigmatization.

Cutsforth's critique may have accelerated the shift to a day-class model, but its republication coincided with other developments. Until the 1950s, more than 80% of the blind children in the United States who were provided education were enrolled in residential schools (Lowenfeld, 1956). That this pattern was shortly reversed Lowenfeld attributed to parents, who "knew and made known their children's needs," and educational officials, who "responded by increasingly providing services on the local level" (p. vi).

Although some critics of today's "Full Inclusion" movement (e.g., Fuchs & Fuchs, 1994) suggest that opposition comes from blind persons, as well as from the Deaf community, only the latter has an investment in maintenance of residential schools for transmission of culture.

Adaptive Instruction, Integration, and Independence

With new waves of European immigration, the heterogeneity of American school children and urging of settlement leaders were forcing school officials to address the reality of diversity among students, as we saw. Although many did not finish, or even begin, secondary schooling, the elementary had become in fact the *common school*. Forming special classes for students with "exceptional" needs was congruent with a general thrust toward providing for all by diversifying—some would say "sorting" (Spring, 1972). But the nation was yet a long way from achieving either the goal of universal schooling or that of accommodating to diverse needs of pupils.

Blindness represented a clear case of students who were demonstrably educable and who could learn the same content as their seeing peers if taught in a specialized manner. Klein had from the beginning favored instruction for all blind pupils in regular schools, but despite a national preference for maintaining children in their own communities, the low incidence of blindness in Austria, as in other nations, influenced continued reliance on centralized schools well into the present century (Taylor & Taylor, 1960, p. 87). In Japan, the number of residential schools for blind and for deaf students increased from four in 1897 to 38 in 1907 (Tsujimura, 1979, p. 7), attributable to low incidence rather than ideological considerations favoring centralized schooling. Denmark's Royal Institute for the Blind, authorized in 1811 but not opened until 1857, though organized by a private philanthropic society, was supported through government grants (Taylor & Taylor, 1960, p. 125). Two Finnish schools were opened in 1865 and 1870, also with government support. In Norway, an Act of Parliament in 1881 authorized the state to assume operation of schools for blind pupils, as well as deaf pupils and those with retardation, if the private agencies that had established them were unable to continue their support (Taylor & Taylor, 1960, p. 326).

Legislation adopted in several European nations assigning responsibility to government began to favor a more dispersed, localized approach. The Elementary Education (Blind and Deaf Children) Act of 1893 gave each Local Education Authority (LEA) in England and Wales responsibility to educate blind (ages 5–16) and deaf (ages 7–16) students in "centres" certified by the Ministry of Education (Taylor & Taylor, 1960, p. 147). Still, while some precedent for day schools had been established, congregate centralization remained the norm in Britain, on the European continent, and throughout the world. While day classes had become more numerous in the 20th century, residential school enrollment had increased more.

The greater number of American blind students also continued to be served in residential schools, of which there were 65 in the United States in the late 1930s. However, in 1900 Frank Hall demonstrated a different approach in the Chicago public schools, paralleling developments in teaching deaf pupils and the ungraded classes being set up for "backward" and otherwise difficult-to-teach pupils, but distinctive in encouraging blind children's interaction with typical peers. While special classes were established, provision was made for pupils to share in general school experiences, permitting social integration in combination with specialized instruction. This set the pattern that was adopted as other major cities instituted programs (Farrell, 1956, p. 57). In Ohio, the Cincinnati School District assumed responsibility in 1905 for operation of a class that two sisters, Georgia and Florence Trader, had begun a year earlier, located in the public library (Ohio Department of Education, 1985). New York's classes were instituted in 1909, the same year Robert Irwin established Cleveland's. By 1938, 25 American cities operated day classes, enrolling approximately 500 students (Irwin, 1938).

While responsibility for instruction of blind students had increasingly come to be assumed in many nations by public education, advocacy for the rights of blind persons transcended issues of schooling. In 1918, in the United States, financial investment in services for blind persons approximated $31 million, but the "services were scattered, diffuse, lacking in common goals or standards" (Koestler, 1976, p. 8). The remaining hurdles were segregation in residential schools; the limited number of books available in braille; the limited number of persons who had learned to use braille; insufficient opportunities to be self-supporting; lack of financial security for persons who were dependent; and lack of access to "devices to simplify . . . daily routines" (p. 9). A key organization formed in 1921 to work on all these fronts was the American Foundation for the Blind, and beginning in 1924, Helen Keller was its most effective ambassador.

In this she worked closely with Robert B. Irwin, blind since the age of 5, who had come to the organization's headquarters having, with Edward Allen, pioneered the extension of specialized instruction to pupils with low vision. Irwin (1955) strongly believed that blind children should learn "in the company of the seeing." The classes he set up in Cleveland in 1909, therefore, though specialized, were intended to encourage children's involvement in the regular school program, as Hall had demonstrated in Chicago. Enthused by Perkins educator Edward Allen's accounts of visits to British schools, where pupils with some functional vision were provided specialized instruction, Irwin (as did Allen in Boston) began a program of "sight-saving" classes in the Cleveland schools, then assisted in establishing similar programs in seven other Ohio communities. The model was soon adopted throughout the United States (Ohio Department of Education, 1985).

The classes were based on two principles. First, the needs of children with usable vision sufficient for potential print reading were recognized to differ from the needs of children who would need to rely on touch. The existing instructional models were based on the assumption that tactile alternatives must be used; for substantial numbers of children, including pupils in the residential schools, that was not necessarily the case. The second principle was that it was important for children with some functional vision to "conserve" the vision they had. Thus, sight-saving classes were distinguished by environmental modifications, like dimmed lighting, with instructional materials designed to minimize visual demands. The notion of "conserving sight" through such protective arrangments was later discredited, largely through demonstrations of Natalie Barraga (1964) that effective teaching could increase *visual efficiency* without endangering residual vision. Most "blind" children are now recognized to have some functional vision and, of these, a majority are in fact able to read print. Nevertheless, provision for children with low vision marked an important development in providing for children with impaired vision.

The need to provide for students who have some ability to use vision in learning, rather than relying entirely on hearing and touch, was made known largely through the work of Allen and Irwin. Today, the needs of most of these students are addressed in regular classrooms through use of large print, high-contrast materials, and other adaptations. Actually, research evidence indicates that "most learners with low vision can read as comfortably and efficiently by using regular print with or without magnification" (Barraga & Erin, 1992), but conversely, for many with very low vision, braille can be valuable "as either a primary or a supplementary medium" (p. 180) that often can be readily accommodated within the regular education program. Just as seeing persons have become accustomed to braille in the community and the world of work, in elevators and ATMs, it is one of many instructional media to accommodate pupil diversity. However, technological advances, especially in translation of print and other visual information into sound, suggest that the history of blindness has entered a whole new era. Possibly more for children, and adults, who are blind than in the case of any other form of human exceptionality, technology is proving the key to realization of Howe's vision and that of generations of "blind emancipators" themselves.

CHAPTER 6

Mental Retardation, Educability, and Worth

VICISSITUDES OF PROGRESS

Concerning retardation, the 19th century would begin and end in pessimism, though it foreshadowed themes of normalization and inclusion. Hopes for "cure" brought a backlash, and though founded after the models of deafness and blindness as places for teaching and learning, "institution after institution . . . slipped from the noble ideals of its planners into a warehouse of hopelessness and despair" (Ozolins, 1981, p. vii). The IQ was "discovered" and propagators of the new psychometric technology attributed human worth on its basis; conceptions of intelligence influenced and were influenced by beliefs about retardation. Old superstitions yielded to science, but some resurfaced, revived by scientific advance itself: Children formerly believed punishment for parental sin came to be viewed as themselves evil, a menace. The social goal shifted from making "the deviant undeviant" to "sheltering the deviant from society" to "protection of society from the deviant" (White and Wolfensberger, 1969). Persons with retardation became targets of "multiple indictments" (Wallin, 1914).

The issue of cure has been linked with the medical model resulting from physicians' dominance in this field (Wolfensberger, 1975). Failure to cure and dramatically increasing numbers in institutions contributed to a growing negativism, also influenced by Galton's (1869) *Hereditary Genius*, with its message of biological determinism based on genetic endowment. The belief that intelligence, morality, and character were inherited, immutable traits inspired proposals to regulate procreation. And in America waves of immigrants different in appearance, language, and custom from descendants of earlier immigrants were increasingly a concern. Even some progressive social scientists "argued for immigrant restriction to exclude undesirables . . . and advocated eugenics to improve the racial quality of Native Americans" (Violas, 1973, p. 42).

Mental tests found their most enthusiastic proponents in the field of retardation. Unlike Binet (1909), Henry Goddard, director of research at the Vineland Training School for Feebleminded Girls and Boys, believed they measured "a single, innate entity" and could be used "to identify in order to recognize limits, segregate, and curtail breeding to prevent further deterioration of an endangered American stock, threatened by immigration from without and by prolific reproduction of its feeble-minded within" (Gould, 1981, p. 159). Goddard's (1912a) went beyond previous genealogical studies in dramatizing the need for social control. Using a surname suggesting good and evil, from the Greek, he and his field workers led by Elizabeth S. Kite sought to locate descendants and trace the dual lineages of a Revolutionary soldier, "Martin Kallikak," from an illicit affair with a barmaid and a subsequent respectable union. Cranial shape and physiognomy were widely considered genetic indicators of breeding, but thinking photographs of "degenerate" descendants did not dramatize his warnings starkly enough, Goddard—or someone—"doctored" them, not the first instance of scientific fraud rationalized by belief, nor the last.

In effect, "three different worlds" have been created for persons with retardation (Tyor & Bell, 1984, p. x). Training schools, conceived as extensions of the common school, became a very different world. While sheer size, numbers, and press to admit persons with more severe impairment were factors, the core difference was one of belief: Residents were no longer expected to leave, lifelong segregation considered in the best interests of both society and residents themselves. Klaber (in Sarason & Doris, 1969) found that, while five of the six facilities he and associates studied were called "schools," only 5–10% of their budgets was spent for "training and education." The institution's function was containment, and so it remained. The "world" of community services yet being created is far from a present reality, but closer to an earlier vision.

EXPERIENCES OF CHILDREN

Throughout history, there have been children described as "dull," "simple," "slow-witted," or "foolish." Such words have found their way into the usage of ridicule and derogation, the stuff of parable, adage, and epigram contrasting folly and wisdom. No one, presumably, would choose such a role, nor would parents choose it for their child. But in rural and village life, a child with delays could experience acceptance, affection, and a sense of worth. Allowances might be made in duties assigned as family routines were established, but to be given responsibilities is to be given respect. In the case of retardation, childhood has long served, wrongly, as a metaphor, but an adult with cognitive impairment is not a child. More than any other people, those labeled retarded have been described, interpreted, "done for," and "done to." While that is true of *all* children, it is most true of children with disabilities, most of all children assigned that label.

It is surprising that few professionals attempted to understand the experience of retardation in a phenomenological sense before Edgerton's (1967) groundbreaking *Cloak of Competence*. Even now, while children with cognitive impairment are frequently research "subjects," their subjective experience is even less familiar than that of most children, although some (e.g., Bogdan & Taylor, 1976, 1994) have enabled persons labeled retarded to share in their own words their experiences, beliefs about themselves and other people, hopes and fears. We have no diaries, interview transcripts, even applicable portrayals in literature to tell us what life was like for a child with retardation in the 19th century. Superintendents' reports tell us little about them as individuals, though they do suggest that many training school residents were not retarded. Most, Howe claimed in 1846 (in Richards, 1935), were maintained in poorhouses, but we can be certain a greater number, when circumstances permitted, lived with their families. For them, the likelihood of growing to maturity in their home communities was, of course, much greater, as were indeed their chances of growing to maturity at all. It is a poignant thought to imagine how this chapter might "read" if it could somehow tell *their* story, in *their* voices.

EXTENSION OF REFORM: HOWE AND SEGUIN

Striking parallels can be seen between the careers and personalities of Edouard Seguin and Samuel Gridley Howe. For both, Sicard's work with deafness was a point of departure, though Seguin was more influenced by Pereire's methods. Both were ardently committed to reform, indeed, involved in radical movements. Both expressed respect for their clients and eschewed coddling. And each undertook great pedagogical challenges, Howe a pupil with neither sight nor hearing and others experiencing both blindness and retardation, Seguin "the idiots" as a class. Both were charismatic figures, like those Blatt (1981) had in mind with his reflections about developers of "spectacular methods." And both could be difficult; their attempt to work together, lasting just three months, was predictably short-lived.

Like Howe, Seguin (1866/1907) believed institutions should be schools, their mission to prepare pupils for return to their communities, as well as sources of knowledge in "all branches of anthropology" (p.75). In fact, he thought these facilities should be located within communities, not isolated or centralized, and small enough that the superintendent could review each pupil's progress daily. Pupils able to live at home could be provided outreach services, but Seguin recognized that some with the most severe

impairments required long-term care. Howe (1848a) tempered his un-
bounded optimism in describing a "very few cases . . . in which the brain
and nervous system have no command over the system of voluntary muscles;
and which consequently are without power of locomotion, without speech,
without any manifestation of intellectual or affective faculties" (p. 6).

Howe deplored the fact that, excepting a short-lived attempt in 1818 to
teach a few pupils with retardation at the American Asylum for the Deaf
and Dumb, they were not provided for, languishing with other "unfortunates." His daughter (Richards, 1935) noted that his own work had inevitably brought her father in contact with "the idiotic and feebleminded," and
success with three blind pupils believed "idiots" convinced him that, if
improvement was possible with those doubly handicapped, it certainly was
attainable for those with sight. Howe was determined that Massachusetts
must have a school, and that it must institute Dix's reforms; having gained
a seat in the legislature, he sponsored a bill mandating care for the insane,
then worked for legislation for persons with retardation. A bill introduced
in 1846 by Judge Horatio Byington called for an investigatory commission,
chaired by Howe, "to inquire into the condition of idiots of the Commonwealth of Massachusetts," and enabling legislation was enacted when the
legislature overrode the governor's veto. Supported by endorsements from
Sumner and Mann, Howe's (1848b) eloquence won the day:

> Massachusetts admits the right of all her citizens to a share in the blessings of
> education. . . . And will she no longer neglect the poor idiots—the most wretched
> of all who are born to her—those who are usually abandoned by their fellows
> . . . and shall our Commonwealth continue to bury the humble talent of lowly
> children committed to her Motherly care and let it rot in the earth. (p. 411)

An annual appropriation of $2,500 was authorized for an experimental
program, first located in a wing at Perkins. In 1850, Howe and his associates obtained a charter of incorporation, and the next year the Massachusetts School for Idiotic and Feeble-minded Youth was established, which
Howe intermittently ran for the next 25 years, relocated in Waverly. He also
participated in nascent organizational efforts but like Seguin dissociated
himself from the leadership group as its views diverged from his own. Howe
seems not to have met Seguin in the course of his European visits, but his
commission cited Sumner's report of his work. Seguin himself, due to political unrest in France following the 1848 Revolution, had relocated in
America, where for four years he had been working to establish a practice
in Cleveland when Hervey Wilbur brought him to the new training school
in Albany. He then accepted an invitation from Howe, who though enthusiastic in his praise, was resigned to his inevitable departure. Why their col-

laboration was so short is not clear, but Seguin did not share all Howe's enthusiasms, such as phrenology.

Edouard Onesimus Seguin (1812–1880) was in his mid-twenties when he took on his first "idiotic boy" at the Bicetre, under Esquirol's supervision, and determined to devote himself totally to that work. When an annex was set aside as a school, in 1842, he was made its director. In 1879, the year before his death, when he spoke at a conference at the institution in Media, Pennsylvania, the local press hailed him as the "progenitor of the present system of treatment of imbecility" and the "parent of the efforts for the elevation of this class."[1] The latter encomium acknowledged his advocacy, the former his *physiological method,* which while consonant with the "somatic style" of the neuropsychiatry of his day (Hale, 1971), and derived from the sense-realist philosophers who influenced Itard and Pereire, was a new invention.

Seguin's innovations resulted more from belief than from arduous study of the work of others (Talbot, 1964). Characteristically, he resonated to Saint-Simonism, named for Henri de Saint-Simon (1760–1825), who like Lafayette had joined in the American struggle for independence and whose *Nouveau Christianisme* (1825) propounded amelioration of the lot of the poor through collective self-sacrifice by the more privileged. After the 1789 Revolution, Saint-Simonism briefly assumed proportions of a movement, attracting idealistic young Frenchmen like Isaac and Eugene Pereire and feminists like Claire Démar (Perrot & Martin-Fugier, 1990), but internal dissension reduced it to a small communal sect, which dissolved when its leaders were tried and condemned. Seguin left the movement, and his homeland, for political reasons, but it was apparently a dispute with management that led to his leaving his post at the Bicetre. Scheerenberger (1983) comments that his continuing difficulties working with others were due to his overly sensitive nature, but he could also be a sharp critic of the status quo; visiting the Bicetre 30 years later, Seguin (1880) sardonically likened the leadership to Rip van Winkle. Reflecting the spirit of Saint-Simonism, Seguin (1843) placed his work in the context of efforts with deaf and blind persons, for whom

> hearing has been replaced by sight, sight by touch, speech by pantomime, in short, those born blind and those born deaf have become human beings. I did not have to look about me very long to find a class of unfortunates more to be pitied than these: a class displaced, a separate category, and nevertheless confused but lately with convicts sentenced to compulsory labor, still mixed in today with the insane and the epileptic; I mean the idiots. (pp. 1–2)

---

[1]Newspaper reports and other unreferenced sources cited in this chapter were located in the archives maintained at the Elwyn Institute, in Media, Pennsylvania.

When the Association of Medical Officers of American Institutions for Idiotic and Feeble-minded Persons was formed in 1876, Seguin was elected its first president. But his would not be the dominant voice, nor would Howe's call for separation and diffusion be heeded. Instead, Isaac Kerlin's vision of institutions as "cities of refuge," "havens dedicated to incompetency," would prevail (Scheerenberger, 1983, p. 128). Both died before this retreat from the era of education gained full momentum; by 1898, Vineland's superintendent, E. R. Johnston, could pronounce that "the child is to be with us throughout his life; correct education for him must fit him for the institution" (p. 98).

INSTITUTIONAL MODELS

Programs in Europe

Other Europeans had advocated education for persons with retardation, and though the career of one would end in ignominy, his impact was great. Seguin had been preceded by a century of scattered efforts by physicians, clergy, and occasional educators and lay reformers in Austria and Switzerland, and most notably by Vincent de Paul's work in "two huge receptacles" in Paris, the Bicetre and Salpêtrière (Kanner, 1964). But retardation was a peripheral interest of the French alienists; Wallin (1914) later observed that, while it appeared that France would become the premier influence as it had been in deafness and blindness, after Seguin's departure little focused work continued there. Instead, it was a Swiss physician who sensed that the time was ripe for a full-scale movement.

Johann Jacob Guggenbuhl (1816–1863), moved by the sight of a person with cretinism "mumbling the Lord's Prayer at a wayside cross" (Kanner, 1964, p. 78), believed he had a divine calling to devote his life to ameliorating the condition. He noted that cretinism was not found in high elevations; thus, in 1842, with financial backing, he built the Abendberg, the first educational facility for persons with retardation on a mountain summit. He believed that with favorable climate, a health regimen of good diet and exercise, and training, cretinism could be cured. At first the program was exemplary, combining moral management and skilled instruction; Howe, among its many visitors, proclaimed, "The Holy Mount, it should be called" (Kanner, 1964, p. 25). But accepting invitations from all over to promote it caused Guggenbuhl to neglect his program. By the early 1850s, reports of its deterioration brought investigations and withdrawal of support. He was finally denounced as a fraud and, for his propensity to characterize his role as Providential, a hypocrite. At his death, at 47, he was eulogized only with faint praise for raising awareness of retardation, but despite the ultimate tragedy of his life, nation after nation began programs modeled on the Abendberg.

In England, a small Abendberg-inspired program in Bath on Avon begun in 1846 by two sisters, the Misses White, was incorporated in the Magdalen Hospital, opened in the 17th century for patients with leprosy but since the 18th a "repository" like the Bicetre. Following visits to the Abendberg, the Reverend Andrew Reed (1787–1862), founder of three nonsectarian orphanages, opened the "Asylum for Idiots" at Highgate in 1851, which later, relocated at Earlswood in Surrey, became the Royal Earlswood Asylum, the largest of the European institutions, where Langdon Down and W. J. Little served. In Scotland, Sir John and Lady Jane Ogilvy, whose son had benefited from treatment at the Abendberg, opened a facility on their estate near Dundee in 1854 under the aegis of the Scottish Board of Lunacy. Shortly after, a physician named Brodies, author of *The Education of the Imbecile and the Improvement of Invalid Youth* (1856), began another near Falkirk, followed in 1867 by a third, Columbia Lodge, near Edinburgh. In Ireland, an 1861 census having identified 7,033 "defectives," the Stewart Institution opened in 1869 (Kanner, 1964).

In the Netherlands, the queen's personal interest resulted in a program for 21 boys and 10 girls considered educable, which led to a larger facility for 70 children at The Hague. In Switzerland, disillusionment followed Guggenbuhl's exposure, but in 1857 Dr. C. G. Jung (1794–1864), grandfather of the originator of Analytical Psychology, with his own resources founded the Institute of Hope for "backward children" (Wehr, 1987, p. 16). Over the next half-century, 18 Swiss institutions were established (the Abendberg having long been converted to other uses) as religious or benevolent society enterprises, with varying degrees of government support. Scandinavian programs, which later introduced the revolutionary concept of *normalization*, were also based on the Abendberg model, but with such notable innovations as women superintendents in Sweden and Norway's compulsory education policies encompassing children with retardation (Kanner, 1964).

As Reed's example suggests, care of orphans often led to awareness of those with delays. A later instance, in another part of the world, was the aftermath of a disastrous earthquake in Japan in 1890, resulting in more than 10,000 deaths. Within a network of "welfare institutions" established for orphaned children, a child welfare worker, R. Ishii, saw the need for a "department for feebleminded children," the first in the Eastern Hemisphere (Tsujimira, 1979). The key role of physicians was more an American phenomenon (Rosen et al., 1976); in Europe diverse individuals were involved, often with patronage. The historically significant role of clergy was exemplified by Reed in England; in France, Jean Bost (1817–1881), ordained after a military career, opened an orphanage in 1854 at Laforce, called the *famille evangelique.* Finding two of the 75 girls living there delayed, he took them into his home, beginning the first of several homelike facilities he founded. His story is illustrative of the involvement of clergy as an extension of humanitarian care for orphaned children, as that of Seguin and many others reflects the medical heritage.

A third stream involved educators of deaf children. While Seguin drew inspiration from Epée's dedication and Pereire's methods, Carl Wilhelm Saegert, director of Berlin's Institution for Deaf-Mutes, was concerned for deaf children with retardation who were ineligible for admission. In 1845 he began to teach them privately, gaining state support in 1848 when their number had grown to more than 50, the beginning of what became by 1885 a network of more than 30 schools throughout Germany. (An American visitor, Edouard Seguin [1880], found the German institutions, and those in Belgium and the Netherlands, excessively rigorous and lacking in music, gymnastics, and opportunities for "relaxation by playthings and pleasure" [p. 86].) By 1917, Germany had about 100 such facilities (Kanner, 1964, pp. 54–55), but day classes were increasingly preferred.

A Latvian teacher of the deaf, Frederick Platz, opened an "institution for remedial education" but soon died. As other widows had done (Heinicke's) or attempted to do (Pereire's), Theresa Platz carried on her husband's work, disseminating techniques to Slavic countries. Traditions of humane care in eastern European nations seem to have been less influenced by demonology (Kanner, 1964, p. 61), and programs were small; Ireland (1877) noted that, of two in Russia, one served 20 residents, the other just 10. By this time, the dominant model in the United States was the large, centralized institution.

Growth and Change in American Institutions

Within four decades of the opening of Howe's school, others were established in 14 states with two in New York, all led by physicians. Constituted as the Superintendents of the American Institutions for the Improvement of Idiots and Feeble Minded Children, they campaigned to raise their fellow physicians' awareness through communications like one in 1876 whose signators were "Geo. Brown of Barre, Massachusetts; G. A. Doren of Columbus, Ohio; I. N. Kerlin of Media, Pennsylvania; H. M. Knight of Lakeville, Connecticut; E. Seguin of New York; Henry Tuck of Boston; &c &c &c." From the first "tentative experiments" (Fernald, 1893, p. 209), by 1888 there were more than 20 institutions, housing about 4,000 residents (Rosen et al., 1976, p. xviii).

That estimate was made by Hervey Backus Wilbur (1820–1883), who in July 1848, the year of Howe's appeal, took into his Barre, Massachusetts, home the 7-year-old son of a distinguished lawyer, the first pupil in America's first private school for children with retardation. While remaining a strong member of the leadership group, he expressed his own beliefs; at its 1877 conference he was the first to criticize Down's ethnic classification. Like Seguin, who thought he best followed his own precepts, Wilbur (1852) believed his pupils could develop to their fullest potential through proper instruction: "At the base of all our efforts lies the principle, that the human attributes of intelligence, sensitivities, and will are not absolutely wanting in an idiot, but dormant and undeveloped" (p. 17). Having begun a tradition of small, private alternatives, he was called in 1851 to head a new public asylum in Albany, New York. Though controversies arose over management and care of residents, apparently despite Wilbur's efforts, the facility, relocated at Syracuse in 1855, was a model for Canadian and European institutions, as well as others in the United States. Dr. and Mrs. George Brown had assumed leadership of the school at Barre, with Katherine Wood Brown (1827–1907) the guiding spirit and a constant voice for normalizing experiences, as the positive tone of her "Reminiscences" (1896, in Rosen et al., 1976) suggests.

With the New York Asylum for Idiots, as it was renamed when moved to Syracuse, New York was the first state to provide full funding for institutional training (Shuttleworth & Potts, 1924). It admitted 7- to 14-year-old children who were not "greatly deformed" or epileptic, and Letchworth's (1903/1974) descriptions of the residents and their educational program imply that few if any were severely impaired; we shall see that leaders tried to hold the line in this regard. Also in 1848, in Connecticut, a single senate vote thwarted a commission's modest request for partial funding, to be complemented by private sources. The rejection represented what Fernald (1893) described as a "settled conviction of a large majority of the citizens of the Commonwealth that idiots were a class so utterly helpless that it was a waste of time even to collect any statistics regarding them" (p. 209). However, 10 years after that setback a commission member, Henry M. Knight (1827– 1880), gave up his medical practice and, like Wilbur, set up a school in his home while continuing to advocate for support. In 1861, legislation authorized the Connecticut School for Imbeciles, with Knight as its superintendent, a role he held until his death.

The Ohio Asylum for Idiotic and Imbecilic Youth began in 1857, like the school for the blind, in a rented cottage in Columbus. Its superintendent, G. A. Doren, would join Knight, Hervey and C. T. Wilbur, Brown, Kerlin, and Seguin to found the Association of Medical Officers of American Institutions for Idiotic and Feeble-Minded Persons. Moved in 1868 to a partially completed structure, it was soon the largest American institution, renamed in 1898 the Ohio Institution for Feebleminded Youth (later the Columbus State School). Subsequent opening of Orient State Institute in

1926 on a farm annex and another in prototypically rural Apple Creek illustrate a trend to locate institutions in remote settings.

As they grew in size, facilities departed further from the vision of Howe
and Seguin. In 1879, Superintendent Kerlin (1880) reported that the Pennsylvania institution admitted 60 and discharged 32. The report of residents'
status was revealing: 162 boys and 71 girls were "under treatment/in training" while 20 boys and 26 girls were described as "stationary" and 19 boys
and 18 girls as "deteriorating . . . through *age* or disease" (emphasis added).
By 1881 the facility was so crowded that Kerlin protested his inability, despite wide notoriety of the case and offers of financial assistance, to admit
two "feeble-minded" children of a multiproblem family of a widower unable to care for his variously afflicted brood. The Pennsylvania Training
School for Feebleminded Children, now Elwyn Institute (honoring its first
president), opened in 1855, in Germantown, outside Philadelphia; financial difficulties and dissension nearly forced it to close within its first year.
This institution, whose role would be pivotal in successive shifts in con-
ceptualization of services, reflected European influences: that of Kern's
school in Leipzig, founded in 1846, Reed's in England, and Seguin's, based
on George Sumner's reports and Dr. Elwyn's own observations of Hervey's
Seguin-inspired program. Through Sumner he was also in contact with
Howe, who sent his star instructor with a letter of introduction.

J. B. Richards (1817–1886) was commended to Howe by Mann, who
was impressed by his work at the New York House of Refuge. Like Howe
an ardent abolitionist, this missionary's son was confident that, like the
hardened young felons he had taught, children with retardation could learn.
Based on Sumner's reports and Seguin's own now well-established reputation, Howe thought him the best model for his new instructor, who accordingly was dispatched abroad. But Richards felt he gained little from
the experience, except confirmation of his own approach, which combined
physical activity, imitation, use of actual objects as in Pestalozzi's object
teaching, repeated practice, monitoring of progress, personal involvement,
and nonpunitive obedience training. While their approaches were quite
similar, he seems not to have had much interest in Seguin's theorizing;
when the enterprise in Pennsylvania again brought them together they did
not get along, though the brevity of his tenure—less than a year—was not
entirely due to his failings as an administrator. For the remaining three
decades of his life he had little success in realizing his vision, having been
succeeded by Seguin, who after about 12 days moved on to start a school
in New York (M. Rosen, 1993 personal communication). The operation
needed greater managerial acumen than either of these gifted educators
could provide.

That ability was provided by Joseph Parrish (1818–1891), a professor of obstetrics in the Philadelphia College of Medicine and a Quaker, who succeeded in resolving the internal conflicts and fiscal crisis; he was also able to communicate his conviction that children with retardation could benefit from schooling, a belief not readily accepted, as we saw, even in the case of deafness and blindness. In 1859, as his success was rewarded with an additional appropriation from the state legislature, the entire operation was moved in Conestoga wagons to nearby Media. Parrish resigned in 1863 to serve as inspector of camps and hospitals during the Civil War, after which he devoted himself to the treatment and public understanding of alcoholism.

His successor, Isaac Newton Kerlin (1834–1893), over the next three decades became the dominant force in the field of retardation in North America. Like Dorothea Dix, who was a strong supporter of his work, he energetically promoted the expansion of institutions, not only maintaining that they were far preferable to the neglect experienced by most children with retardation, but also that those children could not be served in the common schools. He was also convinced better care could be provided in a good institution—like Elwyn, which offered crafts, recreation, music and, in 1879, added a kindergarten—than at home (Scheerenberger, 1983, p. 123). Kerlin was, like Howe, a leader in whom conviction combined with personal force and persuasiveness. It would be his vision, not Howe's, that shaped the emerging network of institutions, increasingly perceived as serving an essential function in American society. While some leaders used their authority in what we today view as most unfortunate ways, their positive contributions should be recognized. Of Walter Fernald (1859–1924), as of Isaac Kerlin, both assessments are true.

Fernald, appointed to head the Massachusetts School for the Feeble-minded in 1887, provided key intellectual and political leadership toward a return to education. Through lectures at Tufts and Harvard, and many publications, he advanced training for professionals in the field. But early in his career, his were among the harshest indictments, which he later retracted, speaking in positive, humane terms about persons with retardation, opposing compulsory sterilization, and calling for services for families and in schools to enable children to remain in their homes. He opposed reliance on mental tests, stressing the need to evaluate an individual's functioning in social contexts, and during a period of sustained pessimism maintained that those with severe impairment could learn. His proposals influenced comprehensive service policies in Massachusetts that presaged national reforms. To understand how one of Fernald's intellect and humanity could have characterized retardation with terms like "burden," "menace," "parasitic," and "predatory" (Fernald, 1912), we must consider changes in the social and intellectual climate.

INTERPRETATIONS OF MENTAL RETARDATION

"Unfortunates" long comprised an undifferentiated mass, the word implying poverty and deviance. Deviance has sometimes been ascribed to social conditions, but often "mental and moral defectives" themselves have been blamed for conditions troubling society. The Poor Laws distinguished the "deserving" from the "undeserving" poor, the latter's state reflecting failing of character, the former's no fault of their own, but perceived needs for social control coexisted with benevolence. In the Age of Reason, "mental alienation," which encompassed retardation, suggested a clear need for containment (Foucault, 1965).

Natural Laws

Just before the dawn of radical hereditarianism, Ireland (1877) wrote that, while most forms of retardation have a biological basis and are accompanied by physical indicators, some may be acquired through trauma or deprivation. The more general view attributed retardation to hereditary transmission, even liberals like Howe invoking moralistic explanations; he was convinced that the presence of defect revealed hereditary taint, chastisement for violation of natural laws. Though her study of deafness on Martha's Vineyard convinced Groce (1992) that such views were not universal among 19th-century New Englanders, reformers implicated intemperance (Ms. Dix's villain), consanguinous marriage, and other proscribed sexual behavior, especially masturbation, to which Howe (1848b) devoted extensive discussion in his treatise on causes. For him it followed that this scourge of humankind, thus caused, could be eliminated if people obeyed the laws ordained by their Creator. That belief echoes through generations of iatrogenic guilt.

While his more enlightened ideas would not prevail, this propensity to ascribe blame became more invidious as it gained "scientific" support. What changed was the attitude toward the child, a reworking of that of centuries earlier, from innocent victim to despised threat. In 1879, the *National Baptist* reported that, while marriage of "kindred" seemed not as frequently the cause of defect as had been supposed, evidence of violation of natural laws was manifest in children themselves, citing a child who "seemed to have no moral nature" but delighted in inflicting pain. Drunkenness or a "vicious disease" (syphilis or tuberculosis), the article noted, or fright or injury of the mother during pregnancy, seemed the "most marked" causes. Citing information from Elwyn, the *Springfield Republican* reported that cretinism resulted from "ancestral pauperism and malnutrition rather than from an enfeebled or simply vicious inheritance." Recurrence of the word *vicious* is revealing, in light of the indictment to come. Explanations increasingly linked sensual excess, tuberculosis, and retardation. Summarizing "the conditions of idiots of the Commonwealth of Massachusetts," Howe (1848a) noted that, of 359 cases of "congenital idiocy"

> one or both of the immediate progenitors of the unfortunate sufferers had in some way widely departed from the conditions of health and violated the natural laws . . . [that is,] . . . one or the other, or both of them, were very unhealthy or scrofulous; or they were hereditarily predisposed to affections of the brain, causing occasional insanity; or they had intermarried with blood relatives; or they had been intemperate, or had been guilty of sensual excesses which impaired their constitution. (p. 34)

Scheerenberger (1983) cites a report by the Committee on Provisions for Idiotic and Feeble-Minded Persons, in 1886, implicating alcoholism in 34% of "idiocy" and tuberculosis in 56%. While differentiating epilepsy, the report associated it with retardation, mental illness, and antisocial behavior. The need for self-control is stressed, but social control is implied. Intermarriage of consumptives was imprudent, while epileptics should refrain from marriage altogether since that "dread disease, or its co-relations of chorea, insanity, and idiocy" was so frequently inherited. A "family history of alcoholism," clearly linked as it was with "causes of epilepsy, nervous disease, and crime in the same inheritance, is an argument for the restraint of alcoholic inebriety" (pp. 112–113).

A Philadelphia paper reported in 1884 that "consumption and venereal troubles are the two chief sources of imbecility in children," the third being intemperance. Bad living yields bad fruit, and their numbers were increasing inexorably. In 1888, the *Christian Register*, citing 1880 census data, described the estimated 78,000 "imbecile, idiotic, or feeble-minded" persons as "a vast army of the idiotic and the weak-minded . . . the effect and the product of causes—crime, alcoholism, licentiousness, epileptic and neurotic diseases—which are more dangerous to the life of the nation than any armed host on the globe." And where, the writer rhetorically asked, is this army quartered? Lamentably, only about 3% were in institutions, others yet languishing in almshouses, but many dangerously maintained in the community. The public must be protected, but since institutions were costly visitors were urged to see for themselves why they were so essential. While pity and approbation were the expected reactions, some, experiencing shock and revulsion, pondered the need for draconian measures; after visiting New York's Children's Hospital and Home for Idiots at Randall's Island, columnist "Brick" Pomeroy called frankly for "Euthanasia" to spare the severely afflicted their suffering and society the burden of their care.

Mind and Body

Physical differences were often wrongly interpreted as evidence of retardation, but cretinism stimulated ultimately successful ameliorative measures. As with other highly visible forms of deviance, superstitious associations had been made, and sometimes persons with cretinism were venerated. Its prevalence in certain regions, especially in the valleys of Switzerland, interested physicians and prompted Napoleon to relocate families, and in 1891 George Murray developed the first means of correcting the underlying thyroid deficiency.

In 1866, the same year that Seguin (1866/1907) termed it "furfuraceous cretinism," Down (1866) identified a condition he called "mongolian idiocy." While concepts of race embodied in his ethnic classification are repugnant today, they were consistent with beliefs of his day, and as Sarason and Doris (1969) noted, Down saw variations within races as "arguments in favor of the unity of the human species" (p. 365). He attributed departures from racial type to "retrogression," reflecting the then influential Darwin-inspired "degeneration theory." Based on susceptibility to the disease, he thought tuberculosis the hereditary factor predisposing this congenital defect. Children with Down syndrome were long presumed uneducable, unable to manage outside of institutions, and unlikely to reach adulthood. In "A General Review of Mongolian Idiocy," E. A. Whitney, a later Elwyn superintendent, and coauthors (1930) concluded from their survey of hypothesized causes—reversion (degeneration), syphilis, exhaustion (due to parental age), alcoholism, and diverse biological factors—that no definitive cause had been established. (The presence of 47 chromosomes, Trisomy 21, was discovered nearly 30 years later.) "With institutional training," they noted, "they are capable of slight development in the simpler tasks," but not of academic learning (p. 15). The situation is a most discouraging one, they concluded, pronouncing it just as well that about 40% died during the first five years of life.

Another profound influence proved astonishingly durable. Broadly, it was the notion that one's inner nature might be discerned on the basis of physical characteristics, most notably through measurement of heads. Franz Joseph Gall (1758–1828), a contemporary of Rush, Tuke, and Pinel, could not have anticipated the enormous popular interest his work would attract but saw evidence in his brain anatomy research supporting observations in prisons and asylums, where he assumed mental traits were well established. Though he shared his observations through lecturing, it was J. K. Spurzheim (1776–1832) who coined the term *phrenology* and brought it to America, in 1832, where it was enthusiastically received.

Based like other 19th-century views of intellect on faculty psychology, phrenology proposed that the exterior shape of the skull conforms to that of the brain; that a number of discrete mental faculties or functions comprise the mind; and that these are differentially located such that unusual endowments are reflected in unusual exterior structure. Spurzheim expanded the list proposed by Reid and Stewart of the Scottish functional school to a total of 37, differentiating the affective (propensities and sentiments) from the intellectual (perceptive and reflective) faculties. Boring (1950) summarized the extraordinary role of this pseudoscience: "At one time there were twenty-nine phrenological societies in Great Britain and several journals. The *Journal of Phrenology* . . . was born in Edinburgh in 1823 and died in Philadelphia only in 1911. Phrenology had flourished for a century!" (p. 57). The fascination with craniometry took even more bizarre forms, as Gould (1981) described, such as the extensive skull collection amassed by Dr. Samuel George Morton of Philadelphia. It was an early manifestation of a persistent theme: the attempt to rate the differential worth of men and, egregiously, of the respective genders, races, ethnic origins, and social classes represented among humankind, as well, which emerged again in the psychometric movement. Persons with retardation would continue to inspire and be victimized by such efforts.

Recapitulation theory and Cesare Lombroso's (1835–1909) theory of "the criminal man," based on atavistic stigmata, were two other anthropometric ideas that affected beliefs about retardation. These were respectively notions, as Gould (1981) noted, about "the ape in all of us" and "the ape in some of us," the former implying relative worth of groups by virtue of evolutionary progress (white males of northern European origin being most advanced), the latter associating criminality with primitive, "ape-like" features. An 1879 newspaper account of a meeting of the Pennsylvania State Medical Society (addressed by "Dr. Seguin, of Paris"), at Elwyn, highlighted one case with particularly Lombrosian overtones. This child, known as the "gorilla boy," was reportedly only presumed to be human, lacking civilized qualities of any sort.

In Lombroso's (1896) "epileptoid model," which delineated criminal epileptics, criminal moral imbeciles, born criminals, criminaloids or occasional criminals, and criminals by passion, "almost every 'born criminal' suffers from epilepsy to some degree" (Gould, 1981, p. 134). Maintaining that such propensity could be detected in young children, his followers urged early prescreening and isolation. Research at the Elwyn laboratory led Kerlin (1885) himself to conclude that brain formation of persons with retardation tended to be similar to that of criminals and to advance the notion of *congenital moral imbecility*, which he thought could be detected early so the child could be confined before old enough to commit crime. The idea reemerged in the form of the "defective delinquent" (Fernald, 1912) and, more sweepingly, Terman (1916, p. 11) echoed the warning of fellow Clark alumnus Goddard (1914): "*Every feeble-minded person is a potential criminal*" (p. 11). Howe's belief that retardation was an evil (as Bell believed of deafness) never transmogrified to belief that the person was evil, but he readily accepted the notion that differences in head size and shape could account for differences in intellect. Samuel Bayer Woodward, Worcester State Hospital's superintendent, also believed in violation of natural laws with respect to causation and phrenology with respect to differential manifestations of mental illness, but like Howe, imputed evil to the affliction, not the afflicted (Rosen et al., 1976).

These ideas had a twofold impact, linking mental defect with moral defect and strengthening enormously the biological determinism that impeded education and amelioration of social conditions, leading to calls for permanent institutionalization and sterilization. By the mid-1920s, 24 states had enacted sterilization laws, and more than 27,000 women had been sterilized. Chief Justice Oliver Wendell Holmes, summarizing the majority opinion in a landmark case before the U.S. Supreme Court, *Buck v. Bell*, likened compulsory sterilization to vaccinations required for the good of society.

Differentiation and Educability

The term *idiocy* was used generically until Jean Etienne Dominique Esquirol (1782–1840), like Itard, Pinel's student, differentiated it as "the utmost limit of human degradation. Here, the intellectual and moral faculties are almost null. . . . Incapable of attention, idiots can not control their senses. They hear, but do not understand; they see but do not regard. Having no ideas, and thinking not, they have nothing to desire; therefore have no need of sign, or of speech" (Esquirol, 1845, p. 467). While supporting Seguin, Esquirol thought "idiots . . . are what they must remain for the rest of their lives" (in Boyd, 1914, p. 91).

Citing the literal meaning, Seguin believed "the idiotic child was one isolated from the social world by grave cerebral incapacity, by severe sensory deprivation, or by a combination of mental and physical defects" (Talbot, 1964, p. viii). Agreeing that there were degrees of "backwardness," Seguin (1843) summarized in a famous dictum that "*L'idiot est un individu qui ne sait rien, ne peut rien, ne veut rien, et chaque idiot rapproche plus ou moins de ce summum d'incapacité*" (p. 107), which Howe (1848b) invoked (paraphrasing that the idiot "knows nothing, can do nothing, cannot even desire to do anything") in presenting a discouraging picture of severe impairment. But he stressed its rarity; "fools," are a "higher class" and a much larger one who, though having "only the faintest glimmer of reason, and very imperfect speech," can voluntarily move, as well as feel and think, while the far more numerous "simpletons" need only guidance in social interactions (pp. 6–7). This three-tiered structure anticipated later terminology: *educable*, *trainable*, and *custodial*. Seguin's (1866/1907) qualification—"when the idiot does not seem to make any progress" (p. 66)—implies a sense of challenge, rather than of futility, which he expressed from the beginning:

> Esquirol has said that idiocy is an incurable disease. . . . I share that opinion, and I know that self-respecting doctors do not boast of curing it; besides, who talks of therapeutic measures for idiots now? However . . . if a cure for those born deaf or blind had been insisted upon, we would not have today the two schools which bring the greatest honor to our country. While waiting for medicine to restore sight and hearing, teaching supplied those two senses. While waiting for medicine to cure idiots, I have undertaken to see that they participate in the benefits of education. (Seguin, 1843, p. 2)

Others recognized differential needs but were less inclusive. Felix Voisin (1794–1872), who had supervised Seguin, listed four classifications: feeble-minded; normal but poorly instructed; those showing "evil *propensitie*" or character abnormality; and those predisposed to mental problems by a parent's insanity. The Orthophrenic Institution, a private school he opened in 1837, provided differential *orthophrenic treatment* for each class of patients (though not "idiots"), but monetary problems forced its closing (Scheerenberger, 1983). England's Duncan and Millard (1866), who distinguished eight levels, and Ireland (1877) saw the distinction between imbecility and idiocy as one of degree. A danger in classifications lies in their implicit continuum of decreasing educability, relegating some individuals to custodial care; Elise H. Martens (1934) later allayed educators' concerns with assurance that "the lowest cases . . . never reach the public school, for they are essentially incapable of learning," and even those "of higher intelligence but still seriously abnormal, show clearly that they cannot adjust to the group life of the classroom" (p. 15). Both groups were long excluded, though Howe, despite his discouraging description of severe impairment, emphasized their common humanity and the importance of intervention:

> We agree with Esquirol, that idiocy is not a disease. We go further, and maintain that it is impossible to fix the point at which idiocy ends and reason begins. . . . Now we claim for idiots a place in the human family. We maintain that they have the germs of the human faculties and sentiments, which in most cases may be developed. Indeed, the number of persons left by any society in a state of idiocy, is one test of the degree of advancement of that society in true and Christian civilization. (quoted in Bremner, 1971, p. 783)

Hervey Wilbur (1852) similarly emphasized, in his second annual report, that while some students presented greater challenges, all could learn:

A certain portion of the younger and more backward pupils are placed in what may be termed the nursery department . . . these children are watched carefully with reference to their habits of body and mind, to the best mode of commencing our course of instruction with them—the most appropriate first steps in their pupilage. Every means . . . are [*sic*] attempted to attract their attention, to exercise their senses, to awaken perceptions, to excite the curiosity and encourage their imitative faculty. (quoted in Bremner, 1970, p. 757)

Maintaining that the word *idiot* should be used in its original sense and that the institution was better called "Asylum for the Innocents," Kerlin nonetheless recognized that the least impaired residents made the best impression. While a report of a tour in conjunction with the 1878 Convention of Poor Directors and Board of Charities described some inmates as "almost totally deficient in respect to intellect," it noted that many "taken from alms houses . . . [were] deaf and mute children and many more simply without family," placed by a Quaker agency. With Elwyn's population growing dramatically, Kerlin was at pains to remind the public of its mission: to "provide an educational home for children of weak, or feeble minds," not an "asylum for paralytic and epileptic idiocy," who presented, with the "morally unsound," a hopeless prognosis. Growing criticism was implied in the *Delaware Advocate*'s questioning, in 1881, of construction to house the "lowest grade of Idiots and Epileptics . . . unfortunately so deeply afflicted that human skill and patience are powerless to do anything for them, except to protect them." "Repulsive and unresponsive as most of these semblances of humanity are," that charity had overlooked them was, to the writer, understandable. Concerned for the entire enterprise, Kerlin found it advisable to separate these "unresponsive" residents.

EDUCABILITY AND LIMITS OF IMPROVEMENT

While humane care was essential, Seguin insisted that treatment involved more than keeping clients "happy," a notion unjustly ascribed to John Charles Bucknill, an associate of Tuke, who thought happiness gained with "usefulness" (Scheerenberger, 1983, p. 82). William W. Ireland (1832–1909) and John Langdon Haydon Down (1826–1896), best known for their work on etiology and classification, had definite ideas about training and, like Seguin, emphasized kind but firm discipline; Down's (1877) counsel that the child must "be taught to subordinate his will to that of another . . . [and] to learn obedience; that right-doing brings pleasure, and that wrong-doing is followed by its deprivation" (p. 139) reflected Itard's lasting influence and presaged systematic use of natural reinforcers. Ireland's (1877) approach drew from Itard, Seguin, and also Pestalozzi, though he favored maternal direction in the early years, with training beginning at age 7. Considering communicative impairment the prime diagnostic indicator of retardation, both accorded language training more prominence than did Seguin, emphasizing that appropriate instruction could be provided only in institutions. Down (1877) advised that "intelligent children will not take part in the amusements and games of feeble-minded ones" (p. 130); thus, attempts to integrate them would result in social isolation. But both advocated training in functional skills, with the goal of maximum vocational independence.

There was growing uncertainty as to whatever "improvement" could be attained was worth the investment. In 1879, the *Springfield Republican* reported that, of the estimated 40,000 or more feeble-minded persons in the United States, about 15,000 were provided training, through which they can achieve a "higher intelligence" than without it: "Some may be cured; almost all improved; but few are hopeless." In a letter to the *New York Times*, L. P. Brockett, M.D., who had eulogized Seguin (as had his son, Edward, also a physician, and Hervey Wilbur), and who had addressed the issue as an authority in his own right (Brockett, 1856), sought to clarify what was possible. According to Seguin's theory, he explained, most persons with retardation have experienced delayed development and need stimulation. Under conditions of ideal treatment, rarely found except in Mrs. Seguin's work at the New York school, he asserted that "complete recoveries" were possible for 8–18%, while 30% could attain "partial" and 40% "considerable" recovery. The remaining 20%, with paralysis, epilepsy, and "other bad heredity," could not be expected to improve.

But the *Delaware Advocate* charged in 1881 that there had been "ridiculous overwrought statements of remarkable 'recoveries' and cures," and the *Philadelphia Times* headlined an 1885 piece on Elwyn "Children All Their Days." Notions of cure and recovery, and a growing mystique, obscured Seguin's contributions; experiences in the increasingly crowded institutions did not yield the hoped-for results as administrators tried to apply his individualized approach en masse. No one thought him a Guggenbuhl, but disappointing results, given the climate, caused even leaders committed to education to look critically at Seguin's writing. Of their countryman, Binet and Simon (1907) wrote, "Seguin impresses us as an empiric endowed with great personal talent, which he has not succeeded in embodying clearly in his works. These contain some pages of good sense, with many obscurities, and many absurdities" (pp. 3–4).

Seguin provides a link between sense-realist philosophers and the study of sensory processes in psychology's early years, as in Preyer's training experiments with hearing and color vision reported in *The Senses and the Will*,

published in 1888 soon after Seguin's death. Of this German physiologist
who turned to child psychology, Fechner, and Wundt, Boring (1950) observed "the 'new' psychology was really physiological psychology" (p. 425).
Seguin's "physiological method" happened to be consonant with it, but
Montessori's scholarly grounding in the area was far more thorough, her
pedagogy continuing to rest on this narrow base after psychology had grown
beyond it.

Extending Itard's belief that dormant senses could be systematically
aroused and enlisted in the service of learning, Seguin postulated an "un-
broken circle" connecting each sense impression with a mental act (reflection) and a function (expression); that training strengthened these connections; and that training of one sense transferred to another and generalized
to the "impression-reflection-expression circle in intellectual and social activities" (Talbot, 1964, p. 116). While drawing on Sicard's methods, Itard
had also been influenced by Condillac's concept that learning is based on
sensory information, but not sharing Condillac's view of the primacy of the
tactile sense, he neglected touch, which Seguin thought "determined the
disappointing outcome of his experiment" (p. 25). While benefiting from
Itard's counsel, Seguin's ideas evolved from his own experience, culminating
in the 1866 publication of *Idiocy and Its Treatment by the Physiological Method*
(1866/1907), containing such case examples as "Psycho-Physiological Training of an Idiotic Hand."

Through his Saint-Simonist connections, Seguin also knew of Pereire's
work and analyzed what he could learn of his techniques, especially his concept (after Condillac) that the senses "are all variations of the sense of touch"
(Talbot, 1964, p. 18) and his adaptations to the pupil's abilities and interests. Like Pereire and Rollin, Seguin (1866/1907) stressed the *unity* of physical, social, and intellectual development, with education "the ensemble of
the means of developing harmoniously and effectively the moral, intellectual, and physical capabilities" (p. 32). He invoked both dimensions of the
concept of *moral education*: humane treatment and training of personal habits and social behavior. The onus was thus on both teacher and pupil in
developing values and responsibility. He emphasized that

> the idiot is endowed with a moral nature sensitive to the eulogy, reproach,
> command, menace, even to imaginary punishment. He sympathizes with the
> pains he can understand; he loves those who love him; he tries to please those
> who please him; his sense of duty and propriety is limited, but perfect in its
> kind; his egotism is moderate; his possessiveness and retentive propensities
> sufficient; his courage, if not Samsonian, is not aggressive, and may easily be
> cultivated. As a collective body, idiotic children are . . . equal in order and de-
> cency . . . to any collection of children in the land. (pp. 64–65)

While this language may sound paternalistic, his use of the word *idiot* had no pejorative connotation. He emphasized that teachers must strive to draw out each child's inherent moral nature, just as they draw out the child's interest and curiosity in mental training. After Rousseau, he stressed that children should be encouraged to explore their world, even at the risk of a broken dish. (Montessori, his direct intellectual heir, counseled use of actual, breakable dishes in her *casas dei bambini*.) In Rousseau's *Emile* (1762/ 1963) he saw guidelines applicable for all children, including his own pupils: "He wants to touch and handle everything; do not check these movements which teach him valuable lessons . . . he learns by looking, feeling, listening, and above all . . . by judging with the eye what sensations [objects] would cause to his hand" (p. 32). Clearly, Seguin's "permissiveness" did not imply absence of discipline or demands (nor had Rousseau's, nor would Montessori's). To the contrary, genuine love is expressed in the responsible exercise of authority, strategic expression of feeling, and consistent guidance. Seguin's (1866/1907) definition of moral treatment involves a very directive role, requiring.

> systematic action of a will upon another, in view of its improvement; in view for an idiot, of his socialization. It takes possession of him from his entrance in to his exit from the institution; from his opening to his shutting his eyes; from his acts of animal life to the exercise of his intellectual faculties. It gives a social meaning, a moral bearing of everything about him. The influences . . . come upon him from prearranged circumstances, from prepared association with his fellows, and, above all, directly from the superior will which plans and directs the whole treatment. (pp. 148–149)

Thus, while encouraging spontaneous activity, when necessary he would exploit that "superior will," permitting no doubt about what must be done: Command, he wrote, "is expressed by attitude, corroborated by gesture, animated by physiognomy, flashed by the look, made passionate by the voice, commented upon by the accent, strengthened by the articulation, imposed by the emphasis, and carried by the whole power of the stronger on the weaker will" (Sequin, 1866/1907, pp. 157–158). Anticipating the "token economies" often used by today's special educators, he allowed pupils to redeem "tickets" earned for good conduct in order to use a garden on Saturdays (French, 1932), but stressed the need to set priorities, ensuring that objectives were attainable. His dictum, "let us only command at first that which we have the power of enforcing" (p. 161), is excellent classroom management advice for teachers and sound parenting counsel. His advice to both is, like Howe's, to eschew "deleterious tenderness," for "a mawkish sensibility opposes itself to any effect at improvement" (p. 153). Compassion meant respect, not low expectations: "To make the child feel . . . loved and . . . eager to love in his turn, is the end of our teaching as it has been its beginning . . . if they have been loved, they are loving in all the degree of human power conformable with their limited synergy" (p. 170). Love, in this sense, *is* enough.

Authority, "the moral power of command," must not be used arbitrarily, "but by a law of descending gradation, it becomes from immediate, mediate, contingent, negative, etc." (Sequin, 1866/1907, p. 63), roughly analogous to prompt hierarchies. The goal is not mere compliance but eventual self-directed activity. The most intrusive form, *immediate command*, involves "the forms of command which can directly touch the child" (e.g., standing directly in front of the pupil and leaving no alternative but to comply; he did not describe physical intervention). It should be used only when less direct methods—"the look"—were not effective. Anticipating another "best practice" concept, he counseled, "What we cannot command, another child will incite; what we cannot explain to a child, he will imitate from another; what a group cannot do after our command, will be done after the example of a small child" (p. 151).

"The physiological method," Seguin (1880) summarized, "trains the organs to exercise their functions, and conversely, exercises the functions to develop their organs" (p. 26). That principle was translated narrowly in institutions into manual training activities. At Elwyn, according to a newspaper report, the "underlying principle is the training of the hand as the means of developing the intelligence." This was to be accomplished through a program of crafts and practical arts, from bead-stringing to sewing and broom-making, and group exercises with Indian clubs and dumb-bells. More critically, as Kerlin (1891) stressed in *The Manual of Elwyn*, caretakers had to be enjoined to refrain from "severities or meanness toward the children" such as "the passionate smacking, rapping of knuckles, pulling of ears, kicking, pinching, scolding, teasing, threatening, etc." (pp. 25–26).

Seguin, like Montessori, is identified today with certain instructional materials. But like hers, Seguin's was a comprehensive pedagogical system, and though both contributed significantly to the development of specialized methods, the approaches of both were predicated on principles applicable to all children. Seguin believed that instruction must be based on observation, consider the "whole child," and emphasize activity and experience with real things, and that "even the most defective child had some spark of understanding upon which learning could be built" (Talbot, 1964, p. 115). Alfred Binet, though critical of his scientific contributions, shared many of Seguin's beliefs and in fact borrowed some of his "tasks" for the scales he developed. Consideration of his influence requires consideration of another development that profoundly affected persons with retardation.

MEASURING INTELLIGENCE

Mental testing emerged from the confluence of Darwinism, child study, and efforts to establish psychology as a science, the dominant concerns of which—basic processes and individual differences (Cronbach, 1957)—came together in psychometric conceptions of intelligence. Such conceptions were predicated on the belief that intelligence could be defined operationally and measured, yielding a technology for discriminating among individuals. What could be inferred from tests depended on assumptions about the construct and empirical evidence of relationships between test results and other data, such as school performance and, were there such, independent measures of "true" intelligence.

Francis Galton (1822–1911), Darwin's cousin, was the first to develop both a formal means to measure abilities and a statistical means of presenting scores. This work, conducted in his laboratory in the South Kensington Museum, was an outgrowth of his studies of "families of eminence" and gained considerable popular notariety. His concept of a bell-shaped distribution portrayed intellect as a trait present in persons in varying degrees; what was measured later shifted from such skills as motor coordination and sensory discrimination, but the notion that people are differentially endowed with some basic underlying ability persisted. His student, Karl Pearson, pursued the application of statistical analysis, seeking to demonstrate relationships between ability scores and other variables. James McKeen Cattell, who in 1890 introduced the term *mental test*, extended Galton's "mental anthropometry" and developed a set of 50 tests at his laboratory at the University of Pennsylvania, measuring such characteristics, still considered in neurological evaluations of persons who have experienced cardiovascular accident or traumatic brain injury, as rate of movement, reaction time, attention, and memory (Boring, 1950).

Test development occurred in various quarters, as psychologists worked to establish an empirical base. The early work, while atheoretical, was not independent of ideology, one issue being the scientific respectability of applied research. Theories that emerged reflected two major themes with important ideological implications: (1) whether intellectual capacity is predetermined and immutable or can be influenced by environmental factors (i.e., "nature versus nurture") and (2) whether it is a single attribute or comprised diverse abilities. At the time testing was introduced in America, hereditary and unitary views were already contributing to a growing negativism concerning retardation (Sarason & Doris, 1969, p. 275).

Having published, with Victor Henri, studies involving measurement of individual differences conducted in France's first psychological laboratory, which he founded at the Sorbonne in 1889, and having founded the nation's first psychological journal, Alfred Binet (1857–1911) was "France's great psychologist of that generation, . . . an experimentalist after the French fashion of stressing individual differences more than apparatus and the techniques for dealing with the average faculties" (Boring, 1950, p. 573). Interest in "higher" faculties led him to address problems involving schooling and to develop an assessment approach involving scrupulously detailed, verbatim recording of responses. His collaboration with Theophile Simon aimed to develop a means to address a practical problem posed by the Minister of Public Instruction in 1904: identifying needs for differential instruction for pupils not benefiting from the regular curriculum.

While the scope of the resulting "ladder for the measurement of intelligence" would soon extend, it was intended as but one component of a multifaceted evaluation as a base for instruction of pupils experiencing learning difficulties (Binet & Simon, 1916). He considered formal testing an extension of comprehensive observation, an aid in classification but an insufficient basis for the individualized, "experimental" approach to teaching he thought essential. While his early research involved perception and memory, he recognized the critical role in schooling of verbal abilities and, especially, *judgment*: "otherwise called good sense, practical sense, initiative, the faculty of adapting one's self to circumstances" (p. 42). For children with retardation, he rejected Seguin's sensory-motor training, favoring "mental orthopedics," which involved training in memory, reasoning, perception, problem solving, and attention (Doll, 1962).

The Binet-Simon scale, introduced in 1905, comprised graduated tasks intended to be as independent of instructional experience as possible. A 1908 revision grouped the tasks according to the age at which they were typically passed, introducing the term *mental age*, which the German psychologist William Stern suggested in 1911 would yield a more stable index if divided by chronological age. In their 1916 revision, which embedded mental testing within Spearman's theory of general intelligence, Terman and his associates added the convention of multiplying by 100, yielding an *intelligence quotient* (*IQ*). Lewis M. Terman (1877–1956), a normal school product, was one of the circle of bright young men attracted to study with Hall. Soon after obtaining his Ph.D., in 1905, he became head of Stanford's psychology department; his Stanford Revision of the Binet Scale, undertaken in 1937 with Maud Merrill, became the "golden standard" for IQ measurement. The other contribution for which he is best known was a longitudinal study, begun in 1921, of 1,500 gifted children, the famous *Genetic Studies of Genius*, comprising four volumes, a fifth in progress when he died. Promulgation of the Binet scale had been accelerated by translations by two other Clark alumni, Henry Goddard (1910) and Frederick Kuhlman (1911). Kuhlman, whose

1903 thesis, "An Experimental Study of Mental Deficiency," reflected his growing interest in that field, was director of research at the Minnesota School for the Feeble-Minded in Faribault, where he established a teacher training program, extended the age range encompassed by test items and, with Rose Anderson, devised the Kuhlman-Anderson Intelligence Test, soon widely adopted in schools.

Although skeptical of Decroly's report that scores paralleled observational ratings and school performance, Goddard found as did Kuhlman that, despite variability, teachers' rankings were significantly correlated with mental age scores (Sarason & Doris, 1969). His published translation of the scales in 1910, standardized with American children, featured a classification scheme he had proposed a year earlier, now based on mental age equivalents: *Idiots* had a mental age of 2 years or less, that of *imbeciles* ranged from 3 to 7, and that of *morons* did not exceed 12 years, each with subgroupings of low, medium, and high-grade "defectives." Establishment of a mental age of 12 as the cutoff for determination of feeble-mindedness, based on findings with institutional subjects, was an interpretative flaw not immediately recognized, but as this concept was applied with the Army Alpha Test in 1917 under the direction of Robert M. Yerkes, it appeared that nearly half the draftees were feeble-minded (Gould, 1981). (Despite improved standardization procedures, some still argued that if most American adults have the mentality of a 14–year-old, access to higher education ought to be carefully restricted.) While pursuing investigations in Darwinian interpretations of human behavior in his Yale primatology laboratory, Yerkes served with Thorndike on the Committee on Inheritance of Mental Traits of the American Eugenics Record Office, established in 1910. (Bell chaired its Committee on Heredity of Deafmutism.)

The eugenic linkage was based on "exaggerated faith in the validity of IQ tests and in the existence of a measurable human quality known as human intelligence [and] . . . the pretentious claim that we can separate conceptually the influences of heredity and environment and calculate the relative importance of each in determining test-taking abilities" (Blum, 1980, p. 275). Concerning retardation, by 1913, Haskell (1944) commented, "the damage was done. The infallibility of the Binet test, of the psychometric method in general, of the mental age, of the I.Q. soon to follow, all this became a fetish to be worshipped and protected from all doubt and attack" (p. 114). And there were attacks. Walter Lippmann, in a series of six articles in the *New Republic* in 1922, criticized the fundamental assumptions of the psychometric movement, insisting that what tests measured was "an unanalyzable mixture of native capacity, acquired habits and stored-up knowledge, and no tester knows at any minute what he is testing":

The claim that we have learned to *measure hereditary intelligence* has no scientific foundation. We cannot measure intelligence when we have never defined it, and we cannot speak of its hereditary basis after it has been indistinguishably fused with a thousand educational and environmental influences from the time of conception to the school age. [IQ testing] . . . in the hands of men who hold this dogma [of fixed, innate intelligence] could not but lead to an intellectual caste system in which the task of education had given way to the doctrine of predestination and infant damnation. (quoted in Steel, 1980, pp. 207–208)

Subsequent tracking and exclusion from schooling, implying a fear of contamination rationalized by professions of concern for the presumably less endowed, proved such concerns well warranted. While Goddard modified his views, other leaders in the field of psychometrics became ever more adamant in calling for sorting, educational and societal. Thorndike (1940) continued to the end of his career to advocate selective breeding, whereby "the able and good . . . beget and rear offspring. . . . One sure service (about the only one) which the inferior and vicious can perform is to prevent their genes from survival" (p. 957). Echoing Galton and Pearson, Lippmann's principal adversary in the *New Republic* debate, Terman (1924) warned that "the fecundity of the family stocks from which our gifted children come appears to be definitely on the wane" (p. 363).

Notions of racial differences in evolutionary advancement had hardened by the 1920s, and by the 1930s relied heavily on IQ tests. While over time Terman's hereditarianism and belief in inherent race differences also wavered, that was not true of all influential psychologists. Henry E. Garrett, Thorndike's student and a president of the American Psychological Association, highlighted Goddard's (1912a) not-yet-discredited Kallikak study in his 1955 *General Psychology* text, material that he retained in the 1961 edition, in the context of alleged racial differences in intellect revealed by IQ tests. Even as the civil rights movement gathered force, and test bias was exposed, Garrett promulgated pamphlets proclaiming the intellectual inferiority of African Americans and warning of the threat of "miscegenation." In fairness, while social scientists are clearly not immune to transparently racist notions, hereditarianism is not tantamount to racism, nor is psychometrics inherently its tool. But the attempt to undergird racism with "scientific" respectability, which reemerged in the 1990s, has arguably been the worst mischief to come of the psychometric movement.

The idea that intelligence is innate, unitary, and immutable was summarized in 1925 by Pearson's heir in Britain, Cyril Burt (1940): "Intelligence is . . . distinguished from attainments—which are acquired and not inborn; from special abilities—which are limited and not general; and from temperament or character—which are, in their essence, emotional rather than intellectual" (p. 281). His position concerning the first was supported by an impressive array of data from twin studies. Apologists at first dismissed inconsistencies Kamin (1974) found in reanalyzing Burt's data, but further analyses demonstrated incontrovertibly that he had fabricated much of it, even inventing "investigators," one of the greatest frauds in the history of science. A biographer (Hearnshaw, 1979) attributed his actions to near-pathological depression over the ascendancy of liberal, behavioral, and environmentally oriented perspectives and decline in reliance on IQ testing in British schools. In any case, his scientific legacy continued through H. J. Eysenck and R. B. Cattell, whose dissertations he directed, and an American psychologist, Arthur Jensen, whose thesis of inherent intellectual differences aggravated racial tensions already exacerbated by reports of disproportionate representation of African-American pupils labeled mildly retarded and placed in special classes. We return to this most troubling issue in Chapter 10.

DAY CLASSES

It was inevitable that Seguin's interests would extend to general education, but it was not at all inevitable that schools would include pupils with retardation. The idea was advanced early for children with impaired hearing, but there is no indication that it was considered for those with impaired intellect. The residential school model was firmly in place in both instances, but in the latter it was supported by social, as well as pedagogical, considerations. We saw that many deaf persons believe that true with deafness, though in a different way. In both instances, interestingly, day classes originated in Germany.

European Beginnings

In an 1820 pamphlet, the first publication on education of children with retardation, Johann Traugott Weise (1793–1859) recommended that Hilfsklassen (special classes) be formed in Hilfsschules (Auxiliary Schools) (Scheerenberger, 1983, p. 83). Nearly four decades passed before the first was opened, at Halle in Saxony, in the year of Weise's death. The concept's appeal can be attributed to a general view among Germans that the Volksschule should teach all children, though that very argument could be used to oppose specialized instruction for some. But the long delay was due mainly to the novelty of the notion that children with retardation could benefit from instruction at all; the models that had only just come into existence involved segregation rather than inclusion in society, asylum rather than exposure to the world, and confinement in a controlled milieu. In America, institutions continued to be considered "indispensable" for "the blind, the deaf, the mentally deficient, and the socially maladjusted or juvenile delinquents," as well as

> two other groups . . . found in a type of residential institution which has the double function of providing both hospitalization and education . . . (1) crippled children who are in need of hospital care, and (2) epileptics, for whom long-term treatment is important. . . . When the handicap is a double or triple one, for example, in the case of the deaf-blind, the cripple-feeble-minded, or the the deaf-blind-feeble-minded, the problem becomes increasingly compli-cated. (U.S. Dept. of the Interior, Office of Handicapped Children, 1928, 1939, pp. 1–20)

While American institutions struggled to maintain a focus on individu-als with good prognosis, those in Europe were considered appropriate for only the most severely impaired (Maennel, 1909). Fernald (1904) remarked that many pupils in Auxiliary Schools he visited functioned at a lower level than most in American institutions, and Charles Bernstein (1920), notable for his innovative community-based training, reported that the vast major-ity of admissions to the facility in Rome, New York—about 80%—were "morons or borderline cases" (p. 1). More readily received in Europe, where retardation was viewed less negatively, the day-class concept spread to other countries: Norway (1874); Switzerland (1888); Prussia (1892); Austria (1895); England (1898); Denmark, Holland, and Belgium (1900); Sweden (1904); and France (1909). In Italy, deSanctis incorporated Montessori's methods in a day "asylum school" he opened in Rome in 1899 for 40 poor children with retardation (Kanner, 1964). The goal of auxiliary education was, as for all students, that pupils "become useful members of society" (Maennel, 1909, p. 84). Distinctive aspects involved organizing instruction in consideration of the "demands of mental energy required," as well as physical exertion (i.e., no afternoon session, since many pupils had to walk some distance); stimulation of each "different side of the child's nature"; and standardized curriculum, "the same subject . . . taught in every class at the same time" (pp. 134–136).

In Britain, indirect support for day classes had come in the form of sup-port for care for children with retardation at home. Seeing that as desirable, Duncan and Millard (1866) advised parents to provide good physical care, exercise, and habit training, guided by kindness and respect expressed through positive expectations (Scheerenberger, 1983, p. 82). G. E. Shuttle-worth (1899) reported that London's first day class was formed in 1892; by 1899, with responsibility formally assigned to the schools through Parlia-mentary act, the enterprise in London alone extended to more than 2,000 pupils, taught by 86 teachers in 43 school locations (implying an average class size of 23). That information, shared in the *Journal of Psycho-Aesthenics*, the organ of what became the American Association on Mental Deficiency (now Mental Retardation), was the only reference that year to day classes. But the following year it included a report on the first American classes, formed in 1896 in Providence, Rhode Island (Esten, 1900), and a paper (Channing, 1900) urging enrollment beginning at age 3 or 4.

Elizabeth Farrell's Ungraded Classes

Noting that Howe had envisioned the education of exceptional children as a "link in the chain of common schools," Wallin (1914, p. 29) saw in Auxiliary Schools a model for the United States. Another model for instruction for pupils with retardation, he suggested, was the classes for "refractory and truant" pupils instituted in New York (1874) and for "backward" pupils in Cleveland (1879). The main concern appears to have been with pupils who didn't seem to "fit," irrespective of cause (Ysseldyke & Algozzine, 1982). It was less an issue of retardation than one of cultural difference and problem behavior, factors that continued to influence which pupils were placed. Having herself set up an experimental class at the Henry Street Settlement, Lillian Wald persuaded the New York school system to engage a teacher, recommending 19–year-old Elizabeth E. Farrell (1870–1932), later co-founder, in 1922, and first president of the International Council for Exceptional Children. The class she was assigned in 1889, Farrell (1908–1909) recalled, simply

> grew out of conditions in a neighborhood which furnished many serious problems in truancy and discipline (and) . . . was made up of the odds and ends of a large school. There were over-age children, so-called naughty children, and the dull and stupid children. They were taken from any and every school grade. The ages ranged from eight to sixteen years. They were the children who could not get along in school. They were typical of a large number of children who even today are forced directly or indirectly out of school; they were the children who were interested in street life; many of them earned a good deal of money in one way or another. While some . . . had been in trouble with the police, as a class they could not be characterized as criminal. They had varied interests but the school, as they found it, had little or nothing for them. If these boys were to be kept in school they had to be interested. They had to be shown that school could be more than mere study of books in which they had no interest. They had to be convinced that to attend school was a privilege not a punishment. This "about face" on the part of these boys was accomplished after many months. (pp. 91–92)

Working from no particular theory of learning or of retardation, Farrell adopted a pragmatic approach drawn from experience teaching in an ungraded rural school. In 1906 she was appointed head of the newly formed Department of Ungraded Classes, formalized in 1908 as a citywide special education program. At the time of her death in 1932, it comprised a teaching staff of about 500, the Psychoeducational Clinic, and a program of home visitation, staffed at first with volunteer social workers but since 1917 by full-time visiting teachers. There had by no means been a marked shift to a day-class model; by 1917 all but four states had at least one institution and some had several. To Farrell (1908–1909), the priority was quite different from that expressed by their leaders, which was to find children with retardation and segregate them. While seeing a "need for further classification," she believed schools should respond to pupils in their diversity, a philosophy expressed in the names of the organization she founded, the Ungraded Class Teachers' Association, and of its journal: *Ungraded.*

Institutional leaders' opinions about the role of day classes were summarized by the superintendent of the Training School at Vineland. Formerly called the New Jersey Home for the Education and Care of Feeble-Minded Boys and Girls, that program had begun in the home of the Reverend S. Olin Garrison (1853–1900), a larger facility purchased through donations as referrals multiplied. Garrison's successor, E. R. Johnstone (1870–1946), who led the institution for more than four decades, inaugurated a research department, a teacher training program, and an influential journal, the *Training School Bulletin.* Johnstone (1908) supported the special-class idea, but saw it mainly as a "clearing house" for "not only the slightly blind and partially deaf" but also, "the incorrigibles, the mental deficients, and cripples. . . . The only thing to do is to give them the best of care and training possible. Keep them in the special classes until they become too old for further care in school, and then they must be sent to the institutions for safety" (p. 115). Whether for their safety or ours he did not say.

The special class is then a holding operation and a clearinghouse. But were the classes fulfilling such roles, and were pupils given "the best of care and training"? The New York schools turned to an expert, Johnstone's director of the Department of Psychological Research, to evaluate the program. Henry Goddard (1912b) noted the steady increase in the number of these classes in New York, from 14 in 1906 to 131 at the end of the 1911–1912 school year, housed in 95 schools and enrolling about 2,500 pupils. But he calculated, based on a presumably conservative prevalence rate, about six times that number should be placed. The district must improve its efforts to identify its feebleminded pupils for placement in the ungraded classes. But there were problems with the classes, the most basic concerning what was taught. Is it worthwhile, he asked, to attempt to teach these pupils to read, write, and cipher? Though some can learn such skills, the instructional content should be vastly different from the regular curriculum. A related concern involved qualifications of the teachers. To address these ills, Goddard recommended that more supervisors be appointed.

Each of these ideas has a ring of familiarity, for the concerns identified are concerns today. Though she must have appreciated the implied endorsement of her department's role, Farrell (1914) bristled. Allowing that greater attention should be devoted to identifying eligible pupils, she disagreed vigorously with the recommendation of how that should be done: entirely by means of the scales for measuring intelligence Goddard was enthusiastically promulgating. Her response is studded with quotations from American and European leaders, including Binet himself, concerning limitations of the tests: The technology had not been perfected, results were sometimes misleadingly low, the procedure was costly in staff time. But her main concerns were those of Fernald and Binet, that such tests do not provide a complete picture of the pupil and are an insufficient basis for planning instruction.

While agreeing that it was important for pupils to learn to do household work, she stressed that their abilities were quite diverse; the curriculum must address these differences, not deny opportunities based on classification. The teachers, for their part, would continue to seek additional training, an area to which Farrell made important contributions, having begun an in-service program in 1911 and taught a course at the University of Pennsylvania in 1912. She subsequently lectured at New York University, developed a training program at the Oswego Normal School, her alma mater, and from 1916 until her death taught special education methods and administration courses at Teachers College, Columbia University (Warner, 1944). In noting that building principals were not knowledgeable about the program, Goddard had both hit a nerve and identified a problem that has persisted; while the rest of a school's instructional program was overseen by the principal, ungraded class teachers were supervised by "special inspectors." Farrell (1914) may have felt a degree of investment in this separation, as have many of her successors through the years, but concluded that the consultant had provided only "a series of doses prescribed for present ills," rather than a broad vision:

> The service given by Rousseau to general education, by Pestalozzi to the education of poor children, by Horace Mann to public education in the United States, is similar to that expected from Dr. Goddard for the education of mentally defective children when he was employed by the School Inquiry Committee to investigate the aim, methods, and results of ungraded class work. To be unable to see the forest for the trees is sad. To have missed the vision is sadder still. (p. 45)

Farrell (1915) herself presented data supporting the role of the ungraded classes in preparing pupils for the "larger world of affairs." Only 4% of 350 former pupils were in institutions, 54.8% were employed, and 8.8% of those not working were reported able to do so. Even the 24.6% living with their families reportedly made an economic contribution. Her own vision, expressed posthumously in the New York City Board of Education Schools Report for 1944, clearly differed from Goddard's, at least at that point in his career:

> We need a staff at the Psycho-Educational Clinic that will grow in number and in quality. . . . We need enough ungraded classes to care for all needy children. We need to teach them better. We need the research in teaching technique and in subject matter which sufficient and adequate supervision can make possible. These are our needs. They can and will be satisfied when it is perceived distinctly that adjustment in school is the only guarantee we have of adjustment in the larger world of affairs. If we do not achieve with each child success commensurate with his powers and his abilities we may be certain that we insure failure and its concommitant maladjustments. (p. 120)

"What Is Special About Special Education?"

This now-familiar question would be formally posed in the 1960s, especially with respect to pupils labeled mildly retarded (Dunn, 1968). In the formative years, public school provisions were positive alternatives to exclusion, while presumably beneficial for regular teachers and typical pupils. But how would the experiences of those placed be different from those they would have had through the regular curriculum? Though that question seemed to receive little attention, classes proliferated. Wallin's (1914) *The Mental Health of the School Child*, reporting the first national survey of public school arrangements for exceptional pupils, noted that several states had formed classes for "slow," "mentally defective," or "backward" pupils, but while state support for institutional placement was commonly provided, most special classes were formed through local initiatives without state subsidy. In 1929, with 16 states having enacted at least permissive legislation, 266 districts had established 2,552 classes, enrolling 46,625 pupils with retardation. Though that enrollment nearly doubled by 1934, with classes in 427 communities, it represented a small minority of those presumably eligible. In New York, the number of classes statewide increased from about 50 in 1918 to 1,039 in the 1935–1936 school year, 535 of which were in New York City, and then remained stable at that level through 1944, with about 100 additional units in New York City being offset by decreases elsewhere in the state (New York City Board of Education, 1944).

"That special classes are an accepted fact is attested by their increase in number," proclaimed a New York Schools bulletin (1944, p. 3). Elise Martens (1934) recommended that schools provide for about 90% of children with retardation, who could become fairly independent through special-class instruction, excluding those considered "uneducable" and "unable to adjust" (p. 15). But the reality differed in two respects: considerably more than 10% were excluded and, even with rapid postwar expansion, the number of classes did not approach that presumably required to accommodate all eligible pupils. As Sarason and Doris (1969) observed, while those assigned met IQ criteria, "it will come as no surprise to the reader familiar with urban education to learn that the other major basis for special class placement was misbehavior" (p. 54). The principal concern of school officials being management, not differential classification, diagnostic criteria were used to justify placement decisions originating with teachers' referrals for difficult behavior. Wallin (1924), like Farrell, believed special-class assignment should be based on educational needs, rather than IQ eligibility, and that the goal for many should be return to regular class.

As in England, these classes differed mainly in size and in pupils' age span. In New York, standards stipulated a maximum class size of 18 students if the age range exceeded four years, but if the age span were smaller 22 could be enrolled, as many as 25 if a large school grouped more homogeneously. This rather large class size was nevertheless smaller than that of regular classes and much smaller than those in institutions, where, according to Martens (1934), ratios of one teacher for 70 pupils were common. However, while Farrell's ungraded-class concept explicitly addressed the wide variability among pupils, some teachers simply provided "whole-group" instruction for a smaller number. Concerned about this tendency, inspectors (Goldstein & Peyser, 1933) urged that teachers "must not be conditioned to a fixed pattern of attitude and procedure" (p. 17). They also expressed concern that inappropriate placement accounted in some degree for the wide variability, recommending that pupils with physical disabilities or who were "mentally maladjusted" be placed in other classes "suited to their needs" (p. 17).

Except for eclectic borrowing from Seguin and Montessori, no distinctive pedagogy had emerged in America, but in Europe another physician-turned-educator, Ovide Decroly (1871–1932), left his practice in Paris in 1901 to open a school for children with retardation in his native Belgium, the first of several in which he pioneered methods soon adopted by other European special educators. In its use of games, active learning, activities based on individual children's interests, and experience with real objects, his approach showed Pestalozzian influence. Pupils learned mathematical concepts through counting and measuring things in their environment and integrated reading and writing in developing their own books. His "centers of interest" anticipated today's learning centers and thematic organization of content as units but, like Montessori's classroom arrangement, reflected concerns of living, developed around the basic needs of food, protection from the elements, defense against common dangers, and work (Hamaide, 1924). Also like her believing his methods appropriate for all, he turned his attention to general education (Decroly & Decroly, 1932). His work had little impact in America until translated by Alice Descourdes, whose own text, *The Education of Mentally Defective Children* (1928), stressed "natural activity," "perceptual knowledge and sensory training," "correlation or concentration" (activities organized around a central theme), individualization, and "the utilitarian character of the teaching"—that is, practical skills aimed earning a living (pp. 54–55).

American institutions provided training in work skills, but it was limited to institutional living and often in the service of the facility. Increased emphasis on preparation for the broader world of work was influenced by an individual who represented a bridge between institution and school. As a teacher in New York, Meta L. Anderson (1878–1942) had seen needs for individualized instruction, which led her to take a summer class at Vineland. Noting her abilities, Johnstone and H. H. Godeland commended her to the Newark school district, where in 1910 she extended special classes to the secondary level, with individualized methods of occupational preparation described in her text, *Education of Defectives in the Public Schools* (1917). After a year in Serbia as head of Reconstruction Aid, she returned in 1920 to head Newark's program, earning a Ph.D. at New York University in 1922 and becoming the first educator to serve as president of the American Association on Mental Deficiency (Irvine, 1978).

In October 1934, the U.S. Office of Education sponsored a three–day conference on the education of pupils with retardation, led by Elise H. Martens, chief of its Section on Exceptional Children and Youth. The resulting report (Martens, 1935) stated that objectives and specialized curricula should be based on educating each child:

> (1) . . . *in keeping with with his capacities, limitations, and interests*; (2) . . . *for achievement on his own level*, without attempting to force him into activities beyond his abilities; (3) . . . *for some participation in the world's work* and also *for participation in those social and cultural values which are within his reach*; and (4) . . . with *full consideration of the best interests of all children.* (p. 134)

These broad principles left considerable room for interpretations, which Scheerenberger (1983) grouped as reflecting three schools: conservatives (who focused on limitations and emphasized habit training), progressives (who emphasized social experiences as well as preparation for adult living), and those, like Wallin, advocating "a more flexible approach" of remediation for pupils able to return to regular classes, but academic as well as personal-social adjustment preparation for all (p. 206). Conservatives' thinking was influenced by economic conditions; as one educator (Berry, 1923) stated, "The folly of attempting to make skilled laborers out of this type of individual, when twenty percent of the normal population gainfully employed are engaged in unskilled labor, is self evident" (p. 133). The development of instructional methodology had become a focus of scholarship as well as policy, however, as discussed in Chapter 9. But many children with retardation were excluded from school, while the majority who were in school did not receive special education, the former a matter of policy, the latter of limited resources.

Gesell (1924) stressed that, although retardation cannot be cured, in all but the most severe cases "it will respond very definitely to treatment" (p. 275), by which he meant *education*, beginning in infancy, emphasizing personal habits and social skills, and aimed at ultimate employability within the community where, with support of agencies, relatives, and "self-appointed friends," the person's life can be "relatively contented and safe" (p. 276). Today's conceptions and goals, while more ambitious than contentedness and safety, do not seem altogether different. Should they be? Scheerenberger (1987) concluded that the "quarter century of progress" (1960–1985) was, despite impressive medical advances, social programs, and new educational opportunities, also "a period of uncertainty [in which] promise far outweighed progress" (p. 259). Psychological theory and research concerning intellectual impairment long reflected a "difference orientation" (Zigler, 1966), a normative rather than a "competence" view (Biklen & Duchan, 1994). Does what society now calls "mental retardation" make some people, and some children, different in fundamental ways? Recalling Howe's affirmation, "*They are us,*" we might more usefully ask: What does a child—any child—need in order to feel, and to be, valued and valuable, loved and competent, maximally independent yet part of a social network? In any event, study of retardation led to identification of "new categories," discussed in Chapter 9, which in turn influenced policies and practices affecting children labeled mentally retarded.

CHAPTER 7

Body, Mind, and Spirit: Children's Physical and Health Impairments

CULTURAL IMAGERY AND SOCIAL FORCES

To differ from the norm physically has often been thought to signify mental deviation, the "handicap" thus imposed by others. Prejudice and myth have also impugned the social and moral qualities of persons with physical impairments; they were to be feared and avoided. Examples abound in fairy tale and fiction: an evil character uses a prosthesis, walks with an abnormal gait, is unusually large or small in stature, or is distinguished by "fits," facial disfigurement, or abnormal appendages (Thurer, 1980). But images of impotence and fragility are also found, and of endearing qualities of "cuteness," the person reduced to the status of a pet or permanent child. Helplessness and dependency in a child are acceptable, even expected, but while the "poster child" strategy has been successful in appealing to sympathy, children with disabilities grow up to become adults.

Stereotypes are challenged when one known to have begun life normally experiences impairment, which occurred on a massive scale, as Cruickshank observed, in the wake of World War II, a "maiming war" (in Aiello, 1976). As with other areas of exceptionality, self-advocacy has had profound impact. Successful campaigns for elimination of architectural and other physical barriers have reminded those who are "temporarily able-bodied" that physical disability is not something that affects just an unfortunate few; it is part of the universal human condition. So too with illness, in Susan Sontag's (1978) phrase "the night side of life, a more onerous citizenship." She explains: "Everyone who is born holds dual citizenship, in the kingdom of the well and in the kingdom of the sick. Although we all prefer to use only the good passport, sooner or later each of us is obliged, at least for a spell, to identify ourselves as citizens of that other place" (p. 3). It may be that deep knowledge that motivates some to try to distance themselves from infirmity, whether through barriers, consciously or unconsciously imposed, or even benign sympathy.

While progress has been greatly enhanced by public education, civil rights legislation, and technological advances, medicine has had a central role in the history of services for children with physical impairments, for unlike other disabilities theirs are explicitly medically determined and defined. But no child's essential characteristics are medical in nature. Historical events have served to shift the focus of attention to successive medical conditions, influenced social policy as well as philanthropy, led to provisions for schooling, and inspired public health measures. Virulent strains of influenza have been responsible for epidemics of encephalitis like that of 1918, and often death; the 1918 "flu" pandemic caused more deaths in a single year than did the bubonic plague during its 4-year devastation of Europe (Henig, 1992). Fear of infection gripped all nations; in England, "in church, trains, and other public places people wore antiseptic masks of flesh-colored gauze over nose and mouth" (Graves & Hodge, 1940/1963, p. 23). Between 20 and 40 million deaths, more than twice the number of World War I fatalities, occurred among the approximately 2 billion people throughout the world who contracted influenza that winter.

Events such as epidemics, wars, and population shifts have sometimes generated or exacerbated hostilities associated with impaired health, even the tendency to blame the victim and interpret illness as divine retribution. Such has been the case with tuberculosis and cancer, and is today, with blame implicit in labels like "AIDS babies" and "crack kids." Medical and public health advances have been immeasurably important in treating, even potentially or actually preventing, many threats to life and health, but changes in societal attitude do not necessarily follow immediately. And for children, in any case, much more than a medical situation is involved by virtue of the nature of childhood.

EXPERIENCES OF CHILDREN

Pale and haggard faces, lank and bony figures, children with the countenances of old men, deformities with irons upon their limbs, boys of stunted growth, and others whose meagre legs would hardly bear their stooping bodies, all crowded on the view together; there were the bleared eye, the hare-lip, the crooked foot, and every ugliness or distortion that told of unnatural aversion conceived by parents for their offspring, or of young lives which, from the earliest dawn of infancy, had been been one horrible endurance of cruelty and neglect. There were little faces which should have been handsome, darkened with the scowl of sullen dogged suffering; there was childhood with the light of its eye quenched, its beauty gone, and its helplessness alone remaining; there were vicious-faced boys brooding, with leaden eyes, like malefactors in a jail; and there were young creatures on whom the sins of their frail parents had descended, weeping even for the mercenary nurses they had known, and lonesome even in their loneliness. With every kindly sympathy and affection blasted in its birth, with every young and healthy feeling flogged and starved down, with every revengeful passion that can fester in swollen hearts, eating its evil way to their core in silence, what an incipient Hell was breeding there! (Dickens, 1839/1978, pp. 151–152)

Dickens's portrait of the pupils of Dotheboys Hall may have stung his contemporaries, but it should not have strained their credulity. Such scenes in "schools" for rejected children, whether entrepreneurial or charitable operations, were not uncommon in England in the 1830s. They provided a means of abandonment often far crueler than that practiced in the Dark Ages, and the novelist intended to disabuse anyone of the notion that children remanded to the tender mercies of a Wackford Squeers would be beneficiaries of "the kindness of strangers" (Boswell, 1988). Of the church-run "ragged schools" he confessed, "My heart so sinks within me when I go into these scenes, that I almost lose the hope of ever seeing them changed" (in Kaplan, 1988). For each sunny Tiny Tim in Dickens's world there were many more lame Smikes, "dispirited and hopeless" (p. 143). But both archetypes shared poverty, and in America as in Europe a child with orthopedic impairment and of poor family, like Anne Sullivan's brother Jimmy, was likely to die for lack of treatment or from infection incurred in a crowded almshouse.

"Children circulated restlessly" in New York's almshouse hospital, where in 1810 "most wards were a hodgepodge of ages and sexes, of disabilities and ailments" (Rosenberg, 1987, p. 17). But unless already in almhouses, few sick children saw the inside of a hospital. Even as general hospitals emerged—in Philadelphia (1752), New York (organized in the 1770s and opened in the 1790s), and Boston (1821), hospital care was far removed from the experience of most Americans. The preponderance of early 19th century hospital patients were poor: Irish immigrants, sailors and "fallen women" with venereal diseases, and persons thought insane. Since colonial times, a child of intact family who became ill was put to bed, but rarely seen by a doctor (though in the Plymouth colony some persons with reputations for medical knowledge "probably took 'patients' into their homes" (Demos, 1970, p. 80). Treatments were based on traditional wisdom, but since recovery was in God's hands the most efficacious treatment was prayer. Such diseases as scarlet fever often left a child with impaired vision or hearing, or both, and sometimes with orthopedic impairments. Others incurred crippling injury in the course of work or play, more often the former. Often the cause could only be surmised. Although children's impairments might have economic consequences, and long-term implications in terms of a daughter's marriageability or a son's independence, they were often regarded with resignation, as misfortunes that, depending on a family's resources, might have greater or lesser impact.

FOUR OVERVIEWS

Physical impairments are extraordinarily diverse, in adults as well as in children, as is their impact on life experiences. It is beyond the scope of this chapter to review the historical information bearing on all the neuromotor, orthopedic, and health impairments that children experience. Certain conditions, however, have had unique significance in the history of services for children.

Epilepsy (Convulsive Disorder)

We considered the historical background of convulsive disorder in Chapter 1 as prototypic of the linking of science and superstition. Though the list of famous historical figures with epilepsy is impressive—it includes Socrates, Alexander the Great, Napoleon Bonaparte, Vincent Van Gogh, and Alfred Nobel—convulsive disorder was long associated with retardation, one of the 10 types of "idiocy" in Ireland's (1877) classification scheme. Until Charcot distinguished it from hysteria, it was also confused with psychic disturbance. Advances in neurology led to a more accurate understanding, as John H. Jackson correctly attributed the cause of seizures to excessive electrochemical discharge of nerve cells in the brain. Still, such influential physicians as Moses Alan Starr (1904) described a pessimistic prognostic picture. The prevailing American view—as of retardation, mental illness, congenital deformity, sensory impairment, constitutional weakness, predisposition to diseases (especially tuberculosis), "pauperism," and criminality—attributed it to "degenerative inheritance." The American Breeders Association in 1913 targeted all these "socially unfit classes" to be "'eliminated from the human stock if we would maintain or raise the level of quality essential to the progress of the nation and our race'" (in Scheerenberger, 1983, p. 154).

As confinement in institutions was endorsed, some, like the Minnesota School for the Feeble-minded and Colony for Epileptics, formed separate units, and separate facilities began to appear, the first in the United States a private facility for children under 14, opened in Baldwinsville, Massachusetts, in 1882 (Sarason & Doris, 1969, p. 251). Ohio's, founded in 1891, was the first state institution; by 1932 eight more states had established such facilities (Bremner, 1970, p. 864). Although day classes were introduced, first in Cleveland, in 1906, institutional placement continued to be far more frequent, and Cleveland's program was in fact shortly abandoned. It was thought that children should be placed as early as the condition was diagnosed, with the expectation that the colony would be their permanent home, as the Ohio Hospital for Epileptics 1896 annual report suggests:

> The children . . . adapt themselves more readily to their new surroundings . . . until the Hospital becomes in fact, as well as name, a real home to them. The major part of those who are unfortunately destined to bear their afflictions indefinitely will become permanent residents, and should be fitted by education and training of a mental, as well as manual, character to become useful members of the colony. (quoted in Bremner, 1970, p. 865)

Amid such fatalism there were more hopeful indications. That same report stressed that "those who have the good fortune to recover should not be deprived of the advantages of school life during their residence here" (p. 865). Moreover, as further advances in neurology confirmed Jackson's hypotheses, medications for seizure control advanced from Locock's use of bromides in 1857, to Hauptmann's introduction of phenobarbitol in 1912, to the first nonsedative medication, diphenylhydantoin, developed by Merritt and Putnam in 1937, a major breakthrough. By the 1960s, a variety of anticonvulsant medications were differentially prescribed, based on the individual's unique situation.

Cerebral Palsy

Two paradoxical consequences of the belief that "epileptics and paralytics" represented forms of severe retardation were, first their exclusion from training schools based on presumed uneducability, and then, as these became essentially custodial receptacles, their confinement. In spite of medical advances by the 1860s, old assumptions continued to prevail; the superintendents of the ever-expanding American institutions long assumed neither condition amenable to education. Prenatal and perinatal causes of birth defects associated with cerebral palsy had been identified by W. J. Little, who defined its etiology and characteristics in 1862—hence the designation "Little's disease." His observations concerning histories of prematurity and difficulties in delivery among children at the Earlswood Asylum led to improved prenatal and perinatal care, if not immediately to realization that many were not cognitively impaired. Children with cerebral palsy have constituted the largest single "group" of children with physical disabilities identified as eligible for special education, though many do not need or receive special education. In view of its great diversity, this developmental disability is a broad rubric encompassing varying degrees and types of motor impairment, usually involving abnormal tone and impaired voluntary control of muscle groups affected, depending on location of the brain lesion.

Cerebral palsy was not a focus of the first school programs for children with physical impairment, though no doubt some with mild motor involvement were among those enrolled, while others were in regular classes. This began to change after World War II. In the United States, the individual most responsible for focusing attention on the educational needs of children with cerebral palsy, and in promoting a key role for the then still new field of physical therapy, was Winthrop M. Phelps, an orthopedic surgeon. In a private school in Baltimore, Phelps trained numerous teachers and therapists, advocating strongly for individualized physical management to enhance mobility and prevent deformities. But he was keenly aware that the needs of children transcended physical care.

In England, a large-scale study of 3,700 children with cerebral palsy (Dunsdon, 1952) revealed wide variation in learning needs, though the investigator recommended separate schools to provide more functional training than was available in the regular curriculum. The first of several British schools specifically for pupils with cerebral palsy (in Britain, the term *spastics* has typically been used), St. Margaret's in Croydon, was founded in 1947 by a private organization (Taylor & Taylor, 1960, p. 149). In Scotland, the Westerlea School for Educable Spastics was established in Edinburgh in 1948, two years after the Scottish Council for the Care of Spastics (p. 398), a counterpart of the United Cerebral Palsy Association (UCPA) organized in the United States in 1949.

Other nations instituted similar programs during this period, such as the "Children's Castle" hospital in Helsinki, Finland, founded in 1918, which in 1948 added a school for children with cerebral palsy that also enrolled pupils with congenital malformations (Taylor & Taylor, 1960, pp. 175–176). Other programs that emerged in Europe after World War II included one in Portugal, established in 1958 (p. 378). Many such facilities were residential and geared to older children, but the nursery classes soon introduced by such agencies in the United States as the Society for Crippled Children allowed children to live at home. In addition to providing a range of services, that agency, UCPA, and others worldwide undertook significant programs of advocacy to promote understanding of cerebral palsy, especially when the war had ended.

Curiously, these advances may have obscured the reality that neurological impairment can affect a child's perceptual processes, learning style, cognitive abilities, and socioemotional development. That concern was, at all events, expressed by William Cruickshank (1949), who cautioned that so much emphasis was placed on physical management that many parents and professionals assumed that the child's needs were exclusively physical. He stressed the importance of comprehensive services across the life span, and the program of research he and his students at Syracuse University instituted addressed children's learning and socioemotional needs (e.g., Cruickshank, 1952). His observations that impaired perception in some children with cerebral palsy, where there was known brain injury, interfered with academic learning led him to investigate similar interfering patterns in instances of suspected minimal impairment. The importance of this work, based on formulations of Alfred Strauss, in the early development of programs for pupils with learning disabilities, is discussed in Chapter 9.

But cerebral palsy encompasses such great diversity that no generalizations are warranted about educational issues. Mobility and communication needs in themselves indicate the need not for special education but rather for adaptive strategies or equipment. Vision and hearing acuity, as well as perceptual processing, are more likely to be impaired than in the general population, but many do not experience such difficulties. Persons with cerebral palsy, like those with deafness or blindness, reflect the full range of intellectual ability. One's physical involvement may be severe, with significant impairment of mobility, communication, and self-care skills. Intellectual ability, even special talents, may be masked, as Christy Brown's (1955) autobiographical *My Left Foot*, the basis for an enormously effective film, with the Irish poet portrayed by Daniel Day-Lewis, illustrates:

> I used to lie on my back all the time in the kitchen or, on bright warm days, out in the garden, a little bundle of crooked muscles and twisted nerves, surrounded by a family that loved me and hoped for me and that made me part of their own warmth and humanity. I was lonely, imprisoned in a world of my own, unable to communicate with others, cut off, separated from them as though a glass wall stood between my existence and theirs, thrusting me beyond the sphere of their lives and activities. (pp. 13–14)
>
> [At 16], I began to be not merely miserable and gloomy, but also resentful. I resented the world as a whole because of my crooked mouth, twisted hands and useless limbs. I looked about at all that was normal and perfect about me, and asked myself for the hundredth time why was I made different, why should I have been given the same feelings, the same needs and sensitivities as other people along with a practically functionless body. (pp. 82–83)

Historically, provisions for children were made in response to public health concerns, to disease rather than neuromotor or orthopedic impairments. While illness may also have the effect of depressing a child's cognitive skills, should that occur it often reflects the psychological impact of being sick for extended periods, of pain, lethargy, or weakness, perhaps anger, fear, or sadness. Tuberculosis became, as Sontag (1978) wrote, a metaphor for qualities ranging from spirituality and asceticism to sensuality and eroticism; it is in fact, however, a physical condition caused by infection.

Tuberculosis

This disease that can be traced throughout history experienced a resurgence in the form of drug-resistant strains early in the 1990s after public health measures in industrialized nations had seemed effective in significantly controlling its prevalence and impact. Always much feared and poetically characterized as "Captain of all the men of death" (Dubos & Dubos, 1952), it was long considered the most dangerous of all diseases. But in the 19th and early 20th centuries it became the greatest single medical challenge, responsible for an estimated one billion deaths. Over the centuries many treatments had been tried but none were effective, for until Robert Koch isolated the tubercle bacillus in 1882 its cause was unknown. What was well known was the weakening, wasting, fevered body resulting from "consumption," as pulmonary tuberculosis was called. The best hope was thought to lie in attention to hygiene and climate.

The belief that a child's frailty or lethargy was a dangerous sign coincided with changing mores, as early 19th century European physicians warned that neglecting physical exercise and reading novels might jeopardize mental stability (Foucault, 1965). In America, a growing interest in hygiene was expressed in educational trends, as well as fashions and customs. Rush was an early advocate of physical exercise for everyone, including persons with mental illness and retardation. Mann advocated inclusion of hygiene and physiology in the common school curriculum, and Howe thought physical education a priority for blind children. An influential early psychiatrist, Amariah Brigham (1833/1973), cautioned that parents' overemphasis on intellectual training, to the neglect of physical exercise, increased children's susceptibility to illness. Vigorous activity, once thought immodest, even dangerous, gained popularity in the 1830s and 1840s, an early version of "wellness" supported by a strong temperance movement. It was desirable even for "ladies" to be healthy and robust, and active recreational pursuits were no longer viewed as idle, and hence evil, pastimes.

Also encouraged by Romanticism's reverence for nature and idealization of childhood, the belief that recreation was good for children and that a healthy body was linked with learning and with character influenced reformers concerned about delinquency, as well as those concerned about child labor. Wholesome outdoor pursuits were supposed to have the dual preventive virtues of keeping children healthy and out of trouble. Despite these trends, which after all had limited impact on the lives of poor people and certainly did not slow the pace of industrialization and urbanization, "consumption" became increasingly prevalent. Even after Koch's discovery, prevalence increased, as did fatalities, especially in the crowded cities and in Native American villages and boarding schools.

In 1908, the year the Federal Indian Health Program was instituted, 11.16% of the annual mortality in the United States was attributed to tuberculosis, not counting the virtual decimation of Native Americans, among whom its "ravages . . . were especially widespread" (Thomas et al., 1993, p. 372). As late as 1913, between 5 and 15% of American children were believed to have active tuberculosis (Dubos & Dubos, 1952). As the search for cure continued, the greater concern was how to stop its spread. America's first tuberculosis sanitorium, following European models, was established by Dr. Edward Livingston Trudeau, in 1885, in Saranac Lake, New York. But attention to conditions associated with industrialization and urbanization was more important in the crusade to prevent its spread than were sanitoria (Bates, 1992).

The focus on containment constituted a mixed blessing, for while "the general public was disinterested in Indian people" contained on reservations (Thomas et al., 1993, p. 372), fear contributed to calls to restrict immigration. Jacob Riis's (1902) graphic portrayals attacked the tenements, yet purveyed ethnic stereotypes; nativists were already inclined to blame the victim. Novelist Ernest Poole's (1903) description of New York's "lung block" (in Bremner, 1970, p. 886) was intended to raise awareness of the devastating impact of tenement life, but the people he described were, after all, Italians or other "foreigners." The Immigration Act of 1924 excluded persons "afflicted with idiocy, insanity, imbecility, feeble-mindedness, epilepsy, constitutional psychopathic inferiority, chronic alcoholism, tuberculosis in any form, or a loathesome or dangerous contagious disease" (U.S. Statutes at Large, 68th Congress, 1925), and tuberculosis is yet grounds for exclusion of immigrants. But it is no longer believed linked with other feared forms of deviance, the evidence for such linkage having of course been spurious. As we noted in Chapter 6, tubercular parents were believed a cause of retardation since mortality rates in institutions often resulting from tuberculosis greatly exceeded that of the general population. But disease spreads in crowded environments, and residents were not provided quality health care. A person with either condition might have been pitied, but was nevertheless a pariah.

Most children's hospitals, like New York's St. Mary's, which opened in 1870, would not admit children with contagious diseases or "chronic incurables" (Letchworth, 1903/1974). But some were established for children with nonpulmonary tuberculosis (i.e., bone and joint, spinal, or skin abscesses), such as the Sea Breeze Hospital at Coney Island, opened in 1904 by the New York Association for Improving the Conditions of the Poor (Teller, 1988). Since tuberculosis was most often contracted in childhood, "preventoria" were established, the first in Lakewood, New Jersey, in 1909, where siblings could be sent when a case was discovered, but it had to relocate due to opposition of area residents fearful of contagion (p. 110). Urged by reformers like Lillian Wald, whose "Nurses' Settlement" provided infected pupils instruction and families guidance on prevention, schools began to institute programs.

The model that emerged was the open-air school, where children could be taught as well as treated. The first such program in Europe, the Open Air-Recovery School, was established in 1904, in Charlottenburg, a suburb of Berlin (Frampton & Powell, 1938). This model spread throughout Germany and to other nations, especially Italy and England. It was introduced in Canada in 1910. Permissive legislation in Scotland, in 1906, resulted in construction of several schools "of a semi-open air type" (Taylor & Taylor, 1960, p. 397). In Europe, most such schools, like the sanatoria, tended to be located in rural areas, in the forests, or in the mountains. (So high and remote is one sanatorium, Hans Castorp's cousin tells him in Mann's *The Magic Mountain*, that "they have to bring their bodies down on bob-sleds in the winter" [1927, p. 7].) In Yugoslavia, "forest schools" for "delicate" children (anemic, undernourished, or tubercular) were established after World War I. But in America, where people at risk were concentrated in large cities, most open air schools were located in urban centers, sometimes on the roof of a tenement.

When Dr. William H. Maxwell, New York City schools' superintendent, assigned a teacher to the Sea Breeze facility, the first hospital class was formed (New York City Board of Education, 1941), followed in January 1908 by an "out-of-door school" sponsored by the Providence League for the Suppression of Tuberculosis. Under public school auspices, day classes were next established in Providence for pretubercular and malnourished children and those with "lowered vitality," or who were "undervitalized." Later in that year, Boston and New York instituted programs for children with chronic respiratory problems, heart disease, anemia, and scrofula. The Boston Outdoor School, for children 4 through 16, was on the roof of the Refectory Building in Franklin Park (in Bremner, 1970, p. 930). By 1911, 35 American cities had out-of-door schools, which by 1916 served about 1,000 children. The concept of the fresh-air class was an attempt to respond to health needs, while instruction was provided in order to prevent educational loss for pupils "not sick enough to be put in a hospital, but still too weak to keep pace with the normals" (Frampton & Powell, 1938, p. 147). Proposals that because of nutritional needs lunches be provided for the pupils were controversial since feeding children would constitute a significant departure from the traditional role of the school and was not common until the 1930s. An immediate solution came through involvement of charity groups (Dubos & Dubos, 1952).

Once its cause had been discovered and as public health measures were introduced, the campaign to eradicate tuberculosis was worldwide. The increased attention to needs for specialized schooling for children with physical and health impairments in general to which these efforts contributed occurred not only in Europe and America but also in other nations. In Japan, as early as 1918, a movement began to provide education and vocational training in conjunction with medical treatment (Tsujimura, 1979), but the children were recognized to have diverse needs. In Tokyo's Municipal Komei School, "physically weak" pupils were separated from those with orthopedic impairments, the groups comprising two distinct dimensions of the school's program. This was for many years Japan's only special school for pupils with physical impairments, but it influenced schools throughout the country to form day classes for both "crippled" and "physically weak" children.

The tendency for programs initiated in response to tuberculosis to stimulate provisions for children with other problems was replicated in many countries, as programs established for children with "chronic weakness" or "lowered vitality" adapted to changing needs. By midcentury, tuberculosis was no longer the focus of specialized schooling and was thought no longer a major public health problem in "developed" nations. As we know, it has not been conquered after all but has returned with even greater virulence where poverty, overcrowding, and malnutrition exist.

Poliomyelitis

A quasi-clinical model of a different sort emerged in the 1940s in response to poliomyelitis, known as "infantile paralysis," a condition that Americans knew had affected their president's mobility, though few knew how much. Described in the mid-1800s as a debility of the lower extremities, following the first clinical account by Michael Underwood, a London pediatrician, it had undoubtedly existed throughout history; abnormalities found in prehistoric skeletal remains suggest what may be polio effects. Scriptural references to "lameness" do not permit certainty that post-polio effects were involved, but that is clearly a possibility in some instances, and the discussions of Hippocrates probably encompassed polio-related impairments. But polio was overshadowed by the devastating pestilences and epidemics that accompanied the changing environments to which humankind had to learn to adapt (Paul, 1971); in the past as today, endemic diarrheal disease due to inadequate nutrition and health care was so commonly implicated in widespread mortality in childhood that other conditions were overlooked. When children were left with impaired mobility following an illness, the causal connection was not understood; lameness in a child of previously normal movement was attributed to a probable fall or to a chill, rather than infection. In his memoirs, Sir Walter Scott attributed his lameness to infantile fever (Lockhart, 1837) and eventually sequellae of childhood disease were more generally recognized.

Poliomyelitis is the "only *common* disease in which sudden paralysis in a previously healthy infant or young child can occur" (Paul, 1971, p. 40). The suddenness with which a child may be struck, together with the debilitating effects, made it much feared as in the 1930s and 1940s more than 10,000 paralytic cases a year were reported in the United States, at least one-third resulting in permanent crippling deformity. But the epidemic was worldwide, in actuality pandemic. As a young nurse working in Australia's bush country, Elizabeth Kenney (1886–1952) adopted an unconventional approach of necessity with her first case, a 2–year-old girl in great pain, but as she applied it with others it became a source of great hope and the subject of great controversy.

At the First International Polio Conference in New York in 1948, Edward Streck, a psychiatrist, stressed the psychological implications for a child of the standard practice of immobilizing muscles to prevent their pulling against weaker ones, the child placed in a passive position manipulated by adults. Instead, Kenney manipulated the affected muscles. "She knew very little about the concept of poliomyelitis as an acute viral disease which must inevitably run its course," Paul (1971, p. 340) comments, "but she certainly knew about the business of handling the paralyzed child." Though physicians had invited her to the United States in 1940, many regarded her ideas with suspicion. In Wilfrid Sheed's (1973) novel *People Will Always Be Kind*, a doctor responds to his 16–year-old patient's hopeful inquiries, "'Yes, well, she's done some very useful work. Mostly for cutting down atrophy. That's about all she's proved so far. . . . I'm sorry, Brian, but those people give me a swift pain. Nurse Kenny, too, if it comes to that. Just another exhibitionist, raising false hopes in sick people. Put your faith in real doctors, Brian. And in your own fighting spirit'" (p. 28). (Brian was not greatly reassured.) Kenney (1941) insisted, "Let my record speak." Begun as a ward in the Minneapolis General Hospital, the Kenney Institute, which now specializes in rehabilitation of neuromotor impairments resulting from stroke, arthritis, and spinal cord injury, became world-famous for Kenney's success in facilitating more normalized functioning.

The rise in polio's worldwide prevalence, well before the American epidemic in the 1940s, created a sudden and urgent need for home- and hospital-based tutoring. It also inspired hospital schools for children and youth with post-polio sequellae, such as France's first school for children with orthopedic impairments, established in 1919 at St. Fargeau par Ponthierry (Taylor & Taylor, 1960, p. 199). Greece's Asclepion Sanitarium, (founded in 1954) on the island of Leros near a tuberculosis hospital founded two years earlier, initially served polio patients, each facility operating its own school program. We shall return to the topic of schools in hospitals, an important development in the history of special education. Young people today probably cannot appreciate the impact poliomyelitis had on families before the contributions of Salk and Sabin. But older persons well remember the fear of the paralyzing disease that was epidemic when they were young, and many yet bear lasting physical reminders, as well as vivid memories of interrupted lives.

MORTALITY AND RISK IN CHILDHOOD

Social Policy

Policy developments most significantly affecting exceptional children early in the 20th century were those that affected children and families in general. The first White House Conference on the Care of Dependent Children, in 1909, led to formation of the Child Welfare League and of the Children's Bureau within the Department of Labor. It also yielded a ringing affirmation of the importance for dependent children of *family*, and of the need to support "worthy" and "deserving" mothers where families experience adversity:

> Home life is the highest and finest product of civilization. It is the great molding force of mind and character. Children should not be deprived of it except for urgent and compelling reasons. Children of parents of worthy character, suffering from temporary misfortune and children of reasonably efficient and deserving mothers who are without the support of the normal breadwinner, should, as a rule, be kept with their parents, such aid being given as may be necessary to maintain suitable homes for the rearing of the children. (White House Conference, 1909, p. 9)

This event culminated more than a century of determined volunteerism—mainly by women—on behalf of children and families. The virtually innumerable 19th-century women's charitable societies had worked for relief of widows and care of orphans, abolition of slavery, temperance, parks and playgrounds, sanitation and municipal services, and a host of other causes (Scott, 1992), including suffrage, finally realized in the United States with passage in 1920 of the 19th Amendment to the Constitution. A most significant legislative event affecting both women and children was enactment, the next year, of the Sheppard-Towner Act, which authorized grants-in-aid to the states for the promotion of maternal and infant health and welfare, administered under the Children's Bureau. Some opponents, believing the events connected, accused legislators of capitulating out of fear of the "women's vote." Vigorously attacked in the *Journal of the American Medical Association* as an "imported socialistic scheme," the act's constitutionality was challenged, but upheld by the Supreme Court (Bremner, 1970, p. 1020). Some 70 years later, while progress had been made, issues of inequity, unaccessibility, and unaffordability of health care generally, and maternal and child health care in particular, yet challenge the nation.

Causes of Disabling and Fatal Conditions of Children

As we saw, many diseases to which children were highly vulnerable had been identified well before the 19th century. Rush reported occurrence in North America of scarlet fever, delineated in Europe in the 17th century, yet it increased in prevalence, often resulting in deafness or orthopedic impairment as children continued to be at risk for this as for other potentially fatal or disabling infectious diseases, such as meningitis. Three of every four American deaths in the 19th century occurred before the age of 12, but the very early years were especially tenuous; of every thousand newborns in England and America in the 1880s and 1890s, about 150 did not survive to their first birthday; in some countries the rate was as high as 40% (Holt & McIntosh, 1933). In 1923, Gesell stated that more than a third of American deaths occurred before age 6, "ten times as many in the first half decade of life as in the full decade from five to fifteen years" (p. 25). In 1912, Wallin (1912a) told the American Association for Study and Prevention of Infant Mortality that house flies were a major cause of the 49,000 infant deaths from cholera reported annually. He was also critical of mothers, recommending that those who could breast-feed their infant but did not be fined, and warning of the harm of alcohol, both to the fetus and as it impaired maternal caregiving. (Dorris [1989] cites William Sullivan's report that in 1899 the rate of mortality for infants of alcoholic women was 56%, more than twice that for nondrinking women.)

Birth itself constituted serious risks for both mother and newborn. In 1913, by conservative estimates, more than 15,000 American women died in childbirth, making it second only to tuberculosis as a cause of death in adult women (Gesell, 1923). Today, an infant born significantly preterm or at very low birthweight, even less than 1,000 grams, or with other complications is considered at *biological risk* (Tjossem, 1976). However, the baby's chances of surviving, and even of thriving, have been immeasurably enhanced by technology. In times past, most such newborns died, and most who did not perish immediately experienced continued stress throughout their usually very short lives. But dramatic recent progress is counterbalanced by continued high infant mortality, most alarmingly in large urban centers in the United States. "The fundamental causes of infantile mortality may be summed up as poverty and ignorance," wrote Dr. Ira Wile in 1910 (in Bremner, 1970, p. 965), but a major factor continues to be inequitable availability of maternal care. At the same time, survival of the event of birth is a factor in the prevalence of disability in children, for many experience impairment, sometimes multiple or involving continued dependence on technology.

Some congenital conditions, such as hemophilia, muscular dystrophy, sickle cell disease, and cystic fibrosis, are known to have a hereditary basis, while in other instances that is less certain. One now sees many children and also adults with myelomeningocele, generally termed spina bifida, a congenital malformation of the posterior vertebrae resulting in varying degrees of impaired sensation and mobility due to spinal cord damage. But this is an increase in survival. Insertion of a shunt permits removal of cerebrospinal fluid from the cranial cavity, which otherwise caused hydrocephaly and usually death. Though some diseases that had left children with impaired sight or hearing or with respiratory, cardiac, or neurological impairments have been effectively conquered, childhood illness, especially during the period traditionally termed "infancy" (about the first seven years), is yet a cause of disability. In some instances, means of prevention are known but are not accessible to all.

Risk was exacerbated by institutional living, inspections frequently revealing a host of untreated problems, as well as impetigo and trachoma resulting from unsanitary conditions and shared toilet articles. After a Child Welfare League inspection of Thornwell, a Presbyterian orphanage in South Carolina in 1928, the Reverend H. W. Hopkirk reported that of 320 children four had incipient tuberculosis, several had enlarged tonsils or adenoids, 70 showed symptoms of pellagra due to dietary deficiencies, while others were underweight (Thurston, 1930, pp. 215–216). Poor nutrition was a common finding; in one account (Trotzkey, 1930) children with special health needs were lumped into a general category of "underweights," without differentiation as to health status.

Though crippling accidents have throughout history resulted in serious disability, head and spinal cord injury were first addressed as areas of rehabilitation and prevention late in the 19th century by William Osler (Ohry & Ohry-Kassay, 1989). Such injuries still are frequent, despite laws requiring car seats for infants and young children, and growing acceptance of the wearing of helmets when cycling. While many children incur neurological damage as a result of falls, the cause of such damage, or death, is often a bullet, especially in America where guns are readily available. And in addition to children who bear lasting effects of sexual abuse are many with permanent physical and neurological damage resulting from being hit, shaken, burned, or otherwise mistreated; in 1991, 2,694,000 American children were reported as abused or neglected (American Humane Association, 1992).

Hospitals for Children

Physical disability knows no socioeconomic boundaries, but while all children are vulnerable, and while wealth and privilege cannot guarantee a child's health or even survival, poverty has always massively increased the degree of risk. Since Augustus, and probably earlier, there have been attempts to provide care for children we now describe as at environmental risk. In England between 1700 and 1825, 154 foundling hospitals were created to reduce the high rate of infant mortality and to provide care for "bastard and poor" children (New York City Board of Education, 1941). As we saw, such efforts were generally not successful. We can be certain that many, probably most, of the countless children cared for by Vincent de Paul (1581–1660) and the Sisters of Charity were sick or had orthopedic or sensory impairments. Since some of those with retardation he undertook to teach surely had physical impairments, we could by stretching a point place the beginning of special education for children with physical disabilities in the priory of Saint-Lazure.

Pediatric hospitals did not appear until the 19th century, by the end of which most large European and American cities had facilities for children. The first orthopedic hospital in Europe, opened in Denmark in 1898, like others that followed, treated adults as well as children. Several such facilities opened in America after the Civil War, some specifically for children, but often specialized and selective: Most would not admit children with cerebral palsy, epilepsy, or tuberculosis; in the 1890s, Lillian Wald and Mary Brewster, also a nurse, had to convince hospital authorities in New York to admit patients with typhoid fever (Howe, 1976). Albany's Child's Hospital treated children with crippling conditions resulting from poor nutrition, bone or joint tuberculosis, spinal injury, or abuse, as in an instance of a baby given an overdose of morphine by a "depraved" mother (Letchworth, 1903/1974).

The New York Society for the Relief of the Ruptured and Crippled was founded in 1863 to treat patients believed curable, about half of whom at any given time were children, some as young as 4, with diagnoses including club foot, swollen joints, hip disease, and paralysis resulting from spinal injury. Letchworth (1903/1974) noted that *all cases* were reported "cured and discharged," most within a few months. Its remarkable (if unlikely) cure record aside, two notable facts about the hospital were its work in design and construction of braces and its accessibility, due to an elevator, to persons with impaired mobility. The New York Orthopedic Hospital opened in 1866, a year after the city's Opthalmic Hospital, and in 1875 the first combination home and hospital for crippled children was founded in Minnesota (New York City Board of Education, 1941, pp. 5–6). The first of the Shriners' Hospitals was opened by Atlanta's Scottish Rite Masons in 1915, its mission to "reclaim from dependence and disease many hopelessly crippled" (Allen, 1924), but there were some stipulations: "Children will be admitted . . . regardless of creed or fraternal affiliations. They will be treated and cared for absolutely free. The principal requirements are that they be capable of improvement, that they be of normal mentality, and that they be unable to pay for medical services and treatment given" (p. 239).

Founding of Philadelphia's Home of the Merciful Saviour in 1884 represented a step forward in terms of recognition of public responsibility. But as one author (Eberle, 1914/1922) observed, such homes "still treated the cripple as an unfortunate best taken apart from the world altogether, and consequently educated him only for his own mental health and that he might be happy and useful within the little artificial charity-given world of the institution where he must live and die because the world outside had no place for him" (p. 59). Boston's Industrial School for Crippled and Deformed Children, however, was founded in 1893 in the belief that "if cripples could be educated as a matter of charity, they could also be educated for the purposes of taking them out of the charity class, in which, except for the utterly maimed few, they emphatically do not belong" (p. 59). Similar training schools were soon established in New York, Philadelphia, and Cleveland.

St. Mary's Hospital, established by the Episcopal Church in New York in 1870, served only children, most between 2 and 14. While lacking anything like today's child life programs, this was one of the first to consider the child clientele with respect to decor and provision of toys and play materials. But St. Mary's also provided for infants, and there were indications that, whatever children's physical symptoms might indicate, being hospitalized so early in life subjected them to even greater risk. Physical problems have many ramifications for children's psychological development, but this has been demonstrated most dramatically in the case of very young children experiencing hospitalization.

Children in Hospitals

As we have noted, while hospices have been provided for centuries, young children have never fared well in such arrangements. That was still true in the 1880s, when Dr. Abraham Jacobi, a strong advocate of pediatric training, charged that most "nurseries" for sick children "succeed in so keeping and nursing their little inmates, that those admitted in health are soon taken sick, and those taken sick die" (in Bremner, 1970, p. 832). René Spitz (1945) recounted the appalling story revealed in hospital records: Most young children did not survive the cure. Hospitalization and placement in foundling homes established after the Civil War entailed removal from the home, a form of institutional placement albeit intended as temporary, and while the rate of death among persons in institutions ranged from 35 to an appalling 75%, commonly exceeding 50% for children under 2, for infants less than a year old it neared 100% (Bowlby, 1945). H. D. Chapin (1908), a pediatrician, reported the extremely high incidence of infant mortality in the hospitals of New York City: "Unless the infant is quickly discharged after the acute symptoms subside there is nearly always a slow, but progressive weight loss which bears an inverse ratio to age, being especially marked under 6 months. If the atrophy gets beyond a certain point no change of environment or food will save the patient" (p. 491).

Despite Chapin's photographic documentation of marasmus (later termed failure to thrive) and the effectiveness of a program he implemented for prompt discharge for recuperative care through an organization of trained families known as the Speedwell Society, standard hospital practice remained basically unchanged until Spitz (1945, 1946) described what he termed *hospitalism* observed in infants maintained in a foundling home. Contrasting the deterioration of these infants with the health and well-being of counterparts whose (incarcerated) mothers had daily contact with their babies, he argued that it was not hospitalization per se, but maternal deprivation that accounted for the malnutrition, weight loss, and apathy he observed. Spitz's descriptions revealed that the foundling home infants were otherwise deprived; kept much of the time in their cribs, they had little stimulation, caretakers even adopting the expedient of covering the crib sides with sheets to lessen the likelihood of a crying infant setting off others. Staff-convenience practices, a far cry from moral management, later became notorious in institutions of all kinds.

The term *failure to thrive* first appeared in 1933, in the 10th edition of *Holt's Diseases of Infancy and Childhood*, although L. E. Holt had used the phrase "cease to thrive" in the first edition, in 1899. While observing that the high rate of mortality of hospitalized infants involved malnutrition, he noted that that often had no known organic cause. Later, a "mixed" type, with organic problems exacerbated by inadequate nurture, was recognized. Chapin (1908) had maintained that deterioration could occur among infants in their own homes, and subsequent investigations linked developmental delays to disturbed mother-infant relationship (e.g., Coleman & Provence, 1957; Powell, Brasel, & Blizzard, 1967). But extended hospitalization placed even babies with healthy attachment at extreme risk. In a landmark monograph published by the World Health Organization, John Bowlby (1945), a British psychoanalyst influenced by Melanie Klein's concept of the "infantile depressive position" (Young-Bruehl, 1988), reported his findings in English hospitals as confirming the link between deficient caloric intake and emotional deprivation. Bakwin (1949) vividly described the characteristics of infants hospitalized for extended periods:

> listlessness, emaciation and pallor, relative immobility, quietness, unresponsiveness to stimulation like a smile or coo, indifferent appetite, failure to gain weight properly despite the ingestion of diets, which, in the home, are entirely adequate, frequent stools, poor sleep, and appearance of unhappiness, proneness to fatal episodes, absence of sucking habits. The hospital infant is pale . . . facial expression is unhappy . . . muscle tone is poor . . . there is no interest in environment, lying quietly in bed, rarely crying and moving very little. (p. 512)

Hospitalization could have devastating effects on infants, but it could also be traumatic for older children. Protracted hospital stays have become uncommon, and practices in care of children have changed dramatically, but such changes were late in coming. Most hospitals now encourage a mother to be with her hospitalized child and otherwise attempt to normalize the child's experience. But as recently as the 1960s, when the American Association for the Care of Children in Hospitals, now the Association for the Care of Children's Health (ACCH), was founded, it was standard practice for young children to be separated from families. Robert and Suzanne Massie (1975), authors of *Nicholas and Alexandra*, and themselves parents of a child with hemophilia, described their experiences with hospitals where "the rules were against . . . familiarity. In defiance of all reasonableness and humanity, parents were often treated as pariahs; or, at best, as annoying hindrances [by] cold-eyed nurses, residents, and even doctors" (p. 33).

The concept of child life education was born in the 1960s in response to concerns that children's emotional needs associated with hospital experiences were not addressed. Emma Plank (1905–1990), ACCH co-founder with five other women representing North American hospitals, was aware of the often traumatic impact on a child of simply being in a place where people hurt and even die. Child life educators must be trained professionals who understand children's fears and fantasies, she wrote in *Working with Children in Hospitals* (1962). They are not occupational therapists, but neither are they merely "play ladies," a term, she quipped, which in German refers to prostitutes. (This determined Viennese, trained by Montessori and also as one of Anna Freud's "child experts," also had a sense of humor.)

Child life educators employ an eclectic mix of play and art therapy techniques, reassuring talk, tutoring, and supportive friendship to allay children's fears of surgery, stress of separation, anticipation of pain, and boredom.

Schooling for children in hospitals, as with the facilities for children with emotional problems described in Chapter 8, was an afterthought, even in programs that were called schools, like the Boston Outdoor School, described as "primarily a hospital, or day camp, under the eye of nurse and doctors; but . . . necessarily also a school" (in Bremner, 1970, p. 930). For most children, hospitalization meant an interruption, presumably a short one, and by the mid-20th century, many states authorized tutoring for "home-bound and hospitalized children" to keep up with studies. On the other hand, chronic health conditions sometimes constituted a basis for exclusion from schooling altogether, and some hospitals themselves formed schools, operation of which was later assumed by a school system. A program founded in 1908 by Sir Henry Gauvain at the Lord Mayor Treloar Hospital in Alton, for example, came under English school management in 1912 (Taylor & Taylor, 1960). But despite advances, the educational neglect of children with orthopedic impairments and the medical neglect of children of the poor continued to be major child welfare concerns.

SETTLEMENT WORKERS AND VOLUNTEERS

The first English school for children with physical disabilities was established by voluntary organizations, in 1851, at Marylebone, followed in 1865 by one at Kensington (Taylor & Taylor, 1960, p. 147). In the late 1860s, a "cripples' nursery" was formed in London; with a second opened in 1890, the two served just 46 children from 3 to 8 years of age. At about this time, another philanthropic project, the Moore Street Home for Crippled Orphan Boys, the first of six such small residential programs established in England, was initiated in London to train boys age 8–13 in such trades as jewelry and boot-making. The boys had to be ambulatory, with crutches if needed, and otherwise present "favorable prospects" for using the training to make a living (New York City Board of Education, 1941). The Dr. Barnado's Home for Crippled Children, started in London in 1886, opened branches in Northern Ireland, one for boys and one for girls (Taylor & Taylor, 1960, p. 342). In 1888, the Invalid Children's Aid Association was formed to provide home visiting for chronically ill children or those with severe physical impairment. Although schools were legislatively empowered in 1899 "to provide training for physically and mentally defective and epileptic children" (Taylor & Taylor, 1960, p. 342), they were not required to do so for another two decades. While the English tradition of voluntarism remained strong, responsibility shifted to public auspices.

That was not the case in Switzerland where most such institutions, like a residential school for children with orthopedic impairments established in 1864, remained under religious denominations or "non-denominational humanitarian associations" (Taylor & Taylor, 1960, p. 452). In Denmark, the Reverend Hans Knudsen in 1898 added an orthopedic hospital and elementary and vocational schools to the rehabilitation facility for adults with neuromotor impairments he had founded in 1872 (p. 125). Finland's Society for the Care of Cripples also included elementary and industrial schools, as did the Cripples' Institute in Belfast, founded in 1888 (p. 342). In Britain and America the continued emphasis on home visiting is attributable to the key role of settlement leaders: Lillian Wald and Jane Addams, in New York and Chicago, and in England, Mary Ward. Mrs. Humphrey Ward (1851–1920), novelist and niece of Thomas Carlyle, saw in her work with English settlements and "play centres" a means of practicing a social gospel. Through her efforts the first school for children with physical disabilities established by a school board, the Invalid Children's School, was begun at Tavistock Place, at the Passmore Edwards Settlement, in 1899 (New York City Board of Education, 1941). The settlement movement had actually begun in 1884, with founding of London's Toynbee Hall, which inspired Jane Addams and other visiting American reformers.

Lillian Wald and the "Nurse's Settlement"

"Crime, disease, and poverty were not new at the turn of the century. . . . What was new was the increased number of indignant reformers . . . who joined with . . . middle-class pioneers who had begun settlement work in the tenement districts of many of the nation's largest eastern cities in the 1880s and 1890s" (Pratte, 1973, p. 61). Settlement workers campaigned for laws to regulate child labor and ensure that children would remain in school, as well as school policies to address their needs more effectively. Herself a nurse, Lillian Wald (1867–1940) was particularly concerned by the neglect of medical needs of New York's poor immigrants, whose children were routinely excluded from school for health problems that could be readily treated. In her play "At Home on Henry Street" (in Coss, 1989), Claire Coss portrays Wald as ironically contrasting the alacrity with which policymakers later took up "war preparedness" with their slowness to provide for children: "For years we struggle to have school nurses. With the flick of a pen, we have military training in our schools" (p. 26). Recalling the beginning of that struggle, she recounts—as she seems to have done for all who would hear—the story of "'little Louie, the deplorable condition of whose scalp is denying him the blessings of education'" (Wald, 1915, quoted in Howe, 1976, p. 93).

Begun in a fifth-floor apartment shared with Mary Brewster, the Nurse's Settlement relocated to a house on Henry Street, its full-time staff of 11 in 1898 including Lavinia Duck and eight other nurses. By 1900, there were 15, increased to 27 by 1906, the name changed, to avoid stigma, to the Henry Street Settlement (Howe, 1976, p. 93). Gaining substantial philanthropic support, especially from Jacob Schiff, Wald extended her campaign to the policy arena, persuading the city to adopt her "district nurse" model of public nursing and the New York schools, after a trial in 1902 with a nurse on loan, to appoint 12 (Bremner, 1970, p. 812). Urging nurses to be alert to violations of health policies as an extension "'from the individual to the collective interest'" (in Coss, 1989, p. 67), she counseled "'when you see an individual suffering, you help that person on the spot. Then you work to remove the cause'" (p. 26). Through her urging, Helen Hartley Jennings, a trustee, endowed the Department of Nursing and Health at Teachers College, Columbia University, which, under Adelaide ("General") Nutting, "emphasized the modern social, preventive, and educational aspects of the field" (Cremin et al., 1954, p. 55).

Though an astute campaigner, comfortable with millionaires and power brokers, Wald identified personally with her immigrant neighbors. By 1916, though her Visiting Nurses Service comprised over 100 nurses, with an annual budget of $150,000, Irving Howe (1976) tells us that "the Settlement kept its personal tone, run along the principles of anarchic matriarchy" (p. 94), while Wald herself was "a figure of legend, known and adored on every street" (p. 90). With activist-attorney Florence Kelly, she campaigned for the Children's Bureau established in 1912 through a bill signed by President Taft, which under Julia Lathrop, a Hull House social worker, was charged with a broad range of issues, including infant mortality, juvenile justice, child labor, and children with disabilities.

Jane Addams and Hull House

During these years, Lillian Wald's famous counterpart in Chicago, Jane Addams (1860–1935), was countering hostility toward immigrants, while herself living among these families and responding to their needs. With Ellen Gates Starr, she began Hull House in 1889 in an old mansion on Chicago's near west side. A frequent and popular lecturer at Chautauqua, where her *Twenty Years at Hull House* was first published in 1911, she urged that quintessentially native American audience in a 1905 address "to break out still further into the world about you till it includes the man who seems quite unlike ourselves" (in Morrison, 1974, p. 60). In this xenophobic time, she insisted that it was important to understand the diverse cultures and traditions from which these recent European immigrants had come, that fear and revulsion of impoverished immigrants resulted from not knowing them as individuals, thus not realizing how much all people have in common.

Although illness caused her to abandon plans to be trained as a nurse, and her work is not identified as was Wald's primarily with health issues, they were regularly encountered at Hull House. That children's physical as well as emotional problems often resulted from the sheer struggle families experienced for survival was evident in the stories of three children in its "impromptu kindergarten:" "'one had fallen out of a third-storey window, another had been burned, and the third had a curved spine due to the fact that for three years he had been tied all day long to the leg of the kitchen table, only released at noon by his older brother who hastily ran in from a neighboring factory to share his lunch with him'" (in Tims, 1961, p. 51). Recognizing that parental ignorance was a barrier, as in the case of an infant with cleft palate whose mother allowed him to die of neglect when returned to her (Addams, 1911), she advocated preparing young women for parenthood. But just as infant mortality was linked with deprivation of maternal affection, she stressed the need for love and understanding "in that second birth at adolescence" (p. 246).

Addams, like Wald a pacifist, was co-recipient of the Nobel peace prize in 1931 and a strong advocate for the rights of children and suffrage for women. A close associate of Dewey, who served on her board, she shared his view of education as life but thought schooling often unconnected with people's lives. Like other settlement workers, she conducted instruction for adults, as well as children, but insisted on the importance, and justice, of providing cultural and recreational opportunities, rather than just functional training. "We have the curious notion," she told the National Education Association in 1897, "that it is not possible for the mass of mankind to have interests and experiences of themselves which are worth anything" (Addams, 1897, p. 109).

Hull House inspired other programs in Chicago, such as Dr. Graham Taylor's Chicago Common and Mary McDowell's University Settlement, as well as spread of the concept to other cities. While extraordinarily influential in advancing this movement, which epitomized progressivism, Addams saw it as "only one manifestation of that wider humanitarian movement which throughout Christendom, but preeminently in England, is endeavoring to embody itself, not in a sect, but in society itself" (Tims, 1961, p. 48). Like England's Beatrice and Sydney Webb, as much as American progressivists, Addams believed "social engineering" and governmental initiative at the local community level essential spurs for the "inevitability of gradualism" to bring about social justice (p. 72).

WAR, DISABILITY,
AND THE ALLIED HEALTH PROFESSIONS

Like other helping professions, social work, which has had a major role in working with children with disabilities and their families, received impetus from war. In the postwar climate of the 1920s, the settlement movement declined, such efforts thought suspect, possibly "un-American" (Allen, 1931). The growing influence of psychoanalysis also oriented the field more toward individual casework than reform (Borenzweig, 1971), and there were many injured and shell-shocked veterans in need of counseling. Children have always been tragic victims of wars, a grim fact that led Montessori (1949/1972) to campaign for world peace through education. It also led Addams, Wald, and Helen Keller to risk their own reputations in opposing the "war preparedness" that led to dispatch of American expeditionary forces. In the second world conflict, children uprooted, orphaned, or emotionally damaged by war inspired Anna Freud to find ways of helping children cope, and Bruno Bettelheim drew insights from his own experiences in war in treating disturbed children. As we discuss in Chapter 9, rehabilitative work with head-injured veterans led to specialized instruction for children with learning disabilities.

Thus, for persons with disabilities, war has had paradoxical benefits. Koestler (1976) found "sad irony in the fact that war, which has robbed so many of their sight, has often brought boons to blind people in its wake" (p. 7). For deaf persons war had demographic consequences that furthered cultural identification, for "undraftable deaf men found themselves in great demand. A peculiar consequence . . . was the creation of a large deaf community in Akron, Ohio" drawn by the rubber industry (Van Cleve & Crouch, 1989, p. 163). In both world wars and the Korean conflict, psychological evaluation of recruits heightened awareness of retardation, often a basis for rejection; as Sarason and Doris (1969) wrote, "There is apparently (and unfortunately) nothing like a war to force a society to look at its human resources" (p. 10). Nonetheless, many with retardation did in fact serve, while World War II brought unprecedented employment opportunity to many of those rejected—though after the war most were, as Doll (1962) had predicted, "quickly shuffled back to poverty and dependency" (p. 66). Certain services provided today for children originated or became professionalized in war. While such application came later, the professions identified as *allied health* emerged in consequence of the American Civil War and the First World War.

Nursing

Florence Nightingale is surely the name most closely identified with the nursing profession, the origins of which are in fact termed the "pre-Nightingale" (up to 1860) and "Nightingale" (1860–1900) periods (Stewart, 1944). She may have exaggerated the contrast between her idea of a trained nurse and those they would supplant, who were "too old, too weak, too drunken, too dirty, too stolid, or too bad to do anything else" (in Seymer, 1954, p. 274). But hospital nursing was drudgery: "The line between nursing and domestic service could hardly be drawn in the mid-nineteenth century" (Rosenberg, 1987, p. 214). Women had cared for the sick in voluntary capacity since antiquity, but the feminization of nursing paralleled that of teaching. Orders like the Sisters of Charity and Mercy had long been involved in hospital work, and in the early 1800s, Protestant "lady volunteers" began to assume some tasks formerly done, presumably less well and with less dedication, by paid male employees in hospitals like St. Luke's in New York, Boston's Children's Hospital, and the Episcopal hospitals of Philadelphia (p. 219).

While efforts for improvement had been in evidence as part of the general reform movements of the early 19th century, the Civil War revolutionized the quality of hospital care in America. By its end more than 200 hospitals in the Union alone treated more than 1 million men, with a death rate of less then 10% (Rosenberg, 1987). The professionalized order and sanitation beginning to characterize both American and British hospitals have been attributed to Nightingale's effectiveness in invoking statistics and new medical knowledge to support her recommendations for ordered, professional care. Similarly, though the needs for both improved working conditions and trained nurses had been noted earlier, she was instrumental in starting the first English training schools in the 1860s. In America, catalyzed by the Civil War, the first three schools were opened in 1873, and by 1880 15 schools had produced about 300 graduates (p. 219).

It has been suggested that Nightingale saw in nursing what Peabody saw in "child gardening": the full expression of women's role. But as with teaching, that is a myth. While some physicians and hospital administrators used this argument to convince reluctant colleagues who perceived a possible threat to the doctor's authority, it is more likely that the field opened to women, as did teaching, because they could be hired for lower pay and nursing, like teaching, provided more respectable employment than other options. Young women had to suffer drudgery and indignities at the hands of sometimes imperious male physicians in their preparation, but "after two years of exhausting work the nursing graduate could look forward to a lifetime of respectable self-employment" (Rosenberg, 1987, p. 223). Middle-class virtues of "ladylike" conduct, compliance, and "refinement" were sought in candidates (p. 225), but while the experience of hospitalization itself was also increasingly perceived as "respectable," the preponderance of child patients at the turn of the century, at least in the large general hospitals, represented "a social class far lower than that of their nurses and physicians" (p. 303). Pediatric nursing was formalized in training programs later than certain other specialties, psychiatric nursing having begun to be seen as a specialty as early as 1882 (Stewart, 1944).

Physical and Occupational Therapy

Like speech language therapy, physical and occupational therapies are essential services for many children with physical disabilities. As immigration created a perceived need for "speech teachers," as discussed in Chapter 9, the Great War was responsible for the emergence of these two other specialties, though they had different antecedents. In 1917, based on recommendations of a committee of physicians appointed by the surgeon general, the Division of Special Hospitals and Physical Reconstruction was created to administer the Reconstruction Aide program, modeled after efforts begun in Europe. In September 1918, it was placed under the supervision of Marguerite Sanderson, who, with Drs. F. B. Grainger, E. G. Brackett, and J. E. Goldthwait, had organized units at Walter Reed Hospital to prepare trainees for transfer overseas. When Sanderson was assigned to coordinate work in Europe, Mary McMillan, an American who had worked in England with an orthopedic surgeon, was appointed Head Reconstruction Aide, later organizing the largest of the seven emergency programs formed to train "Re-Aides," at Reed College in Oregon (American Physical Therapy Association [APTA], 1979).

"*Kinési-Thérapie,*" or *physiotherapy*, "has been practiced since the beginning of the world, yet was born in the World War," wrote Grainger (1923, in APTA, 1979, p. 1). He referred to the "component parts of physiotherapy" (p. 2)—the ancient practices of massage and of relief through bathing (hydrotherapy), to which various antecedents of electrotherapy, some controversial, began to be added by the 17th and 18th centuries, later complemented by mechanical means, passive manipulation, and corrective exercise. While these were taught as specialized branches, the training instituted in response to the wartime emergency covered the gamut, as well as content in such fields as anatomy, physiology, chemistry, and physics. In American army hospitals and camps alone, not counting work overseas, from 1918 to 1920, the training enabled "about 86,000 disabled soldiers to have the benefit of over three and one-half million treatments" (McMillan, 1921, p. 9).

Following the war, the field was promoted in Scandinavia, Britain, and the Commonwealth, as well as with formation in 1920 of the American Women's Physical Therapeutic Association (its name soon changed so as not to exclude the very few males). Concern for professional identity was expressed in efforts to develop training and licensure standards, distinguish the field from nursing and physical education (in which many therapists had prior training), and agree on a suitable title from among such proposed alternatives as "physical therapeutics." In Europe, the term *physiotherapy* was more generally used, and though American workers referred to themselves as physical therapists, the national organization used physiotherapy for many years in its name and publications.

Therapists generally work in close conjunction with physicians, their services prescribed following orthopedic surgery and for persons whose mobility is impaired as a result of disease or injury; needing to use prosthetic or orthotic aids; with abnormal tone, posture, or movement; or needing to regain or maintain motor function during hospitalization or convalescence. When polio was epidemic, therapists had major roles in rehabilitation and, as we noted, Phelps promoted their involvement with children with cerebral palsy. They now work in diverse settings, from neonatal intensive care units to centers providing geriatric care, in sports medicine and in schools. They are key team members in working with patients, including infants and children, who have incurred head or spinal cord injury. While most are generally prepared, increasing numbers pursue a pediatric specialization.

While physical therapy is specifically indicated for persons with physical impairment, occupational therapy has had broad application with exceptional populations. Begun as a facet of rehabilitation of adults, it had early antecedents; Philippe Pinel, impressed by reports of its use in Saragossa, Spain, made *work* a component of his moral treatment reforms. This concept was distinct from training in a trade, like that done in schools for blind or deaf pupils and in some for pupils with impaired mobility. It also differed from the labor, ostensibly to build character but often in the service of the institution, imposed in reformatories and in institutions for persons with retardation (though the stated intent was similar). The first "workshop" to exploit the therapeutic use of crafts was established in Chicago in 1908, followed by "curative workshops" in Boston and Philadelphia, and in the Netherlands and Britain, the latter pioneered by Elizabeth Casson. Rather than training, the idea of *occupational* therapy refers to involvement in "occupations" appropriate to the client's needs in the present, the work instrumental, not an end in itself. In psychiatric contexts, the therapist's role is not merely to keep the client "occupied," but to provide activites that help clients work through conflict, redirect aggression, and gain self-esteem and ego strength.

Progressivist themes—humanistic values, faith in work, and enthusiasm for scientific research—can be seen in the early development of the field

(Schwartz, 1992) and, like progressivism, especially in education, it reflects American Pragmatism as an underlying philosophical base (Breines, 1986). However, it was the conflict in Europe that created an urgent need for therapists. General John J. Pershing, Allied Expeditionary Force Commander, called for 1,000 of the reconstruction aides, soon followed by many more, to help in rehabilitation work by "teaching hand-crafts to the convalescent soldiers" (Christensen, 1991). As with physical therapy, "By and large they were women because their work was perceived as being of a subservient nature," and was assumed to meet only a temporary need (p. 15). Even when instituted in peacetime hospitals consequent to the Industrial Rehabilitation Act, the field had to struggle for recognition, which prompted formation of the National Society for the Promotion of Occupational Therapy (now the American Occupational Therapy Association) in 1917 (Dunton & Light, 1950). Its founders' diverse backgrounds suggest notions of the identity of the new profession: "George Barton and Thomas Kidner were architects. Eleanor Clarke Slagle was a social worker. William Rush Dunton was a physician, and Susan Tracy and Susan Johnson were nurses. Isabel Newton (Barton) . . . was a stenographer" (Christensen, 1991, p. 8).

World War II brought occupational therapy greater recognition, but its very diversity fragmented the field (Breines, 1986); a schism existed between practitioners who identified it with psychiatric work and tuberculosis and those whose wartime experience had oriented them toward orthopedic and neuromotor disability (Christensen, 1991, p. 28). By the 1950s, however, therapists were becoming identified with treatment of children in both psychiatric and rehabilitation agencies. Since therapeutic activities are designed to have functional utility in enabling clients to acquire skills needed for daily living, for an adult with impaired motor functioning, skills for personal care, food preparation, use of adaptive equipment, and so forth, may be emphasized. For a child, age-appropriate self-care activities are involved, with particular emphasis on fine motor skills and perceptual-motor coordination.

Increasingly since the 1950s and 1960s, occupational therapy, like physical therapy, has been provided in specialized school programs for children with physical disabilities, usually on a "cluster," or center, model. When P.L. 94–142, which identified these as related services, extended education to all children with disabilities, irrespective of nature or severity, and mandated placement in the Least Restrictive Environment, four problems arose that continue to pose difficulties for school districts: cost of therapy services; unavailability of sufficient numbers of practitioners, especially with pediatric and school-based experience and interests; difficulties in integrating therapeutic goals within a unified Individualized Education Program (IEP); and logistical concerns associated with dispersing students needing services in "home schools" rather than segregated centers (Christensen, 1991).

SCHOOL HEALTH SERVICES

The concept of medical affiliation with schools, for which Lillian Wald fought in New York, was also spurred by settlements in other cities. In the 1870s, a few urban districts introduced medical inspections. In 1894, Boston appointed 50 school physicians, a practice adopted soon thereafter in Chicago, New York, and Philadelphia. At the turn of the century, Gesell & Gesell (1912) noted, only eight American school districts had medical inspections, but within a decade over 400 cities introduced the practice, as well as vision and dental screening. Still, Wallin (1914) pointed out that America lagged far behind Europe, where school physicians had been assigned since 1868 in Sweden, followed by France and Germany.

John Edward Wallace Wallin (1876–1969), recipient of a Yale Ph.D. and one of the first school psychologists, was certainly one of the first Americans to provide analyses of special education programs that were both scholarly and practical. The psychoeducational clinic he established at the University of Pittsburgh in 1912, inspired by a visit to the Vineland Training School, was one of the first in America and the first of eight clinics he directed in schools, community agencies, and universities. That he continues to be honored is evidenced by the Council for Exceptional Children's annual award in his name to a succession of the most revered American leaders in special education.

Concerned about health needs of pupils in ungraded classes, Wallin (1924) advocated strenuously for medical and dental clinics but emphasized that these were secondary to the central focus of specialized instruction. Although they have medical needs, he stated, a "large percentage of subnormal children are purely educational and not medical cases. Their mental development depends almost entirely upon proper pedagogical training and little if at all, upon medication or surgical interference" (p. 18). His landmark book, *The Education of Handicapped Children* (1924), documented progress worldwide and expressed views about the role of education, especially for pupils with retardation, that departed from the dominant biological determinism. Rejecting hereditarianism's implications for social control as opposed to environmental amelioration, he proposed a differentiated educational approach, with the goal of returning many students to regular classes and including those children to whom the term *trainable* would later be applied. Though endorsing mental testing, he was among the first to note its limitations (Wallin, 1912b), believing like Farrell that individual needs rather than statistical eligibility should determine educational placement.

While his writing reflects a balance of objectivity and humanitarianism admirable in any era but especially so in the early decades of the 20th century, series editor Cubberly's introduction to the 1924 book seems jarringly at odds with its author's beliefs, declaring its contribution would be to reduce the "social menace of those children who enter school life in a handicapped physical or mental condition" (p. viii). But Wallin himself reflected views of the day in terminology, in recounting without comment founding of schools for "the colored blind," and noting in an earlier work (Wallin, 1914) that "a child abnormal in body probably cannot remain normal in mind; he will tend, as has been said, to become morally perverse and criminal" (p. 9) (though this was to stress the need for psychoeducational clinics, for which he argued compellingly, citing high prevalence of disease, orthopedic impairments, and vision, hearing, and dental problems). Nor was Wallin's (1912b) research on epilepsy free of contemporary myths, although it is revealing concerning both beliefs about epilepsy and the impact of mental testing. His study of more than 300 residents of the New Jersey State Village for Epileptics at Skillman employed the Binet-Simon scale. While critiquing the measure and noting that his sample "may" not be representative (of which we can be certain), he reported it revealed, using Goddard's term, that most epileptics were morons.

Nevertheless, Wallin exerted extraordinary positive influence on the introduction of services in schools and in countering negative expectations and prejudices. Like Farrell, he believed schools should exclude no child and should serve an essential role, through psychoeducational clinics, in identifying special needs and providing appropriate services, not simply in classifying and separating those with problems. Concerning nature versus nurture, he advanced an "euthenics" position (Wallin, 1914) emphasizing environmental influences on children's physical and mental health, as well as intellectual potential. While he did not hold out hope for cure of retardation, he argued in the tradition of Seguin that "mental improvement" could be expected as a result of effective teaching.

Another early advocate of health services in schools literally embodied the linkage of medicine, psychology, and education. Child study came to full flower in the long and productive career of Arnold Gesell (1880–1961), who, though also trained in medicine, was the first individual officially identified as a school psychologist (Fagan, 1987). He had previously been a teacher and a principal in Wisconsin, and then an instructor at the Los Angeles State Normal School (Ames, 1989). Best known for his documentation of norms for all domains of typical infant, child, and adolescent development, Gesell also greatly influenced the understanding of atypicality. While he is considered here in the context of school health services, the scope of his work was enormous, and in fact very few of his more than 400 publications specifically addressed children's physical or health problems (Ames,

1989). Still, his minutely detailed documentations of the course of development proved essential to our knowledge of physical, as well as mental, emotional, and social growth, and a basis for *developmental diagnosis* (Gesell & Amatruda, 1941) in assessing developmental progress and problems of individual children.

The accolade "greatest modern student of the child" (Gesell & Gesell, 1912, p. 342), with which he acknowledged his mentor, is one many later professionals might bestow on Gesell himself. He is commonly identified with a school of developmental psychology labelled *maturationist*, as distinguished from the *environmentalist* tradition of behaviorism, and as the principal successor to Hall, whom he credited with linking biology to psychology by applying "the concepts of evolution to the mind of the child and of the race" (Gesell, 1948, p. 224). Thus, the intellectual succession proceeded from Darwin to Hall and then to Gesell, and it is on that basis that his portrayal of the course of development has been criticized; his description of "ages and stages" would seem to ascribe little importance to environmental influence, while neglecting individual variability. Yet, in his writings, collected and edited by his long-time collaborator, Louise Bates Ames (1989), there is evidence to support her assertion that for Gesell, as for Piaget, "*interaction* is the crux of the matter" (p. 9). And, while believing genetic influence dominant, he insisted that "no two infants were ever born alike" (Gesell, 1949, p. 548).

The events that led to founding of the Yale Clinic of Child Development, now the Gesell Institute of Human Development, involved an attractive counter-offer to one proffered by fellow Clark alumnus Lewis Terman combining state-level responsibilities with a Stanford faculty appointment. Offer of a full professorship in Child Hygiene at Yale, along with appointment as Connecticut State Director of Child Hygiene, was one he could not refuse, not least since it enabled him to complete medical studies and remain in close proximity to Clark and his mentor (Fagan, 1987). While Gesell was an early advocate for school health services, his conception of what these entailed went beyond routine medical inspection and provision of school nurses. He urged preventive measures, such as attention to nutrition, as well as prompt identification and timely treatment of health problems, especially in the preschool years and in kindergarten (Gesell, 1923). Further, he extended the scope of school health to encompass *mental* hygiene, emphasizing prevention of problems: "Child Hygiene, as Dr. Gesell interpreted it, appeared to include the physical, psychological, and educational well-being of the child" (Ames, 1989, p. 53). Notwithstanding his long-standing interest in retardation and occasional papers on specific medical problems and syndromes, his major concerns were for all children, rather than for certain groups.

AGENCIES, SCHOOLS, AND SPECIAL CLASSES

With the shift from a charity model to an approach geared to future employability, a parallel shift occurred in location of services, from hospital or clinic to day classes. This mirrored trends in other areas, especially hearing and vision, and reflected the renewed commitment to maintaining family integrity in the interests of the child, affirmed in the 1909 White House Conference. While Massachusetts's 1851 compulsory attendance law included "crippled" children, public school provisions for children with orthopedic impairments were introduced in America in Chicago in 1899. New York established its first class in 1906, at P.S. 104 in Manhattan (New York City Board of Education, 1941, p. 6). Like the open-air classes for pupils with "lowered vitality" or active tuberculosis, and programs for pupils with epilepsy, some other specialized arrangements were introduced, such as New York's classes for children with heart problems resulting from rheumatic fever, formed in 1907. But most often, in most nations, children with orthopedic or health impairments, depending on severity and issues of contagion, were tutored in hospitals or at home, enrolled in regular classes if that was thought feasible, or not schooled at all. A committee of physicians reported that many of the 958 pupils in New York with epilepsy were excluded from school in 1936 for "other than medical reasons" (New York City Board of Education, 1941).

New York's classes began outside the purview of the public schools in 1898 by the Children's Aid Society, and in 1900 the Guild for Crippled Children of the Poor of New York was organized, with an auxiliary given special responsibility for the many children with physical impairments on Manhattan's lower east side (New York City Board of Education, 1941, pp. 5–6). Collaboration with local philanthropy had European precedents; Berlin's Association for the Care and Training of Mentally Deficient Children provided food and clothing for needy children in Auxiliary Schools, as well as day care and assistance with vocational placement (Maennel, 1909). In 1900, a group of Cleveland women known as the Sunbeam Circle began a kindergarten at the Alta House Settlement in the city's Little Italy. The success of this venture inspired the women to raise funds to buy a cottage and hire a teacher for a small group of older pupils to provide instruction interspersed with rest and "corrective treatments" (Ohio Department of Education, 1985, p. 10), eventually provided by physical and occupational therapists. This demonstration that the children could negotiate the physical demands of school persuaded the district to assume responsibility, and in 1910, a building (Sunbeam School, a name retained when the program was relocated) was provided and teachers assigned. The Sunbeam Circle provided hot lunches and a public nurse, persuading a brewery to supply transportation via horse-drawn wagons. State legislation enacted in 1913 provided up to $150 per child per year reimbursement for such programs (p. 12).

Paralleling these developments, advocacy efforts culminated in 1921 in the founding of the National Society for Crippled Children, in Toledo, Ohio, principally through the leadership of Edgar Fiske "Daddy" Allen (1862–1937), an industrialist whose son had died after being injured by a streetcar (Allen, 1924). The original group, representing 46 Rotary Clubs in Ohio, had advocated so successfully for public awareness and medical, educational, and rehabilitative services that their "Ohio Plan" formed the basis for state legislation, Ohio's "Act to Provide Medical and Surgical Treatment of Crippled Children" (1919), and was emulated in other states. Though Canadian representation came in 1920, the first actual international congress was held in conjunction with Rotary International's 1927 convention in Belgium. By the 1930s, other civic groups had joined in supporting the new organization, which continued active fund raising, resulting in hospital construction; visiting teachers provided instruction and vocational training in these hospitals. The society's philosophy was set forth, in 1931, as "The Crippled Child's Bill of Rights," summarized in the tenth provision that

> not only for its own sake, but for the benefit of Society as a whole, every crippled child has the right to the best body which modern science can help it to secure; the best mind which modern education can provide; the best training which modern vocational guidance can give; the best position in life which his physical condition, perfected as best it may be, will permit, and the best opportunity for spiritual development which its environment affords. (p. 25)

Beginning in the 1940s, local affiliates of the society and of the United Cerebral Palsy Association formed nursery classes, which with therapies and social services for families have generally been fee-based, following a sliding scale in consideration of income and third-party reimbursement. After enactment of P.L. 94-142, responsibility for operation of many preschool programs began to shift to public schools, depending on state policy and often local initiative. Amendments enacted in 1986 (P.L. 99-457) extended provision of services to eligible children beginning at age 3.

As in the case of deafness and blindness, special educational programs for children with physical disabilities, in the United States as in other nations, were usually centralized. The logic, though no longer acceptable, continues to be invoked: Buildings must be accessible, and it is more economical to centralize therapy services. While the idea of "centers" adapted to accommodate pupils who use wheelchairs or other adaptive equipment, where services can be conveniently clustered, appears reasonable, it segregates, not on the basis of educational needs but on the basis of physical characteristics. In the United States, federal legislation (Section 504 of the Rehabilitation Act of 1977 and the Americans with Disabilities Act of 1990) ruled such segregation a violation of civil rights under the Constitution. Use of a wheelchair or need for specialized therapies does not in itself dictate what school a student should attend, or whether the student should be taught in a regular or special class. Many students with physical impairments, given access, assistive and adaptive technology, or other supports, find the demands and opportunities of "regular" education more appropriate than those in a special setting. Thus, and in view of their great diversity, it is difficult to argue that pupils with physical disabilities need a certain form of specialized instruction.

It happened that an innovative method not devised specifically for exceptional children, though the school bearing its name has enrolled many (Semel, 1992), was piloted with students with physical disabilities. Helen Parkhurst (1887–1973), having worked as an assistant to Montessori, adapted her concepts in an "Individual System" of individual contracts and learning centers, with pupils assigned to "jobs" with worksheets to complete at their own pace in "subject laboratories." The plan was piloted with children at the Upway Field School for Crippled Children in Pittsfield prior to its introduction in the Dalton (Massachusetts) High School. Parkhurst lectured worldwide on the Dalton Plan, and the first issue of *Progressive Education*, in 1924, featured experiments with the plan in England (Cremin, 1961, p. 248). She herself established the private Dalton School in New York City, in 1920, published *Education on the Dalton Plan* (1922), and produced radio and television programs for and about children. The story of the Dalton Plan suggests that "individualized instruction, an important current in progressive education" (Semel, 1992, p. 31) is appropriate not only for pupils with disabilities, but for all pupils.

Manifestations of physical and health impairment in children have changed in response to medical and public health developments, influencing the kinds of services and educational approaches provided. The open air school, with its quasi-hospital regimen of rest, nursing, exercise, and nutrition, responded to tuberculosis and pre-tubercular conditions. A different kind of quasi-clinical model was introduced with provision of therapies for post-polio patients and pupils with cerebral palsy and orthopedic impairments, as well as a multitude of medical syndromes. In the United States, the initial focus of state-coordinated Crippled Children's Services programs established under Title V of the Social Security Act of 1935 was orthopedic impairments, but "by 1958 orthopedic problems constituted less than 50% of the reported diagnoses. Better neonatal survival rates meant more children with cystic fibrosis, neurologic deficits, congenital malformations, and inborn errors of metabolism" (Farel, 1988, p. 70). Continuing medical research will yield means of prevention and cure for many more problems, and educational needs will change accordingly.

In recent years, issues of concern have involved children with severe and multiple impairments affecting cognitive ability, those with special health care needs who may be dependent on life-support technology, and those who are HIV-positive or have AIDS. Fetal Alcohol Syndrome/Fetal Alcohol Effect (FAS/FAE) and prenatal exposure to cocaine have presented major challenges. Certain biological conditions, autism and traumatic head injury, have been "reclassified" for educational purposes but, like others such as Tourette syndrome and Attention Deficit Disorder, still pose educational problems. Finally, while children of poverty continue to be at greatest risk for physical and health impairments, as they have been throughout history, many medical syndromes know no boundaries of class and, moreover, children with physical and health impairments represent a universal human reality in which, in Susan Sontag's (1978) words, we all "hold citizenship." All these statements also apply to children who are the topic of the next chapter.

CHAPTER 8

Feared Victims: Dependent, Neglected, Disturbed, and Delinquent Youth

Emotional disturbance in children must always have existed, yet it is "properly a twentieth century phenomenon" (Despert, 1965, p. 8). Long before alienists differentiated mental illness from retardation, Galen had identified such conditions as hysteria, depression, and hallucinations, but these were considered adult maladies. Esquirol (1838) gave the first description of childhood psychosis but proposed no differentiated treatment. Emil Kraepelin acknowledged but did not elaborate on childhood disturbances, though Hermann Emminghaus's *Psychic Disturbances of Children,* published in 1887, discussed pathogenic family and school influences—revolutionary at a time when biogenic views were dominant—but the work was largely ignored (Alexander & Selesnik, 1966). Early in the 20th century, psychiatric publications began to address childhood problems, culminating in 1935 in Kanner's *Child Psychiatry,* a major stimulus for services for children.

Certain accounts of Jesus casting out demons involved children, some of whom must have been disturbed, as were many "bewitched" children of the Middle Ages. The 12–year-old boy who began the first Children's Crusade, in 1212, was no doubt delusional (Baker & Traphagen, 1935). Some groups even today think a child whose behavior is deviant is possessed, but even if no occult forces are actually suspected, he "has the devil in him." Historically, a willful child, one who disobeyed, lied, stole, or committed cruel acts, did so out of contrariness. Children were expected to be obedient, grateful, and kind—to be "good"—and not to pout, sulk, or whine, but to be "happy." While parents were charged with keeping their children in line, at some point, often at age 7, they themselves were held responsible for their actions.

In 18th-century France, many incorrigible children were incarcerated, classified as "insubordinate" or "guilty." Similar provisions were made in the German *Zuchthausern,* houses of correction, introduced in Hamburg early

223

in the 17th century (Foucault, 1965, p. 43). A system of prisons, poorhouses, and workhouses was established in England for the purpose of managing the poor, which is to say confining them, adults and children, in massive numbers in the numerous "brideswells." "By 1774, pauperism—genuine poverty, as opposed to habitual vagrancy—had assumed alarming proportions. There is probably no other period in English history in which the social classes were so clearly divided" (Jones, 1972, p. 17). Each of the 15,000 parishes in England and Wales was designated a poor-law union and required to establish a workhouse. In such Dickensian settings, children were hidden away with physically and mentally infirm adults, as over and over we see reference to the poor as a dangerous—even a vicious—class, to children of the poor as objects of pity but also of fear.

INNOCENT VICTIMS AND WILLFUL BURDENS

Mind Cure

If children were responsible for their own actions then certainly adults were. Eccentricity was tolerated in one who was not dangerous, but many yet wondered what forces might be at work in one behaving oddly, subject to dark moods, or with unaccountable somatic complaints. Though certain predispositions were generally attributed to morbid heredity, the belief lingered that the ability to draw on inner resources to control one's thoughts and feelings, even one's body, was a sign of spiritual strength and character. Either way, with such strictures a disturbed family member was a source of shame (Corbin, 1990). The search for the locus of inner resources led Aristotle to locate the soul in the heart, and Galen to place it in the brain, which came to be considered the organ of the mind, critical to understanding insanity as illness (Altschule, 1957). The mind-body relationship is still not well understood, but "psychosomatic" illnesses are seldom dismissed as "all in the mind." Some physical complaints have been reported by sufferers in response to discovery of the condition (Shorter, 1992). "Spleen, vapors, and melancholia" in 18th-century European women have been ascribed to changes in their social status associated with less romantic, economically motivated male attitudes toward marriage, while such phenomena as millennial hysteria and witch-hunting have been metaphorically termed collective psychosis (Rosen, 1968).

If conditions can make one sick, might sick persons will themselves to wellness? This theme, familiar today in holistic medicine, was expressed in the "mind cures" popular in this century's first decade, bridging transcendentalism and Freudian psychology (Hale, 1971). They were anticipated by Phineas P. Quimby's assertions that it was patients' faith in their doctors that enabled cures to be effected. (Voltaire had quipped that the art of medicine consists in amusing the patient while nature cures the disease; Quimby thought the patient must do more than let nature take its course.) While some were charlatans, most early New England "curists," certainly Mary Baker Eddy, who broke with Quimby, were quite sincere (as have been adherents of Norman Vincent Peale's positive thinking and of today's self-help notions). Though long antedated by more sophisticated versions in Eastern mysticism, Quimby's ideas paralleled an interest in what we now call parapsychological phenomena, in England shared by a circle of intellectuals centered around Elizabeth Barrett Browning and novelist-politician Edward Bulwer-Lytton (Porter, 1972). Though it was not a religion per se, spiritualism's popularity can be accounted for, like much in the 19th century, by the challenge of science to faith.

Although the interest applied mainly to adult affairs, children were certainly affected. In 1848, in Hydesville, New York, the "rappings" in the Fox home created a sensation that became a craze, for though the young Fox sisters admitted their hoax, mediums flourished as people sought to enlist their powers to communicate with deceased loved ones and receive guidance from the spirit world. Communities grew up around practicing mediums, and some, like Lily Dale in New York, still attract the faithful and the curious. The phenomenon cannot be dismissed as but another instance of exploitation of fools by knaves; it was coterminous with a broad spiritual awakening within established churches and interest in such ideas as the Swedenborgian spirit world. But reflection and contemplation are luxuries mainly available to the relatively comfortable. No doubt many troubled persons found comfort and strength in spiritualism or mind cure, but the core issues involved external impact of deviant behavior. That is so today, even where children are concerned.

Counting Lunatics

Moral management reforms were slow to spread; those in Paris, Boring (1950) noted, "had not even extended . . . to the French provinces at the time of Pinel's death in 1826" (p. 51). In America, Quaker humanitarianism was evident in early asylums for persons experiencing mental illness, but with growing concentration of populations in cities awareness of deviance both increased and took a less altruistic tone, factors that led to the establishment of the Worcester State Hospital in Massachusetts (Grob, 1965). The campaign for a hospital for "lunatics and other sick persons" begun in 1810 by James Jackson and John C. Warren, eminent Boston physicians, was grounded in ostensibly altruistic injunctions that "when in distress . . . every man becomes our neighbor" and aiding the unfortunate is "the first of duties in Christian countries." But recognizing that the principal concern of Boston's philanthropists was *Boston*, their appeal raised the alarming specter of "significant numbers of nameless, faceless people existing outside the network of traditional institutions" (Dalzell, 1987, p. 13).

That the facility established at Worcester, near Boston, was built and operated with public support was due to the efforts of Horace Mann, who in 1829 undertook a survey to ascertain the number of lunatics in Massachusetts. He located 289 such persons: 78 in poorhouses, 37 in their families' homes, 19 in jails, 10 in the McLean Mental Hospital, the rest in almshouses like Charlestown's, convincing the legislature of the need for an appropriate facility. Opened in 1833, Worcester State Hospital became a model for others, like one in New York in 1839. The legislature, moved by Dorothea Dix's report of the many insane persons languishing in jails and workhouses, authorized expansion of the Worcester hospital in 1841, by which time there were 11 mental hospitals in the United States. By 1844, there were 24, as well as one in Ontario and one in Nova Scotia (Deutsch, 1949). Much of that expansion, and founding of additional European hospitals, is attributable to the influence of one reformer.

Dorothea Lynde Dix (1802–1887) left an unhappy home situation in Maine at age 12 to live in Boston with her grandfather, Dr. Elijah Dix, one of two main sources of inspiration for the life of service she would lead. The other was the Reverend William Ellery Channing, leading abolitionist and center of "organized benevolence in Boston" (Donald, 1960), who referred her to Howe, Sumner, and Mann. Having begun, at 14, to teach, she opened a school in Worcester. Channing's children were among those of other eminent families enrolled in one she later began in Boston, to which, concerned about the lack of free education for poor children, she added a charity component with his assistance (Wilson, 1975). Ill health forced her to close her school in 1838, though she continued to write for children and in 1841 agreed to teach a Sunday School class in the East Cambridge House of Correction. Appalled by the conditions under which mentally ill persons were maintained there and in other almshouses, jails, and asylums she visited, she began a crusade through "memorials" to state legislatures. Her 1848 memorial to the U.S. Congress proposed, since existing facilities could provide for only one-twelfth of the insane persons in the land, federal assistance through land grants for states to establish public institutions. Moved by her indefatigable lobbying, Congress passed an act in 1854 that would have apportioned 2,225,000 acres of public land for that purpose; President Pierce's veto, ostensibly on constitutional grounds, was probably motivated more by fear that such federal involvement might dry up local "fountains of charity" (Bremner, 1970, p. 789).

While disagreement continued as to the federal role in amelioration, there was growing consensus concerning the causes of insanity; in the Victorian mind there was little doubt that mental aberration was transmitted to children by parents. Esquirol's view was endorsed by eminent physicians like James Cowles Prichard, who wrote of a predisposition to insanity that must have presented a secret worry among thoughtful, responsible persons with familial "taint" (Gay, 1984, pp. 17–18). In France, as the fear of mental illness grew during the 19th century, so did the shame associated with it: "A 'deranged daughter' could easily discourage her sisters' suitors" (Perrot & Martin-Fugier, 1990, p. 148).

Worcester's first superintendent, Samuel Bayard Woodward, shared the belief in violation of natural laws as the principal cause of defect—which, since drunkenness was one of the major violations, was not without substantiation. The connection with birth defect was established well before the terms Fetal Alcohol Syndrome (FAS) and Fetal Alcohol Effect (FAE) were introduced in the 1970s. At the height of the 18th century's "gin epidemic," the British Royal College of Physicians observed a marked increase in mortality of newborns of drinking mothers (Dorris, 1989). Alcohol consumption during pregnancy had been linked with birth defect since antiquity; the Greeks cast the link within the context of physical health, 19th-century reformers within a moral context. The pre-Darwinian Zeitgeist was also receptive to the idea that nurture was important, and while Dix, Howe, and Woodward pointed the finger of blame at parental intemperance for congenital defect, they saw its adverse effects on parenting. Thus alcohol placed children at double jeopardy, and intemperance, considered a problem of the lower classes, was among the major reform campaigns of the 1830s and 1840s.

Moral Management and the Family Metaphor

Moral treatment's patronizing aspect was increasingly dominant as services became, in both senses, increasingly institutionalized. By midcentury, mental hospitals underwent a transition paralleling that soon to occur in institutions for persons with retardation. American society was also less tolerant of odd behavior and more inclined to see talking to oneself, dressing oddly, or reclusiveness as reason for confinement. The family metaphor now applied was not what Howe had in mind for, treated as dependent children, incarcerated against their will, hospitalized persons could be released from the "family" of the state only if their own promised to care for them (Dwyer, 1987). Commitment meant loss of rights and status and, in Europe as in America, often involved women, especially unmarried women, "who contributed less . . . to the family's well-being" (Corbin, 1990, p. 658). While most Americans who were committed were poor, a more affluent woman whose manner or attire was eccentric or who practiced spiritualism was also a candidate, most states accepting the husband's or father's petition with a physician's certification. Even in states requiring a public hearing, like Illinois where in 1875 a jury supported her son's claim that Mary Todd Lincoln was insane, it was waived if the medical superintendent concurred. A wife's commitment sometimes resulted from marital conflict, the case with Elizabeth Ware Packard, who would not conform to her minister husband's narrow religiosity; when released and divorced, she campaigned for commitment law reforms (Sapinsley, 1991).

Filling rapidly with poor people, especially Irish immigrants, the prototypical hospital at Worcester had by midcentury become basically custodial. Moral therapy was intended as an educational intervention to help patients learn acceptable attitudes and behaviors, as Amariah Brigham, superintendent of the Lunatic Asylum at Utica, New York, described in "Schools in Lunatic Asylums" (1845). (Brigham, among the "Original 13" founders of the American Psychiatric Association, was a co-founder in 1880 of the short-lived National Association for the Protection of the Insane and the Prevention of Insanity [Deutsch, 1949].) But as confidence in this optimistic approach decreased, asylums remained orderly but provided little treatment; large institutions came to bear more resemblance to Bedlam than to Tuke's Retreat. This grim reality was brought to public attention by Clifford Whittingham Beers (1876–1943), who, in *A Mind That Found Itself* (1908), described the brutal conditions he had witnessed and experienced, having been committed following a nervous breakdown in 1900. In 1909, Beers, with William James and Adolph Meyer, founded the National Committee for Mental Hygiene. (Sadistic abuse of psychiatric patients of course continued; while "hydrotherapy" was a common 19th-century treatment, there have been appalling accounts by rueful former attendants of "moving" naked inmates around in the 1950s with firehoses, to relieve boredom.)

A key figure in the nascent mental hygiene movement, Adolph Meyer (1866–1950) applied his neurological training gained in Zurich, Berlin, Paris, and London to work with mental illness. In 1913, he founded America's first psychiatric teaching hospital, the Phipps Clinic at Johns Hopkins, based on the model Esquirol pioneered. While in the popular mind insanity reflected moral degeneracy, at least moral weakness, psychiatry was experiencing an organic era (Lewis, 1941); Meyer attacked both. Stressing the unity of mind and body and the need to understand mental illness as sickness rather than evidence of moral failure, he also criticized the brain localization theories and typologies being advanced in neurology, psychiatry, and criminology. He was thus quick to recognize the implications of Freud's work for the understanding of children and emotional conflicts in adolescence, and consequently for healthy child-rearing and pedagogy. Rejecting the pessimism inherent in biologically deterministic views, he maintained that psychopathology could be explained on the basis of "learned dynamic habit patterns" (Hale, 1971, p. 18).

His wife, Mary Brook Meyer (1868–1939), could be considered the first psychiatric social worker, having introduced the practice of assessing clients' living environments to better understand their needs. Children's behavior problems are now understood as involving malfunctioning "ecosystems," rather than residing in the child alone, though American special education policy excludes "social maladjustment" in determining children's eligibility, unless caused by emotional disturbance. Youthful norm-violating behavior continues to be an apparently intractable problem, with concerns for the young person secondary to concern for the perceived threat posed to general safety and stability. This theme runs through early work with delinquents. And 19th-century adults may have been unaware of children's psychological problems, but they did know that children needed a place to live and adults to care for them. More than adult psychiatry, ameliorative work with children with emotional or behavioral disorders evolved from early programs for delinquent and dependent children.

ASYLUMS FOR ORPHANS

When death from infectious disease was common, adults were also at risk, and orphaned children were typically taken in by relatives; poverty often made it necessary for even healthy parents to give up a child, sometimes several. It was thus with Annie Sullivan and her brother and sister, who experienced a mother's death and a father's inability to provide for their support. Colonial practice based on the Poor Laws placed the onus on family and community, and strong traditions of independence and individualism retarded national policy concerning dependent children. But the Catholic Church had a long tradition in the area, the first American orphanage having been founded by Ursuline nuns in 1728, and Protestant and Jewish organizations soon saw it within their purview (Curti, 1964). As states assumed responsibility for delinquents, religious bodies founded asylums for children whose mothers had died in childbirth or who were orphaned as a result of work accident on a farm or in a mine, or of disease. By 1830, mainly in response to typhus, yellow fever, and cholera epidemics, 15 private orphanages had opened, followed by another 23 in the 1830s and 30 more in the 1840s (Rothman, 1971, p. 76).

Many represented a blend of benevolent outreach and community responsibility, in the sense of care for one's own, a religious group undertaking services for orphaned or otherwise needy children of its members. In Cleveland, Ohio, for example, the Martha Washington and Dorcas Society, a women's church group, founded the Protestant Orphanage (now Beech Brook) in the 1850s. Two Catholic orphanages were founded: St. Mary's Female Asylum in 1851 by the Ladies of the Sacred Heart to provide for the many orphaned Irish girls in the community, and St. Vincent's Orphan Asylum for boys in 1853 by the Sisters of Charity (later merged as Parmadale). The Cleveland Jewish Orphan Asylum (now Bellefaire) was founded in 1868 through efforts of the city's large Reform German community (Polster, 1990, p. 12).

The Parsons Child and Family Center, a treatment agency in Albany, New York, began in the 1820s, when church women concerned for the numerous "ragged, starving children who wandered the streets begging for food and at times eating garbage" constituted themselves as the Ladies Orphan Society (*Hapless Children*, n.d., p. 3). Despite the expected low costs of such an enterprise—less than New York City's average of 13 cents per week per child—the idea of a home for orphaned children needed leadership, soon provided by Orissa Heely, grieving over the death of her newborn infant and abandonment by her husband, and a teacher friend, Eliza Wilcox. Begun in 1829, the project soon expanded to include destitute children whether orphaned or not, and the numbers grew rapidly. The next year the Society for the Relief of Orphan and Destitute Children in the City of Albany was formally constituted, supported by two-dollar memberships supplemented by a small public subsidy.

While philosophy regarding placement came to favor adoption and foster care, the advent of the mental hygiene movement and the influence of psychoanalysis created awareness that some children needed planned group living and treatment. Thus, many facilities begun as orphan asylums converted their mission. The shift occurred over decades, however, so that by the 1960s it was not unusual for a "Home" to number among its residents young people who had simply grown up there, as well as troubled youngsters who needed a secure, nurturing environment, but something more. Administrators were advised that institutional care of orphans was no longer needed since "the orphan has almost disappeared."

There are only 1/16th as many orphans in the United States as there were as late as 1920 even though the child population is much larger. Greater advances in medical science and health have resulted in this phenomenon. Only a small percentage of mothers die in child-birth today as contrasted with 1920 or even 1935. Industrial and farm accidents have been greatly reduced and epidemics and plagues have been eliminated. (Child Welfare League of America, 1960, pp. 7–8)

While the Social Security Act of 1935 enabled as of 1960 1,400,000 fatherless children, more than 60%, to live with the surviving parent or a relative, what *was* needed was professional treatment for "troubled children, problem children, emotionally disturbed children, children who need to have their capacity to love and be loved restored" (p. 8). In the 19th century, the concepts of childhood disturbance and treatment were unknown, though there were surely needy children. What was known was that children left homeless needed a place to live and adults to care for them and nurture their moral and spiritual development. The Civil War impacted this situation enormously. While the toll resulting from actual killing was great, many more fatalities resulted from infectious disease. A great many of those who perished were themselves little more than children, but many children were left orphaned or fatherless with mothers whose efforts to provide for their care failed or resulted in the mother's own early death. Available facilities were rapidly overwhelmed. While each orphan asylum that would later convert to residential treatment has its unique story, one in Berea, Ohio, is illustrative.[1]

John Baldwin, having discovered a rich lode of sandstone on his property, imported German workers known for their skill in sandstone mining who, with their families, established a community with common language, tradition, and affiliation with the German Methodist Church. But as the conflict between North and South raged, they "marched together with their native countrymen" and some did not return. Left with limited options for family support, some widows found night work cleaning unheated streetcars and office buildings in nearby Cleveland. Many of the men who did return to mine the quarry contracted lung disease. On both counts, tuberculosis took its toll, leaving a number of children full orphans. Sympathetic neighbors supplied food and clothing, but there were now children needing shelter. Thus, in 1864, Drs. Jacob Rothweiler, William Nast, and William Ahrens founded the German Methodist Orphan Asylum "to receive orphans or other children . . . in order to care for their bodies and minds in the best possible manner, and to educate and fit them for their temporal and eternal welfare." The first child, 9-year-old Marie Bletch, entered on May 1, 1864, followed by seven more the next day. At its most numerous its 60,000 members constituted about 1% of German Americans, but American German Methodism was a dynamic sect; until 1933, its Central Conference supported the asylum through donations solicited via *Der Christliche Apologiste*, a weekly publication. (Impressively, what became Baldwin-Wallace College was established in the same community through this means.)

---

[1]This information was obtained from the Archives of the Berea Children's Home and Family Services, Berea, Ohio.

Until 1930, 75 or more children were housed in a large, congregate building completed in 1891, with an addition in 1902, both designed by August Klotzbach, who had lived 11 years in the home. The Manual Training School was added in 1908. A cottage system was fully adopted in 1942, the campus of the Methodist Children's Home, as it had been renamed, comprising six cottages, the original structure used for offices and activities, and a nearby 144-acre farm with farmhouse, where gardening and chicken-raising produced income as well as work experience. Trade training was emphasized, sometimes leading to an apprenticeship, as it did for architect Klotzbach, who recalled, "Just as discipline in all families was sterner . . . , so likewise, it was more severe in the Asylum. But, rigid and often harsh as it was, it somehow turned out sturdy men and women." Daily life allowed little time for play, much for religious training, and much more for work, older boys serving as "overseers." Children were nourished on wholesome, if spartan, fare, bathed in the river nearby, and put to bed and awakened early. Such a routine, standard in asylums, was often accompanied by an oppressive regimentation that bred resentment, but most of this agency's alumni seemed to recall it with affection, many maintaining life-long connections. In such homes work was thought essential to the development of character, and training for work essential for children's "temporal welfare."

These views did not change radically, but demands began to ease in response to changing views of childhood in the society as well as changes in the situations of children admitted. A former housemother recalled in 1954 that none of the 18 girls in her care were full orphans, but most came from "broken homes," and while needing discipline, they needed understanding more, and some flexibility in management. While the home was part of the community—a resident recalled that townspeople celebrated Christmas with the children—inevitable tensions developed with the local schools, and a campus school was initiated in 1965 as a component of the agency's treatment program.

MANAGEMENT OF DELINQUENTS

As we saw, under Roman law rebellious sons could be banished from the household, and "removal" in one form or another is a prototypic response to children who disturb family life. Responsibility for child-rearing has in virtually all societies belonged to the family, more or less shared by neighbors or elders; an African adage is that "it takes a whole village to raise a child." In Europe and America, children without parents to supervise them, or whose parents were unable to do so, represented a broader problem than rebellious sons, one that grew in magnitude in response to events—famines, epidemics, wars—and with industrialization.

English Reformatories

The forced-work programs begun in 18th-century Europe included not only those on the street but also troublesome youth of respectable families. Even in late 19th century France, a surprisingly large proportion of youth placed by their fathers in reform schools were girls, "whom they feared would become pregnant or who were guilty of 'misbehavior,' the main reason cited for sending young women away" (Perrot & Martin-Fugier, 1990, p. 159). The practice of placing a difficult child in a setting better able to exercise control had taken various forms, such as apprenticeship under a tough master. But the idea of a training school was first tried in Rome in 1704 by Pope Clement XI, who established a hall in the Hospital of Saint Michael "for 'correction and instruction of profligate youth, that they who when idle were injurious, may when taught become useful to the state'" (in Tappan, 1949, p. 438).

By the late 18th century, street urchins of the sort Dickens made memorable were a major concern in London, where a culture of criminality spawned many institutions like Fagin's school for young thieves. Street crime was specialized work, entailing a broad range of "trades," as Hughes (1987) noted, "as though the Industrial Revolution, breeding an ever-expanding range of products and specialists to make them, had brought forth an equal army of specialists to steal them" (p. 171). Like all cultures, this one had its own shared language:

> The most dexterous were the *files* and *buzz-gloaks*, or pickpockets. . . . Larger schools (whose ten-year-old initiates were known as *erriffs*, a straight word for young canaries, or *academy buzz-nappers*) were a favorite topic of London journalists. They taught the art of *fogle-hunting* (drawing out handkerchiefs), *bung-diving* (taking purses), *speaking to the tattler* (lifting a watch . . .), and *chiving the froe* (cutting off a woman's pocket with a razor). (p. 172)

The children of transported criminal parents were also a concern, but reformers saw in them hope for preventing enculturation into criminal life. In 1788, the Philanthropic Society of London began a program called the New Asylum for the Prevention of Vice and Misery among the Poor, placing children picked up on the street in cottages to be trained in gardening, tailoring, and shoemaking (Barnes & Teeters, 1945). As numbers grew, and the need to separate boys and girls became evident, a large building was obtained in 1792 at St. George's Fields in Southwark with dormitories and workshops. In addition to fiscal problems, disciplinary concerns multiplied as boys who had actually engaged in crime came to predominate; returned runaways smuggled in weapons and soon girls were "absconding" for liaisons with the boys. But the society managed to continue and in 1806 was officially sanctioned by Parliament. Under Sydney Turner, effective but not unduly repressive discipline was introduced, along with differential treatment: Children who had committed no criminal offense were trained in "The Manufactury," others were first "softened" in "The Reform." Especially "bad boys" considered incorrigible could be "expelled," which meant transfer to prison (Carlebach, 1970, p. 14). Turner recommended adoption of an agricultural colony concept, like that at Mettray in France, and accordingly in 1849 the program relocated to Redhill in Surrey, south of London, where residents (now only boys) lived in houses with staff.

Parkhurst Prison for Boys, established in 1838, was from its inception a penal institution rather than a reformatory, intended to deter young offenders from further crime, as well as potential micreants. Its predecessors were the notorious prison hulks Dickens vividly described in *Great Expectations*, one of which had been set aside for juveniles, with prison dress, leg irons, and harsh discipline. Parkhurst's governor, Robert Woolcombe, thought "the constant infliction of summary punishment" counterproductive, and differentiated "probationary class" and "ordinary class" inmates from the "refractory class," who "received very rough treatment" (Carlebach, 1970, p. 27). His successor, Captain George Hall, initiated a system of incentives and improved medical and nutritional provisions. Reports of released inmates transported to Australia indicated generally favorable adjustment, but opening of more reformatories impacted the number, and nature, of Parkhurst inmates; though they represented the hardest cases, their declining numbers meant reduced support. With a change in leadership, empty cells were filled with female convicts, and in 1864 the last 78 boys were transferred to a facility at Dartmoor.

The Parkhurst experience served to frame the debate concerning management of delinquency in England. Real advances toward enlightened treatment were obscured by images of leg-irons and of the military guard imposed after an escape attempt by 34 boys. But opponents attacked the very concept of incarceration of the young, also favoring "voluntary" (philanthropic) rather than state control. The most vocal of these, Mary Carpenter (1807–1877), was "a brilliant, volatile, passionate and arrogant woman whose life, work and prejudices were to dominate the history of the management of juvenile delinquency" (Carlebach, 1970, p. 40). This clergyman's daughter found in children of the poor and in delinquency causes to which to devote her considerable talent and energies. Experiences with the Ragged School she founded in 1846 led her to call for free day schools for destitute children, industrial "feeding" schools for neglected children, and reformatory schools for those who had committed crimes. Imprisonment, she maintained, was never warranted.

At the core of her crusade was the uniqueness of childhood. The problem of delinquency was generally viewed as entirely one of social class; "official inquiries into crime, drunkenness, prisons, and transportation that were held between 1815 and 1840 tended to confirm the same view of crime: that its class nature mattered more than its causes" (Hughes, 1987, p. 167). But Carpenter asserted that children of any class might commit delinquent acts, the difference lying in the family support available to the more privileged child. Lacking such resources, a child experienced one of two situations, both more likely to corrupt than redeem: if he or she was apprehended, corruption would result from imprisonment; if not, antisocial behavior would escalate until a professional criminal was made. What was needed was an approach recognizing the nature of childhood, focusing on the individual, and crossing lines of class.

She seems to have supported her attack on Parkhurst with misleading information, prompting a response by Joshua Jebb, Director of Convict Prisons, who feared her stressing the "children of the State" stigma would affect public sentiment to the detriment of the children. Owing to her self-confessed "unwillingness to own herself in the wrong" (Carlebach, 1970, p. 52), she was undeterred and her adamant opposition to child imprisonment was instrumental in bringing about reform legislation. But while effective in articulating sound principles of reformatory management, she was not able to put them into practice at the Red Lodge Reformatory for Girls she founded in 1854, the first in England. Whether because she was a better critic than implementer or because her charges were more intractable than anticipated, little in the way of reform seems to have been accomplished. Visitors' reports cautiously hinted at problems, but their diffidence and tendency to exonerate Carpenter might be attributed to fear of her retributive pen; their tone changed after her death, expressing total dissatisfaction with conditions of the school.

Since the Reformatory Schools Act of 1854 was relatively nonspecific concerning operation, leaders shared their views. Hardwick Reformatory's Barwick Lloyd Baker endorsed rigorous conditions, for short terms, with training as laborers but minimal instruction. While insisting that the experience must not be perceived as pleasant, he agreed with Matthew Davenport Hill that discipline should be kind as well as firm. Based on the Redhill experience, Turner emphasized that, in a family-like cottage model, direct-care staff were critical, also endorsing agriculture as the best avenue to achieve the dual purpose of work preparation and character building. While some boys might be apprenticed or conscripted in the army, he thought for most the best plan was removal from the circumstances that had led to their difficulties through transportation to one of the colonies (Carlebach, 1970).

Dispersion and Deportation

Dispersion of delinquents was predicated on two motives: a genuine desire to help young people redirect their lives, and a wish to be rid of the problem, reminiscent of "passing on" of unfortunates from town to town. Howe's opposition to reformatories was consistent with his ideas about family; to Mann, concerning a proposed reformatory at Lancaster, he wrote, "We have thousands and thousands of natural reform schools, viz. virtuous families, in which they ought to be received and reformed" (in Richards, 1909, p. 330). Arguing that "Viciously Disposed Youth Should Not Be Brought Together, But Put Far Asunder" (p. 189), rather than centralized confinement, which breeds antisocial behavior, small farms should be "hired, where boys could be 'colonized,' under the care of plain substantial farmers, and their *wives* and *families*" (p. 513). Of the many urban children of poverty "transported" to such wholesome settings, as we saw in Chapter 3, few were in need of reform.

In England, recidivism was a problem for which, for adult criminals, transportation seemed an ideal solution; Australia could "swallow a whole class . . . whose existence was one of the prime sociological beliefs of late Georgian and early Victorian England . . . English lawmakers wished not only to get rid of the 'criminal class' but if possible to forget about it" (Hughes, 1987, p. 1). Despite his popularity, Dickens's insistence that criminality was a consequence of poverty did not change dominant views that crime, vagrancy, alcoholism, and immorality were simply lower-class characteristics (Kaplan, 1988). Whatever the actual number of "reformed" youth who found their way to one of the colonies, juvenile offenders were among the vast numbers of felons transported to Australia. Nearly one-fifth of the convicts arriving at Hobart between January and September of 1834, Hughes (1987) tells us, were juveniles. Altogether, "more than 2,000 such boys were transported to Van Diemen's Land and went to the reformatory at Point Puer," for children between 9 and 18, "to be schooled, taught trades, instructed in the truths of Christianity, and punished" (p. 409). Though transportation from Parkhurst was officially an extension of punishment, good behavior could earn a boy a "probationary pass" or even a "ticket-of-leave." But a "bad boy" was in for rough treatment.

Religious instruction under a succession of chaplains, through enforced daily devotionals and hymn-singing, proved largely ineffectual, as did the rudimentary academic instruction, but opportunities to learn a trade were apparently at least as good as the boys would have had in England. Work was very hard, mainly serving adult needs, and fatigue after a grueling day could not have yielded enthusiastic scholars. Like today's reform facilities, "Point Puer had not one but two social systems: an official one imposed by the commandant and the chaplain, and a tribal one invented by the boys" (Hughes, 1987, p. 411). Despite harsh punishments for offenses like lying and stealing, peer pressures to commit them in the interests of the group were strong. A boy needed to maintain "a middle way" to survive (p. 412).

Houses of Refuge

In the American colonies, "children were simply not supposed to be delinquent" (Teeters & Reinemann, 1950, p. 64) and most had families, but in time among the throngs of immigrants seeking work were hundreds of children "sold" as indentured servants, a form of industrial enslavement that increased with industrialization. This did enable some to receive training, even apprenticeship, but failure to adhere to the terms of the contract or misbehavior meant jail; most indentured children simply continued to be exploited as cheap labor (Felt, 1971). English-style almshouses provided shelter for indigent children but not effective regulation of those inclined to act out, and whether in jail or almshouse children were mixed with adult criminals or persons with all manner of problems. As alternatives, reformers would create an "institutional web" (Foucault, 1977) of special schools, reformatories, mental hospitals, and orphanages; for young offenders such an alternative was the House of Refuge. Conceived by John Griscom, a Quaker influenced by Pestalozzi and Oberlin, these were intended to serve the child's needs, even more importantly than protecting society. Griscom's New York House of Refuge, opened in 1825, was followed in 1827 by Boston's Municipal House of Reformation for Juvenile Offenders and one in Philadelphia, whose board president, John Sergeant, stressed that "the Refuge is not a place of punishment," nor is it

> a provision simply nor even principally, for the security of society against offense, by the confinement of culprits, nor for inflicting the vengeance of society upon offenders as a terror to those who may be inclined to do evil. . . . but, in the accents of kindness and compassion, invites the children of poverty and ignorance whose wondering and misguided steps are leading them to swift destruction, to come to a home where they will be sheltered from temptation and led into the ways of usefulness and virtue. (in Snedden, 1907, p. 12)

Houses of Refuge were an improvement over imprisonment, in that young offenders were not thrown in with hardened criminals, but the effect was much the same. The vision articulated by Sergeant was not realized; despite the intent to provide training in a trade, work was done on contract, children essentially providing cheap labor (Hawes, 1971). Like the buildings, discipline was prison-like, with liberal use of corporal punishment, all receiving the same treatment irrespective of offense (Snedden, 1907, p. 12).

Colonies and Cottages

A major concern among social problems attendant on urbanization and industrialization were "potential hordes of street urchins" whose propensity for crime seemed to be growing (Brenzel, 1980, p. 199). In England, evangelical tracts and Dickens's novels portrayed the city, with its "poverty, lack of work, dislocation, vile housing, addiction, the death of hope," as a breeding ground for crime (Hughes, 1987, p. 167). Reformers on both sides of the Atlantic "combined a pressing need to control the urban poor with what they considered benevolent care of the deprived" (Brenzel, 1980, p. 199). Child labor was thought an effective means of control, since children would be kept off the street, although in America, "many . . . who ended up working were not homeless wanderers, but children whose wages added to the meagre incomes of their families" (Felt, 1971, p. 41). As in other areas, Americans sought to learn how the problem was dealt with in Europe. To that end, in 1854 the Massachusetts legislature, contemplating a school for girls, dispatched a commission led by Francis Fay to visit programs in Germany (Das Rauhe Haus, in Hamburg), France (Ecole Agricole, in Mettray), and England (the Royal Philanthropic, in Surrey). These shared the philosophy that delinquency had environmental causes and thus sought to create homelike living arrangements in pastoral settings, providing training and religious instruction. That model would be adopted in America, in most instances providing secular education.

The idea of approximating family-like arrangements through cottage living originated at Mettray, near Tours, where in 1839 Judge Frederic Auguste Demetz began a colony on land a friend had donated, together with money for construction. Convinced that young miscreants could be reclaimed, Demetz was impressed by the goal of the houses of refuge he had been sent to inspect but thought agriculture held the best hope, by involving youth in honest labor, close to nature. The first inmates having been selected from the prison at Frontrevault in 1840, the plant comprised a chapel and six three-story houses, each with a workshop, a school, and dormitories, the boys grouped in family units supervised by masters. Work was by intent hard and discipline strict, with the ever-present threat of return to prison, but democratic in that peers chosen by the boys monitored rewards and punishments (Teeters & Reinemann, 1950). Some thought the regimentation demoralizing; Foucault (1977) called it "the disciplinary form at its most extreme, the model in which are concentrated all the coercive technologies of behavior . . . 'cloister, prison, school, regiment'" (p. 293). In France as in England, the idea of incarceration of youth was itself controversial; by the end of the century "it was far more common to denounce not youthful offenders but ill treatment by beastly parents, whom it was proposed to relieve of their responsibilities" (Perrot & Martin-Fugier, 1990, p. 159).

A municipal reformatory for boys opened in New Orleans in 1845, followed in 1849 by others in Rochester and Baltimore, tempered the house of refuge approach, but these also were prisonlike in construction and in operation. The concept that emerged expressed the faith that the common school could be extended to "make sober, hard-working children out of the footloose young" (Felt, 1971, p 41), serving a dual purpose reflected in programs today: to provide for needs that could not be met through ordinary schooling, and to protect society by removing and segregating deviant pupils (Katz, 1968). The first such extension was a facility for boys opened at Westborough, Massachusetts, in 1847, later named the Lyman School for Boys. Further extension reflected fears that, since social stability depended on the "angel in the house," an ideal of domesticity, submission, purity, and piety—qualities singularly lacking in some young females—the family, and thus the society, was endangered.

Pursuant to the Fay Commission's recommendations, the State Industrial School for Girls opened in 1856 in Lancaster, about 50 miles from Boston, the first "family style" institution in North America. Brenzel's (1980) study analyzes the social forces that influenced its character during its first half-century. "Lancaster fused the twin nineteenth-century emphases on schools and families. Through the combination of schooling and reform, the girls . . . would be saved so they could fill the appropriate female role within the family" (p. 197). Cottages, where each had her own small room with a common recreation area, surrounded a chapel, but despite the homelike features the brick buildings unmistakably comprised an institution, where "the girls were to be sheltered, educated, and gently incarcerated" (p. 202). Most were very poor, placed through probate court sentence or by their families for "stubborn, wayward, and potentially degenerate behavior; vagrancy, running away, and staying out late at night continued to be the most frequent female juvenile crimes" (p. 203). By the 1850s, after the Potato Famine of 1845, more than half Boston's population was foreign-born, mostly Irish (Handlin & Handlin, 1971), as were almost all foreign-born Lancaster inmates. Despite Catholic leaders' concerns about anti-Catholic and anti-Irish bias in the common schools, this arm of the system represented nearly the only option for a poor family. By 1900 about 6% were African-American.

Although its first superintendent, Bradford Peirce, expressed an idealistic vision, "reform ideology," Brenzel (1980) comments, "blended together the confused motives of benevolence and social control" (p. 197). That girls were increasingly indentured as domestics at 16 suggests more of a holding operation than the reform effort originally envisioned. The change in mission to training young women for "service" responded to a growing demand, but it also implied lowered expectations associated with a more general, and more sinister, shift occurring in American reform work. While society depended on feminine virtue for stability, female criminality and wantonness constituted a serious danger, and as with retardation there was movement away from the environmental faith that had inspired programs like Lancaster. Views like that expressed in the Howe-Sanborn Report in 1865, "General Causes of the Existence of Dependents, Destructives, and the Like," for the Massachusetts State Board of Charities, that drunkenness at the time of conception transmitted evil qualities to children hardened to ascribe inherent evil to the child. With poverty seen more as result than cause, since "most delinquent poor children suffered the 'permanence of taint'" (Brenzel, 1980, p. 208), "the concern shifted from saving children to classifying types of depravity" (p. 205).

Lancaster at first intermixed the girls, irrespective of age or type of offense, but soon younger girls were separated from those "considered more tainted, harder, and less-redeemable" (Brenzel, 1980, p. 208). As in the larger society, the classification system instituted was based on hereditarian and class-biased premises. Moreover, Lancaster was being compelled to concentrate on older, and tougher, "cases" (a term increasingly used). The State Primary School was opened in 1886 in Monson, Massachusetts, in the former almshouse, to house younger dependent children, but its inmate population also soon changed and it closed within a decade. State-legislated deinstitutionalization finally closed Lancaster in 1976. Its story, Brenzel concludes, reveals the "decline of hopes for reform into a desire for social control" and is "a drama about the devastating effects upon families of poverty and public charity . . . [that] offers an overarching view of reformers. . . . the initial exuberance and optimism of the founders abruptly ended. In their stead came fatigue, disillusionment, pessimism, and anger" (p. 212).

In the same year the girls' reformatory was opened, one for boys was established in another Lancaster, in Ohio. Initially, the "cottages" were large log cabins, each housing as many as 40 boys supervised by "Elder Brothers." As at Mettray, agriculture was the main endeavor, work was hard, and days were long. Sundays were devoted to religious services and reflection. Also like Ecole Agricole, discipline was strict; attempted escape was punished by two weeks' confinement in a dark cell, with the threat of return to prison sometimes carried out (Barnes & Teeters, 1945, p. 913). Reformatories that followed tended, like the two Lancasters, to be located in remote settings, with no opportunity for heterosexual contact and with rigid, monot-

onous routine and militaristic regimentation. Though conceived as extensions of the common school, with truancy often a factor leading to placement,
most American reform "schools" provided no real educational program for
the 23,901 children they housed (Caddey, 1963). By 1925, the number of
schools had nearly doubled, to 158, and the number of inmates, 84,317,
more than trebled. Howe had called for dispersion, but centralization was
the norm, and while the avowed goal was reform, punishment and deter-
rence were implicit objectives. Mainly, society had to be protected from
these, as from other, deviants.

In practice, delinquent youth, like those with retardation, were treated
as a menace and considered inherently bad and basically intractable. The
view that they were "born criminals" was widespread by 1925, but in that
year an authoritative change in perception is suggested by, of all people, Cyril
Burt (1925), who concluded, based on a study of 200 cases, that there was
"no sharp line of cleavage by which the delinquent may be marked off from
the non-delinquent":

> This graded continuity, the normal melting into the abnormal by almost imper-
> ceptible shades, is entirely in accord with what we now know of most other
> forms of mental deviation. The insane, the neurotic, the mentally deficient are,
> none of them, to be thought of as types apart, anomalous specimens separated
> from the ordinary man by a profound and definite gap; the extreme cases merge
> into the borderline, as the borderline merges into the average, with no sudden
> break or transition. It is the same with the moral faults of children; they run in
> an uninterrupted series, from the most heartless and persistent crimes . . . up
> to the mere occasional naughtiness to which the most virtuous will at times
> give way. The line of demarcation is thus an arbitrary line. (pp. 13–14)

That Burt (1925) differentiated delinquency as "a social rather than a
psychological concept" (p. 15) from retardation is interesting, for as we saw
these were commonly linked. It was generally reported that offenders' scores
on the new mental tests tended to be lower than average, which we could
attribute in some measure to culture bias. "The defective mental equipment
of juvenile offenders as a class," W. D. Morrison wrote in 1898, "originates
either in a defective physical basis of mental life or in inherited mental incom-
petence, or in the evil effects of abnormal mental surroundings" (p. 116).
Significantly, considering the tenor of the times, he argued for differential
arrangements for younger children. In 1893, he reported, "forty-seven infants under six years of age were committed to industrial schools in England,
and 347 boys and girls between the age of six and eight" (p. 290). Allowing
that "evil habits" develop very early, he thought such schools neither geared
to the needs of children so young nor likely to effect reform due to the influence of older youth.

While including "cautious adoption of practicable eugenic measures" (p. 587) among his suggestions for prevention, Burt (1925) also called for improved environmental conditions and recreational opportunities. The effect of heredity, stated this staunch hereditarian, is at most indirect. Inherited "weaknesses . . . may favor a moral lapse in later life; they in no way constitute a fatal and inexorable propulsion towards it" (p. 56). He recommended intervention when signs of difficulty first appeared and comprehensive psychological study of the youth involved in delinquent behavior, considering past history and present situation, with specific recommendations systematically followed up through continued observation.

CHILD GUIDANCE, JUVENILE JUSTICE, AND MENTAL HEALTH

As we saw, Hall's child-study approach, while seeking to change schooling, was not aimed at changing children. Instead, it implied a fatalistic belief that children would simply be as they are, and it was a task for psychologists and educators to know children as they are. But child study was taking a different form in some American and British agencies, involving comprehensive studies of children in trouble, as Burt recommended, sometimes in cooperation with the courts, and developing alternative schooling arrangements.

Guidance Centers and Psychoeducational Clinics

Psychological services for children began in 1896 with Lightner Witmer's clinic for the psychoeducational study and treatment of children at the University of Pennsylvania. When in March of that year a teacher brought a 14–year-old pupil with a puzzling spelling problem to the university, Witmer (1909) recalled his own early attempts as a preparatory school teacher in Philadelphia to remediate a student's language difficulties. The process he used in attempting to identify the precise nature of the boy's problem leading to steps in remediation, which he subsequently called the *clinical method*, seems to have expressed his own notion of the application of psychology to such problems (Fagan, 1985). While Hall's child study involved normative description, with special attention to children showing indications of advanced ability, Witmer (1909) applied his *orthogenics* with those having learning and behavioral difficulties, including some the institution at Media had rejected as uneducable. Still, he believed his approach applicable for all children. Over the next 30 years, case studies like that of his first client were published in the *Psychological Clinic*, a journal intended to focus on the individual child, not only those with problems, which accordingly by its eighth volume was subtitled *A Journal of Orthogenics for the Normal Development of Every Child* (French, 1990, p. 4).

Another important figure in launching the child guidance concept, which in the 1920s assumed the proportions of yet another movement, was Dr. Thomas W. Salmon. Concerned that societal factors placed the mental life of many children at risk, Salmon convened a conference in March 1921 at Lakewood, New Jersey. The outcome was a five-year demonstration, under the joint auspices of the Commonwealth Fund and the National Committee for Mental Hygiene, of community child guidance clinics, marking a redirection in the spirit of Witmer from the deterministic views of the age (Deutsch, 1949).

Witmer's model stimulated a network of clinics in institutions, as well as in universities and public schools. In the unit E. R. Johnstone established at the Vineland Training School, where Edgar Doll would pioneer in assessing adaptive behavior, Goddard translated and normed the Binet-Simon scales, which Frederick Kuhlman extended at the clinic founded by his predecessor, A. R. T. Wylie, at Minnesota's Fairbault School for the Feebleminded. While mental testing was a priority interest in these settings, that was initially not the case with school-based clinics. The first, Chicago's Department of Scientific Pedagogy and Child Study, formed in 1899, followed Hall's normative approach, using for assessment anthropometric measures such as cranial widths. Although the new field of psychometrics had been expected to have major significance for education, especially given its origins in Binet's effort to address a practical educational problem, it at first had little impact in schools or in Witmer's clinic; neither adopted the Binet-type procedures as readily as did their counterparts in institutions (Wallin, 1955). Few professionals were trained to use or interpret the new tests, nor were there provisions for credentialing qualified testers (Fagan, 1985).

By the 1920s, this began to change as both mental testing and psychoeducational clinics became familiar parts of the educational landscape. Wallin had reported in 1914 that there were 26 child-study clinics in universities, more than 20 in institutions and correctional or vocational training centers, and 19 in school districts, others contracting with agencies for pupil diagnostic evaluations. By 1930, use of tests to determine special class eligibility had become standard in large districts. Testing is, of course, only one facet of psychology's application to education; Hildreth (1930) expressed the great faith in its potential: "Not every educational problem is solved automatically by the application of some well-known law of psychology. Many otherwise baffling situations may, however, be reduced to comparatively simple terms by the application of psychological techniques" (p. 9). Wickman (1928) found teachers and mental health professionals had profoundly disparate perceptions of children's behavior, but while mental hygiene and curriculum were included in Hildreth's list of 11 such "problems," school psychologists' (Witmer had coined the term in 1897) responsibilities increasingly emphasized a gate-keeping role they had not necessarily sought.

While scientific identity, rather than application, was the goal of the American Psychological Association (APA), which Hall founded in 1892, Witmer's legacy was evident at its 1917 meeting with forming of the American Association of Clinical Psychologists (AACP), which in 1919 became APA's first division, the Clinical Section. The American Association of Applied Psychology (AAAP) was formed separately in 1937, with sections reflecting venues of application: Clinical, Educational, Consulting, Industrial and Business; the Military section was added in 1944. A need for unity during the war years led to merger of AAAP with APA, its 19 charter divisions including the Division of School Psychologists (Fagan, 1985). The National Association of School Psychologists (NASP) was founded in 1969, while another specialization, school counseling, had become involved in pupil guidance, though primarily academic and vocational, with increasing responsibilities for group testing.

The child guidance approach was also being applied in connection with the new concept of a separate juvenile justice system. Maintaining that immigrant children, like their elders, had needs beyond mere survival, and to discourage delinquency, Jane Addams (1909) had argued for parks and playgrounds in the cities. But insisting that youth who did break the law should be handled differently than adult criminals, she persuaded the Illinois legislature in 1899 to establish not only separate hearings, as was already done in several states, but special courts, as provided in England since 1873. These were mandated in 1908, and a 1920 act required "metropolitan magistrates," selected for their qualifications to hear juvenile cases, sitting with two laypersons, one of whom must be a woman. Though the system was, and is, imperfect, such early judges as the Honorable Ben B. Lindsey of the Denver Juvenile Court introduced humane and constructive procedures in handling young offenders (Hall, 1926, p. 25).

William Healy's (1869–1963) concern for the frightened youth he observed in Chicago courtrooms took him in 1905 to Witmer's clinic and to Vineland to consult with Goddard. In 1909, with philanthropic support, he founded the Juvenile Psychopathic Institute in Chicago, later called the Illinois Juvenile Research Institute. Diagnostic workups on court-referred youth included reports by home visitors, forerunners of the psychiatric social workers Mary Jarret began to train in 1918 at the Boston Psychopathic Hospital in conjunction with Smith College, from which collaboration the Smith College School for Social Work, the nation's first, evolved. In the 1920s, efforts to intervene with youth presenting problem behavior begun in conjunction with juvenile courts spread to schools, hospitals, and community agencies, Healy himself having in 1916 become director of Boston's Judge Baker Guidance Center, a model for programs that by midcentury were instituted in most large American cities (Bremner, 1971, p. 1,050).

Centers in England adopted the voluntary (i.e., private) model recommended by a commission chaired by the Earl of Feversham, who was appointed in 1927 to head the national Child Guidance Council. It was soon standard for training of social welfare workers to include practica in London's child guidance clinic. While as in the United States clinics coordinated with schools, they provided diagnostic evaluation and consultation rather than specialized instruction. That pattern continued in American schools until the 1960s, when experimental classes for troubled children were formed in collaboration with mental health agencies. In England, Oxford's guidance center added an observation school in 1930 for "problem children," enrolling 48 pupils with "personality disorders" and IQs ranging from 70 to 95. Its team approach, involving a physician in general practice, a psychiatrist, and a social worker, was extended to 175 pupils with retardation in regular schools. Psychologists' roles were limited to evaluations, nor do teachers seem to have been considered full team members (Jones, 1972); role issues were a factor in later criticisms of the "medical model."

Classes for Unrulies

Separation of behaviorally deviant students had actually begun much earlier. American schools in fact formed classes for pupils whose classroom behavior was considered unmanageable before such provisions were made for children with impaired hearing, vision, or health, the first in 1871 in New Haven, Connecticut, followed in 1874 by several in New York. While records of similar classes in other large cities are sketchy, what seems clear is that they were mainly "repositories for all kinds of children who simply did not fit into the regular classroom" (Ysseldyke & Algozzine, 1982, p. 40). Elizabeth Farrell (1908–1909) recalled that her own, and New York's, first "ungraded" class of 8–16-year-olds comprised "the odds and ends of a large school," repeated failures, "so-called naughty children," and some we would call street-wise (pp. 91–92). This experience formed the basis for establishment, under Farrell's leadership, of New York's system of ungraded classes, discussed in Chapter 6. With adoption of mental testing, this concept transmogrified into self-contained classes for pupils with retardation, but management problems were considered at least as much as test score eligibility in placement decisions. Of pupils eligible for placement on the basis of IQ, those presenting behavior problems, which usually precipitated referral in the first place, were most likely to be placed (Sarason & Doris, 1969).

Many special classes continued to represent a catch-all arrangement like Farrell's, but there was growing awareness that the labels applied were inadequate to identify the needs, or simply differences, of pupils. By the 1960s, concerns focused on disproportionate referral and placement of minority pupils; children labeled "slow learners" (among sundry other labels) whose learning problems were *specific*, rather than due to low overall ability; indications that even "appropriately labeled" students might fare as well, or even better, in regular classrooms; and the fact that pupils, once placed in special education, tended to remain there throughout their school careers. Another concern was the exclusion from these classes, and hence from schooling altogether, of children whose measured IQ fell below a certain point. Critical factors were the civil rights movement, litigation and legislation, efficacy research, and parent activism. We noted these issues earlier and return to them in the final chapters. Impetus for classes specifically for pupils considered disturbed or presenting serious behavior problems came less from the schools than from the growing number of residential treatment agencies.

Organizations and Policy Developments

In 1924, the American Orthopsychiatric Association (AOA), was founded, two years after the Council for Exceptional Children (CEC). The organizations differed in membership and scope, the latter dominated by educators, concerned primarily with school issues, and involved with all forms of exceptionality, but among children and youth. The founders of AOA, who included Healy and Karl Menninger, sought to organize mental health professionals, then defined as psychiatrists, clinical psychologists, and psychiatric social workers, involved in treating adults as well as children. Although educators were among the early members, as were practitioners of other disciplines such as nursing, their status on the orthopsychiatric team led by the psychiatrist was long considered ancillary. Pursuant to a study sponsored by the National Committee on Mental Hygiene and the Commonwealth Fund, the American Association of Psychiatric Clinics for Children was formed in 1945, with Dr. H. Frederick Allen its first president, to formulate and monitor standards for treatment facilities for children.

As with retardation, the Kennedy administration began a bold departure in social policy relating to mental health, especially concerning children. Under the Social Security Amendments of 1965 (P.L. 89-97), a study funded at the level of $1 million was undertaken to determine how resources for children might better be coordinated. The resulting report, *Crisis in Child Mental Health: Challenge for the 1970s*, was published in 1970 by the Joint Commission on Mental Health of Children (JCMHC), representing 46 organizations, including the American Psychiatric Association and the Academy of Child Psychiatry. The new specialty of child psychiatry had begun to impact on school-affiliated guidance clinics, assisting in identifying troubled pupils and providing treatment. One eminent psychiatrist (Pearson, 1954) optimistically predicted that eventually every school would have access to the expertise of a psychoanalytically trained child psychiatrist!

Many did provide consultation to schools, like Dr. Oscar Markey, whose association with Bellefaire, which converted to residential treatment in 1924, led to affiliations with several school districts (Polster, 1990). Such involvement also reflected a growing interest in prevention, which Smiley Blanton (1925) reported was the major focus of the Minneapolis Child Guidance Clinic. While in the 1920s collaboration between mental health workers and educators focused on aberrant behavior, by the late 1940s it addressed prevention of such problems and promotion of positive mental health. The theme of the 1950 White House Conference on Children and Youth expressed an ambitious goal: *A Healthy Personality for Every Child*, referencing E. H. Erikson's (1950) psychosocial stages in the development of "ego identity." Beliefs about what constituted a healthy personality and how it could be promoted had changed dramatically within a relatively short time, as had the way troubled children were viewed.

Influence of Psychoanalysis

The eugenics movement brought together diverse sources of injunctions to seek the virtuous life, such as temperance, censorship, and sexual restraint, expressed in guides for the young to "natural laws." Bearing such subtitles as "Nature's Secrets Revealed: Scientific Knowledge of the Laws of Sex Life and Heredity, or EUGENICS" (*Safe Counsel*, 1914), these presented a sanitized, moralistic construction of "Vital Information for the Married and Marriageable of All Ages; a Word at the Right Time to the Boy, Girl, Young Man, Young Woman . . . together with Important Hints on social purity, heredity, physical manhood and womanhood." Youth were enjoined to maintain purity of thought, as well as restraint and continence, but this *fin de siècle* "civilized morality . . . [was] an ideal of conduct, not a description of reality" (Hale, 1971, p. 25). Physicians yet endorsed punitive and cruel, sometimes draconian, measures to suppress children's expression of sexuality and sexual curiosity, the psychic, and sometimes physical, damage of which can only be imagined (Piers, 1978). At the least, many conscientious young people were surely carrying burdens of guilt and fear as America discovered Freud.

The psychoanalytic notion of an intrapsychic battleground implied many challenging possibilities, not least of which being that the line between normality and deviance, health and illness, was not a sharp demarcation. Freud did not "discover" the unconscious, nor did he invent the notion that understanding of one's childhood experiences is crucial to understanding oneself as an adult, as in Wordsworth's line, "The child is father to the man." Romantic and Victorian writers' self-revelations made the 19th century, in Peter Gay's (1988) phrase, "an age of Hamlets" (p. 129), and autobiographies invariably began with accounts of the author's childhood (Perrot & Martin-Fugier, 1990). But Freud broke new ground in describing the vicissitudes of childhood and their influence on the adult personality. While he left to others, especially his daughter, the treatment of children, his theories had profound implications for the understanding of processes and problems of children's personality development.

As is well known, some were shocked by his assertions about childhood sexuality, which was, in psychoanalytic terms, an object of repression and denial. Many intellectuals were concerned with freeing the young from repressive forces of society and superego, but by the 1940s progressive education, having become identified with "permissiveness," had gotten a bad name in some circles. Bertrand Russell, whose wife Dora ran one of the "free schools" that sprang up in Britain, advocated complete sexual freedom, and A. S. Neill believed sexuality should be handled with total frankness from earliest childhood. Summerhill was thus often cited as "that dreadful school," as Neill titled his own account, though it was more democratically egalitarian than wildly permissive. Of the "problem children" in whom he specialized, Graves and Hodge (1940/1963) remark drily, "Some turned out sincerely good, a few stayed sincerely bad. Everything got broken" (p. 211). While holding to tenets of accepted morality, G. S. Hall (1904) reacted against the "Puritanical" suppression of pleasure, suggesting that in adolescence "purity of thought was probably impossible" (Hale, 1971, p. 272). In the famous Clark University lectures in September 1909, Freud "confirmed the importance of two of [Hall's] deepest interests—sexuality and childhood" (p. 19).

Freud's description, based on meticulous analysis of case studies, of the origins of neurosis in early experiences (actual or fantasized) and unconscious conflicts would have major ramifications for schooling and child-rearing, indeed virtually all facets of modern life. While the talking cure's techniques of free association and dream analysis were not well suited to work with children, in the case study of Little Hans, whose complaint was a phobia of horses, Freud demonstrated the technique of child treatment via the parent (Furman & Katan, 1969). Other therapeutic approaches have emphasized abreaction through play, a technique first reported by Hermione von Hug-Hellmuth, a Viennese analyst, to understand "the mental life of the child" (Alexander & Selesnick, 1966). In 1932, Melanie Klein

(1882–1960) described use of "play therapy" with children as young as 2 (Young-Bruehl, 1988). Play techniques, especially suited to work with young children, were further refined by such therapists as Virginia Axline (1947), while other expressive modes were also introduced as therapeutic avenues. Music therapy, "the scientific application of music or music activities to attain therapeutic goals" (Lathom & Eagle, 1982, p. 5), now used with all exceptional populations, began as an adjunctive mental health discipline.

Psychoanalysis had great impact on parenting and schooling, but Anna Freud (1964) feared its influence was "piecemeal," each discovery inspiring calls for change in practice, often with unfortunate results, as with misguided notions about total freedom from all restraints. Easing demands on the child's superego to lessen guilt and free creative impulses, while desirable, may generate new anxieties difficult for children to manage, implying the need to help children develop ego strength. But since each event has a particular psychological meaning for each individual child, generalizations based on superficial understanding of psychoanalysis were unwarranted. While "learning inhibition" might explain some pupils' difficulties in reading and mathematics, intrapsychic conflict was unlikely to be implicated in most instances, especially during what Freudians call the latency years. Alluding to her formulation of *developmental lines,* she stressed the need for self-discipline; while it is desirable to relate learning to fantasy and sexual curiosity, "the child needs to do more than merely transfer his energy and interest from his passions to his tasks. He also needs to complete the line of development which leads from play to work, and this implies the ability to pursue an activity, regardless of the pleasure gain of the moment, until a final result has been achieved" (p. 465).

Her thinking was influenced by experiences with children uprooted by war, at Hampstead with an American colleague Dorothy Burlingame, where her case studies of coping in children separated from home and family had implications for providing for children whose families were disrupted by divorce or other events. Co-authored with a professor of law, Joseph Goldstein, and a child psychiatrist, Albert J. Solnit, *Beyond the Best Interests of the Child* (1973), endorsed policies that support permanency in placement and that recognize the primacy of a child's *psychological family.* Her work also offered a theoretical basis for an older notion, associated with moral treatment, that influenced the emergence of therapeutic education.

Therapeutic Milieux

Psychiatric insights had had little impact on the handling of delinquency in America (Zald, 1960). Finding that practices in reformatories in the six states he studied fell far short of professed ideology, Deutsch (1950) identified "10 deadly sins": regimentation, monotony, mass treatment, political influence, insufficient funding, isolation, complacency, excessive physical and psychological punishment, enforced idleness, and "babelism," the use of modern social science language to mask the ugly realities that actually existed. Goffman (1961) termed the last, among other cosmetic attempts to make a favorable impression, "cleaning up the front regions." However, two influential models emulated in many treatment settings evolved from work with delinquent youth, one reflecting the colony tradition and family model, informed by progressivist concepts, the other psychoanalytic influence. Subsequent approaches reflect a combination of the two, modified by ecological and cognitive-behavioral theory, in the form of such concepts as *milieutherapy* (Redl, 1959), *teacher-counselors* (Hobbs, 1964), *Positive Peer Culture* (Trieschman, Whittaker, & Brendtro, 1969), and *Life Space Intervention* (Wood & Long, 1991).

In 1877, when the Reverend Willard Parsons of Sherman, Pennsylvania, asked his congregation to open their homes to children from New York's slums, the Fresh Air Fund was born, with its network of "friendly towns." But finding that members of youth gangs with whom he had been working as a volunteer were not accepted, William Reuben George (1866–1936) set up his own camping program in Freeville, New York, in 1893. Encouraged by its success, George sold his manufacturing business in 1895 in order to operate the camp throughout the year, as a community modeled on the structure of the U.S. government, a "republic" based on the ideals of self-support and responsible citizenship. With the motto "nothing without labor," the Freeville Junior Republic was almost entirely self-sufficient and self-governing (Holl, 1971). Although it was soon emulated in nine other states, George felt that none adhered to the model, which he therefore considered a failure.

However, his beliefs were shared Floyd Starr (1883–1980), founder of the Starr Commonwealth near Albion, Michigan, with affiliates later established in Detroit and in Van Wert and Columbus, Ohio. Like "Daddy" George, "Uncle Floyd" actually carried out the family model Howe had recommended. The Starr Commonwealth Creed, which affirms that "there is no such thing as a bad boy," emphasized the dignity of work, the importance of environment, and the need for "confidence and trust" in working with youth (Fennimore, 1988). That some boys certainly abused that trust is not surprising, nor does it invalidate his credo. But some children's psychological situation is considerably more complex, and psychoanalytic insights eventually informed the Commonwealth, under Larry Brendtro, as well as many other programs. A troubled child may need a parent figure, Bellefaire's Morris ("Fritz") Mayer (1959) agreed, but children in residential treatment have to deal concurrently with four sets of parents: their own, the "care parents" who oversee their daily life, "power parents" who make the rules and control the enterprise, and therapists, who become "transference parents."

August Aichhorn's (1878–1949) application of psychoanalytic concepts in work with delinquent boys, described in *Wayward Youth* (1925/1951), had significant influence and the endorsement of Sigmund Freud, who contributed an introduction. Having established programs at Ober-Hollabrunn in 1918 and St. Andra in 1920 prior to appointment to administer youth services for the City of Vienna, he obtained psychoanalytic training, joining Freud's circle and the Vienna Psychoanalytic Society. Maintaining that children's maladjustment involved the interaction of psychological and sociological phenomena, not disadvantaged circumstances alone, he also insisted that delinquents were not tainted with "hereditary degeneration." Applying psychoanalytic principles, he stressed the importance of analyzing acting-out behavior to determine what intervention was needed and of a group living situation that was reality-based but not governed by arbitrary rules. Most problematic, he stressed the need for a highly trained, professional staff able to understand the individual child's problem and develop an appropriate plan of treatment. His observations concerning dissocial, "institutional children," shared with Anna Freud, with whom he maintained a friendship to the end of his life, influenced her own thinking about permanence. In his experience, relationships with parents were the foundation for character development. While damaged children could be helped through relationship with a trusting adult, he believed most fared better "even in tumultuous families" than if deprived of family relationships by institutional placement (Young-Bruehl, 1988, p. 250).

The term *therapeutic milieu,* suggested by Aichhorn's work, was introduced by Bruno Bettelheim (Bettelheim & Sylvester, 1947) to describe the psychoanalytically informed group-living approach he instituted in 1944 at the Sonia Shankman Orthogenic School. Maintaining that many disturbed children had not learned to love or formed a sense of self, Bettelheim believed a psychologically safe living situation was needed for the child's ego to develop. His ideas, and Aichhorn's, influenced the approach Fritz Redl and David Wineman adopted with acting-out delinquent boys at Detroit's Pioneer House, which emphasized recognition of the importance of the peer group in treatment, described in *Children Who Hate* and *Controls from Within,* published under one cover as *The Aggressive Child* (Redl & Wineman, 1957), a seminal contribution to the development of therapeutic methods. Redl (1959) described a technique called "Life Space Interviewing" for helping a child gain self-control and make effective decisions in conflictual and upsetting situations, subsequently found effective in crisis intervention in school and in camp settings, with groups as well as individual clients (e.g., Morse

& Small, 1959). Another influential early work, *Cottage Six* (Polsky, 1962), described the notion of a "therapeutic youth culture," modified in Brendtro's Positive Peer Culture approach.

Spread of Residential Treatment

Throughout the 19th century, children were placed outside their homes because of parental death or incapacity, need for medical care under confined conditions, retardation, access to education if deaf or blind, or seriously norm-violating behavior. In such situations, most often the first and the last, awareness of psychiatric concepts or a caretaker's perceptiveness sometimes revealed a child with significant emotional problems. In severe instances, such as a child's experiencing hallucinations, the situation bore similarities with known adult pathology; most often, deviant behavior was considered puzzling, disturbing, or simply annoying, depending on the sensitivity of the adult. Symptomatic behaviors probably paralleled those suggested in Bower's (1960) definition, later adopted in American educational policy: unexplained learning difficulties, unsatisfactory relationships, situationally inappropriate behavior or feelings, pervasive unhappiness or depression, unexplained physical complaints.

There were surely instances of extreme disturbance, like that Dorothea Dix saw in a young girl in an almshouse "who suffered the fourfold calamity of being blind, deaf, dumb, and insane" (in Bremner, 1970, vol. 1, p. 777). The girl's screaming, and the violence, fearfulness, self-injuriousness, and other aberrant behavior of a host of other children in Paris's Bicetre, American almshouses, and English brideswells may have represented quite understandable responses to circumstances of impairment, confinement, separation, cruelty, or all in combination. Perhaps Dix's belief that the girl's multiple impairments included "insanity" was correct; we can be quite certain that among children so confined were those experiencing schizophrenia or other serious disturbances, perhaps others with autism. As a general statement, though since Esquirol insanity and idiocy had been differentiated, even if the former was suspected provisions for a child's care (if special care was provided) were made, for good or ill, under the latter rubric. Before the 20th century, psychiatric treatment for children did not exist.

By the early 1960s, about a quarter of a million American children lived in residential institutions, most for extended periods. Based on institutional labels, nearly half (48%) would be inferred to be "dependent and neglected," that is "orphans," while 23% would be classified as delinquent and 24% as mentally retarded. Those considered emotionally disturbed would constitute 3%, with another 2% mentally ill, that is, with diagnoses suggesting severe conditions such as schizophrenia. But classification based on institution "type" is highly misleading, for placement was more often based on the kinds of facilities available than on a child's needs (Caddey, 1963). The largest "category," in particular, as we saw, masked a shift in mission already well under way.

At the time Aichhorn began his work, only a handful of American agencies had been founded (as had the Child Guidance Home in Cincinnati, Ohio, opened in 1920), expressly to provide treatment for seriously disturbed children. In 1913, the Sonia Shankman Orthogenic School was established as part of the University of Chicago's Rush Medical College, later made world-famous by Bettelheim, who became its principal in 1944, later its director (Zimmerman, 1991). The more typical pattern, beginning in the late 1930s, was that of a shift in the mission of agencies established earlier in response to child welfare needs. For example, in the late 1940s, the Evanston Children's Home, operated by the Illinois Children's Home and Aid Society, established in 1907 as a receiving home for young children awaiting placement or with short-term physical needs, shifted to psychotherapeutic intervention for disturbed children. The Menninger Foundation had opened its Southard School in Topeka, Kansas, in 1926 for "feebleminded" children and others who "suffered from organic disease" or "had behavior problems," but in 1940 separated 5- to 15-year-old children with serious emotional disturbance to be afforded psychiatric treatment. Hawthorne-Cedar Knolls School, in Hawthorne, New York, founded by Jacob Schiff in 1906 as the Jewish Protectory and Aid Society, was intended with its cottage plan as a model reformatory; its shift to a treatment orientation, with addition of psychological, psychiatric, and social work components, occurred over two decades (Reid & Hagan, 1952).

New private facilities were also established expressly to provide residential treatment, such as the Emma Pendleton Bradley Home in Providence, Rhode Island, and the Children's Services Center of Wyoming Valley, in Wilkes-Barre, Pennsylvania, opened in 1931 and 1938, respectively. Also, from the 1940s through the 1960s, an extensive network of hospital-based treatment programs for children was created under public and private auspices, a concept Dr. Lauretta Bender pioneered at New York's Bellevue Psychiatric Hospital in 1935. Planning began in 1937 for the Children's Services unit of the University of Michigan's Neuropsychiatric Institute, finally opened in 1949. A children's ward in the Langley Porter Clinic in San Francisco, authorized in 1939, opened in 1944. In Allaire, New Jersey, the Arthur Brisbane Treatment Center, founded in 1946, began as a children's unit of the New Jersey State Hospital (Reid & Hagan, 1952). Michigan's Hawthorne Center, one of the nation's first comprehensive psychiatric treatment facilities for children and adolescents, was established in 1956.

The idea that special education could be a mode of treatment for dis-

turbed children evolved as an afterthought as on-grounds classes were formed
in agencies founded as asylums for orphans and in children's units in hospitals. By 1974, there were 340 residential treatment centers in the United
States, each serving an average of 56 children, a total of more than 19,000
"beds," in addition to 20 state and county and 6 private mental hospitals
exclusively for children under 16 (Witkin, 1974). In most, the initial focus
was individual psychotherapy; the idea that the whole living situation
was potentially therapeutic evolved over time. "The task of the therapeutic
school," wrote George Devereux (1956), "is chiefly to humanize the child"
(p. 52). Nicholas Hobbs (1964), inspired by programs in Scotland, Canada,
and France, reconceptualized it as one of *reeducation.*

Unlike deafness or blindness, where education was the central issue,
disturbance seemed to imply needs for containment and "therapeutic removal," the family having "failed in its socialization task . . . since otherwise
the child would not have to be sent to a therapeutic school in the first place"
(Devereux, 1956, p. 52). "Parentectomy" is a notion that can be understood
in the historical context of attribution and iatrogenic guilt, with constructs
ranging from natural law violation to "schizophrenogenic mothers" and
dysfunctional families. In the orthopsychiatric team model the caseworker's
role was to "work with the parents," usually separately from work with the
child. Increasing recognition that difficulties of "the troubled and troubling
child" (Hobbs, 1982) are contextual and transactional led to concurrent
efforts to support children's coping abilities and change environmental situations they had to cope with, through family therapy in outpatient treatment
and emphasis in residential settings on the child's involvement with, rather
than separation from, family.

While European and American practices have historically been mutually influential (Juul, 1990), some argued that the American "medicalization"
of deviance contrasted sharply with a humanistic model underlying European mental health systems. In the 1960s, the medical model came under
attack; Thomas Szasz (1970), a psychiatrist, described mental illness as a
"myth," a condition "manufactured" by society. American Psychological
Association President George Albee (1968) called the model impractical
from the standpoint of resource availability and allocation. The Joint Commission on Mental Health of Children (1970) concluded that, while nearly
10 million American children and youth needed mental health services, only
one-third of those with severe problems "receive any help at all" (p. 3). (Even
now, Kaufman [1993] estimates that special education serves fewer than
half the students with behavioral problems who could benefit.) Linton (1971)
called basing assistance on diagnosed pathology "probably the most inappropriate model that could be utilized for the vast majority of maladjusted
children" (p. 156). Maintaining, like Hobbs, that relationships with trusted

adults have the greatest impact, he recommended professionalizing the roles of child-care workers and teachers, like the *educateurs* in France and Montreal and *orthopedagogues* in Denmark and the Netherlands.

These ideas were important influences on Project Re-ED (for reeducation of emotionally disturbed children), based in Nashville, Tennessee, and piloted in a tri-state catchment area, later endorsed by the Joint Commission. Based on an ecological conception of child deviance, Re-ED sought to link family, school, and community, primarily through two key staff roles: the *teacher-counselor* and the *liason teacher*. The model has been emulated in other countries—an instance of Juul's mutuality—and in the United States, there is a national network of programs following the Re-ED philosophy. Due to the necessarily restricted impact of school on a child's life space, this ecological approach is difficult to implement in a day-school setting, although it has influenced specific practices and professionals' understanding of troubled children. Whatever the merit of a residential model, the day class, as William Morse (1958) commented when such classes were just beginning, "enables the child to keep one foot in reality" (p. 59).

Public School Special Classes

The first American effort to provide psychiatrically informed, specialized instruction for large numbers of troubled children occurred with the establishment in 1946 of New York's "600" schools, comprising both day schools and residential facilities. This development followed an arrangement with Bellevue Psychiatric Hospital, Lauretta Bender having persuaded the district in 1935 to assign teachers to the children's ward opened the previous year, a precedent later adopted in other cities. While the concept of designating certain schools and agencies, initially according to the city's numbering system, suggests mainly an administrative arrangement, it encouraged educators to incorporate therapeutic principles in instruction. The *clinical teaching* approach Berkowitz and Rothman (1960) described applied psychoanalytic concepts in remediating reading and other skill areas, as well as therapeutic use of other curricular areas, particularly art.

While many such school-agency collaborations were developed (Cohen, 1965), it became more common for school districts to form their own classes, governed by state education standards, with little involvement of mental health systems. By the 1960s, Morse, Cutler, & Fink (1964) identified more than 300 such classes, some informed by varying degrees of psychodynamic, behavioral, or psychoeducational theory, many more using what the researchers characterized as modified "educational," "green thumb," or even "primitive" methods. Over the next two decades, the number expanded; a 1987 survey of 126 districts providing special class arrangements for students with behavior disorders revealed that virtually all (99.4%) had emerged within just two decades (Grosenick, George, & George, 1987). While most of the classes studied by Morse and colleagues operated on a fairly intuitive basis, by the 1980s many were based on behavioral principles or incorporated "behavior-modification" strategies. But it was becoming clear that children's problems could be understood from diverse perspectives, each having certain implications for intervention. The complexity of the issues and the confusion among educators and mental health professionals were addressed in the early 1970s by William Rhodes and associates through the Conceptual Models Project (Rhodes & Tracy, 1972), which delineated alternative theories and service delivery systems. Today, behavioral and cognitive principles are often integrated, involving such self-management strategies as rehearsal and mediated learning.

In current discussions of inclusion, students labeled "behavior disordered" are a particular concern of the organized teaching profession, and of equal, though differently motivated, concern of leaders in this area of special education. Compared with other exceptional students, many are in fact served in such "restrictive" settings as residential centers and separate day schools (Kaufman, 1993). Perhaps we could benefit from recalling Howe's (1848b) admonition that difficult (in the language of his day, "viciously disposed") youth should not be brought together "but put far asunder!" In any case, it is a truism that the often devastating effects on children of complex societal conditions cannot be addressed by schools alone, which have limited opportunity, and less sanction, for involvement with families and other out-of-school ecosystems. As with physical health needs, other systems exist to address those in the sphere of mental health. But in both areas collaboration, ideally an integrated service system, is made problematic by bureaucratic strictures and funding mechanisms, as well as differing priorities, purposes, and professional orientations. As states curtail funding and actually eliminate programs of treatment for children and youth in conflict or in trouble, investing instead in more and more prisons to incarcerate offenders, the question remains: Who speaks for children?

CHAPTER 9

Children with Communication and Processing Disabilities

If society creates disabilities, the largest classification of exceptional pupils in American schools represents a social construction of massive proportions. In some respects an artifact of school organization, curriculum, and assessment created to account for pupil differences not otherwise explainable, "specific learning disability" is not surprisingly also a controversial construct. Unlike deafness, blindness, and other physical impairment, this "category" is non-existent in most of the world's nations, though the "condition" is presumably present. The areas of learning and communication disorders have in common both high prevalence and certain historical antecedents, which also bear on other impairments involving language processes and now generally believed to be intrinsic, or organic, autism and Attention Deficit Disorder, though each also had unique influences. Their diversity notwithstanding, this chapter is concerned with the "newer" manifestations of exceptionality in children, involving difficulties in communication or in processing information.

Key forces in the emergence of the concept of learning disability have influenced social policy concerning all exceptional children. These have included school restructuring to accommodate pupil diversity; new conceptions of how behavior is linked to neurological processes; growing use of assessment as a basis for intervention with individual pupils; and parent advocacy. Since all but the last presumably had some scientific basis, mainly in research conducted with adults, this chapter begins with an overview of scientific developments, which, as has always been true, both influenced and were influenced by attitudes, beliefs, and values concerning human exceptionality.

EVOLUTION OF A KNOWLEDGE BASE FOR SPECIAL EDUCATION

The Industrial Revolution, as Adam Smith foresaw, brought ever finer division of labor, generally following specialization in means of production and distribution, and in commodities themselves. In the case of human services, a key factor has been the ever-increasing specialization in the perceived needs of clients, patients, and pupils resulting from clinical experiences. This provided stimulus for research, which by early in the 20th century was being done in various settings; by the 1920s, wartime rehabilitation and school psychoeducational clinics were research sites, as were universities, where educational psychology, a new branch of a new science, began to influence special education's increasing focus on learning, instruction, and measurement. While social and political forces arguably had a more important role than scholarship in influencing explanations of differences among children, these influences have been intertwined. At all events, a knowledge base for specialized services emerged in the context of service systems, and these were provided in response to sociopolitical forces.

Early Laboratories

In the 19th century, training schools were the locus for training and research, functions later increasingly done in universities and affiliated centers. Schools for the blind had been laboratories in which Haüy, Braille, Howe, and Waite experimented with line printing and punctiform alternatives. In schools for the deaf, variations of instructional methods were investigated, though Bell departed from this tradition; his tutoring (like Itard's, applying scientific conventions) and genealogical research were done outside the residential schools he opposed, but within those schools continuing scholarship led to important discoveries about the structure of American Sign Language (ASL). A network of institutions for persons with retardation in Europe and America developed research programs, important not only to workers in that field but more generally. In England, the enormous institution at Earlswood provided a laboratory for the investigations of Down, Little, and many others. In American institutions, brains of deceased inmates were weighed and measured, the interest in measurement then shifting to intelligence testing.

In several instances investigations of prison inmates by individuals whose interests were not primarily in retardation *per se* became part of the canon of knowledge in that field. The work of Gall (who also studied asylum inmates), Lombroso, and Richard L. Dugdale had negative impact on attitudes concerning retardation, though in the last instance that is an oversimplification. Dugdale's (1877) study of the lineage of five of the six "Juke" girls, prompted by observations in New York prisons, actually led him to conclude that "environment is the ultimate controlling factor in determining careers, placing heredity itself as an organized result of invariable environment" (p. 66). This Lamarckian view had implications for environmental intervention to interrupt generation-to-generation patterns (Sarason &

Doris, 1969, p. 258). But Arthur Estabrook's (1916) interpretation, using follow-up data from the Eugenics Record Office, was explicitly hereditarian, linked retardation with criminality and licentiousness, and, with Goddard's (1912a) study of the Kallikaks, spawned more "negative eugenics" studies of pseudonymous families.

While the research tradition associated with retardation had clearly become mainly descriptive rather than experimental, the approach pioneered by Itard and Seguin focused on interventions as, we could say, "independent variables" manipulated to achieve instructional goals. Both traditions have continued to guide psychological investigators, many, as Zigler (1966) noted, generating theories to explain what is "different" about persons with cognitive impairment, others concerned more with the efficacy of interventions in changing behavior. As we saw, mental testing and statistical methods, especially for calculating correlation, contributed to the former; once a phenomenon could be made measurable, all manner of descriptive and comparative analyses seemed possible.

But it is a scientific truism that causation cannot be inferred from correlation, and in psychology demonstration of causal relationships in emulation of the "hard sciences" became the ideal. Hall sought to replicate at Johns Hopkins the experimental laboratory Wilhelm Wundt, "the first man who without reservation is properly called a psychologist" (Boring, 1950, pp. 316), established at Leipzig in 1879. Having worked briefly in Hall's laboratory, James McKeen Cattell (1860–1944) appointed himself an assistant in Wundt's to do his dissertation research, then set up his own at the University of Pennsylvania, which Witmer managed when he went to Columbia. In the laboratory he directed there from 1891 until dismissed in 1917 for public expression of his pacifism, Cattell's investigations of physical and mental measurement, and of scientific eminence, reflected Galton's influence, combined with Wundt's experimentalism. In the work of his most famous student can in turn be seen Cattell's influence and that of William James (1842–1910), who, though "not by temperament nor in fact an experimentalist" (p. 508), saw psychology's pedagogical implications.

Study of Learning Processes

The birth of educational psychology brought a divergence of the foundation for much subsequent research involving children with disabilities from Hall's child psychology, which formed the basis for normative descriptions of children's development. Edward Lee Thorndike (1874–1949), stimulated as a Wesleyan undergraduate by James's *Principles of Psychology* (1890), enrolled in his Harvard course "The Relations Between Physiology and Psychology" and, though greatly encouraged by James's support, accepted

Cattell's offer of a fellowship at Columbia. Impressed also by James's *Talks to Teachers* (1899), Thorndike was convinced of psychology's relevance for schooling. Thus, while James was "the pioneer of the 'new' psychology in America" (Boring, 1950, p. 508), and Hall's child study shaped the new "child psychology," parentage of a branch that has often cohabited with, and sometimes subsumed, special education in academia is due to Thorndike.

"It is the province of educational psychology," wrote Thorndike (1914), "to give . . . knowledge of the original nature of man and of the laws of modifiability of learning, in the case of intellect, character and skill" (p. 1). The field explicitly concerns *behavior*, defined as "those activities of thought, feeling, and conduct in the broadest sense which an animal—here, man—exhibits, which . . . are referred by popular usage to intellect, character, skill and temperament. Behavior, then, is . . . inclusive of, conscious life" (p. 2). Thorndike's educational psychology was a psychology of learning and motivation based on three classes of phenomena: "a *situation*, or state of affairs influencing the man [*sic*], a *response* or state of affairs in the man, and a *connection* or bond whereby the latter is the result of the former" (p. 1). He had but recently turned his attention from puzzle-box experiments in James's basement with cats, dogs, and chicks to applications with human learning when the first edition of his *Educational Psychology* appeared in 1903. Publication the next year of *Introduction to the Theory of Mental and Social Measurement*, explaining the application of statistical methods to mental testing, marked his enthusiastic entry into that field.

Thorndike's empirical laws of learning were in the tradition of functional psychology, which, through Dewey, emerged in America from Pragmatism. Concerned with purposeful change, functional psychology sought to go beyond description in asking the question *why*. As applied by J. B. Watson, a product of Chicago's functional school under Frank Angell, it became "behaviorism," a nonmentalistic, stimulus-response model that, its reductionism notwithstanding, had rich implications for interventions with children. The positions of Watson (1928) and Gesell, Hall's successor, were antithetical, the former claiming to be able to shape in the newborn infant virtually any set of abilities and characteristics, the latter insisting that we cannot "mould the child as though he were clay, for he is an individual with inborn propensities, with inherent characteristics" (Gesell, 1940, p. 198). With the later influence of B. F. Skinner and others who saw in the experimental analysis of behavior a foundation for experimental teaching in Itard's tradition, behavioral concepts profoundly influenced intervention approaches with exceptional individuals. Conversely, the normative, maturationist orientation of child study continued to be dominant in general education, particularly for young children. But by the 1960s, other forces were generating interest in intervention, especially for children whose poverty placed them at risk.

Sponsorship of Childhood Disability Research

As teacher preparation moved from residential institutions to higher education institutions, so did the research laboratory, both anticipated when a teacher brought a boy presenting puzzling learning difficulties to Witmer at the University of Pennsylvania. The incident led to the founding of the Psychological Clinic, in 1896, the birth of "clinical psychology," and the start of formal training for special educators. What did not change was the inextricable linkages of client service, research, and training, for practicum in institutions was a core component of Witmer's summer institutes. But until the 1950s, although clinical psychologists like Witmer and Wallin made contributions, academic psychologists seemed to have little interest in retardation (Sarason, 1988) or other areas of disability. Notwithstanding his strong interest in retardation and children's mental and physical health problems, Gesell's focus was normative development. And notwithstanding the ascendancy of learning theory in academic psychology, a review at mid-century (McPherson, 1948) identified just 14 learning studies involving subjects with retardation. Within the next decade, this situation began to change dramatically as academics and their students instituted ambitious research programs in conjunction with institutions.

A series of events in bringing this about began in 1952, with the appointment, through urging of state Special Education Director Ray Graham, of Samuel Kirk to begin a training program at the University of Illinois. With federal and state funding, Kirk (1958) conducted a five-year study of the efficacy of preschool instruction of children with retardation, a landmark in establishing a rationale for early intervention. Again with Graham's support and external funding, Kirk established the Institute for Research on Exceptional Children, its interdisciplinary faculty—including James A. Gallagher, Bernard Farber, Oliver Kolstoe, Lawrence Stolurow, Herbert Goldstein, Merle Karnes, and Clifford Howe—generating, in Kirk's (1984) words, "volumes of research in many areas of exceptionality" (p. 39), addressing issues in instruction-related assessment and intervention and influences on cognitive development. A second center that became renowned for research, policy shaping, and training was established in 1954, with the aid of a federal grant that was, by today's standards, quite modest, in Nashville, Tennessee, at the George Peabody College for Teachers, under Nicholas Hobbs and Lloyd Dunn. As talented faculty and doctoral students were attracted, especially with establishment of the John F. Kennedy Center, Peabody became another seminal source of knowledge, tools for instruction and measurement, and influential scholars and leaders.

In 1963, federal legislation (P.L. 88-164) authorized 13 centers at major research universities for research and training of interdisciplinary personnel. These needs, and needs for demonstrations of comprehensive, life-span services for persons with developmental disabilities, led by 1981 to establishment of 43 centers in 30 states, under the University Affiliated Program created in 1963 pursuant to recommendations of the President's Panel on Mental Retardation. Research in these centers has spanned a broad range of topics bearing on prevention, epidemiology, intervention, and service coordination. Nor has their scope been limited to retardation, but rather has addressed the full range of developmental disabilities. Meanwhile, after intensive lobbying by parents, the Children with Learning Disabilities Act (P.L. 91-230) of 1969 generated research, teacher training, and demonstration centers focused specifically on that area.

As psychoeducational clinics spread into the schools, these too became involved in research, though most lacked sufficient resources even to meet service needs; the "'clinic,'" Fagan (1985) commented, "was often nothing more than a small room and one staff person" (p. 380). Meanwhile, their counterparts in institutions continued in the tradition of Goddard and Kuhlman in the further development and standardization of tests and investigations of their potential uses. But other work, which would lead to a major shift in intervention approaches, was first demonstrated in institutions in the 1950s and 1960s, and some were applying these "behavior modification" techniques with children whose development was very delayed or whose behavior was very deviant, first in institutions and then in schools. Scientific developments contributed importantly to understanding of both learning disabilities and communication disorders. But these converged with other developments, especially parent activism, extension of psychometric methods to reading and other curricular areas, war, and efforts to "Americanize" immigrant children.

COMMUNICATION DISORDERS

As we saw in Chapter 1, various figures of antiquity were known or reputed to have speech impairments, usually characterized, whatever their actual nature, in such a way as to suggest stuttering, which Hippocrates had described and Aristotle ascribed to faulty tongue movement. Amman treated diverse communication disorders, not only "mutism" ascribed to deafness. A text published in 1583 by Jerome Mercurialis (1530–1606), an Italian physician, described voice disorders as well as articulation and *balbuties* (stuttering), distinguishing "natural" from "accidental" etiology of disfluency but recommending "loud, distinct speech" whatever the cause (Berry, 1965, p. 78). The first psychological explanation of stuttering, as a "collision" of simultaneous ideas, was proposed by 18th-century German rationalist philosopher Moses Mendelssohn, grandfather of the composer. It was long recognized that defective speech sometimes resulted from an anatomical impairment, and the 19th century saw advances in surgical intervention for persons with cleft palate and improvements on the obturator, a prosthesis developed by Ambroise Paré.

While an extensive European medical literature on speech impairments existed, stuttering yet seemed to attract most clinical interest. A German physician, Philipp Friedrich Herman Klencke (1813–1881) suggested it was due to lack of harmonious operation of respiration with muscles, as did Alfred Becquerel (1814–1866) of France, himself a stutterer, and James Hurt (1833–1869) of England, whose famous patients included the social reformer and poet Charles Kingsley (Berry, 1965). In educational contexts, however, speech (other than reciting or declaiming) was a focus only in work with deaf children and, in some programs, those with retardation. As still happens, children's delayed or unusual speech associated with undetected hearing loss was often attributed to "feeblemindedness." But "incorrect" speech, often reflecting dialectal influences, was attributed to the ignorance of the inferior classes.

Speaking Correctly

> "Yuh know wat dis's fuh?" he held it up to David's eyes. David examined it more closely. "No. Wot d'yuh do wit' it?" "It c'n catch rats, dot's wot yuh do wit' it. See dis little door? De rat gizz in like dot. . . . Foist yuh put sompin ove' hea, and on 'iz liddle hook. An nen nuh rat gizzin. Dey uz zuh big fat rat inna house, yuh could hear him at night, so my fodder bought dis, an' my mudder put in schmaltz f'om de meat, and nuh rat comes in, an' inna mawingk, I look unner by de woshtob, an'ooh—he was dere, runnin' dis way like dot." (Roth, 1934, p. 49)

By the 19th century, when Melville Bell established himself as a "corrector of defective utterances," proper elocution was a popular preoccupation and becoming a focus of instruction in the American academies and the common schools. Persons were judged by the style, as well as the substance, of their speech, with effective oratory much admired. On the other hand, speech patterns reflecting linguistic influences that deviated from the accepted standard, like Yinglish, Cockney, Gullah, or Cajun, irrespective of their linguistic integrity and distinctive merits, were simply considered inferior, uneducated, or low-class. For "native" and "assimilated" Americans, the new European immigrants epitomized that inferiority; their talk, their manner of dress, indeed everything about them, was strange, vulgar, *foreign*. Since correct English usage and proper diction were considered essential to assimilation, speech became a focus of instruction in New York's

"Steamer" or "vestibule classes" and their counterparts in other cities with large concentrations of recent immigrants.

Recitation retained its central role in the classroom despite progressive influence, with pupils made to take their turn responding to queries, declaiming before the class, and otherwise exposing their utterances to teacher scrutiny and often peer ridicule. In classes formed for immigrant children in the 1890s, "speech teachers" led group breathing exercises, choral speaking, and oral poetry recitation, intended to improve spoken English, evidenced by conformity to certain standards for usage and diction. Even after the flow of immigration had been staunched, through the protectionist 1920s and into the Great Depression, efforts to "Americanize" youth continued. In *A Walker in the City*, literary and social critic Alfred Kazin (1951), recalled the psychological impact on a sensitive young person:

> We were somehow to be a little ashamed of what we were . . . [for] a "refined," "correct," "nice" English was required of us at school that we did not naturally speak, and that our teachers could never be quite sure we would keep. This English was peculiarly the ladder of advancement. Every future young lawyer was known by it. Even the Communists and Socialists on Pitkin Avenue spoke it. It was bright and clean and polished. We were expected to show it off like a new pair of shoes. When the teacher sharply called a question out, then your name, you were expected to leap up, face the class, and eject those new words fluently off the tongue. (p. 22)

The premium placed on "proper" speech was not, of course, a uniquely American phenomenon. As Graves and Hodge (1940/1963) noted in their social history of Great Britain between the wars, many working-class people seeking advancement took advantage of free instruction in "educated speech" provided by the BBC (p. 178). And of course, Professor Henry Higgins's transformation of Eliza Doolittle in Shaw's *Pygmalion* is most visibly (or audibly) an achievement in phonology, a subject of great interest to Shaw, who himself devised a phonetic alphabet. But from a sociolinguistic perspective, to be "nonstandard" is not necessarily to be impaired; the distinction between language difference and disability has continued to be problematic in determining eligibility for special education.

Speech Correction

The new specialists were called on to help pupils who actually did have speech problems. Kazin (1951) himself experienced a "secret ordeal" of disfluency, the remediation of which required participation in a speech clinic, where he "sat in a circle of lispers and cleft palates and foreign accents holding a mirror before my lips and rolling difficult sounds over and over" (p. 24).

Humiliated by his inability to get the words out in class, he felt further stigmatized by being singled out, and further burdened by having to make up work missed on account of weekly trips to the clinic, located at another school.

While New York experimented with a class for "speech defective" children in 1908, the first systematic program was instituted two years later in Chicago, when in response to parents' requests, speech instruction was provided for 1,287 "young stammerers," an early demonstration of the power of parental advocacy. According to Superintendent Ella Flagg Young, the children actually presented a variety of speech difficulties (Moore & Kester, 1958), presumably mostly articulation delays. However their predecessors may have acquired their specialized skills, for this purpose a cadre of 10 young teachers was given "additional" training. In New York, a plan formulated in 1911 called for selected English teachers, with further training, to give 30- 60-minute speech correction lessons to identified pupils, but the program for New York's "thousands of children suffering from defective speech" was not implemented until 1916 with appointment as Director of Speech Improvement of Dr. Frederick Martin, who declared its goal was "wiping out all handicaps and setting a standard for normal American children" (in Moore & Kester, 1958, p. 50). Soon many districts began such programs, often as a facet of psychoeducational clinics.

Although the role of speech specialists had not yet been well delineated, nor had formal training structures been established, a knowledge base was growing. Complementing neuroanatomical and other medical research, experimental psychology's contribution was most apparent in the work of Edward Wheeler Scripture (1864–1945), author of *Stuttering and Lisping* (1912) and other seminal texts, as well as a number of scientific papers. Scripture had done his dissertation (on the association of ideas) under Wundt at Leipzig, before joining Hall's group at Clark, moving next to Yale. There, he continued experimental work in phonetics in collaboration with his wife, May Kirk Scripture (1865–1943), who continued to contribute guides for American speech correctionists after her husband's departure from America (to England), their marriage, and apparently the field of speech science (Berry, 1965). But his work was important to its emergence as a discipline.

Professionalizing the field required accommodating scientific and clinical interests. A key event was a meeting of 11 professors in New York's McAlpin Hotel in December 1925, convened at a conference of the short-lived National Association of Teachers of Speech. It had been arranged at an impromptu gathering in the home of Lee E. Travis in Iowa City, of five persons, including Robert W. West, a later president of the American Speech and Hearing Association (ASHA) and Sara S. Hawk, the first woman in the field to earn a doctorate (West, 1960). The "rump session" led to formation of the Speech Association. Its later designation, the American Society for the Study of Disorders of Speech, reflected its academic focus, but its renaming, in 1934, as the American Speech Correction Association acknowledged affiliation of practitioners. With emergence of audiology as a specialization, the organization was incorporated in 1947 as the American Speech and Hearing Association, and retained the acronym ASHA when in 1978 it became the American Speech-Language-Hearing Association. As now, membership was differentiated from licensure, the latter based on award of the Certificate of Clinical Competence, attained with completion of an accredited university training program.

The first of these, the model for others that followed, was established at the University of Wisconsin in 1914 when J. M. O'Neill opened a "speech clinic" directed by a physician, Smiley Blanton, whose undergraduate major was in "the speech arts" (Moore & Kester, 1958). This university leadership was an important factor in Wisconsin's authorizing statewide assignment of itinerant speech correctionists in schools in 1923, a service pattern soon adopted in other states. By 1959, 39 states, and by 1966 all states, had mandated speech services, generally limited to the elementary level. A survey in 1960 (Bingham, Van Hattum, Faulk, & Taussig, 1961) revealed that 1,462 trained therapists were employed in American schools, working mainly with children in the primary grades (75% of caseload) who had articulation problems (81%), that is, omissions, substitutions, distortions, or additions of certain sounds. Most traveled from school to school, seeing an average of 111 children per week.

P.L. 94–142 changed this situation dramatically, with respect to both age and nature of problem, creating a need for changes in training of specialists. Students eligible for special education, across disability "categories," including those who had been excluded from schooling, had needs for specialized attention in the communicative domain, in addition to those whose primary disability was one of communication. While facilitative work with young pupils not considered "handicapped" has continued, it has necessarily assumed lower priority in the face of legislative mandate. Students with cerebral palsy, autism, Down syndrome, and the dual impairment of deaf-blindness, for example, presented challenging needs, sometimes for augmentative communication, that under the law had to be addressed.

While the focus in schools was speech, the study of language generated models identifying speech as a means of symbolic expression, as brain researchers differentiated language-related processes and linked aphasia with brain injury. Expressive aphasia, more common than receptive, can range in severity from mild interference to essential inability to use language in communication. Acquired aphasia can result from cardiovascular accident or head injury, the principal cause in children. (If congenital, it often results from perinatal complications involving deprivation of oxygen to the brain.) The role of communication specialists in this area began with rehabilitative work with military personnel who incurred head injury in the First World War. World War II brought increased involvement and, for some, inspired interest in childhood disability studies.

Richard L. Schiefelbusch (1984), later director of the Center for Mental Retardation and Human Development at the University of Kansas, credited his experiences in a POW camp, teaching speech classes for fellow prisoners who wished to enhance "their social skills for civilian life," or "seemed to have transaction problems . . . evident in their manner of communicating (voice quality, stuttering, or comprehensibility), in disordered thought functions (illogical sentences, word confusions, or disoriented meanings), and group-related fears and anxieties (stage fright)" (p. 234). He pursued his interests through postwar study, at the University of Kansas and, at Northwestern, under Helmer Myklebust, whose theories of language and learning disabilities evolved from his research on deafness.

That work with children first focused on articulation, disfluency, and voice disorders is implied by the role designation "speech correctionist." The succession of titles—speech therapist, speech pathologist, speech-language pathologist—suggests evolving conceptions of the discipline and its scope. *Speech-language pathology* implies a knowledge base and intervention repertoire encompassing the linguistic areas of morphology, syntax, semantics, and pragmatics, as well as phonology. Since many children's difficulties in learning and social interaction imply underlying language abnormality, the fields of communication disorders and learning disabilities have common models and origins.

LANGUAGE IMPAIRMENT

Wiederholt (1974) noted that, during what he called the "foundation phase" of the field of learning disabilities, investigations mainly involved spoken language. Gall found speech difficulties were often due neither to inability to move the tongue voluntarily nor to memory interference, but to impairment of "the faculty of speech alone" resulting from trauma in specific parts of the brain. Later discrediting of his phrenological notions obscured the significance of Gall's work, though some built on his concepts of brain localization. John Baptiste Bouillaud, through postmortem examination of brain-injured adults, linked anterior lobe lesions with impaired speech and damage to other cortical areas with impaired sensation and movement, functions Gall had localized in the brain stem. Based on research at the Bicetre, Pierre Paul Broca (1824–1880) differentiated functions of the left and right hemispheres, linking impaired speech with lesions in the third frontal convolution. While arguing that some cases could result from damage in other areas, J. H. Jackson extended Broca's hypotheses concerning hierarchically organized reflex arcs as the basis for specialized functions, further pursued by Henry Charlton Bastion. Carl Wernicke's (1845–1905) differentiation of sensory aphasia (receptive language) from apraxia (speech) and "mind-blindness" (central language processing) suggested to Wilbur and others diagnostic distinctions among persons with retardation (Rosen et al., 1976).

Recognizing that language is both a unique human ability and among the most complex, Henry Head differed from the "diagram makers," as he termed them, in insisting that language behavior involves integrated neurological functions. Localization notions were nevertheless relevant to later ideas concerning learning disabilities, especially in suggesting that impairment could be manifest in diverse ways. But Head's work with brain-injured soldiers convinced him that certain functions, like writing, speech, or word memory, and their neural substrates were not specifically isomorphic (Wiederholt, 1974). As in other areas, the critical events that led to eventual applications with children were wars.

War and Rehabilitation

As with other specializations, the Great War brought the new medical specialty of neurology into prominence, with appointment of Dr. Harvey Cushing (1869–1939), pioneer in neurosurgery, as Head of Neurology for the American Expeditionary Forces. But cognitive rehabilitation began in a network of rehabilitation centers in Germany and Austria established for military personnel who had sustained head injury, directed by neurologists like Max Isserlin, who headed a center at Munich, and neurological researchers like Kurt Goldstein of the University of Frankfurt, generally acknowledged as founder of the field of brain injury rehabilitation (Boake, 1991). His center at Frankfurt included medical services, psychological evaluation to identify strengths and deficits, a school where teachers carried out prescribed therapies, and eventually a vocational workshop to assess work potential and facilitate transition to civilian life. Like other German neurological specialists, Goldstein had a particular interest in communication disorders, but he believed brain injury affected other areas of function as well. In *Aftereffects of Brain Injuries in War*, Goldstein (1939/1942) identified five pronounced behavioral characteristics observed in soldiers who had incurred head injury: forced response to stimuli, figure-background confusion, hyperactivity, meticulosity, and catastrophic reaction. When the English translation appeared in 1942, Goldstein himself was among the emigré intellectuals working in the United States.

Following the war, American rehabilitation agencies were located in military hospitals and tended to focus on medical treatment rather than providing comprehensive services, although the staff of one included speech correction teachers. By 1920, as the centers began to close, American interest in brain injury rehabilitation waned until renewed by World War II. At that time, more comprehensive rehabilitation facilities, along the lines of the earlier German model, were established, in the United States, Britain, and the Soviet Union, the last under Alexander Luria, whose work had significant postwar influence on Soviet *defectology* and on L. S. Vygotsky's contributions to theory and practice involving children.

The strongly biological tradition in eastern European nations, Hewett and Forness (1974) suggest, may have originated with a decree of Peter the Great that deformed human or animal specimens be turned over to authorities for study. Organic explanations long dominated, with psychogenic causation simply not acknowledged, and classifications of retardation used such terms as feeblemindedness, debelism, imbecility, and idiotism (Lipkowski, 1973). Although the American testing movement had some impact in the 1920s, Makarenko and other leading educators denounced its premises as anti-Marxist (Korgesaar, 1988). Instead, a diagnostic system based on certain qualitative performance criteria, developed by Vygotsky in the 1930s, guided placement and differential instruction. According to Vygotsky's concept of *disontogenesis*, primary (i.e., biogenic) defects are exacerbated by social factors, leading to secondary defects, the latter addressed through remediation, the former through strengthening compensatory functions (Gindis, 1986).

As in Poland, which had had institutions in Warsaw for blind and for deaf persons since 1841 and 1857, respectively (Taylor & Taylor, 1960, p. 356), sensory impairment had been of long-standing interest in Soviet states; a school for blind children was established in Kiev, in the Ukraine, in 1884 (Holowinsky, 1977). Sections of the defectological department formed in 1929 at the Kiev Pedagogical Institute under A. M. Shcherbyna were devoted to *typholopedagogy* (education of the blind), *surdopedagogy* (deaf), and *logopedagogy* ("deaf-mute"). The considerable interest in the impact of sensory impairment on cognitive functioning extended to children with intact senses but impaired learning ability, but by no means precluded remediation; benefits of early stimulation, demonstrated by A. V. Zaporoshets, became an important theme in intervention with young children.

In postwar America, interest in head injury rehabilitation once again declined as psychiatric work with veterans gained ascendance, a development that affected various disciplines. Clinical psychology gained impetus from the Veteran's Administration but experienced a temporary narrowing of focus, with a widening fissure separating clinicians from research psychologists (Sarason, 1988). In psychiatry, while psychoanalysis had focused attention on psychogenic factors in dysfunctional behavior, biogenic issues continued to be addressed, with implications for treatment encompassing a growing pharmacopoeia of psychotropic drugs (increasingly used with children), electroshock therapy, and, most drastically, lobotomies. In the 20th century, organicity was increasingly considered an important dimension in differential diagnosis of children, to the extent that Barkley (1990) characterized its first six decades "the age of the brain-damaged child" (p. 3).

Strauss Syndrome and Structured Classrooms

While earlier descriptions of children with emotional volatility, high activity level, and attentional problems had been proposed, as Barkley (1990) recounts in his text on Attention Deficit Hyperactivity Disorder (ADHD), the individual most influential in applying findings obtained with brain-injured adults to work with children was Alfred A. Strauss (1897–1957). Earning his medical degree at the University of Heidelberg in 1922, with specializations in psychiatry and neurology, Strauss worked as research associate and outpatient department director of the university's Psychiatric and Neurological Clinic, also conducting a practice and consulting with schools and a children's home. Appointed visiting professor at the University of Barcelona, he helped to establish that city's first child guidance clinics (Gardiner, 1958). Coming to the United States in 1937, he was appointed research psychiatrist at the Wayne County Training School at Northville, Michigan, where he opened an experimental unit for brain-injured children in 1941. The Cove School, which he founded in 1947, at Racine, Wisconsin, adding a day unit in 1950 in Evanston, Illinois, had much influence as a research laboratory, training center, and model program.

Strauss's work merged two theoretical streams in German psychology, the *Gestalt* school and the *orthogenetic theory* of another emigré, Heinz Werner (1890–1964). The former brought a focus on perceptual phenomena and intrinsic processes regulating them, the latter a developmental framework to account for the increasing differentiation of children's perceptual experiences. Werner (1961) described cognitive development as a progression from syncretic to discrete, fostered by symbolic functioning. Collaborative studies with Werner and Newell Kephart of *exogenous* (brain-injured) and *endogenous* children with retardation led Strauss and Laura Lehtinen (1947) to identify a set of characteristics of children with organic brain injury, comprising what came to be termed Strauss syndrome: impulsivity, emotional lability, distractibility, motor disinhibition, figure-ground discrimination problems, perseveration, and hyperactivity. The approach they designed accordingly required a dramatically modified environment, with distracting stimuli minimized (e.g., covered windows, bare walls in drab colors, unbejewelled teachers, individual carrels). Daily routines were predictable, unnecessary change avoided, tasks short and focused, with sensory materials, such as Seguin's and Montessori's, used for pupils to practice matching, discrimination, classification, and sequencing as foundations for academic learning.

These concepts were applied in a quasi-experimental field study by a group in Montgomery County, Maryland, led by William Cruickshank, whose work in the area of cerebral palsy was noted in Chapter 7. Cruickshank had identified patterns in some children with known neurological impairment similar to those Strauss attributed to suspected but unconfirmed impairment. Lacking firm evidence that linked problems in concentrating on a task, paying attention, reading, writing, or other skills essential to school success to mild or minimal neurological dysfunction, it was notoriously difficult for professionals to agree on diagnosis, compounded when they represented diverse disciplines or adhered to diverse theoretical orientations. Were such problems attributable to emotional conflict, as psychodynamic perspectives would suggest? Might they reflect maladaptive responses that had been *learned*, attributable to a child's reinforcement history, as behaviorists might argue? And how important was differential diagnosis when it came to teaching the child?

Consequently, Cruickshank and his associates (Cruickshank, Bentzen, Ratzeberg, & Tannhauser, 1961) designed a project to address two key concerns. First, a team representing various clinical disciplines—psychologists, neurologists, special educators, speech pathologists, among others—was asked to differentiate children whose reported problems in school learning and behavior seemed to have a neurological basis. Second, both groups, one comprising those believed brain-injured, the other, children demonstrating similar behavior but who were consensually judged not brain-injured, were instructed according to the manner Strauss and Lehtinen recommended. The investigators found that the structured environment, special materials, and systematic methods benefited both groups. The legacy of this important study is reflected even today in one of the major controversies in the field: Are "true" learning disabilities only those that have an organic cause?

The project stimulated research and demonstration efforts with pupils who presented behavioral problems in school but who were not believed to have organic pathology. In Arlington, Virginia, Norris Haring and E. L. Phillips (1962) combined the concept of a highly structured setting with behavioral procedures, systematically reinforcing desired behaviors. Frank Hewett's (1968) "engineered classroom," pioneered in Santa Monica, California, further systematized the ongoing charting of behaviors and added hierarchically ordered centers corresponding to pupils' differential "levels," beginning at the most basic level of *attention*. Through a token economy, pupils accumulated symbolic reinforcers they could later trade for concrete ones, such as toys, to learn the relationship between their own appropriate behavior and desired outcomes and to strive for goals and defer gratification —all areas of difficulty for many children with behavioral problems.

Even before a full report had been published, the Montgomery County Project began to influence practice, parents' advocacy having made school officials aware of significant numbers of children whose difficulties in school were not adequately provided for. Ohio undertook a project in 1959, with Cruickshank as consultant, to study effectiveness of the structured-classroom approach for pupils with average intellectual ability (IQ over 80), low achievement, and behavior problems. Its success led in 1962 to standards for Neurologically Handicapped pupils, for whom eligibility determination required a neurological evaluation, originally including an electroencephalogram (EEG), a component later deleted. While other states initially made similar reference to organicity, most began almost immediately to adopt educationally referenced terminology. Ohio renamed this fast-growing program, which had expanded in its first decade from 9 to more than 1,000 classes, *learning and/or behavior disorders* in 1973, later distinguishing *specific learning disability* from *severe behavior handicap* (Ohio Department of Education, 1985).

Strauss and Lehtinen's (1947) notion that "all brain lesions, wherever localized, are followed by a similar kind of disordered behavior" (p. 20), supported by Lashley's theory of *equipotentiality*, was not universally accepted, especially given the variability among children whose problems seemed to have an organic basis. Since actual brain damage was often not found, terms like *minimal brain dysfunction* were proposed, but even with technological advances determining the presence and nature of a possible neurological cause, diagnosis still relies mainly on "soft signs," behavioral indicators revealed through neuropsychological testing. While such assessment is yet in a fairly early stage of development, a pioneer in its use was another emigré, Elizabeth M. Koppitz (1919–1983), a Peabody graduate with a Ph.D. from Ohio State, who herself had a learning difficulty that required her to take more time than most people to complete certain tasks. A skilled diagnostician, she refined scoring and interpretation methods for instruments like the Bender Visual-Motor Gestalt Test, adapting it for use with young children. Her work influenced development of methods used today in evaluating students with Attention Deficit Disorder and traumatic brain injury.

While the concept of Strauss syndrome did not prove durable, elements of the structured classroom were widely adopted and were, for a time, standard practice. Clearly, some elements have been retained, such as an orderly environment in which interfering stimuli are minimized, routines are predictable, and instructional materials are selected for their stimulus characteristics and carefully sequenced. But other notions basic to the still evolving concept of specific learning disability would question the desirability of modes of instruction or an environment qualitatively different from what is provided in the regular classroom, to which these students were expected to return if, indeed, they should leave it in the first place. A related question is whether the difficulties these students have in acquiring skills essential to school success are qualitatively different from those of a great many others.

Literacy and Diagnostic/Remedial Teaching

While learning disabilities can be manifested in various ways, especially performance in mathematics, reading, and written expression, most frequently pupils so identified have reading problems, reportedly presented by about 80% (Mercer, 1994). But since definitional criteria must be satisfied in determining if a pupil is eligible for special education, very few reading problems are ascribed to learning disabilities, particularly to underlying neurological dysfunction (Chall, 1983). While boys identified as learning-disabled far outnumber girls, and far more boys than girls seem to have reading difficulties, *dyslexia* reportedly occurs with equal frequency (Wolff, Michel, Ovrut, & Drake, 1990). A number of factors other than neurological organization influence ease or difficulty with which children learn to read, as well as who is determined to have a learning disability.

Although adult literacy is an urgent national concern in the 1990s, it is not a new one; while reading instruction has traditionally been a responsibility of elementary schools, Gray (1939), more than a half-century ago, cited records of secondary students showing that "from 20 to 30 per cent . . . read so poorly that they can engage in required reading activities only with great difficulty. Indeed, some of them are so much retarded in reading that it is impossible for them to read the books ordinarily used at their respective grade levels" (p. 138). Many explanations have been offered of "Why Johnny can't read." Specialists today view *literacy* in a holistic and interactive sense involving text processing, metacognition, motivation, and communication, rather than as a set of isolated skills. But the field's emergence, which paralleled that of special education, was similarly in response to concern for problems many pupils experienced in school, especially in mastering an ability basic to school learning. The general, and contentious, area of "developmental reading" has been important in identifying causes of poor reading and suggesting avenues for prevention.

Marian Monroe (1932) noted wide variability both among poor readers and in profiles yielded for the same pupils by different diagnostic measures. While she and a few other early specialists believed problems involved interaction of pupil characteristics, teaching methods, and text features, subsequent conceptions located "causative factors of reading disability within the reader" (Lipson & Wixson, 1986, p. 114) and stressed diagnosis and "treatment." The subspecialization of remedial reading reflected a medicalization of such difficulties, paralleling that which occurred in special education. Some conceptions, like Hinshelwood's (1917) notion of congenital "word blindness," attributed difficulties to neurological causes but suggested training to remediate the affected skills in reading or writing. Samuel Orton (1925), proposing that such problems as reversals in cases of dyslexia were due to hemispheric imbalance, coined the term *strephosymbolia*, "twisted symbols," to explain problems in remembering word patterns and in letter orientation. His ideas concerning the role of poorly established hemispheric dominance influenced Anna Gillingham, Bessie Stillman, and Marion Monroe, whose remediational approaches reflect a growing diagnostic movement in education that resulted from extension of standardized testing (Lipson & Wixson, 1986). As the area of learning disabilities emerged, "diagnostic-prescriptive" teaching became its hallmark.

Samuel Kirk, in a sense the "founder" of the concept of specific learning disability, attributed development of *The Illinois Test of Psycholinguistic Abilities* (Kirk, McCarthy, & Kirk, 1968) to the influence of Orton and Monroe. The ITPA model, based on Charles Osgood's tri-level, mediation-integration model of communication, was not intended as a "theory" but as a practical tool for identifying a pupil's strengths and weaknesses in specific areas, as Monroe had proposed. It was, Kirk (1984) cautioned, "only an aid to clinical judgment for children with language and related disorders," and not "for the diagnosis of all ills and educational problems" (p. 38). But the ITPA nevertheless epitomized process-oriented intervention. As we saw in the case of Strauss syndrome, perception and perceptual-motor coordination have been "underlying processes" of particular interest.

Perceptual-Motor Training

The process orientation is based on two key assumptions: that such difficulties reflect an underlying dysfunction in the central nervous system, and that remediation involves strengthening a weak modality, training the child to compensate through use of the strong ones (as do persons who are blind or deaf), or some combination of the two, as in Grace Fernald's (1943) multisensory approach. Thus, a pupil's instructional plan predicated on diagnostic assessment reflects a profile of "intraindividual differences." A number of related constructs have been proposed in recognition of the incontestable fact that most people are better at some things than at others. The extent to which differential skills reflect pervasive differences in temperament is an area that has been extensively explored by developmental psychologists. A related idea, less thoroughly studied but widely accepted, is that of differential "learning styles," which suggests that individuals have preferred learning modalities (e.g., visual, auditory, haptic). Differential abilities do not necessarily imply defect; perhaps the most revolutionary challenge to unitary conceptions of human ability is expressed in Howard Gardner's (1983) theory of "multiple intelligences."

The validity of applying underlying process constructs to the diagnosis and remediation of academic skills depends on four key considerations: existence of the relevant underlying abilities or processes; the accuracy with which they can be assessed; effectiveness of procedures used to train or remediate them; and the transfer of enhanced process function to skills such as reading, writing, spoken language, or calculation. It may be that process functioning can be enhanced without enhancing academic functioning. It may also be that direct instruction of reading, writing, or calculating skills is as effective or even more effective—but certainly more efficient. Research to date has tended to support both these possibilities, although it is certainly also possible that improved diagnostic and/or remedial methods may in the future validate ability training. But some professionals, especially in the academic specialty within physical education concerned with the study of motor behavior, believe improved process functioning desirable in its own right.

A theorist often invoked by that discipline's practitioners is another pioneer in the tradition of Itard and Seguin, Newell C. Kephart (1911–1973). Rather than in education or psychology, Kephart's doctorate was in child welfare, earned at the University of Iowa's Child Welfare Station. Subsequent collaboration, as a "mental health worker," with Strauss at Michigan's Wayne County Training School, greatly influenced his ideas, which epitomize the fundamental features of ability training: They are based on a coherent theory linking underlying processes with behavior that is observable, and therefore able to be assessed and remediated. His thinking reflects the Gestalt influence, combined with D. O. Hebb's theory of neurological organization and Werner's epigenetic principle, integrated with Piaget's theory of an invariant sequence of developmental stages that originate with the newborn's congenitally organized reflex patterns. Those stages are hierarchical, in that attainment of later (higher-order, abstract) functions depends on prior establishment of earlier functions. *Sensorimotor schemata*, which Piaget considered foundations for subsequent "structures," and thus the building blocks of intelligence, are, in a sense, Kephart's "motor concepts."

Kephart's (1971) model depicts a sequence of stages (motor, motor-perceptual, perceptual-motor, perceptual, perceptual-conceptual, conceptual, and conceptual-perceptual) at any of which developmental progress may be interrupted. A breakdown in coordination or integration may be apparent in any of several areas: *body image* (an internalized model of one's own body); *balance*; *kinesthetic figure-ground*, considered basic to visual, tactile, and auditory discrimination; and *laterality*, or an internalized concept of sidedness, problems in which he believed caused distorted or reversed directionality manifest in dyslexic (reading) and dysgraphic (writing) patterns. While most children achieve these skills in the course of development, others imperfectly integrate motor, perceptual, and conceptual learning, manifesting "splinter skills" and impaired ability to generalize. Problems may be seen in inability to track a moving target like a penlight (ocular pursuit, which many optometrists believe essential to reading and amenable to training), and difficulty in tasks based on body image or requiring perceptual-motor coordination, like crossing the body's midline when drawing chalkboard figures; copying certain figures; walking a balance beam; patterned movement, as in simulating "angels in the snow"; traversing an obstacle course; identifying and localizing body parts; and striking a suspended, moving ball with a stick held in various positions. Such tasks were incorporated in a criterion-referenced assessment procedure, the *Purdue Perceptual-Motor Survey* (Roach & Kephart, 1966), for 5- to 10-year-old children.

Kephart's remediation approach involves systematic practice, initiated at the level at which a child's developmental progress appears to be interrupted. Since many children with learning difficulties manifest such problems as reversals and difficulties in "motor planning" or awareness of body boundaries, his methods were—like structured classrooms—readily adopted in the proliferating programs for children with learning disabilities. But his recommended activities, or variations of them, were often applied in fairly eclectic fashion, rather than based on individual child diagnosis. In general, perceptual-motor training may indeed enhance a child's skills, especially in sport and games, but little evidence has been found of transfer to academic skills (Hammill & Weiderholt, 1973).

Another whose diagnostic teaching methods found their way into classrooms for children with learning disabilities in the 1960s and early 1970s was Marianne Frostig, whose *Developmental Test of Visual Perception* (Frostig & Horne, 1964) was designed for children from 3 to 10 years of age as a basis for remediation. While visual perception is certainly important in school learning, however, the causal link Frostig and her associates asserted between "school failure and maladjustment" and problems in visual perception has not been supported by research, nor has the efficacy of perceptual training in remediating difficulties in school learning (Hammill & Weiderholt, 1973). Various underlying processes have been postulated to account for such difficulties. Mann (1979) suggested that the "process explosion" in American psychology at mid-century represented an ancient quest in new guise: the attempt to explain behaviors of particular contemporary interest on the basis of "hypothetical 'inner' events or entity constructs" (p. 14). That quest has by no means been abandoned with respect to our understanding of children's learning problems, but it has not to date yielded results particularly satisfying to educators, parents, or students themselves.

PARENT ADVOCACY
AND THE LEARNING DISABILITIES "MOVEMENT"

Theorists theorize, but parents seek answers to benefit their children, now; thus, it was due to parent advocacy that this field assumed the proportions of a movement. That alternatives were possible that could be implemented within the structure of public education was suggested by privately operated programs offering forms of "educational therapy" based not on psychodynamic but on psychoeducational principles, in the tradition of Witmer's clinical method. Parents who could afford them turned to private alternatives for a troubled or seriously disturbed child excluded from school, or being maintained but not helped, or when more intensive treatment than was considered possible on an outpatient basis seemed indicated. That private facilities are costly and thus burdensome, if not impossible, for families was a critical consideration in P.L. 94–142's mandate for Free Appropriate Public Education (FAPE). Some private programs accommodated children not benefiting from regular instruction, as well as others who were excluded altogether.

The Dubnoff Center for Child Development and Educational Therapy, in North Hollywood, California, has since its inception emphasized "educational therapy" as the major mode of treatment, combined with a strong parent-involvement component. Earlier in its development, the center focused mainly on children considered "brain-damaged," but Belle Dubnoff found an individualized, structured approach, emphasizing movement and creative use of diverse materials, beneficial for other children referred to her, including children with autism and severe emotional disturbance. Having begun with three children in her home, she established the center in collaboration with Marianne Frostig in 1948 to offer "special educational training to children who could not be placed in public schools because of learning disabilities, developmental disabilities, physical handicaps, language and communication disorders and/or emotional or behavioral disturbances, and for whom there is no other appropriate placement" (Frietag, n.d.).

Similarly, the Grove School in Lake Forest, Illinois, now called the Educational Treatment Center for the Exceptional Child, was established mainly for excluded children, but also served others whose needs their parents thought were not being met in schools. In 1958, its founder, educator and religious author Virginia F. Matson (1974), agreed to tutor a boy whose parents had been advised to "put him away." At first tenuously housed in a church, the program soon enrolled 60 children, taught by 15 teachers. Such private resources provided alternatives to institutions for children with severe impairments and to debilitating school failure for those with "mild" learning problems. Even with assurance of the right to a Free Appropriate Public Education, many parents still seek private resources; the 1988 *Directory for Exceptional Children* lists more than 150 private schools in the United States for children with learning disabilities.

Specific learning disability is often identified, compared with other special education categories, as a mild disability, but from the child's and parent's perspective there is nothing mild about the academic, and often social, failure experiences involved. Such experiences are not unique, however; if this accounts for only some difficulties, in learning to read for example, how are those of other unsuccessful readers, the majority, explained? Sleeter (1990) maintains that the American tendency to categorize pupils deemphasizes instruction, reinforces societal sorting, and contributes to self-fulfilling prophecies. By the 1960s, she states, five categories had been created, "differentiated by whether the cause . . . was presumed to be organic, emotional, or environmental, and whether the child was deemed intellectually normal or subnormal . . . called slow learners, mentally retarded, emotionally disturbed, culturally deprived, and learning disabled" (p. 27).

The last group, she charges, originally comprising a vastly predominant population of white, middle-class children, "was created to explain the failure of children from advantaged social groups, and to do so in such a way that it suggested their eventual ability to attain relatively higher status occupations than other low achievers" (Sleeter, 1990, p. 33). Since 1975, however, the demographics of learning disabled (LD) identification and placement have changed radically, especially in large city schools whose LD programs now reportedly enroll a preponderance of generally low-achieving pupils, with low IQ scores, from minority and low-income families (Gottlieb, Gottlieb, & Wishner, 1994). Such shifts reflect continuing concerns about inequity, preference for labels that do not imply irremediable cognitive limitations, and attempts to provide help for many students to whom it may otherwise be unavailable. But great increases in the number of students identified as learning-disabled—from 1.2% of all pupils in 1976–1977 to 3.6% in 1989–1990, more than 2 million, 48.5% of all pupils receiving special education (Mercer, 1994, p. 123)—is cause for concern, as is evidence of inconsistency and arbitrariness in determining eligibility. Controversies notwithstanding, the rapid growth of programs for students with learning disabilities has been largely due to parent activism.

For example, in 1967, virtually on arrival at the vaunted ivory tower of academe, the first author was greeted by a mother demanding, "What are *you* going to do for these children?" The experience was surely not unique, but compared with those of school officials, academics' encounters with parents were mild. Parent activism has been an extraordinarily important factor in the development of services for exceptional children, but seldom has the potential of that force to shape policy and influence practice been as evident as in this area. The concept of *specific* disability that emerged, largely due to parent advocacy, had broader impact reflected in the Individualized Education Program (IEP), which defines appropriate education for each pupil receiving special education. And while the IEP specifies areas where intervention is needed, the Least Restrictive Environment component stipulates provisions for normalization. These were core facets insisted on by parents of children with learning disabilities, together with the stipulation that these pupils are otherwise "normal" and not "defective."

Even as this "invisible handicap" received more attention, definitional agreement was elusive. That was a desired outcome of a meeting convened by the Fund for the Perceptually Handicapped in Chicago's La Salle Hotel on April 6, 1963. While "pioneers of the Learning Disabilities movement" were present, most of the 159 registrants represented local organizations, in 17 states and one Canadian province, begun by parents concerned that their children's difficulties were not understood (Russell, 1973). As Kirk summarized, definitions emphasized either etiology (e.g., minimal brain dysfunction) or manifestations in school (e.g., dyslexia, dysgraphia, etc.); with adoption of his proposed descriptor for pupils with "disorders in development in language, speech, reading, and associated communications skills," the Association for Children with Learning Disabilities (ACLD) was formed. Now the Learning Disabilities Association of America (LDA), most of its 50,000 members are parents. In 1968, the year the National Advisory Committee on Handicapped Children proposed the definition incorporated in the Children with Learning Disability Act of 1969 (later in P.L. 94–142), the Council for Exceptional Children's Division for Children with Learning Disabilities (DCLD) was established. Continuing definitional disagreement led to its constituting itself independently as the Council for Learning Disabilities (CLD), as a new CEC Division for Learning Disabilities (DLD) was formed.

Clearly, the construct has been a highly politicized one, its history influenced by forces in addition to scientific advance. Parent activism has also been an important factor leading to new conceptions of the nature and cause of more pervasive problems, which, like learning disabilities, are now known to persist into adulthood and are generally believed to reflect underlying brain pathology. The most compelling examples are perhaps seen in the case of a condition characterized by highly deviant language and impaired communication, originally termed early infantile autism, and Attention Deficit Disorder, which, though perhaps less dramatic in its impact, is a serious problem for many children and families.

REDEFINITIONS, REDISCOVERIES, AND NEW UNDERSTANDINGS

Autism, clearly, is a condition that has always existed, affecting occasional individuals in every period and culture. It has attracted in the popular mind an amazed, fearful, or bewildered attention (and perhaps engendered mythical or archetypal figures: the alien, the changeling, the child bewitched). And yet it was only in the nineteen-forties that it was medically described—almost simultaneously, as it happened—by Leo Kanner, in Baltimore, and Hans Asperger, in Vienna, both of whom, independently, converged on the term "autism." (Sacks, 1994, p. 106)

This term was an interesting choice, considering views today, for dictionary definitions (e.g., *Webster's Third New International*, p. 147) associate autism with "absorption in need-satisfying or wish-fulfilling fantasy, as a mechanism of escape from reality." That is apparently how Kanner (1943) interpreted the "mental aloneness"—a certain aloof quality he observed—coupled with an "obsessive insistence on sameness." These characteristics, which explained stereotyped mannerisms such as hand-flapping, apparent fascination with objects in preference to human interaction, and speech that if present at all was noncommunicative and idiosyncratic, were described as "autistic disturbances of affective contact," which Kanner allegedly attributed to parental "coldness." (In a report of a follow-up of 11 children among his original patients, however, Kanner [1971] maintained that was a misrepresentation and that he had stated the condition appeared to be inborn.) Belief in psychogenic etiology, congruent with psychoanalytic notions, assumed psychotherapy to be the treatment of choice, with the child or concurrently with the child and mother. Many, like Bettelheim (1967), believed that treatment required "therapeutic removal" of the child from the presumptive source of the condition: the parents. Yet Bettelheim was among those who in the 1960s pioneered a major shift to educational approaches, albeit in residential settings.

Founded in 1953 by Dr. Carl Fenichel in response to parent activism, the League School in Brooklyn, New York, adopted a present-oriented educational approach, in preference to psychotherapeutic probing of the repressed past. The very fact that this was a day school implied rejection of "parentectomy," but as many professionals continued to ascribe autism to poor parenting, parents expressed growing frustration with lack of information, services for their children, and support for themselves. "Most certainly," wrote the parents of one child, "we don't need to be told we have disturbed kids because *we* are uptight or neurotic" (Lapin & Lapin, 1976, p. 287). Two important events leading to recognition that *"parents do not cause autism"* (p. 288) and that families had not been well served by professionals or programs were the founding in 1965 of the National Society for Autistic Children (now Autism Society of America) and the publication by Bernard Rimland, parent of a child with autism, of *Infantile Autism* (1964).

While much about autism is yet puzzling, there is broad consensus supporting Ritvo's (1976) hypothesis "that the personality deficits observed in these children were secondary to their organic brain pathology," which could result from diverse causes (p. 4). Moreover, this spectrum disorder encompasses a range of characteristics and levels of severity, and may be present in combination with such conditions as Rett's and fragile X syndromes, seizure disorder, severe allergies, viral infections, congenital rubella, tuberous sclerosis, and motor incoordination (Freeman, 1993). Accurate diagnostic information is critically important to professionals' and parents' understanding of the child—who will become an adult—with autism. But it cannot convey understanding of the *experience* of autism. While the savant phenomenon is rare, many persons demonstrate unusually acute abilities, such as spatial awareness, hypervisualization, and sensitivity to sound. Donna Williams's account in *Nobody Nowhere* (1992) reveals unusual gifts, as well as experiences shared with many others:

> There upon the pages I felt both angered and found. The echoed speech, the inability to be touched, the walking on tiptoe, the painfulness of sounds, the spinning and jumping, the rocking and repetition mocked my whole life. My head swam with images of the abuse that had been my training. The necessity of creating the characters had torn me apart but saved me from being a statistic. Part of me had complied with my training, the other part had made it through twenty-six years with a private, cut-off world intact. (p. 187)

Although she indeed did experience a mother's abuse and a father's virtual noninvolvement, Ms. Williams recognized that her "difference" was present from the beginning. In *Somebody Somewhere* (1994), she reflected further:

> Autism had had me in its cage for as long as I had ever known. Autism had been there before thought, so that my first thoughts were nothing more than automatic, mirrored repetitions of those of others. Autism had been there before sound so that my first words were the meaningless echo of the conversations of those around me. Autism had been there before words, so that ninety-nine percent of my verbal repertoire was a stored-up collection of literal dictionary definitions and stock phrases. Autism had been there before I'd ever known a

want of my own, so that my first "wants" were copies of those seen in others (a lot of which came from TV). Autism had been there before I'd learned how to use my own muscles, so that every facial expression or pose was a cartoon reflection of those around me. Nothing was connected to self. Without the barest foundations of self I was like a subject under hypnosis, totally susceptible to any programming and reprogramming without question or personal identification. I was in a state of total alienation. This, for me, was autism. (p. 5)

Autism has recently become a familiar word to millions who had never heard of it before, through the movie *Rainman*, Donna Williams's memoirs, interviews with her and other persons of accomplishment who have autism, and Oliver Sacks's (1994) account in the *New Yorker* of his conversations with biologist/engineer Temple Grandin, who has described her own experiences as a person with autism in numerous lectures and in her autobiography (Grandin & Scariano, 1986). Countless students, readers, listeners, and viewers have thereby been helped to understand what it might mean to experience the world, one's sensations, one's self, and other people very differently from the way they themselves do.

There is a difference between understanding that many learning, language, and social interactive difficulties experienced by children have an underlying biological basis and medicalizing such difficulties in the sense of regarding children as "defectives." Like other forms of exceptionality, they represent *differences*, understanding of which can benefit the individual, family members, peers, teachers, and society. Labels may often be more harmful than helpful, but accurate diagnosis also may offer an explanation for the previously unexplainable, and thereby a release from guilt, often a reason for hope: It's nobody's fault, it's all right to be different, and something can be done. As with learning disability, such would seem to be the case with autism, a pervasive developmental disability that may occur in association with other conditions.

The "condition" most frequently reported to co-occur—in about 70% of all cases—is psychometrically defined mental retardation. While this finding suggests a distinction between "low functioning" and "high functioning" individuals—Asperger's syndrome from Kanner's syndrome—it does not necessarily suggest a reliable basis for diagnosis, prognosis, or determining intervention; conventional assessment procedures are of questionable value with individuals who "process" in highly atypical ways. Many people with autism also experience severe allergies, as does Donna Williams, or a history of seizure disorder, but neither is likely to cause autism, nor are they its results; various manifestations can originate from the brain pathology reflected in the motor incoordination and perceptual and cognitive processing differences often associated with autism. And while such manifestations are now generally agreed to be biologically caused, the possible causes are varied and are yet being studied (Freeman, 1993).

In the 1970s, fragile X (Martin-Bell) syndrome began to be described in the medical literature as a chromosomal condition, second only to Down syndrome as a cause of retardation. The "brittle" quality, or even separation, of the X chromosome of the 23rd pair results from a recessive gene and, like all X chromosomal abnormalities, occurs more frequently in males, who are also far more likely to have intellectual impairment. However, girls as well as boys may present behavioral manifestations, often attributed to "hyperactivity" and not addressed by physicians or educators, such as motor incoordination, severe language delay, hand-flapping or other stereotypy, lack of eye contact, and difficulty in tolerating change or accommodating their own learning schemata to typical classroom structures, as with autism. Whether fragile X can be a "cause" of autism, or may be a concurrent condition, is arguable, but it is not considered a "subtype," as are Rett's syndrome or Heller's syndrome (American Psychiatric Association, 1987).

Another genetic condition, identified a century earlier than fragile X but even more recently linked to autism, and characterized by quite different features, is tuberous sclerosis. In addition to a history of seizure activity, those features include benign tumors, most frequently of the brain but also of other organs and of eyes and extremities, and skin lesions or rashes. Delayed language and motor development observed in many children with tuberous sclerosis, together with difficulties in tolerating overstimulating or unpredictable situations, suggests a link with autism, which indeed reportedly occurs far more frequently in these children than in the general population, though "the mechanism of this association remains to be elucidated" (Smalley, Tanguay, Smith, & Guitterez, 1992, p. 352). In this instance, symptoms associated with autism, including developmental delay, sleep disturbance, hyperactivity, and volatility, may be sequellae of early and persistent seizuring resulting from a brain tumor.

Attention Deficit Disorder/Attention Deficit Hyperactivity Disorder (ADD/ADHD) is another instance of a diagnosis sometimes welcomed because it seems to explain the inexplicable—a child's inattention, erratic and unpredictable behavior, impulsivity, mood swings, unresponsiveness to contingencies parents find effective for most children, and inconsistency in the quality of performance of tasks at home and at school. Again, such patterns have probably been present in some children at any time in history, but ADD was first officially described in 1980 in the American Psychiatric Association's *Diagnostic and Statistical Manual* (DSM-III) as a distinct disorder (at this time, as two disorders: ADD "with or without hyperactivity"). Though a "reconceptualization . . . from the DSM-II category Hyperkinetic Reaction of Childhood," it provided much more specific diagnostic criteria (Barkley, 1990, p. 21).

As was true of Strauss syndrome, all the characteristics associated with ADHD can be presented by "normal" children, which has brought challenges that this is yet another social construct. However, voluminous research data that have accumulated since the 1970s and the testimony of parents and children themselves argue compellingly that ADHD is "real." As a matter of parenting and of professional practice, that is extremely important for many reasons, not least of which is the appropriateness of psychopharmacological intervention. In the 1970s, critics charged widespread misuse of drug management, essentially providing a means of social control predicated on a "myth" of the hyperactive child (Schrag & Divoky, 1975). While the issue still is troubling, predominant medical views are that, unless contraindicated (by tic disorders, Tourette syndrome, or certain other conditions), such stimulant medications as Ritalin, properly administered and monitored, combined with training (e.g., cognitive-behavior modification), reportedly enhance most children's social and academic functioning, even into the adolescent years (Barkley, 1990).

Yet, ADHD is also in a sense socially constructed, as are all forms of human exceptionality. While diagnostic criteria exist, they are arbitrary and inconsistently interpreted, which accounts for widely variable prevalence rates. (DSM III-R estimates 3–5%.) Moreover, cultural factors and family contexts may affect both children's manifestation of symptoms and adults' tolerance (or intolerance) of those symptoms (Barkley, 1990, p. 61). ADHD is currently recognized in Section 504 of the 1973 Rehabilitation Act and the Americans with Disabilities Act of 1990 (ADA), if one or more life functions is affected, but not (explicitly) in the Education of the Handicapped Act, amended as the IDEA. Thus, pupils diagnosed as having ADHD are not thereby considered eligible for special education, but they cannot be discriminated against, often requiring schools to provide services under their "504 Plan." The fact that ADHD is presently not a special education "category" does not disqualify students from special education based on an IEP— many have been found to meet the criteria for one of the IDEA categories, most frequently learning disability, serious emotional disability, or health impairment. But many parents consider such requirements artificial, masking the unique needs of children with ADD/ADHD.

Unlike "learning disability," "specific language disability," and other descriptive constructs—arguably "mental retardation"—that provide a kind of pedagogical catch-all rather than an explanation, certain biologically based constructs suggest a basis not only for understanding, but also for intervention. In some instances, they also pose a paradox, as Barkley (1990) writes of ADHD, in a "society founded on egalitarian ideals and an economic meritocracy . . . [since] deficiencies in behavioral self-regulation arise early in childhood . . . are amplified by conditions of social disadvantage; and predispose afflicted individuals to a high risk of educational, social, and occupational underachievement" (p. 38). In turning to the question of how the lessons of history can inform policy and practice concerning children a society considers exceptional, we begin with certain assumptions, perhaps banal, but critical: (1) Children are indeed biologically diverse; (2) some differences place children at significant risk; however, (3) a child's destiny is not determined by biology but by myriad transactional life experiences in successive social contexts, most basically that of family; (4) while human diversity is inevitable, and desirable, its meaning is culturally determined; thus, (5) what a society considers "handicapping," in children as in adults, is in most instances symptomatic of social injustice, intolerance of diversity, or unimaginative or myopic use of resources—and thus preventable.

CHAPTER 10

Dimensions of a "New History"

"THE CENTURY OF THE CHILD"

The Individuals with Disabilities Education Act and the Americans with Disabilities Act suggest in their very titles how radically the context of human exceptionality has changed. England's Idiots Act of 1886 was repealed in 1913 by the Mental Deficiency Act, but terms like *deficiency* are no longer so readily applied to human beings. New language conventions acknowledge distinctions between disability and person, and between one's characteristics and barriers imposed by others; while some disabilities may be preventable, *all* associated handicaps can be ameliorated, if not eliminated. But even as barriers are removed, children remain inevitably handicapped by their very dependence and inability to choose the circumstances of their birth or nurture. The "Children's Century" had been envisioned as a time when the implications of that dependence would be fully recognized.

Thus, the First White House Conference on Children affirmed a societal commitment to *family*, a commitment maintained as President Wilson, declaring 1919 the Year of the Child, convened the second. The third produced the Children's Charter, which explicitly referenced exceptional children. With the United Nations' Declaration of the Rights of the Child, adopted in 1959, the idea of children's rights was presumably no longer a "minor enthusiasm" of a few reformers, but a worldwide cause. In its Third Declaration, in 1974, the U.N. Children's Fund affirmed that "the child who is physically, mentally or socially handicapped shall be given the special treatment, education and care required by his particular condition." But the gap between rhetoric and reality is nowhere more cruel than in society's tolerance of conditions that put children in harm's way. Today, more than half the incidence of childhood disability worldwide results from malnutrition, viral and bacterial infections, and communicable disease (Marfo, 1986). In America, one child in four is born into poverty, many go without immunization, most are affected by violence—physically or, given its ubiquitous nature, psychologically. These conditions, with prenatal exposure to drugs or toxic environmental elements, HIV-AIDS, exploitation in its many forms, and lack of hope for a better future—for many, for any future at all—describe not the beginning of the Century of the Child, but its end. Society creates disability in more than one sense.

"Services" have expanded dramatically, though not commensurate with their need, and while it would be gratifying to believe otherwise, we have seen that neither benevolence nor science has consistently served children with or at risk for disabilities well. Often, calamitous events like wars, devastating in their impact on children, have paradoxically stimulated action. Yet, though calls for children's rights have rung hollow and movements have faltered, they suggest a pattern of progress, expressed in social policy and in new paradigms for understanding both exceptionality and childhood. A comprehensive analysis of medical discoveries, technological advances, advocacy, and policy developments is beyond the scope of this final chapter. But among the lessons to be drawn from history are several overarching themes suggesting a foundation for a new history.

DIVERSITY: THE CONTEXT
OF CHILDHOOD EXCEPTIONALITY

The present "era" of services began with the century, but where children were concerned 1919—the Year of the Child—began a decade of paradox. Progressive reformers yet sought to improve the quality of life for children of the new European-Americans. Some, like Addams, Wald, and Florence Kelley, joined ranks with African-American leaders, in the NAACP and its forerunner Niagara Movement, in seeking racial justice in schooling as in other areas of American society. While white America's attitudes toward DuBois's "talented tenth" ranged from patronization to disbelief, feelings about the "submerged tenth" ranged from apathy to virulence (Lewis, 1993). Though progressive reforms continued, notably compulsory education and child labor legislation, the movement faded with its loss of social focus (Cremin, 1961). The idealism and national sense of mission President Wilson hoped to sustain seemed to evaporate with the Armistice; "normalcy" involved suppression of ideas and hostility toward all who were "different," thus a threat (Allen, 1931). Protectionism and eugenics converged with psychometrics in a scientific racism anything but celebratory with respect to human diversity, which impacted directly on children and their schooling.

Psychometric Sorting and Subsystems of "Diversification"

As school enrollments swelled, so did the numbers of casualties. In 1909, in *Laggards in Our Schools*, Leonard P. Ayres had called for more economical alternatives to grade repetition for the 33.7% of elementary pupils he reported academically deficient. Estimating that more than half the pupils in large urban districts had mental and physical problems associated with poverty, and citing Connecticut's adoption of the Snellen chart in 1899, Wallin (1914) called for systematic screening to identify vision, health, and hearing problems. While recommending special "orthophrenic" classes for pupils who needed them, he also argued for a more flexible curriculum and organizational structures to accommodate remedial instruction. As we saw, progressivism's social-settlement facet was an important force in urging schools to provide both health services and special classes, perceived need for which grew in parallel fashion to increased pupil heterogeneity.

Tests seemed to offer an "objective" system of sorting to reduce this diversity to manageable proportions. Despite general enthusiasm about ability tests, concerns were raised, most famously by Walter Lippmann as noted in Chapter 6. Nor were all educationists sanguine about the trend toward their wide adoption. Dewey (1916) believed that while tests might reveal talents of some pupils, they should not be used to close doors of opportunity for others. W. C. Bagley (1925), a prominent critic of progressivism, cautioned that tests could only suggest to the educator where to begin, not prescribe or limit goals; improperly used, they were potential instruments of social Darwinism, a concern that subsequent educational tracking and exclusion have shown to be warranted. Such responses have often implied fear of contamination, rationalized with professions of concern for the presumptively less fortunate or less well-endowed, educationally defined as slow to learn, difficult to control, or likely to need special care. Or make others uncomfortable: the Wisconsin Supreme Court ruled in 1919 that "a mentally normal, blind child could be barred from school since his/her handicap had a depressing and nauseating effect on teachers and children" (Hensley, 1973, pp. 3).

While by 1918 all states had enacted compulsory education laws, exclusion policies soon followed; special education had come to mean "special place," but a more urgent concern was those children for whom schools provided no place at all. A half-century later, a Children's Defense Fund study (Washington Research Project, 1974), reported that, in addition to a "far greater number who are technically in school but who benefit little or not at all" (p. 2), nearly 2 million children and youth of school age, three-quarters of a million 13 or younger, were not enrolled in school. The investigators concluded

> that if a child is not white, or is white but not middle class, does not speak English, is poor, needs special help with seeing, hearing, walking, reading, learning, adjusting, growing up, is pregnant or married at age 15, is not smart enough

or is too smart, then, in many places, school officials decide school is not the place for that child. In sum, out of school children share a common characteristic of *differentness* by virtue of race, income, physical, mental, or emotional "handicap," and age. They are, for the most part, out of school not by choice, but because they have been *excluded*. It is as if many school officials have decided that certain groups of children are beyond their responsibility and are expendable. Not only do they exclude these children, they frequently do so arbitrarily, discriminantly, and with impunity. (p. 4)

Schools had adopted policies of "conditional nurture," and as in medieval times what placed a child at risk was differentness. Disability, though not the only basis, provided one means of delineating who should be excluded and, ironically though not surprisingly, as compulsory education was mandated, states and local districts codified criteria for exclusion on the basis of "inability to benefit." Such policies, formulated in the 1920s, had by the early 1970s become, if anything, more firmly entrenched. Protypical was the explanation of Superintendent William J. O'Shea (1926) that New York's ungraded classes were not appropriate for all children with retardation. "Exclusion cases" included those with a measured IQ lower than 50, or higher in those who, "because of other special defects or physical disabilities can not profit by the type of instruction suitable to the majority of children in ungraded classes," who varied "as far from the typical ungraded-class pupil as the retarded child varies from the normal" (p. 38). Classes formed for those who "didn't fit" now excluded pupils who "didn't fit" those classes, with Wallin's and Farrell's belief that schools should serve all children a decidedly minority opinion.

New York's exclusion cases included children with epilepsy, postencephalitis, chorea, and "psychopathic personality or actual psychoses," as well as "deviant physical growth" patterns, like those with "mongolian features . . . unfortunate individuals who can be recognized by the physical stigmata . . . and small stocky build. They are always seriously retarded in intelligence, and it has been useless to attempt instruction except on the very lowest level. . . . Obviously, such training can at present be better provided in the homes of children or in institutions" (O'Shea, 1926, pp. 38–39). Elimination of exclusionary policies, often codified in legislation, culminated decades of advocacy by parents, sadly not always joined by special educators, excepting such rare leaders as Richard Hungerford, of the Detroit and then New York districts (Blatt, 1975). In Cuyahoga County, Ohio, where school officials had concluded that instruction of "'low mentals' . . . does not lie within the sphere of 'education'" (Schmidt, 1970, p. 52), a group of parents formed "community classes," lobbied for state enabling legislation, and began a network that became the Association for Retarded Children (now Citizens) (Turnbull & Turnbull, 1990). By 1954, more than 30,000 people were active in groups advocating for persons with mental retardation (Stevens, 1954). Landmark court decisions—*PARC et al. v. Commonwealth of Pennsylvania* (1971) and *Mills v. Board of Education* (1972)—established precedent for Free Appropriate Public Education (FAPE), the cornerstone of P.L. 94-142, and *zero exclusion*.

Crucially, FAPE encompassed the principle of Least Restrictive Environment, for steadily increasing numbers of pupils had been placed in separate programs. Automotive transportation had contributed to schools' ability to provide alternatives to residential settings, but that capability, combined with growing psychometric expertise, contributed to the ascendancy of the segregated special class model. By the 1920s, about two-thirds of large American school districts had such classes (Abraham, 1972); with this enhanced diagnostic capability, the number placed grew from about 26,000 in 1922 to 357,000 in 1948, slightly more than 1.2% of all pupils. Over the next decade, that nearly doubled, and by 1968 it had reached 2.2 million, the most dramatic postwar increase being in classes for children identified as mentally retarded: from 87,000 in 1948 to 390,000 in 1963 (Farber, 1968).

While school psychology's purview and its practitioners' expertise have never been restricted to testing, the school psychologist's role became increasingly restricted to diagnostic evaluation to determine eligibility for special education (and for inclusion in school), often the basis for state funding allocations. While it ranges widely, depending on needs of the individual student, the average annual per-pupil cost for special education is today about twice that for regular education students, but about 13% of that cost is for assessment. In the 1985–1986 school year, the number of pupils found eligible based on evaluation had reached 4.1 million, and 4.8 million in 1990–1991, not including those in gifted programs. Since many more did not meet required criteria, the cost of simply determining which pupils were eligible had become staggering (Moore, 1988).

A third factor in the growth of special classes, though its impact was at first slight, was another critical outcome of the 1930 White House Conference: creation of a department of special education in the Office of Education, with Elise Martens appointed in 1931 senior officer. Though assisted only by a part-time secretary for most of the two decades she held this post, and though other priorities preoccupied government, Martens worked to sustain attention to the needs of exceptional children through her ubiquitous pamphlets and leadership in organizing conferences (Aiello, 1976). Addressing one such conference in 1934, in the depth of the Depression, First Lady Eleanor Roosevelt warned that the cost to society of appropriate, differential instruction for exceptional children was far less than the cost of not providing it. While that theme has since become familiar, the Depression slowed momentum in the growth of services.

The postwar "boom," amplified during the Kennedy and Johnson administrations, reflected in increasing prevalence of special classes, led to debate concerning two key issues: effectiveness of such arrangements, and soundness—and fairness—of placement decisions. The former gave rise to numerous efficacy studies, which yielded ambiguous results with regard to social adjustment: Rejection and isolation of exceptional pupils was often observed in mainstream situations, yet special placement was often associated with low self-esteem, stigma, and restriction of models. Further, lower expectancy was often linked with special class instruction, and generally, though not invariably, academic performance indices favored regular class placement. But many factors made such comparisons suspect, principally the fact that pupils were quite purposefully, not randomly, assigned to the respective "treatments" (Gallagher, 1994).

As the civil rights movement gathered force, of even more urgent concern was the question of which students were referred by teachers for "suspected handicaps" and subsequently placed, and which students were more or less likely to be identified as gifted. Dunn (1968) saw probable discrimination in schools' tendency to label and segregate disproportionate numbers of minority pupils, writing that 60 to 80% of the enrollments in classes for pupils with mild retardation were "children from low status backgrounds—including Afro-Americans, American Indians, Mexicans, and Puerto Rican Americans; those from nonstandard English speaking, broken, disorganized, and inadequate homes; and children from other non-middle class environments" (p. 6). Mercer (1973) pointed out that many children able to cope with everyday life were labeled retarded "because they have not had the opportunity to learn the cognitive skills necessary to pass Anglo oriented intelligence tests" (p. 44).

Students of the history of American culture cannot fail to see parallels in majority attitudes toward, and hence opportunities provided for, persons with disabilities and persons of color. Just as DuBois thought Booker Washington's vocationally oriented training a trap for African Americans and the route to continued subservience (Lewis, 1993), John Carlin and other leaders of the Deaf community criticized "the lack of encouragement for deaf people to advance beyond manual trades" (Leakey, 1993, p. 86). Lane (1992) has delineated other striking parallels between Anglo-colonialist beliefs and policies concerning people of color and majority (i.e., English-speaking) attitudes and policies concerning deaf persons as a linguistic minority. Cultural deafness represents a special case, where educational "integration" has often meant denial of equity; for many other children considered exceptional, separate placement has meant segregated, thus inherently *unequal*, education.

While diversity in American society is increasingly multifaceted and complex, the core "American Dilemma" has continued to be a matter of black and white. In his classic study, Gunnar Myrdal (1944) noted the paradox "that the official political creed of America denounced, in general but vigorous terms, all forms of suppression and discrimination, and affirmed human equality" (p. 50), yet suppression, discrimination, and inequality have in this instance been accepted and maintained. From the time of the Revolution to the Civil War, in the North where schooling was available at all for African-American children, it was available through separate schools, most philanthropic but some public, like the New York African Free Schools. Even Boston, the first city to offer public education for black children, maintained separate facilities until state legislation forbidding such distinctions was enacted in 1855 (Bullock, 1967). Teachers of both races dispatched by missionary societies to Freedmen's Schools formed during Reconstruction were greeted hostilely, often terrorized, by native whites, but found adults hungry to learn, and parents determined that their children have that opportunity (Litwack, 1979).

A century later the U.S. Supreme Court, reversing *Plessy v. Ferguson*, ruled that separate is *not* equal. But did special education provide a means to perpetuate educational, and hence societal, segregation both of children with disabilities and of those *judged* to be different, and accordingly *labeled* as having disabilities? Carrier (1986) argues that the *Brown* ruling led "a number of school systems . . . to find other ways of sorting pupils, and many introduced or expanded ability grouping and increased provision for the mildly retarded and to a lesser extent the emotionally disturbed" (p. 302). Despite P.L. 94-142's mandates for nonbiased, multifactored evaluation, conducted with informed parental consent, a report by the National Academy of Sciences Panel (Heller, Holtzman, & Messick, 1982) revealed continued disproportionate percentages of minority and disadvantaged children— especially boys—placed in special classes. More than twice as many minority and lower SES children as middle-class, nonminority children continued to be reported placed due to learning and behavior problems (Ysseldyke, Algozzine, Richey, & Graden, 1982). But issues of equity and justice transcend special education; as Artiles and Trent (1994) concluded, "we find ourselves still grappling with the issue of overrepresentation and the problem of serving, equitably and effectively, children whose problems, in some cases, are more complex and stressful than the problems of the children described by Dunn" (p. 432).

The question of special education's efficacy cannot be answered simply, but clearly problems have been identified. In its *Eleventh Annual Report to Congress on the Implementation of the Education of the Handicapped Act,* the U.S. Office (now Department) of Education (USDOE) (1989) reported that the number of residential placements of children, having dropped significantly following implementation of P.L. 94–142 and as a facet of general deinstitutionalization, had remained steady for a decade. But monitoring teams reported that removal of pupils based on category of disability and the local district's service system was common, often without evidence that a student's IEP could be implemented only in a separate facility. Moreover, despite the provision for FAPE through age 21, the dropout rate of special education students was higher than that of the general school population, with only 59.5% graduating, and students with disabilities had inordinately high rates of unemployment on leaving school or graduating. The report indicated that the number referred because of suspected learning disabilities had increased, and USDOE's (1993) report for the 1991–1992 school year revealed that this category comprised 5.2% of the public school enrollment, more than half the special education enrollment. Shifts in categorical prevalence suggest a certain arbitrariness, but for the considerable proportion of the pupils assigned this label who do not complete school—36% in 1991—outcomes of separate instruction as a strategy to manage diversity, irrespective of categorical label, appeared less than optimal.

From Zero Exclusion to Full Inclusion

The so-called judgment or non-normative categories make up the vast majority of pupils determined eligible for special education, not only in the United States but in other industrialized nations (e.g., Brennan, 1985; McGee, 1990). Most versions of the so-called Regular Education Initiative (REI), proposed by former USOE Assistant Secretary Madeline Will (1986), have primarily concerned these pupils (e.g., Reynolds, Wang, & Walberg, 1987). Their rationale has included the considerable expenditure and arbitrariness entailed in determining eligibility, negative impact of labeling and segregation—social as well as instructional—of pupils found eligible, and the lack of provisions to address individual needs of pupils *not* found eligible, a broad group mainly comprising children of low-income and minority families often described as "at-risk." The concept entails a presumably more effective use of resources to address the individual needs of a greater number of pupils, within the context of a broader curricular framework, in such a way as to minimize stigma associated with removal from the educational mainstream. It entails a "restructuring" (Reynolds, et al., 1987) of the whole educational enterprise, at the least operational changes in the ways schools are arranged and pupils and teachers assigned, if not a fundamental paradigm shift concerning the role of schooling itself (Skrtic, 1991).

Although much discussed (in the special education literature, at any rate), seemingly responsive to calls in the 1980s for broad educational reforms, and widely endorsed, at least in spirit, "the REI was a *special* education initiative" that, except in certain states, brought "little concomitant change in general education programs" (Fuchs & Fuchs, 1994, p. 299). Its limited impact was attributed, at least in part, to the lack of involvement in discussion on the part of general educators. By the mid-1990s, however, calls for *inclusion*, a far more dramatic response to pupil diversity, got the endorsement of policymakers (National Association of State Boards of Education, 1992), and the concerned attention of the organized teaching profession. To some, it appeared that, in "radicalizing" the REI, full inclusionists may have revitalized special education reform, but in their "extremist" rhetoric and "uncompromising" advocacy for "students with severe intellectual disabilities," they jeopardized special education and its relationship to the broader enterprise of schooling (Fuchs & Fuchs, 1994, p. 303–304).

P.L. 94-142's mandate for zero exclusion had meant a radical departure from past practice, but barely two decades later the idea that even children with the most severe forms of disability could learn and could benefit from schooling was no longer revolutionary. Children formerly categorized as "unable to benefit from education," who warranted bare mention in textbooks as "custodial cases," were now identified in school records, as well as journals and texts, as *students*. The designation "trainable," as distinct from "educable," though not totally erased, was no longer legally defensible; *all* children with disabilities must be provided a Free Appropriate Public Education (FAPE), based on an Individualized Education Program (IEP), in the Least Restrictive Environment (LRE). The federal legislation represented a triumph of advocacy, achieved through a series of key court rulings, for every child's right to education.

The advocates were, as always, parents, but in this instance joined by an unlikely collection of professionals, initially a preponderance of behavioral psychologists and lawyers, with a steadily expanding diversity of practitioners and scholars, as well as a steadily growing number of persons with disabilities. In 1975, the American Association for the Severely and Profoundly Handicapped (AAESPH), now the Association for Persons with Severe Handicaps (TASH), was formed in Kansas City, its members electing Norris G. Haring its first president. Begun as an informal network of about 30 applied researchers, some of whom had been enlisted as expert witnesses in right-to-education litigation, the organization grew within just two decades to more than 9,000 members. In the context of a growing societal belief in the compensatory powers of early education, TASH members have been among those with particular interest in the potential benefit of intervention early in life for children with cognitive and physical impairments.

EARLY INTERVENTION
AND THE "NEW ENVIRONMENTALISM"

While the decade of the 1920s was a time of protectivism and intolerance, it paradoxically saw growing attention to children's special needs, reflected in such developments as psychoeducational clinics and treatment programs for troubled children—indeed, the birth of yet another small "movement," focused on children's mental health. The attention of child study leaders, now informed by psychoanalytic discoveries, turned to the first five years of life. Between 1923 and 1927, Arnold Gesell, having himself initiated what he called a "Guidance Nursery School" in 1918, published 13 articles on "the nursery school movement" and the potential of nursery education to prevent later emotional and behavioral problems (Ames, 1989, p. 36). Dewey's famous laboratory school, established in 1896, had in fact included preschool children, but in the 1920s several nursery schools were developed as facilities for demonstration, training, and research. In addition to Gesell's, reestablished in 1926 as the Guidance Nursery of the Yale Psycho-clinic, others included the Merrill-Palmer School's (later Institute) in Detroit, Abigail Eliot's Ruggles Street Nursery School in Boston, and Harriet M. Johnson's nursery in New York, later called Bank Street (p. 134).

By the end of the decade, Gesell (1930) averred that nursery education had moved from "a 'no man's land' to an 'every man's land': Psychologists, psychiatrists, kindergartners, primary school teachers, home economics and social workers, public health leaders, mothers' clubs, and mental hygiene organizations have found themselves side by side in the new interest in the preschool child" (p. 143). With respect to diversity, the interest was in children's individuality, pursued through child study, with a dual aim of promoting each child's positive development and of identifying potential problems. Nursery education was a child-centered enterprise but, like the Infant School a century earlier, it was enlisted to serve societal needs. And like special education, its spread was halted by the Depression and renewed by war, the Lanham Act of 1940 providing nurseries for children of women employed in defense work. But as the nursery and the kindergarten ideas continued to evolve, they reflected a benign, nurturing attitude toward young children in their diversity, captured by James Hymes's (1955) phrase "the child development point of view."

In the 1960s, another perspective on the role of early education vis-à-vis child diversity emerged, heralded by publication of J. McV. Hunt's *Intelligence and Experience* (1961) and Benjamin Bloom's *Stability and Change in Human Characteristics* (1964): Effective intervention early in life could change the course of children's subsequent development. This new environmentalism had its beginnings in a classic study (Skeels & Dye, 1939), extended to a larger sample (Skeels, 1941), reporting striking IQ differences in children attributable to differences in early nurture. After two years, children in the experimental group showed an average gain of 27.5 IQ points, while controls, initially somewhat higher in IQ than their counterparts, showed a substantial loss. This suggested a revolutionary notion, and most authorities, considering intelligence innate and immutable, and consequently retardation irreversible and permanent, reacted with skepticism to these reports from the Iowa Child Welfare Station. Nevertheless, a few other reports suggested a degree of cautious optimism concerning environmental influences on early development, heightened by Kirk's (1958) demonstration of significant gains made by preschool children with IQs ranging from 45 to 80.

By the mid-1960s, when Skeels (1966) reported compelling evidence of long-term differences in the adult status of the original subjects, the potential of early intervention to change children seemed nearly limitless, giving rise to a "first generation" of efficacy research focused on measuring children's developmental gains (Guralnick & Bennet, 1992). Could early intervention solve the "problem" of diversity by eliminating it? Even if such a goal were desirable, certainly few, if any, thought the central nervous system infinitely malleable. And some leaders saw reason for concern that, in focusing narrowly on questionable measures of intellect, the "environmental mystique" (Zigler, 1970), reductionist in its view of children and families, might endanger the early intervention enterprise itself. Reports that IQ advantages of children in Head Start were not sustained (Cicerelli, Evans, & Schiller, 1969) suggested that such concerns were not unfounded; as the bureaucratic machinery of the War on Poverty was being effectively dismantled, Project Head Start was, in fact, at considerable risk. As we know, it survived and is generally considered a highly effective social program, the potential of which has yet to be fully exploited.

In any event, as a parallel development to these efforts to change the futures of young children at environmental risk, the late 1960s saw the birth of early intervention with infants, toddlers, and preschool age children with identified disabilities, furthered by creation of the Handicapped Children's Early Education Program (HCEEP) in 1968. While biologically based conditions, such as blindness and cerebral palsy, could not be "cured" through early educational and therapeutic intervention, model programs funded by HCEEP, through its First Chance network, led to new understanding of childhood diversity and the meaning of efficacy for children and families, and consequently to reconceptualization of an old idea.

Collaboration

In Chapter 3, we reflected on the relationship of teacher and exceptional pupil, epitomized by the joint achievement of Helen Keller, who was not "cured" but liberated, and Anne Sullivan Macy. We have also traced a pattern of *integration* of persons with disabilities into the broader society, which as a societal goal has important implications for education and other services for children. In the United States, a succession of court rulings stemming from the pivotal *Brown* decision accelerated the trend toward integration, culminating in the judicial doctrine of Least Restrictive Alternative, operationalized under P.L. 94-142 as Least Restrictive Environment. Presumably, the story of increasing, albeit mandated, collaboration between general and special educators is familiar to readers, although it is still unfolding. Other dimensions of collaboration that have emerged as key elements in the short history of early intervention—about three decades—involve relationships among professionals, service systems, certainly children themselves, and professionals with families. This overarching concept appears to be a core facet of a new historical context in which exceptional children will grow to adulthood.

That a team is something more than the collective expertise of its members is a truism; yet as diverse specializations emerged to address specific needs of children with disabilities, role identities and prerogatives often superseded other concerns. This specificity of role and responsibility has extended to service systems, each of which—for example, educational, medical, child protection and advocacy, mental health, juvenile justice—has operated in accordance with its own particular mandates, ethical codes, and fiscal constraints and mechanisms. As in all areas of human affairs, things seem to have been simpler in the past; however, the mandated *service coordination* and increasingly preferred *transdisciplinary-team* approach that have emerged during the short history of early intervention would appear to offer better models for empowering families to enhance their own, and their child's, quality of life. These concepts indeed represented a departure from earlier conceptions of the relationship between professionals and families:

> "Let's wait awhile' is freqently heard from the lips of a parent who realizes that the little deaf or blind child needs the education which the State School provides, but who is reluctant to part with him so young. He is still a baby—only six years old. In four or five years he will be better able to take care of himself and the separation may not be so hard. But remember, too, that in four or five

years he will have lost the opportunity for the *early* training which is so important. The younger the child the easier it is for him to adapt himself to new ways of learning. Unless you can in your own home provide that which he needs in the preparatory stages of the work, then permit the State school to teach him as early as it will admit him. (Martens, 1932, p. 12)

The most striking contrast between past and present educational arrangements for children with disabilities is that today most live at home with families (Turnbull & Turnbull, 1990). Since the 1950s, parents have rarely been enjoined to give over responsibility for care and instruction of their child, either to the state or to private agencies, nor is blame for the child's difficulties—as in instances of autism and Attention Deficit Disorder—as commonly ascribed to parents. Until quite recently, professionals hoped that parents would do as little harm as possible in the early years of a child's life until their own ameliorative work could commence. Some offered advice toward that end, notably Howe, who professed a family model to be infinitely preferable to centralized institutions. But the "family model" that had taken root was often one of subjugation and denial of human rights (Blatt, Ozolins, & McNally, 1979). The relationship between professionals and parents was, in any case, a one-sided one, predicated on the presumed superior knowledge of the former.

Over time, a succession of events cast the relationship in a different light. It will be recalled that, historically, instruction of children with impaired hearing emerged in response to efforts of their parents, well-to-do and influential ones, to be sure, whether it was a matter of finding and paying a tutor, lobbying for legislation, enlisting a respected advocate in their child's cause, even founding a school. Fathers like Cogswell and Hubbard were not to be patronized; they were the *patrons*. A century later, as American parents of children whose IQs excluded them from school formed community classes, similar developments occurred in other countries. In Ireland, "parents, friends, and professionals concerned with mental handicap formed themselves into voluntary associations and began to establish schools which were subsequently recognized by the Department of Education as special national schools" (McGee, 1990, p. 52). The pattern that emerged, spreading to a broader representation of families, was one of parents' seeking, and bringing about, services for children with disabilities where none had previously existed, or where provisions were seen as inadequate. The litany is long, as we have seen, involving children with speech impairments, retardation, cerebral palsy and other physical disabilities, emotional problems, severe and multiple disabilities, learning disabilities, and more recently autism, traumatic brain injury, Attention Deficit Disorder, Tourette syndrome, and specialized health care needs.

In advocating for their children, parents were redefining their relationship with professionals, as well as their child's needs. P.L. 94-142 attempted formally to define the relationship on the basis of parental rights but did little to bridge the distance between home and school. The parent who questions school recommendations, or requests services at variance with a district's standard arrangements (e.g., "supportive aids and services" for a child in a regular classroom), has often been branded a "problem." Professionals often express discouragement at their difficulty in getting parents to attend meetings, respond to requests, or sign the IEP, confirmed in successive USOE reports to Congress. With experience gained through early intervention, the relationship of professionals and families intended by the *Individualized Family Service Plan* may herald a new, collaborative context, and thus a "new history."

CODA

Among the challenging ideas emerging in connection with the philosophy of inclusion of children with disabilities within the context of societal, and educational, diversity, two in particular suggest that at the very core of a "new history," if such it will be, are exceptional children themselves. The first, *constructivism*, has been increasingly discussed in conjunction with inclusive early education for typical children and those with disabilities (e.g., Mallory & New, 1994), the second, often referred to as *interpretivism*, within the multidisciplinary field of "disability studies" (Ferguson, Ferguson, & Taylor, 1992). It may be that these represent fundamental paradigm shifts affecting all children, and adults, including those with disabilities.

Constructivist conceptions of children's learning as spontaneous, self-directed, and internally organized seem on the surface contradictory to the interventionist tradition of specialized instruction for children with disabilities. Indeed, such instruction has been intended for pupils whose needs were not met through conventional approaches, and the historical record is replete with references to "training"—to comply with adult wishes, to unlearn undesirable habits and acquire acceptable ones, to develop character and eschew vice through honest labor, to imitate the speech and social conventions favored by instructors, sometimes to learn a trade. Yet we have seen that such notions, in their time, did not differ markedly from expectations for the role of education for most other children. Moreover, history not only reveals common philosophical origins, anticipating the constructivist approaches now endorsed in early childhood education, at least through the primary years (Mallory & New, 1994), but striking instances of specialized pedagogy's embracing such practices prior to their adoption in general education. These have included early embracing of Pestalozzian methods and respect for children's inner nature and resources, in fact the "Quixotic" notion (Seguin, 1880, p. 3) that children be educated "for themselves," in recognition, as Burton Blatt (1981) expressed, that all can learn and all are worthy.

Interpretivist conceptions of disability, too, have striking resonance in Diderot's *Letter* (1749/1965) and as revealed in the emerging Deaf scholarship; the critiques by 19th-century Deaf leaders and by Thomas Cutsforth; Robert Scott's *The Making of Blind Men* (1969), Helen Keller's rich legacy, and many other accounts based on personal experience, written by persons with disabilities, or so labeled. As scholars continue to learn "insiders' perspectives," more exceptional individuals—notably Temple Grandin, Donna Williams, Kim Peek, and other persons with autism—tell their own stories, in their own voices. Two young men with Down syndrome, Jason Kingsley and Mitchell Levitz (1994), have recently shared their experiences, and their friendship, by sharing their conversations. Though also filtered through the lens of maturity, such accounts bring us closer to an understanding of how exceptionality was experienced during childhood, and, more importantly, of whose "history" it indeed is. To the extent that the work of future historians of exceptionality in children, informed by "insiders' views," can recount an end to "laws against the poor" and policies inimical to children, realization of every child's right to unconditional nurture, and society's recognition of the paradoxical inseparability of diversity and common humanity, it will describe a new history.

> I sit alone at night and look out into the night, and I wonder if I can make it in the world or if I will have a nice life. But for me I know that I have to do it for myself. For I am the only one who can make that come true. You see I feel like there is another person inside me, just waiting to get out.

> Some things are easier than others. Some things are harder than others for different people. Some people are good at one thing but not good at other things. . . . So I made up my mind the only way to beat this fear is to keep writing. It doesn't matter what I write but I have to keep trying over and over again.
>
> (Selections from *Student Journal*, Literacy Volunteers of Massachusetts).

References

Ablon, J. (1984). *The little people in America: The social dimensions of dwarfism*. New York: Praeger.

Abraham, W. (1972). The early years: Prologue to tomorrow. In J. B. Jordan (Ed.), *Exceptional child education at the bicentennial: A parade of progress* (pp. 26–31). Reston, VA: Council for Exceptional Children.

Abt, I. (1965). *Abt-Garrison history of pediatrics*. Philadelphia: W. B. Saunders.

Act to provide medical and surgical treatment for crippled children. Ohio, *Legislative Acts* CVIII 134–136 (1919).

Adams, M. E. (1927). Sarah Fuller. *American Annals of the Deaf, 72*, 432–436.

Addams, J. (1897). Foreign born children in the primary grades. In *NEA Proceedings*. Chicago: University of Chicago Press.

Addams, J. (1909). *The spirit of youth and the city streets*. New York: Macmillan.

Addams, J. (1911). *Twenty years at Hull House*. Chautauqua, NY: Chautauqua Press.

Aichhorn, A. (1951). *Wayward youth*. New York: Viking Press.

Aiello, B. (1976). Especially for special educators: A sense of our own history. In J. B. Jordan (Ed.), *Exceptional child education at the bicentennial: A parade of progress* (pp. 16–25). Reston, VA: Council for Exceptional Children.

Albee, G. (1968). Conceptual models and manpower requirements in psychology. *American Psychologist, 23*, 317–320.

Albert, J. S. (1981). The Allen School: An alternative nineteenth-century education, 1818–1852. *Harvard Educational Review, 51*(4), 565–576.

Alexander, F. G., & Selesnick, S. T. (1966). *The history of psychiatry: An evaluation of psychiatric thought and practice from prehistoric times to the present*. New York: Harper & Row.

Allen, E. F. (1924). Have hope. In H. E. Abt (Ed.), *The care, cure, and education of the crippled child*. Elyria, OH: Society for Crippled Children.

Allen, F. L. (1931). *Only yesterday: An informal history of the 1920s*. New York: Harper & Brothers.

Altschule, M. D. (1957). *Roots of modern psychiatry*. New York: Grune & Stratton.

American Humane Association. (1992, Jan.-Feb.). Genesis. *The national humane review*.

American Physical Therapy Association. (1979). *The beginnings: Physical therapy and the APTA*. Alexandria, VA: APTA.

American Psychiatric Association. (1987). *Diagnostic and statistical manual of mental disorders* (3rd ed., rev.). Washington, DC: APA.

Ames, L. B. (1989). *Arnold Gesell—Themes of his work*. New York: Plenum.

Anagnos, M. (1882). *Education of the blind: Historical sketch of its origin, rise, and progress*. Boston: Rand, Avery.

Anbinder, T. (1992). *Nativism and slavery: The Northern Know-nothings and the politics of the 1850s*. New York: Oxford University Press.

Anderson, M. (1917). *Education of defectives in the public schools*. New York: World Book Co.

Aries, P. (1962). *Centuries of childhood: A social history of family life*. New York: Alfred A. Knopf.

Aristotle. (n.d.). *Politics* (B. Jowett, Trans.). New York: Carleton House.

Aristotle. (1910). Historia animalium. In J. A. Smith & W. D. Ross (Trans.), *The works of Aristotle. Vol. 4: Historia animalium*. Oxford: Clarendon Press.

Artiles, A. J., & Trent, S. C. (1994). Overrepresentation of minority students in special education: A continuing debate. *Journal of Special Education, 27*(4), 410–437.

Axline, V. M. (1947). *Play therapy*. Boston: Houghton Mifflin.

Ayres, L. P. (1909). *Laggards in our schools: A study of retardation and its elimination in city school systems*. New York: Charities Publications Committee.

Bacon, F. (1900). *Advancement of learning and Novum organum*. New York: Colonial Press. (Original work published 1620)

Bagley, W. C. (1925). *Determinism in education*. New York: Nelson.

Baker, H. J., & Traphagen, V. (1935). *The diagnosis and treatment of behavior problem children*. New York: Macmillan.

Bakwin, H. (1949). Emotional deprivation in infants. *Journal of Pediatrics, 35*, 512.

Ball, T. S. (1971). *Itard, Seguin, and Kephart: Sensory education—A learning interpretation*. Columbus, OH: Merrill.

Barker, J., & Barmatz, H. (1975). Eye function. In W. Frankenburg & B. Camp (Eds.), *Pediatric screening tests*. Springfield, IL: Charles C. Thomas.

Barkley, R. A. (1990). *Attention Deficit Hyperactivity Disorder: A handbook for diagnosis and treatment*. New York: Guilford Press.

Barnes, H. E., & Teeters, N. K. (1945). *New horizons in criminology*. New York: Prentice-Hall.

Barr, M. W. (1910). *Mental defectives: Their history, treatment and training*. Philadelphia: P. Blackstone's Son & Co.

Barraga, N. (1964). *Increased visual behavior in low vision children*. New York: American Foundation for the Blind.

Barraga, N., & Erin, J. (1992). *Visual handicaps and learning* (3rd ed.). Austin, TX: PRO-ED.

Barton, W. E. (1987). *The history and influence of the American Psychiatric Association*. Washington, DC: American Psychiatric Association Press.

Bates, B. (1992). *Bargaining for life: A social history of tuberculosis, 1876–1938*. Philadelphia: University of Pennsylvania Press.

Battiscombe, G. (1975). *Shaftesbury: The Great Reformer: 1801–1885*. Boston: Houghton Mifflin.

Bedell, M. (1980). *The Alcotts: Biography of a family*. New York: Clarkson N. Potter.

Beers, C. W. (1908). *A mind that found itself: An autobiography*. New York: Longmans, Green.

Behr, A. L. (1978). *New perspectives in South African education*. Durban: Butterworths.

Bell, A. G. (1883). *Memoir upon the formation of a deaf variety of the human race*. New Haven, CT: National Academy of Science.

Bell, A. G. (1885). Is there a correlation between defects of the senses? *Science, 5*, 127–129.

Bender, R. (1970). *The conquest of deafness*. Cleveland, OH: Case Western Reserve University Press.

Berens, C. (1938). What organizations for the blind can do in preventing blindness. In H. Lende (Ed.), *What of the blind? A survey of the development and scope of present-day work with the blind* (pp. 17–34). New York: American Foundation for the Blind.

Berkowitz, P. H., & Rothman, E. P. (1960). *The disturbed child: Recognition and psychoeducational therapy in the classroom*. New York: New York University Press.

Bernstein, C. (1920). Colony and extra-institution care for the feebleminded, *Mental Hygiene, 4*, 1–29.

Berry, C. (1923). The mentally retarded child in the public schools. *Journal of Psycho-Asthenics, 28*, 129–136.

Berry, M. F. (1965). Historical vignettes of leadership in speech and hearing: III. Stuttering. *Journal of the American Speech and Hearing Association, 7*(3), 78–79.

Best, H. (1914). *The deaf: Their position in society and the provision for their education in the United States*. New York: Thomas Y. Crowell.

Best, H. (1919). *The blind: Their condition and the work being done for them in the United States*. New York: Macmillan.

Bettelheim, B. (1967). *The empty fortress*. New York: Free Press.

Bettelheim, B., & Sylvester, E. (1947). A therapeutic milieu. *American Journal of Orthopsychiatry, 18*, 191–206.

Biklen, D., & Duchan, J. F. (1994). "I am intelligent": The social construction of mental retardation. *Journal of the Association for Persons with Severe Handicaps, 19*(3), 173–184.

Binet, A. (1909). *Les idées modernes sur les enfants*. Paris: Flammarion.

Binet, A., & Simon, T. (1907). *Mentally defective children* (W. B. Drummond, Trans.). London: E. Arnold.

Binet, A., & Simon, T. (1916). *The development of intelligence in children* (E. S. Kite, Trans.). Baltimore: Williams & Wilkins.

Bingham, D., Van Hattum, R., Faulk, M., & Taussig, E. (1961). Program organization and management. *Journal of Speech and Hearing Disorders Monograph, 8*, 33–49.

Blanton, S. (1925). The function of the mental hygiene clinic in the schools and colleges. In *The child, the clinic and the court* (pp. 93–101). New York: New Republic.

Blatt, B. (1975). Toward an understanding of people with special needs. In J. M. Kauffman & J. S. Payne (Eds.), *Mental retardation: Introduction and personal perspectives*. Columbus, OH: Merrill.

Blatt, B. (1981). *In and out of mental retardation: Essays on educability, disability, and human policy*. Baltimore: University Park Press.

Blatt, B., Ozolins, A., & McNally, J. (1979). *The family papers: A return to purgatory*. New York: Longman.

Blee, K. M. (1991). *Women of the Klan: Racism and gender in the 1920s*. Berkeley: University of California Press.

Blinderman, A. (1976). *Three early champions of education: Benjamin Franklin, Benjamin Rush, and Noah Webster*. Bloomington, IN: Phi Delta Kappa.

Bloom, B. S. (1964). *Stability and change in human characteristics.* New York: Wiley.

Blum, J. S. (1980). Review of *Cyril Burt, psychologist*, by L. S. Hearnshaw. *Harvard Educational Review, 50*(2), 275–280.

Boake, C. (1991). History of cognitive rehabilitation following head injury. In J. Kreutzer & P. Wehman (Eds.), *Cognitive rehabilitation*. Baltimore: Paul Brookes.

Boas, G. (1966). *The cult of childhood*. London: University of London.

Boatner, M. T. (1959). *Voice of the deaf: A biography of Edward Miner Gallaudet*. Washington, DC: Public Affairs Press.

Bogdan, R. (1988). *Freak show: Exhibiting human oddities for amusement and profit*. Chicago: Univ. of Chicago Press.

Bogdan, R., & Taylor, S. (1976). The judged, not the judges: An insider's view of mental retardation. *American Psychologist, 31*, 47–52.

Bogdan, R., & Taylor, S. (1994). *The social meaning of mental retardation: Two life stories*. New York: Teachers College Press.

Bonet, J. P. (1620). *Reduccion de las letras y arte para enseñar a hablar a los mudos*. Madrid: Abarca de Angelo.

Boorstin, D. J. (1958). *The Americans: The colonial experience*. New York: Random House.

Borenzweig, H. (1971). Social work and psychoanalytic theory: A historical analysis, *Social Work, 16*(1), 7–16.

Boring, E. G. (1950). *A history of experimental psychology* (2nd ed.). New York: Appleton-Century-Crofts.

Boswell, J. (1988). *The kindness of strangers: The abandonment of children in western Europe from late antiquity to the Renaissance*. New York: Pantheon Books.

Bower, E. M. (1960). *Early identification of emotionally disturbed children*. Springfield, IL: Charles C. Thomas.

Bowlby, J. (1945). *Maternal care and mental health* (Ed. 2, Monograph Series No. 2). Geneva, Switzerland: World Health Organization.

Boyd, W. (1914). *From Locke to Montessori*. New York: Henry Holt.

Braudel, F. (1979). *The structures of everday life: The limits of the possible. Civilization and capitalism, 15th–18th century (Vol. 1)*. New York: Harper & Row.

Braunstein, P. (1988). Toward intimacy: The fourteenth and fifteenth centuries. In G. Duby (Ed.), *A history of private life. II. Revelations of the medieval world* (pp. 535–630). Cambridge, MA: Harvard University Press.

Breasted, J. H. (1954). *The conquest of civilization* (rev. ed.). New York: Harper and Row.

Breines, E. B. (1986). Pragmatism, a philosophical foundation for occupational therapy, 1900–1927 and 1968–1985: Implications for specialization and education. New York: New York University Press.

Bremner, R. H. (Ed.). (1970). *Children and youth in America: A documentary history, Vol. 1, 1600–1865; Vol II, 1866–1932.* Cambridge, MA: Harvard University Press.

Brennan, W. K. (1985). *Curriculum for special needs.* Milton Keynes, U.K.: Open University Press.

Brenzel, B. (1980). Domestication as reform: A study of the socialization of wayward girls, 1856–1905. *Harvard Educational Review, 50*(2), 196–213.

Breunig, H. L. (1990). The legacy of Dr. Bell. *Volta Review, 92*(4), 84–96.

Brickman, W. W. (1983). Introduction to the study of the learned ladies of the sixteenth and seventeenth centuries. In B. F. Nel, G. S. Jackson, & D. S. Rajah (Eds.), *The changing world of education* (pp. 3–19). Durban: Butterworths.

Brigham, A. (1973). Remarks on the influence of mental cultivation and mental excitement upon health. In *The beginnings of mental hygiene in America: Three selected essays, 1833–1850.* New York: Arno Press. (Original work published 1833)

Brigham, A. (1845). Schools in lunatic asylums. *American Journal of Insanity, 1,* 326–340.

Brill, R. G. (1984). *International congresses on education of the deaf: An analytical history, 1878–1980.* Washington, DC: Gallaudet College Press.

Brockett, L. P. (1856, May). Idiots and institutions for their training. *American Journal of Education,* pp. 601–613.

Brown, C. W. (1896). Reminiscences. *Journal of Psycho-Asthenics, 2*(1), 134–140.

Brown, C. (1955). *My left foot.* New York: Simon & Schuster.

Bruce, R. V. (1973). *Alexander Graham Bell and the conquest of solitude.* Boston: Little, Brown.

Bullock, H. D. (1967). *A history of Negro education in the South: From 1619 to the present.* Cambridge, MA: Harvard University Press.

Bulwer, J. (1644). *Chirologia, or the natural language of the hand.* London: T. Harper.

Bulwer, J. (1648). *Philocophus or the deafe and dumbe man's friend.* London: Humphrey Mosely.

Burt, C. (1925). *The young delinquent.* New York: D. Appleton and Company.

Burt, C. (1940). *The factors of the mind.* London: University of London Press.

Butler, A. (1901). Saving the children. Report of Committee on Destitute and Neglected Children. In *Proceedings, 1901 conference on charities and corrections* (pp. 205–213).

Caddey, J. W. (1963). *The church related residential treatment center for emotionally disturbed children.* Unpublished thesis, Oberlin Graduate School of Theology, Oberlin, OH.

Campbell, J. K. (1967). *Col. Parker: The children's crusader.* New York: Teachers College Press.

Carlebach, J. (1970). *Caring for children in trouble.* London: Routledge & Kegan Paul.

Carrier, J. G. (1986). *Learning disability: Social class and the construction of inequality in American education.* Westport, CT: Greenwood Press.

Chall, J. S. (1983). Literacy: Trends and explanations. *Educational Researcher, 12,* 3–8.

Channing, W. (1900). Special classes for mentally defective school children. *Journal of Psycho-Asthenics, 5,* 40–45.

Chapin, H. D. (1908). A plan of dealing with atrophic infants and children. *Archives Pediatrics, 25,* 491.

Chevigny, H., & Braverman, S. (1950). *The adjustment of the blind.* New Haven: Yale University Press.

Child Welfare League of America, Inc. (1960). *Report of Survey of The Methodist Children's Home, Berea, OH.* New York: Child Welfare League of America, Inc.

Christensen, E. (1991). *A proud heritage: The American Occupational Therapy Association at seventy-five.* Rockville, MD: AOTA.

Cicerelli, V. G., Evans, J. W., & Schiller, J. S. (1969). *The impact of Head Start on children's cognitive and affective development: Preliminary report.* Washington, DC: Office of Economic Opportunity.

Cleugh, J. (1975). *The Medici: A tale of fifteen generations.* New York: Doubleday.

Clifford, D. P. (1979). *Mine eyes have seen the glory: A biography of Julia Ward Howe.* Boston: Little, Brown.

Cohen, R. S. (1965). Therapeutic education and day treatment: A new professional liaison. *Exceptional Children, 32,* 23–28.

Coleman, R. W., & Provence, S. (1957). Environmental retardation (hospitalism) in infants living in families. *Pediatrics, 19,* 285.

Connor, F. P. (1976). The past is prologue: Teacher preparation in special education. *Exceptional Children, 42,* 366–378.

Connor, L. P. (1992). *The history of the Lexington School for the Deaf (1864–1985).* New York: Lexington School for the Deaf.

Corbin, A. (1990). Backstage. In M. Perrot (Ed.), *A history of private life: IV. From the fires of revolution to the great war* (pp. 451–667). Cambridge, MA: Harvard University Press.

Cornett, O. (1990). The century-old wisdom of Alexander Graham Bell. *Volta Review, 92*(3), 145–153.

Coss, C. (1989). *Lillian D. Wald: Progressive activist.* New York: Feminist Press at The City University of New York.

Costin, L. B. (1979). *Child welfare: Policies and practice.* New York: McGraw-Hill.

Cranston, M. (1991). *The noble savage: Jean-Jacques Rousseau, 1754–1762.* Chicago: University of Chicago Press.

Cremin, L. A. (1961). *The transformation of the school: Progressivism in American education, 1876–1957.* New York: Random House.

Cremin, L. A., Shannon, D. A., & Townsend, M. E. (1954). *A history of Teachers College Columbia University.* New York: Columbia University Press.

Cronbach, L. J. (1957). The two disciplines of scientific psychology. *American Psychologist, 12,* 671–684.

Crouch, B. A. (1986). Alienation and the mid-nineteenth century American Deaf community: A response. *American Annals of the Deaf, 131*(5), 322–324.

Cruickshank, W. M. (1949). The emotional needs of crippled and non-crippled children. *Exceptional Children, 16,* 33–40.

Cruickshank, W. M. (1952). A study of the relation of physical disability to social adjustment. *American Journal of Occupational Therapy, 6,* 100–109.

Cruickshank, W. M., Bentzen, F., Ratzeberg, F., & Tannhauser, M. A. (1961). *A teaching method for brain-injured and hyperactive children.* Syracuse: Syracuse University Press.

Cubberly, E. P. (1909). *Changing conceptions of education.* Boston: Houghton Mifflin.

Cubberly, E. P. (1922). *Public education in the United States.* Boston: Houghton Mifflin.

Curti, M. (1964). *The growth of American thought* (3rd ed.). New York: Harper & Row.

Curtiss, S. (1977). *Genie: A psycholinguistic study of a modern-day "wild child".* New York: Academic Press.

Cutsforth, T. D. (1933). *The blind in school and society: A psychological study.* New York and London: D. Appleton and Company.

Dalzell, R. F., Jr. (1987). *Enterprising elite: The Boston Associates and the world they made.* Cambridge, MA: Harvard University Press.

De Carlo, L. M. (1964). *The deaf.* Englewood Cliffs, NJ: Prentice-Hall.

Decroly, O., & Decroly, S. (1932). Manual work in education. *The new era in home and school, 13,* 105–107.

deMause, L. (Ed.). (1974). *The history of childhood.* New York: The Psycho-history Press.

Demos, J. (1970). *A little commonwealth: Family life in Plymouth colony.* New York: Oxford University Press.

Descourdes, A. (1928). *The education of mentally defective children* (E. Ross, Trans.). New York: Heath.

Despert, J. L. (1965). *The emotionally disturbed child: Then and now.* New York: Brunner.

Deutsch, A. (1949). *The mentally ill in America: A history of their care and treatment from colonial times* (2nd ed.). New York: Columbia University Press.

Deutsch, A. (1950). *Our rejected children.* Boston: Little, Brown.

Devereux, G. (1956). *Therapeutic education: Its theoretical bases and practice.* New York: Harper & Brothers.

Dewey, J. (1916). *Democracy and education.* New York: Macmillan.

Dickens, C. (1907). *American notes and pictures from Italy.* New York: E. P. Dutton.

Dickens, C. (1978). *Nicholas Nickleby.* New York: Penguin English Library. (Original work published 1839)

Diderot, D. (1965). *Lettre sur les aveugles à l'usage de ceux qui voient.* In P. H. Meyer, *Diderot studies.* Geneva: Librarie Druz. (Original work published 1749)

Dix, D. (1843). *Memorial to the legislature of Massachusetts.* Boston: Munroe and Frances.

Doll, E. A. (1962). A historical survey of research and management of mental retardation in the United States. In E. P. Trapp & P. Himelstein (Eds.), *Readings on the exceptional child: Research and theory.* New York: Appleton-Century-Crofts.

Donald, D. (1960). *Charles Sumner and the coming of the Civil War.* New York: Alfred A. Knopf.

Dorris, M. (1989). *The broken cord.* New York: Harper & Row.

Down, J. L. H. (1866). Observations on an ethnic classification of idiots. *Journal of Mental Science, 13,* 121–123.

Down, J. L. H. (1877). *Mental affections of children and youth.* London: J. & A. Churchill.

Downs, R. B. (1975). *Heinrich Pestalozzi: Father of modern pedagogy.* Boston: G. K. Hall.

Dubos, R., & Dubos, J. (1952). *The white plague: Tuberculosis, man and society.* Boston: Little, Brown.

Duby, G. (1988). Introduction: Private power, public power. In G. Duby (Ed.), *A history of private life, II: Revelations of the medieval world* (pp. 3–31). Cambridge, MA: Harvard University Press.

Dugdale, R. (1877). *The Jukes: A study in crime, pauperism, disease, and heredity.* New York: G. P. Putnam.

Duncan, P., & Millard, W. (1866). *A manual for the classification, training, and education of the feeble-minded, imbecile, and idiotic.* London: Longmans, Green.

Dunn, L. M. (1968). Special education for the mildly retarded: Is much of it justifiable? *Exceptional Children, 35,* 5–22.

Dunsdon, M. I. (1952). *The educability of cerebral palsied children.* London: National Foundation for Education Research in England and Wales, Nervines Educational Publishing Co., Ltd.

Dunton, W. R., & Light, S. (1950). *Occupational therapy: Principles and practices.* Springfield, IL: Charles C. Thomas.

Durant, W. (1944). *Caesar and Christ.* New York: Simon and Schuster.

Dwyer, E. (1987). *Homes for the mad: Life inside two nineteenth-century asylums.* New Brunswick: Rutgers University Press.

Eberle, L. (1914/1922). The maimed, the halt, and the race, *Hospital Social Service,* 6(August), 59–63.

Edgerton, R. B. (1967). *The cloak of competence: Stigma in the lives of the mentally retarded.* Berkeley: University of California Press.

Eliot, C. W. (1893). Can school programs be shortened and enriched? *National Education Association Proceedings* (pp. 617–625). Washington, DC: NEA.

Erikson, E. H. (1950). *Childhood and society.* New York: W. W. Norton.

Esquirol, J. E. (1838). *Des maladies mentales: Considerées sous les hygieniques, et medico-legaux, 1772–1840.* Paris: Bailliere.

Esquirol, J. E. (1845). *Treatise on insanity* (E. K. Hunt, Trans.). Philadelphia: Lee & Blanchard.

Estabrook, A. H. (1916). *The Jukes in 1915.* Washington, DC: Carnegie Institute.

Esten, R. A. (1900). Backward children in public schools. *Journal of Psycho-Asthenics, 5,* 40–45.

Fagan, T. K. (1985). Sources for the delivery of school psychological services during 1890–1930. *School Psychology Review, 14*(3), 378–382.

Fagan, T. (1987). Gesell: The first school psychologist, Part I: The road to Connecticut. *School Psychology Review, 16*(1), 103–107.

Farber, B. (1968). *Mental retardation: Its social context and social consequences.* Boston: Houghton Mifflin.

Farel, A. M. (1988). Public health in early intervention: Historic foundations for contemporary training. *Infants & Young Children, 1*(1), 63–70.

Farrell, E. K. (1908–1909). Special classes in the New York City schools. *Journal of Psycho-Asthenics, 13,* 91–96.

Farrell, E. K. (1914). A study of the School Inquiry Report on ungraded classes. *The Psychological Clinic, 8*(2,3,4).

Farrell, E. K. (1915). A preliminary report on the careers of three hundred fifty children who have left ungraded classes. *Journal of Psycho-Asthenics, 20,* 20–26.

Farrell, G. (1956). *The story of blindness.* Cambridge: Harvard University Press.

Fay, E. A. (Ed.). (1893). *Histories of American schools for the deaf.* Washington, DC: Volta Bureau.

Fay, E. A. (1898). *Marriages of the deaf in America.* Washington, DC: Gibson Brothers.

Felt, J. P. (1971). Children at work. In T. R. Frazier (Ed.), *The underside of American history.* New York: Harcourt Brace Jovanovich.

Fennimore, K. J. (1988). *Faith made visible: The history of Floyd Starr & his school.* Albion, MI: Starr Commonwealth.

Ferguson, P. M., Ferguson, D. L., & Taylor, S. J. (Eds.). (1992). *Interpreting disability: A qualitative reader.* New York: Teachers College Press.

Fernald, G. M. (1943). *Remedial techniques in basic school subjects.* New York: McGraw-Hill.

Fernald, W. E. (1893). The history of the treatment of the feeble-minded. In *Proceedings of the Twentieth National Conference of Charities and Corrections,* pp. 203–221.

Fernald, W. E. (1904). Care of the feeble-minded. In *Proceedings of the National Conference on Charities and Corrections, 31*(3).

Fernald, W. E. (1912). The burden of feeble-mindedness. *Journal of Psycho-Asthenics, 17,* 87–111.

Flexer, C. (1994). *Facilitating hearing and listening in young children.* San Diego, CA: Singular Publishing Group.

Foucault, M. (1965). *Madness and civilization.* New York: Random House.

Foucault, M. (1977). *Discipline and punish.* New York: Pantheon.

Frampton, M. E., & Kerney, E. (1953). *The residential school: Its history, continuation, and future.* New York: New York Institute for the Education of the Blind.

Frampton, M. E., & Powell, H. G. (1938). *Education of the handicapped, v. I: History.* Yonkers-on-Hudson, NY: World Book Company.

Frazier, T. (Ed.). (1971). *Underside of American history.* New York: Harcourt Brace Jovanovich.

Freeman, B. J. (1993). The syndrome of autism: Update and guidelines for diagnosis. *Infants & Young Children, 6*(2), 1–11.

French, J. L. (1990). History of school psychology. In T. B. Gutkin & C. R. Reynolds (Eds.), *The handbook of school psychology* (2nd ed., pp. 3–20). New York: John Wiley & Sons.

French, R. S. (1932). *From Homer to Helen Keller: A social and educational study of the blind.* New York: American Foundation for the Blind.

Freud, A. (1964). Psychoanalytic knowledge and its application to children's services. *The writings of Anna Freud,* Vol. V. (pp. 460–469). New York: International Universities Press.

Freund, E. D. (1959). *Crusader for light: Julius R. Friedlander.* Philadelphia: Dorrance.

Frietag, G. (n.d.). *The Dubnoff Center for Child Development and Educational Therapy* [Mimeo]. North Hollywood, CA.

Frostig, M., & Horne, D. (1964). *The Frostig program for the development of visual perception.* Chicago: Follett.

Fuchs, D., & Fuchs, L. S. (1994). Inclusive schools movement and the radicalization of special education reform. *Exceptional Children, 60,* 294–309.

Furman, R. A., & Katan, A. (1969). *A therapeutic nursery school.* New York: International Universities Press.

Gallagher, J. J. (1994). The pull of societal forces on special education. *Journal of Special Education, 27*(4), 521–530.

Gallaudet, E. M. (1888). *Life of Thomas Hopkins Gallaudet.* New York: Henry Holt and Company.

Gallaudet, E. M. (1983). *History of the college for the deaf, 1857–1907.* Washington, DC: Gallaudet College Press.

Gallaudet, T. H. (1817). A sermon delivered at the opening of the Connecticut Asylum for the Education and Instruction of Deaf and Dumb Persons. Hartford, CT.

Galt, J. M. (1846). *The treatment of insanity.* New York: Harper & Brothers.

Galton, F. (1869). *Hereditary genius.* London: Macmillan.

Gannon, J. R. (1981). *Deaf heritage: A narrative history of deaf America.* Silver Spring, MD: National Association of the Deaf.

Gardiner, R. A. (1958). Alfred A. Strauss, 1897–1957. *Exceptional Children, 24,* 373–375.

Gardner, H. (1983). *Frames of mind: The theory of multiple intelligences.* New York: Basic Books.

Garrett, H. (1955). *Educational psychology.* New York: American Book Co.

Gay, P. (1984). *The bourgeois experience: Victoria to Freud. Vol. I: The education of the senses.* New York: Oxford University Press.

Gay, P. (1988). *Freud: A life for our time.* New York: W. W. Norton.

Gérando, J.-M. de. (1827). *De L'Education des sourds-muets de naissance.* Paris: Chez Mequiqnon L'Aine Pere, Editeur.

Gesell, A. (1923). *The preschool child from the standpoint of public hygiene and education.* Boston: Houghton Mifflin.

Gesell, A. (1924). The care of intellectually inferior children. In M. V. O'Shea (Ed.), *The child: His nature and his needs* (pp. 261–276). New York: The Children's Foundation.

Gesell, A. (1930). A decade of progress in the mental hygiene of the preschool child. *Annals of the American Academy of Political and Social Sciences, 151,* 143–148.

Gesell, A. (1940). The teacher-pupil relationship in a democracy. *School and Society, 51,* 193–198.

Gesell, A. (1948). *Studies in child development.* New York: Harper.

Gesell, A. (1949). Human infancy and the ontogenesis of behavior. *American Scientist, 37,* 529–553.

Gesell, A., & Amatruda, C. S. (1941). *Developmental diagnosis.* New York: Hoeber.

Gesell, A., & Gesell, B. (1912). *The normal child and primary education.* New York: Ginn & Company.

Gindis, B. (1986). Special education in the Soviet Union: Problems and perspectives. *Journal of Special Education, 20*, 379–384.

Goddard, H. H. (1910). Heredity of feeble-mindedness. *American Breeders Magazine, 1*, 165–178.

Goddard, H. H. (1912a). *The Kallikak family: A study of the heredity of feeblemindedness.* New York: Macmillan.

Goddard, H. H. (1912b). *Report on educational aspects of the public school system of the city of New York to the Committee on School Inquiry of the Board of Estimate and Appointment: Ungraded classes.* New York: Board of Education of the City of New York.

Goddard, H. H. (1914). *Feeble-mindedness: Its causes and consequences.* New York: Macmillan.

Goffman, E. (1961). *Asylums: Essays on the social situation of mental patients and other inmates.* Garden City, NY: Doubleday.

Goldstein, H. M., & Peyser, N. (1933). *Teaching the slow learner.* New York: Board of Education of the City of New York.

Goldstein, J., Freud, A., & Solnit, A. J. (1973). *Beyond the best interests of the child.* New York: Macmillan.

Goldstein, K. (1939/1942). *Aftereffects of brain injuries in war.* New York: Grune & Stratton.

Gottlieb, J., Alter, M., Gottlieb, B. W., & Wishner, J. (1994). Special education in urban America: Its not justifiable for many. *Journal of Special Education, 27*(4), 453–465.

Gould, S. J. (1981). *The mismeasure of man.* New York: W. W. Norton.

Grainger, F. B. (1979). The development of physiotherapy. In American Physical Therapy Association, *The beginnings: Physical therapy and the APTA* (pp. 1–2). Alexandria, VA: APTA. (Original work published 1923)

Grandin, T., & Scariano, M. M. (1986). *Emergence: Labeled autistic.* Novato, CA: Arena Press.

Graves, R., & Hodge, A. (1940/1963). *The long week-end: A social history of Great Britain, 1918–1939.* New York: W.W. Norton.

Gray, W. S. (1939). The language arts—Reading. *Implications of Research for the Classroom Teacher* (Joint yearbook of the American Educational Research Association and the Department of Classroom Teachers). Washington, DC: National Education Association.

Green, F. (1783). *Vox oculis subjecta.* London: Benjamin White.

Greenberg, J. (1988). *Of such small differences.* New York: Henry Holt & Co.

Greenleaf, B. K. (1978). *Children through the ages: A history of childhood.* New York: McGraw-Hill.

Greer, C. (1972). *The great school legend: A revisionist interpretation.* New York: Basic Books.

Grob, G. N. (1965). *The state and the mentally ill.* Chapel Hill, NC: University of North Carolina Press.

Groce, N. E. (1985). *Everyone here spoke sign language: Hereditary deafness on Martha's Vineyard.* Cambridge, MA: Harvard University Press.

Groce, N. E. (1992). "The town fool": An oral history of a mentally retarded individual in small town society. In P. M. Ferguson, D. L. Ferguson, & S. J. Taylor (Eds.), *Interpreting disability: A qualitative reader* (pp. 175–196). New York: Teachers College Press.

Grosenick, J. K., George, M. P., & George, N. L. (1987). A profile of school programs for the behaviorally disordered: Twenty years after Morse, Cutler, and Fink. *Behavioral Disorders, 12*, 159–168.

Guralnick, M., & Bennett, F. C. (Eds.). (1992). *The effectiveness of early intervention*. Orlando, FL: Academic Press.

Hale, N. G. (1971). *Freud and the Americans: The beginnings of psychoanalysis in the United States, 1876–1917*. New York: Oxford University Press.

Hall, G. S. (1904). *Adolescence*. New York: D. Appleton.

Hall, W. C. (1926). *Children's courts*. London: George Allen & Unwin.

Hamaide, A. (1924). *The Decroly class*. New York: E. P. Dutton.

Hammill, D. D., & Weiderholt, L. (1973). Review of the Frostig visual perception test and the related training program. In L. Mann & D. Sabatino (Eds.), *The first review of special education*, Vol. 1. New York: Grune & Stratton.

Handlin, O., & Handlin, M. F. (1971). *Facing life: Youth and the family in American history*. Boston: Little, Brown.

Hapless children. (n.d.). New York: Parsons Child and Family Center.

Haring, N. G., & Phillips, E. L. (1962). *Educating emotionally disturbed children*. New York: McGraw-Hill.

Harrison, E. (1914). *The Montessori method and the kindergarten*. Washington, DC: U.S. Government Printing Office.

Haskell, R. H. (1944). Mental deficiency over a hundred years. *American Journal of Psychiatry, 100*(6), 107–118.

Hawes, J. M. (1971). The treatment of delinquent children. In T. R. Frazier (Ed.), *The underside of American history: Other readings. Vol. 1: To 1877*. New York: Harcourt Brace Jovanovich.

Hawke, D. (1971). *Benjamin Rush*. New York: Bobbs-Merrill.

Hearnshaw, L. S. (1979). *Cyril Burt, psychologist*. New York: Cornell University Press.

Heller, K. A., Holtzman, W. H., & Messick, S. (Eds.). (1982). *Placing children in special education: A strategy for equity*. Washington, DC: National Academy Press.

Henig, R. M. (1992, Nov. 29). Flu pandemic. *The New York Times Magazine*, pp. 28–31, 55+.

Hensley, G. (1973). Special education: No longer handicapped. *Compact, 7*, 3–5.

Hershey, M. (1981). The least restrictive environment for gifted and talented students. *Roeper Review, 4*, 27–28.

Hewes, D. W. (1990). Historical foundations of early childhood teacher training: The evolution of kindergarten teacher preparation. In B. Spodek & O. N. Saracho (Eds.), *Early childhood teacher preparation: Yearbook in early childhood education, Vol. 1* (pp. 1–22). New York: Teachers College Press.

Hewett, F. M. (1968). *The emotionally disturbed child in the classroom*. Boston: Allyn & Bacon.

Hewett, F. M., & Forness, S. R. (1974). *Education of exceptional learners*. Boston: Allyn & Bacon.

Hilbert, C. (1975). *The House of Medici: Its rise and fall.* New York: William Morrow & Co.

Hildreth, G. H. (1930). *Psychological services for school problems.* Yonkers-on-Hudson, NY: World Book Co.

Hinshelwood, J. (1917). *Congenital word blindness.* London: H. K. Lewis.

Hobbs, N. (1964). Mental health's third revolution. *American Journal of Orthopsychiatry, 34*(5), 822–833.

Hobbs, N. (1975). *Issues in the classification of children.* San Francisco: Jossey-Bass.

Hobbs, N. (1982). *The troubled and troubling child.* San Francisco: Jossey-Bass.

Holl, J. M. (1971). *Juvenile reform in the progressive era: William R. George and the Junior Republic Movement.* Ithaca: Cornell University Press.

Hollingworth, L. S. (1924). Provisions for intellectually superior children. In M. V. O'Shea (Ed.), *The child: His nature and his needs* (pp. 277–299). New York: The Children's Foundation.

Holowinsky, I. Z. (1977). Special education in eastern Europe: Training of defectologists and special educators in the Soviet Union. *Journal of Special Education, 11*(4), 469–471.

Holowinsky, I. Z. (1981). Special education in Poland in the 1970s. *Journal of Special Education, 15*(3), 401–405.

Holt, L. E., & McIntosh, R. (1933). *Holt's diseases of infancy and childhood* (10th ed.). New York: D. Appleton-Century Company.

Horn, J. L. (1924). *The education of exceptional children.* New York: Century.

Howe, I. (1976). *World of our fathers.* New York: Simon & Schuster.

Howe, J. W. (1891, August 20). Chautauqua Literary and Scientific Circle Commencement Day address. *Chautauqua Assembly Herald, 16*(26), p. 1.

Howe, M., & Hall, F. H. (1903). *Laura Bridgman—Dr. Howe's famous pupil and what he taught her.* Boston: Little, Brown.

Howe, S. G. (1848a). The causes and prevention of idiocy [special issue]. *Massachusetts Quarterly Review, 3.*

Howe, S. G. (1848b). *Report of commission to inquire into the conditions of idiots of the Commonwealth of Massachusetts.* Boston, MA: Senate Document No. 51.

Howe, S. G. (1875). Perkins Institution and the Massachusetts School for the Blind. *Forty-third Annual Report, 1874,* Boston.

Hudson, A. F. (1893–1894). The union of kindergartens for the deaf. *American Annals of the Deaf, 38,* 277–278; *39,* 25–27.

Hughes, R. (1987). *The fatal shore: The epic of Australia's founding.* New York: Alfred A. Knopf.

Hunt, J. M. (1961). *Intelligence and experience.* New York: Ronald Press.

Hymes, J. (1955). *The child development point of view.* Englewood Cliffs, NJ: Prentice-Hall.

Ireland, W. (1877). *On idiocy and imbecility.* London: J. & A. Churchill.

Irvine, P. (1978). Meta L. Anderson, 1878–1942. *Journal of Special Education, 12*(4).

Irwin, R. B. (1938). The blind and resources for their aid. In H. Lende (Ed.), *What of the blind? A survey of the development and scope of present-day work with the blind* (pp. 3–16). New York: American Foundation for the Blind.

Irwin, R. B. (1955). *As I saw it.* New York: American Foundation for the Blind.

Itard, J. (1804). *Rapport et memoires sur le sauvage de l'Aveyron, l'idiote et le surd-muet.* Paris: F. Alcan.

Itard, J. (1962). *The wild boy of Aveyron* (G. & M. Humphrey, Trans.). New York: Appleton-Century-Crofts. (Original work published 1806)

Johnstone, E. R. (1898). What we do and how we do it. *Journal of Psycho-Asthenics, 2,* 98–105.

Johnstone, E. R. (1908). The functions of the special class. *National Education Association Journal of Proceedings and Address of the 46th Annual Meeting,* pp. 114–118.

Joint Commission on Mental Health of Children. (1970). *Crisis in child mental health: Challenge for the 1970s.* New York: Harper & Row.

Jones, K. (1972). *A history of the mental health services.* London: Routledge & Kegan Paul.

Jordan, D. S. (1908). Report of the committee on eugenics. *American Breeders Association, 4,* 201–208.

Jordan, I., & Karchmer, M. (1986). Patterns of sign use among hearing-impaired students. In A. Schildroth & M. Karchmer (Eds.), *Deaf children in America* (pp. 125–138). Boston: Little, Brown.

Juul, K. D. (1990). Child and youth care in America and Europe: A history of fruitful mutual influences in special education and therapy. *Child and Youth Care Quarterly, 19*(2), p. 91.

Kaestle, C. F. (1973). *The evolution of an urban school system: New York City, 1750–1850.* Cambridge, MA: Harvard University Press.

Kahn, H. A., & Moorhead, H. B. (1973). *Statistics on blindness in the model reporting area 1969–1970* (DHEW Pub. No. [NIH] 73–427). Washington, DC: U.S. Government Printing Office.

Kamin, L. J. (1974). *The science and politics of IQ.* Potomac, MD: Erlbaum.

Kanner, L. (1943). Autistic deviations of affective contact. *Nervous Child, 2,* 217–250.

Kanner, L. (1944). The origins and growth of child psychiatry. *American Journal of Psychiatry, 100,* 139.

Kanner, L. (1964). *History of the care and treatment of the mentally retarded.* Springfield, IL: Charles C. Thomas.

Kanner, L. (1971). Follow-up study of eleven autistic children originally reported in 1943. *Journal of Autism and Childhood Schizophrenia, 1,* 119–145.

Kaplan, F. (1988). *Dickens: A biography.* New York: William Morrow.

Katz, M. B. (1968). *The irony of early school reform: Educational innovation in mid-nineteenth century Massachusetts.* Cambridge, MA: Harvard University Press.

Katz, M. B. (1971). *Class, bureaucracy and schools: The illusion of educational change in America.* New York: Praeger.

Kaufman, J. (1993). *Characteristics of emotional and behavioral disorders of children and youth* (5th ed.). New York: Merrill/Macmillan.

Kazin, A. (1951). *A walker in the city.* New York: Harcourt Brace Jovanovich.

Keller, H. (1903/1976). *The story of my life.* New York: Andor.

Keller, H. (1955). *Teacher: Anne Sullivan Macy.* New York: Andor.

Kenney, E. (1941). *The treatment of infantile paralysis in the acute stage.* Minneapolis: Bruce.

Kephart, N. C. (1971). *The slow learner in the classroom* (2nd ed.). Columbus, OH: Merrill.

Kerlin, I. N. (1880). *Enumeration, classification, and causation of idiocy.* Philadelphia: Collins.

Kerlin, I. N. (1885). Provision for idiotic and feeble-minded children. In I. C. Barrows (Ed.), *Proceedings of the National Conference of Charities and Corrections at the Eleventh Annual Session* (pp. 246–263). Boston: Georgett Ellis.

Kerlin, I. N. (1891). *The manual of Elwyn.* Philadelphia: J. B. Lippincott Co.

Kevles, D. J. (1984). Annals of eugenics (I–IV) *New Yorker, 60,* Oct. 8 (pp. 51–52), 15 (pp. 52–54+), 22 (pp. 92–110+), 29 (pp. 51–52+)

Kingsley, J., & Levitz, M. (1994). *Count us in: Growing up with Down syndrome.* New York: Harcourt Brace Jovanovich.

Kirk, S. A. (1958). *Early education of the mentally retarded.* Urbana: University of Illinois Press.

Kirk, S. A. (1984). Introspection and prophecy. In B. Blatt & R. J. Morris (Eds.), *Perspectives in special education: Personal orientations* (pp. 25–55). Glenview, IL: Scott, Foresman.

Kirk, S. A., McCarthy, J. J., & Kirk, W. D. (1968). *The Illinois Test of Psycholinguistic Abilities* (rev. ed.). Urbana: University of Illinois Press.

Koestler, F. (1976). *The unseen minority: A social history of blindness in the United States.* New York: David McKay.

Korgesaar, J. (1988). On the development of special and remedial education in the Soviet Union. *International Journal of Special Education, 3,* 1–19.

Kozol, J. (1991). *Savage inequalities: Children in America's schools.* New York: Crown.

Kramer, R. (1976). *Maria Montessori: A biography.* New York: G. P. Putnam's Sons.

Kugelmass, J. A. (1951). *Louis Braille.* New York: Julian Messner.

Kuhlman, F. (1911). Binet and Simon's system for measuring intelligence of children. *Journal of Psycho-Asthenics, 15,* 76–92.

Lagemann, E. (1979). *A generation of women: Education in the lives of progressive reformers.* Cambridge: Harvard University Press.

Lamson, M. S. (1881). *Life and education of Laura Dewey Bridgman: The deaf, dumb, and blind girl.* Boston: New England Publishing.

Lane, H. (1976). *The wild boy of Aveyron.* Cambridge, MA: Harvard University Press.

Lane, H. (1984a). *When the mind hears: A history of the deaf.* New York: Random House.

Lane, H. (Ed.). (1984b). *The deaf experience: Classics in language and education* (F. Philips, Trans.). Cambridge, MA: Harvard University Press.

Lane, H. (1992). *The mask of benevolence: Disabling the deaf community.* New York: Alfred A. Knopf.

Lapin, H., & Lapin, C. (1976). The plight of parents in obtaining help for their autistic child and the role of the National Society for Autistic Children. In E. R. Ritvo (Ed.), *Autism: Diagnosis, current research, and management* (pp. 287–298). New York: Spectrum.

La Roncière, C. (1988). Tuscan notables on the eve of the renaissance. In G. Duby

(Ed.), *A history of private life. II. Revelations of the medieval world* (pp. 157–309). Cambridge, MA: Harvard University Press.

Lash, J. (1980). *Helen and teacher.* New York: Dell.

Lathom, W. B., & Eagle, C. T. (1982). *Music therapy for handicapped children: Mentally retarded.* Silver Springs, MD: National Association for Music Therapy.

Lazerson, M. (1971). *The origins of the urban public school.* Cambridge: Harvard University Press.

Leakey, T. A. (1993). Vocational education in the Deaf American and African-American communities. In J. V. Van Cleve (Ed.), *Deaf history unveiled: Interpretations from the new scholarship* (pp. 74–91). Washington, DC: Gallaudet University Press.

Letchworth, W. P. (1974). Homes of homeless children. In R. H. Bremner (Ed.), *Children and youth: Social problems and social policy.* New York: Arno Press. (Original work published 1903)

Lewis, D. L. (1993). *W. E. B. DuBois: Biography of a race, 1868–1919.* New York: Henry Holt.

Lewis, N. D. C. (1941). *A short history of psychiatric achievement: With a forecast for the future.* New York: W. W. Norton.

Lincoln, D. (1903). Special classes for feeble-minded children in the Boston Public Schools. *Journal of Psycho-Asthenics, 7,* 83–93.

Linton, T. E. (1971). The educateur model: A theoretical monograph. *Journal of Special Education, 5*(2), 155–190.

Lipkowski, O. (1973). Special education within a system of public education. *New School, 6,* 8–15.

Lipson, M. Y., & Wixson, K. K. (1986). Reading disability research: An interactionist perspective. *Review of Educational Research, 56*(1), 111–136.

Literacy Volunteers of Massachusetts. (1994). *Student journal: A collection of writings by adult new readers.* Boston: Author.

Litwack, L. F. (1979). *Been in the storm so long: The aftermath of slavery.* New York: Alfred A. Knopf.

Locke, J. (1894). *An essay concerning human understanding, Vol. 1* (A. C. Fraser, Ed.). Oxford: Oxford University Press. (Original work published 1690)

Lockhart, J. G. (Ed.). (1837). *Memoirs of the life of Sir Walter Scott, Vol. 1.* Philadelphia: Carey, Lean, & Blanchard.

Lombroso, C. (1896). Histoire des progres de l'anthropologie et de la sociologie criminelles pendant les années 1895–1896. *Travaux du 4eme Congrès International de l'Anthropogie Criminelle* (pp. 187–199). Geneva.

Lowenfeld, B. (1956). History and development of specialized education for the blind. *American Association of Workers for the Blind,* pp. 15–21.

Lowenfeld, B. (1975). *The changing status of the blind: From separation to integration.* Springfield, IL: Charles C. Thomas.

Mackenzie, C. (1928). *Alexander Graham Bell: The man who contracted space.* New York: Grosset & Dunlap.

Maennel, B. (1909). *Auxiliary education* (E. Sylvester, Trans.). New York: Doubleday.

Mallory, B., & New, R. (1994). *Diversity and developmentally appropriate practices: Challenges for early childhood education.* New York: Teachers College Press.

Mann, L. (1979). *On the trail of process.* New York: Grune & Stratton.

Mann, T. (1927). *The magic mountain* (H. T. Lowe-Porter, Trans.). Garden City, NY: International Collectors Library.

Marfo, K. (1986). *Confronting childhood disability in developing countries.* New York: Praeger.

Marland, S. (1972). *Education of the gifted and talented: A report to the Congress of the United States by the U.S. Commissioner of Education.* Washington, DC: U.S. Government Printing Office.

Martens, E. H. (1932). *Parents' problems with exceptional children* (Office of Education Pamphlet No. 14). Washington, DC: U.S. Government Printing Office.

Martens, E. H. (1934). *Teachers' problems with exceptional children, III: Mentally retarded children* (Office of Education Pamphlet No. 49). Washington, DC: U.S. Government Printing Office.

Martens, E. (1935). A conference on curriculum for mentally retarded children. *Journal of Psycho-Asthenics, 43,* 128–134.

Massie, R., & Massie, S. (1975). *Journey.* New York: Alfred A. Knopf.

Matson, V. F. (1974). *A school for Peter.* Carol Stream, IL: Creation House.

Mayer, M. F. (1959, November). *The parental figures in residential treatment.* Paper presented at the American Association for Children's Residential Centers, Chicago.

McCarthy, J. (1915). *A short history of our own times.* London: Chatto & Windus.

McCullers, C. (1940). *The heart is a lonely hunter.* New York: Houghton Mifflin.

McGee, P. (1990). Special education in Ireland. *European Journal of Special Education, 5*(1), 48–64.

McMillan, M. (1921). Presidential address. *Physical Therapy Review, 1*(2), 2–5.

McPherson, M. (1948). A survey of experimental studies of learning in individuals who achieve subnormal ratings on standardized psychometric measures. *American Journal of Mental Deficiency, 52,* 232–254.

Mead, M. (1955). Theoretical setting—1954. In M. Mead & M. Wolfenstein (Eds.), *Childhood in contemporary cultures* (pp. 3–20). Chicago: University of Chicago Press.

Meltzer, M. (1964). *A light in the dark: The life of Samuel Gridley Howe.* New York: Crowell.

Mercer, C. (1994). Learning disabilities. In N. G. Haring, L. McCormick, & T. G. Haring (Eds.), *Exceptional children and youth: An introduction to special education,* (6th ed., pp. 114–164). New York: Merrill.

Mercer, J. (1973). *Labeling the mentally retarded.* Berkeley: University of California Press.

Michigan School for the Blind. (1882). *First Biennial Report.* Lansing, MI: Author.

Miller, W. E. (1987). *The first liberty: Religion and the American republic.* New York: Alfred A. Knopf.

Monroe, M. (1932). *Children who cannot read.* Chicago: University of Chicago Press.

Montaigne, M. de. (1958). *Complete essays* (D. M. Frame, Trans.). Stanford, CA: Stanford University Press.

Montessori, M. (1964). *Dr. Montessori's own handbook.* Cambridge, MA: Robert Bentley. (Original work published 1914)

Montessori, M. (1965). *Spontaneous activity in education.* New York: Schocken Books. (Original work published 1917)

Montessori, M. (1972). *Education and peace.* Chicago: Henry Regnery Company. (Original work published 1949)

Moore, M. (1988). *Patterns in special education service delivery and cost.* Washington, DC: Decision Resources Corporation. (ERIC No. ED303027)

Moore, P., & Kester, D. G. (1958). Historical notes on speech correction in the pre-Association era. *Journal of Speech and Hearing Disorders, 23*(1), 48–53.

Moores, D. (1987). *Educating the deaf: Philosophy, principles and practices* (3rd ed.). Boston: Houghton Mifflin.

Morrison, T. (1974). *Chautauqua.* Chicago: University of Chicago Press.

Morrison, W. D. (1898). *Juvenile offenders.* New York: D. Appleton.

Morse, W. C. (1958). The program of the children's unit. *Proceedings of the Conference on Inpatient Psychiatric Units for Children,* New York, NY, May 26–29, 1957 (pp. 58–87).

Morse, W. C., Cutler, R. L., & Fink, A. H. (1964). *Public school classes for the emotionally handicapped: A research analysis.* Washington, DC: Council for Exceptional Children.

Morse, W. C., & Small, E. (1959). Group life space interviewing in a therapeutic camp. *American Journal of Orthopsychiatry, 29,* 27–44.

Murray, M. A. (1921). *The witch-cult in Western Europe: A study in anthropology.* Oxford: Clarendon Press.

Myklebust, H. R. (1957). *The psychology of deafness.* New York: Grune and Stratton.

Myrdal, G. (1944). *An American dilemma: The Negro problem and modern democracy* (Vols. 1 & 2). New York: Harper & Brothers.

Naremore, R. C. (1979). Influences of hearing impairment on early language development. *Annals of Otology, Rhinology and Laryngology, 88,* 54–63.

National Association of State Boards of Education. (1992). *The report of the NASBE study group on special education.* Alexandria, VA: Author.

National Commission on the Role of the School and the Community in Improving Adolescent Health. (1990). *Code blue: Uniting for healthier youth.* Washington, DC: National Association of State Boards of Education and the American Medical Association.

New York Board of Regents. (1935). *Report of Regents Commission on Mentally Retarded and Gifted Children to the Board of Regents of the State of New York.* New York: New York Board of Regents.

New York City Board of Education. (1941). *Orthopedically handicapped children* (Report of the Committee for the Study of the Care and Education of Physically Handicapped Children in the Public Schools of the City of New York). New York: Board of Education.

New York City Board of Education. (1944). *Organization of special classes for subnormal children.* Albany, NY: State University of New York Press.

Ohio Department of Education. (1985). *History of special education in Ohio: 1803–1985.* Columbus: Ohio Department of Education.

Ohio Hospital for Epileptics. (1896). *Fifth annual report: Executive documents 1895, I.* Columbus: Author.

Ohio Institution for the Instruction of the Blind. (1842). *Fifth annual report, 1841.* Columbus: Author.

Ohry, A., & Ohry-Kassay, K. (1989). *Spinal cord injuries in the 19th century: Background, research and treatment.* Edinburgh, UK: Churchill Livingston, Robert Stevenson.

Oppenheim, A. L. (1977). *Ancient Mesopotamia: Portrait of a dead civilization* (rev. ed., completed by E. Reiner). Chicago: University of Chicago Press.

Orton, S. T. (1925). Word-blindness in school children. *Archives of neurology and psychiatry, 14,* 582–615.

O'Shea, W. J. (1926). Mentally handicapped children. *Twenty-eighth annual report of the Superintendent of Schools.* New York: Board of Education.

Ozolins, A. (1981). Foreword. In B. Blatt, *In and out of mental retardation: Essays on educability, disability, and human policy* (pp. vii–xii). Baltimore: University Park Press.

Padden, C., & Humphries, T. (1988). *Deaf in America: Voices from a culture.* Cambridge, MA: Harvard University Press.

Parker, F. W. (1894). *Talks on pedagogics.* New York: E. L. Kellogg.

Parkhurst, H. (1922). *Education on the Dalton Plan.* New York: Dutton.

Paul, J. R. (1971). *A history of poliomyelitis.* New Haven: Yale University Press.

Pearson, G. H. J. (1954). *Psychoanalysis and the education of the child.* New York: W. W. Norton.

Perrot, M., & Martin-Fugier, A. (1990). The actors. In M. Perrot (Ed.), *A history of private life: IV. From the fires of revolution to the Great War* (pp. 95–337). Cambridge, MA: Harvard University Press.

Piers, M. W. (1978). *Infanticide.* New York: W. W. Norton.

Pinel, P. (1962). *A treatise on insanity* (D. D. Davis, Trans.). New York: Hafner Book Co. (Original work published 1806)

Plank, E. (1962). *Working with children in hospitals.* Cleveland, OH: Case Western Reserve University Press.

Plato. *The republic.* In I. Edman (Ed.), *The works of Plato* (B. Jowett, Trans.; 1928). New York: Simon & Schuster.

Polsky, H. N. (1962). *Cottage six.* New York: Russell Sage Foundation.

Polster, G. E. (1990). *Inside looking out: The Cleveland Jewish Orphan Asylum, 1868–1924.* Kent, OH: Kent State University Press.

Porter, K. A. (1972). *Through a glass darkly: Spiritualism in the Browning circle.* New York: Octagon Books.

Powell, G. F., Brasel, J. A., & Blizzard, R. M. (1967). Emotional deprivation and growth retardation simulating idiopathic hypopituitarism. *New England Journal of Medicine, 276,* 23.

Powell, T. H., Aiken, J. M., & Smylie, M. A. (1982). Treatment of involuntary euthanasia for severely handicapped newborns: Issues of philosophy and public policy. *Journal of the Association for Persons with Severe Handicaps, 6,* 3–10.

Pratte, R. (1973). *The public school movement: A critical study.* New York: David McKay.

Preston, J. A. (1993). Domestic ideology, school reformers, and female teachers: Schoolteaching becomes women's work in nineteenth-century New England. *New England Quarterly, 66*(4), 531–551.

Pritchard, D. G. (1963). *Education of the handicapped*. London: Routledge & Kegan Paul.

Reagan, T. (1985). The deaf as a linguistic minority: Educational considerations. *Harvard Educational Review, 55*(3), 265–277.

Redl, F. (1959). The concept of a therapeutic milieu. *American Journal of Orthopsychiatry, 29,* 1–18.

Redl, F., & Wineman, D. (1957). *The aggressive child*. Glencoe, IL: The Free Press.

Reid, J. H., & Hagan, H. R. (1952). *Residential treatment of emotionally disturbed children: A descriptive study*. New York: Child Welfare League of America.

Régnier-Bohler, D. (1988). Imagining the self. In G. Duby (Ed.), *A history of private life II: Revelations of the medieval world* (pp. 311–393). Cambridge, MA: Harvard University Press.

Reynolds, M. C., Wang, M., & Walberg, H. (1987). The necessary restructuring of special and regular education. *Exceptional Children, 53,* 391–398.

Rhodes, W. C., & Tracy, M. L. (1972). *A study of child variance. Volume 1: Conceptual models* (Research/Technical Report, Conceptual Project in Emotional Disturbance). Ann Arbor: Institute for the Study of Mental Retardation, University of Michigan. (ERIC No. ED135120)

Richards, L. E. (1909). *Letters and journals of Samuel Gridley Howe, the servant of humanity* (Vol. 2). Boston: Dana Estes & Co.

Richards, L. E. (1935). *Samuel Gridley Howe*. New York: Appleton-Century.

Riis, J. A. (1902). *The children of the poor*. New York: Charles Scribner's Sons.

Rimland, B. (1964). *Infantile autism*. New York: Appleton-Century-Crofts.

Ritvo, E. R. (1976). Autism: From adjective to noun. In E. R. Ritvo (Ed.), *Autism: Diagnosis, current research, and management* (pp. 3–6). New York: Spectrum.

Roach, E. G., & Kephart, N. C. (1966). *The Purdue perceptual-motor survey*. Columbus, OH: Merrill.

Roberts, F. K. (1986). Education for the visually handicapped: A social and educational history. In G. T. Scholl (Ed.), *Foundations of education for blind and visually handicapped children and youth: Theory and practice* (pp. 1–18). New York: American Foundation for the Blind.

Robson, B. (1989). *Pre-school provision for children with special needs*. London: Cassell Educational Limited.

Rodenberg, L. W. (1938). The story of books for the blind. In H. Lende (Ed.), *What of the blind: A survey of the development and scope of present-day work with the blind* (pp. 158–177). New York: American Foundation for the Blind.

Roe, F. W. (1947). *Victorian prose*. New York: Ronald Press.

Rosen, G. (1968). *Madness in society: Chapters in the historical sociology of mental illness*. Chicago: University of Chicago Press.

Rosen, M., Clark, G. R., & Kivitz, M. S. (1976). *The history of mental retardation: Collected papers*. Baltimore: University Park Press.

Rosenberg, C. E. (1987). *The care of strangers: The rise of America's hospital system*. New York: Basic Books.

Ross, I. (1951). *Journey into light: The story of the education of the blind*. New York: Appleton-Century-Crofts.

Ross, D. (1972). *G. Stanley Hall: The psychologist as prophet.* Chicago: University of Chicago Press.

Roth, H. (1934). *Call it sleep.* New York: Cooper Square Publishers.

Rothman, D. (1971). *The discovery of the asylum: Social order and disorder in the new republic.* Boston: Little, Brown.

Rousseau, J.-J. (1963). *Emile.* London: Everyman's Library. (Original work published 1762)

Rowling, M. (1968). *Everyday life in medieval times.* New York: Dorset Press.

Rury, J. L. (1989). Who became teachers? The social characteristics of teachers in American history. In D. Warren (Ed.), *American teachers: Histories of a profession at work* (pp. 9–48). New York: Macmillan.

Rush, B. (1812/1962). *Medical inquiries and observations upon the diseases of the mind.* New York: Hafner. (Facsim. New York: Harper, 1962).

Russell, B. (1970). *Marriage and morals.* New York: Liveright. (Original work published 1929)

Russell, R. W. (1973). *History of ACLD.* Unpublished manuscript, Association for Children with Learning Disabilities.

Sacks, O. (1989). *Seeing voices: A journey into the world of the deaf.* Berkeley: University of California Press.

Sacks, O. (1994). A neurologist's notebook: An anthropologist on Mars. *The New Yorker, 69*(44), 106–125.

Safe counsel. (1914). Marietta, OH: S. A. Mullikin Co.

Sapinsley, B. (1991). *The private war of Mrs. Packard.* New York: Paragon House.

Sapon-Shevin, M. (1994). *Playing favorites: Gifted education and the disruption of community.* Albany: State University of New York Press.

Sarason, S. B. (1988). *The making of an American psychologist: An autobiography.* San Francisco: Jossey-Bass.

Sarason, S. B., & Doris, J. (1969). *Psychological problems in mental deficiency* (4th ed.). New York: Harper & Row.

Schama, S. (1989). *Citizens: A chronicle of the French revolution.* New York: Alfred A. Knopf.

Scheerenberger, R. C. (1983). *A history of mental retardation.* Baltimore: Paul H. Brookes.

Scheerenberger, R. C. (1987). *A history of mental retardation: A quarter century of progress.* Baltimore: Paul H. Brookes.

Schiefelbusch, R. L. (1984). The odyssey of a speech clinician. In B. Blatt & R. J. Morris (Eds.), *Perspectives in special education: Personal orientations* (pp. 233–262). Glenview, IL: Scott, Foresman.

Schmidt, S. N. (1970). *Out of the shadows.* Cleveland, OH: Council for the Retarded Child.

Scholl, G. T., Mulholland, M. E., & Lonergan, A. (1986). Education of the visually handicapped: A selective timeline. In G. T. Scholl (Ed.), *Foundations of education for blind and visually handicapped children and youth.* New York: American Foundation for the Blind.

Schrag, P., & Divoky, D. (1975). *The myth of the hyperactive child.* New York: Pantheon.

Schwartz, H. (1956). *Samuel Gridley Howe, social reformer 1801–1876.* Cambridge, MA: Harvard University Press.

Schwartz, K. B. (1992). Occupational therapy and education: A shared vision. *Journal of Occupational Therapy, 46*(1), 12–18.

Scott, A. F. (1992). *Natural allies: Women's associations in American history.* Urbana, IL: University of Illinois Press.

Scott, R. A. (1969). *The making of blind men: A study of adult socialization.* New York: Russell Sage Foundation.

Scripture, E. W. (1912). *Stuttering and lisping.* New York: Macmillan.

Seguin, E. (1843). *Hygiene et education des idiots.* Paris: Bailliere.

Seguin, E. (1866/1907). *Idiocy and its treatment by the physiological method.* New York: Albany-Brandon Printing.

Seguin, E. (1880). *Report on education (U.S. Commissioner on Education at the Vienna Universal Exhibition).* Washington, DC: U.S. Government Printing Office.

Semel, S. F. (1992). *The Dalton School: The transformation of a progressive school.* New York: Peter Lang.

Seymer, L. R. (1954). *Selected writings of Florence Nightingale.* New York: Macmillan.

Shahar, S. (1990). *Childhood in the middle ages.* London and New York: Routledge.

Sheed, W. (1973). *People will always be kind.* New York: Farrar, Straus & Giroux.

Shorter, E. (1992). *From paralysis to fatigue: A history of psychosomatic illness in the modern era.* New York: The Free Press.

Shuttleworth, G. E. (1899). The elementary education of defective children by "special classes" in London. *Journal of Psycho-Asthenics, 4*, 58–64.

Shuttleworth, G. E., & Potts, W. A. (1924). *Mentally deficient children: Their treatment and training.* London: H. K. Lewis & Co. Ltd.

Silberman, C. E. (1970). *Crisis in the classroom.* New York: Random House.

Silverman, L. K. (1995). Gifted and talented students. In E. L. Meyen & T. M. Skrtic (Eds.), *Special education & student disability: An introduction* (4th ed., pp. 377–413). Denver: Love.

Simons, M. (1988). Montessori, superman, and catwoman. *Educational Theory, 38*(3), 341–349.

Skeels, H. M. (1941). A study of the effects of differential stimulation on mentally retarded children: A follow-up report. *American Journal of Mental Deficiency, 46*, 340–350.

Skeels, H. M. (1966). Adult status of children with contrasting early life experiences. *Monographs of the Society for Research in Child Development, 31*(3), (Whole No. 105).

Skeels, H. M., & Dye, H. B. (1939). A study of the effects of differential stimulation on mentally retarded children. *Proceedings and Addresses of the Sixty-third Annual Session of the American Association on Mental Deficiency, 44*(1), 114–136.

Skrtic, T. M. (1991). The special education paradox: Equity as the way to excellence. *Harvard Educational Review, 61*(2), 148–206.

Skultans, V. (1974). *Madness and morals: Ideas on insanity in the nineteenth-century.* London: Routledge & Kegan Paul.

Sleeter, C. E. (1990). Learning disabilities: The social construction of a special education category. In S. Sigmon (Ed.), *Critical voices on special education: Problems and progress concerning the mildly handicapped* (pp. 21–35). Albany: State University of New York Press.

Smalley, S., Tanguay, P., Smith, M., Gutierrez, G. (1992). Autism and tuberous sclerosis. *Journal of Autism and Developmental Disorders, 22*, 339–352.

Snedden, D. S. (1907). *Administration and educational work of American juvenile reform schools*. New York: Teachers College, Columbia University.

Sontag, S. (1978). *Illness as metaphor*. New York: Farrar, Straus & Giroux.

Soren, D., Ben Khader, A. B. A., & Slima, H. (1990). *Carthage: Uncovering the mysteries and splendors of ancient Tunisia*. New York: Simon & Schuster.

Spencer, H. (1860). *Education*. New York: Appleton.

Spitz, R. (1945). Hospitalism. *Psychoanalytic Study of the Child, 1*, 53–74.

Spitz, R. (1946). Anaclitic depression, an inquiry into the genesis of psychiatric conditions in early childhood. *Psychoanalytic Study of the Child, 2*, 313.

Spring, J. H. (1972). *Education and the rise of the corporate state*. Boston: Beacon Press.

Starr, M. A. (1904). Is epilepsy a functional disease? *Journal of Neuro-Muscular Disorders, 31*, 145–156.

Steel, R. (1980). *Walter Lippmann and the American century*. Boston: Little, Brown.

Stevens, G. D. (1954). Developments in the field of mental deficiency. *Exceptional Children, 21*, 58–62.

Stewart, I. M. (1944). *The education of nurses: Historical foundations of modern trends*. New York: Macmillan.

Stickney, W. (Ed.). (1872). *Autobiography of Amos Kendall*. Boston: Lee & Shepard.

Stokoe, W. C. (1980). Sign language structure. *Annual Review of Anthropology, 9*, 365–390.

Strauss, A. A., & Lehtinen, L. E. (1947). *Psychopathology and education of the brain-injured child* (Vol. 1). New York: Grune & Stratton.

Sumption, M. R., & Luecking, E. M. (1960). *Education of the gifted*. New York: Ronald Press.

Szasz, T. S. (1970). *The manufacture of madness: A comparative study of the Inquisition and the mental health movement*. New York: Harper & Row.

Talbot, M. E. (1964). *Edouard Seguin: A study of an educational approach to the treatment of mentally defective children*. New York: Teachers College Press.

Tanner, D., & Tanner, L. (1990). *History of the school curriculum*. New York: Macmillan.

Tappan, P. (1949). *Juvenile delinquency*. New York: McGraw-Hill.

Taylor, H. (1933). Caroline Ardelia Yale. *Volta Review, 35*, 415–417.

Taylor, J. (Ed.). (1931). *Selected writings of John Hughlings Jackson. Vol. I: On epilepsy and epileptiform convulsions*. London: Hodder & Stoghton.

Taylor, W. W., & Taylor, I. W. (1960). *Special education of physically handicapped children in western Europe*. New York: International Society for the Welfare of Cripples.

Teeters, N. K., & Reinemann, J. O. (1950). *The challenge of delinquency*. New York: Prentice-Hall.

Teller, M. E. (1988). *The tuberculosis movement: A public health campaign in the progressive era.* New York: Greenwood Press.

Temkin, O. (1945). *The falling sickness: A history of epilepsy from the Greeks to the beginnings of modern neurology.* Baltimore: Johns Hopkins University Press.

Terman, L. (1916). *The measurement of intelligence.* Cambridge, MA: Riverside Press.

Terman, L. M. (1924). The conservation of talent. *School and Society, 19,* 363.

Terman, L. M. (1925). *Genetic studies of genius. Vol. 1: Mental and physical traits of a thousand gifted children.* Stanford: Stanford University Press.

Terman, L. M., & Oden, M. (1959). *Genetic studies of genius. Vol. 5: The gifted group at mid-life: Thirty-five years' follow-up of the superior child.* Stanford: Stanford University Press.

Thomas, D. H., Miller, J., White, R., Nabakov, P., & Deloria, P. J. (1993). *The Native Americans: An illustrated history.* Atlanta: Turner Publishing.

Thomas, M. G. (1920). *The first seventy years: Worcester College for the Blind, 1866–1936.* London: National Institute for the Blind.

Thorndike, E. L. (1914). *Educational psychology: Briefer course.* New York: Teachers College, Columbia University.

Thorndike, E. L. (1940). *Human nature and the social order.* New York: Macmillan.

Thurer, S. (1980). Disability and monstrosity: A look at literary distortions of handicapping conditions. *Rehabilitation Literature, 41,* 12–15.

Thurston, H. (1930). *The dependent child.* New York: Columbia University Press.

Tims, M. (1961). *Jane Addams of Hull House, 1860–1935.* New York: Macmillan.

Tjossem, T. (Ed.). (1976). *Intervention strategies for high risk infants and young children.* Baltimore: University Park Press.

Todd, L. P., & Curti, M. (1966). *The rise of the American nation.* New York: Harcourt, Brace & World.

Trieschman, A. E., Whittaker, J. K., & Brendtro, L. K. (1969). *The other 23 hours.* New York: Free Press.

Trotzkey, E. L. (1930). *Institutional care and placing out.* Chicago: The Marks Nathan Jewish Orphan Home.

Tsujimura, Y. (1979). *Summary of the development of special education in Japan.* Tokyo: National Institute of Special Education.

Tucker, R. K. (1991). *The dragon and the cross: The rise and fall of the Ku Klux Klan in middle America.* Hadmen, CT: Archon Books.

Turnbull, A. P., & Turnbull, H. R. (1990). *Families, professionals and exceptionality* (2nd ed.) Columbus, OH: Merrill.

Tyor, P. L., & Bell, L. V. (1984). *Caring for the retarded in America: A history.* Westport, CT: Greenwood Press.

U.S. Department of Education. (1989). *Eleventh annual report to Congress on the implementation of the Education of the Handicapped Act (PL 94–142).* Washington, DC: U.S. Government Printing Office.

U.S. Department of Education. (1993). *Fifteenth annual report to Congress on the implementation of the Education of the Handicapped Act (PL 94–142).* Washington, DC: U.S. Government Printing Office.

U.S. Department of the Interior, Office of Handicapped Children. (1928). *Bulletin No 9.*

U.S. statutes at large, 68th Congress. (1925). Washington, DC: U.S. Government Printing Office.

Van Cleve, J., & Crouch, B. (1989). *A place of their own*. Washington, DC: Gallaudet University Press.

Villey, P. (1927). *L'aveugle dans le monde des voyants: Essai de sociologie*. Paris: Ernest Flammairon.

Violas, P. (1973). Progressive social philosophy: Charles Horton Cooley and Edward Alsworth Ross. In C. J. Karier, P. C. Violas, & J. Spring (Eds.), *Roots of crisis: American education in the twentieth century* (pp. 40–65). Chicago: Rand McNally & Company.

Waite, H. E. (1961). *Make a joyful sound: The romance of Mable Hubbard and Alexander Graham Bell*. Philadelphia: Macrae Smith Company.

Wallin, J. E. W. (1912a). The euthenical and eugenical aspects of infant and child orthogenesis. (Annual Meeting of the American Association for Study and Prevention of Infant Mortality, October 3, Cleveland, OH.) In *Transactions of the Association, 3*, 173–194.

Wallin, J. E. W. (1912b). *Experimental studies of mental defectives: A critique of the Binet-Simon Tests and a contribution to the psychology of epilepsy* (Education and Psychology Monographs No. 7). Baltimore: Warwick & York.

Wallin, J. E. W. (1914). *The mental health of the school child: The psychoeducational clinic in relation to child welfare*. New Haven, CT: Yale University Press.

Wallin, J. E. W. (1924). *The education of handicapped children*. Boston: Houghton Mifflin.

Wallin, J. E. W. (1955). *Education of mentally handicapped children*. New York: Harper & Brothers.

Ward, L. F. (1883). *Dynamic sociology*. New York: Appleton.

Warner, M. L. (1944). Founders of the International Council for Exceptional Children. *Journal of Exceptional Children, 10*, 217–223.

Washington Research Project. (1974). *Children out of school in America*. Washington, DC: Children's Defense Fund.

Watson, J. B. (1928). *Psychological care of infant and child*. New York: Norton.

Weber, L. (1969). *The kindergarten: Its encounter with educational thought*. New York: Teachers College Press.

Wehr, G. (1987). *Jung: A biography*. Boston: Shambhala.

Werner, H. (1961). *Comparative psychology of mental development*. New York: Science Editions.

West, R. W. (1960). The Association in historical perspective. *Journal of the American Speech and Hearing Association, 2*(1), 8–11.

White, W. D., & Wolfensberger, W. (1969). The evolution of dehumanization in our institutions. *Mental Retardation, 7*, 5–9.

Whitney, E. A., Shick, M. M., Bedrossian, E., & Whitney, S. P. (1930). A general review of mongolian idiocy. *Medical Journal and Record, 132*(11), 850–861.

Wickman, E. (1928). *Children's behavior and teachers' attitudes*. New York: Commonwealth Fund.

Wiederholt, J. L. (1974). Historical perspectives on the education of the learning disabled. In L. Mann & D. A. Sabatino (Eds.), *The second review of special education* (pp. 103–152). New York: Grune & Stratton.

Wilbur, H. (1852). *First annual report of the trustees of the New York Asylum for Idiots to the legislature of the state.* Albany, NY: State Printers.

Will, M. (1986). Educating children with learning problems: A shared responsibility. *Exceptional Children, 52,* 411–416.

Williams, D. (1992). *Nobody nowhere: The extraordinary biography of an autistic.* New York: Avon Books.

Williams, D. (1994). *Somebody somewhere: Breaking free from the world of autism.* New York: Random House/Times Books.

Wilson, D. C. (1975). *Stranger and traveler: The story of Dorothea Dix, American reformer.* Boston, Toronto: Little, Brown.

Wishy, B. W. (1968). *The child and the republic: The dawn of modern American child nurture.* Philadelphia: University of Pennsylvania Press.

Witkin, M. J. *Residential treatment centers for emotionally disturbed children 1973–74* (Mental Health Statistical Note No. 130). Washington, DC: U.S. Department of Health, Education, and Welfare.

Witmer, L. (1909). The study and treatment of retardation: A field of applied psychology. *Psychological Bulletin, 6*(4), 121–126.

Wolfensberger, W. (1975). *The origins and nature of our institutional models.* Syracuse, NY: Human Policy Press.

Wolff, P. H., Michel, G. F., Ovrut, M., & Drake, C. (1990). Rate and timing precision of motor coordination in developmental dyslexia. *Developmental Psychology, 26,* 349–359.

Wood, E. J. (1868). *Giants and dwarfs.* London: Richard Bentley.

Wood, M. M., & Long, N. J. (1991). *Life space intervention: Talking with children and youth in crisis.* Austin, TX: PRO-ED.

Woodward, J. (1972). Implications for sociolinguistics research among the deaf. *Sign Language Studies, 1,* 1–7.

Young-Bruehl, E. (1988). *Anna Freud: A biography.* New York: Summit Books.

Ysseldyke, J., & Algozzine, B. (1982). *Critical issues in special and remedial education.* Boston: Houghton Mifflin.

Ysseldyke, J., Algozzine, B., Richey, L., & Graden, J. (1982). Declaring students eligible for learning disability services: Why bother with the data? *Learning Disability Quarterly, 5,* 37–44.

Zald, M. N. (1960). The correctional institution for juvenile offenders: An analysis of organizational "character." *Social Problems, 8,* 57–67.

Zigler, E. F. (1966). Mental retardation: Current issues and approaches. In L. W. Hoffman & M. L. Hoffman (Eds.), *Review of child development research* (Vol. 2, pp. 107–168). New York: Russell Sage Foundation.

Zigler, E. F. (1970). The environmental mystique: Training the intellect vs. development of the child. *Childhood Education, 46,* 8.

Zilboorg, G., with Henry, G. W. (1941). *A history of medical psychology.* New York: W. W. Norton.

Zimmerman, D. P. (1991). *The clinical thought of Bruno Bettelheim: A critical historical review.* Madison, CT: International Universities Press.

Index

NAMES

Ablon, J., 11
Abraham, W., 290
Abt, I., 6, 17
Adams, M. E., 104
Addams, Jane, 73, 208, 209–211, 244, 287
Agricola, Rodolphus, 24, 29
Aichhorn, August, 251
Aiello, B., 188, 290
Aiken, J. M., 3
Albee, George, 254
Albert, J. S., 69, 70
Alcott, Bronson, 67–71, 73
Alexander, F. G., 223, 248
Algozzine, B., 181, 245, 292
Allen, Edgar Fiske, 204, 220
Allen, Edward, 142, 151, 152
Allen, F. L., 79, 211, 287
Allen, Joseph, 70
Allen, Lucy Clark Ware, 70
Altschule, M. D., 224
Amatruda, C. S., 218
Ames, Louise Bates, 217–218, 295
Amman, Jan Conrad, 33, 37, 38, 40, 96
Anagnos, Michael, 106, 131–133, 136, 137, 145–146
Anderson, Meta L., 186
Anderson, Rose, 177
Angell, Frank, 260
Aries, P., 1, 14–15, 22
Aristotle, 4, 6–7, 11, 26, 83, 119, 262
Armitage, Thomas Rhodes, 141
Artiles, A. J., 292
Ashley-Cooper, Anthony, 59
Augustus, 5, 203
Avicenna, 17
Axline, Virginia M., 249
Ayres, Leonard P., 287–288

Bacon, Francis, 26
Bagley, W. C., 288
Baker, H. J., 223
Baker, Henry, 32
Bakwin, H., 206
Ball, T. S., 53, 54
Barker, J., 122
Barkley, R. A., 270, 284–285
Barmatz, H., 122
Barnes, H. E., 233, 240
Barr, M. W., 20
Barraga, Natalie, 152
Barton, W. E., 48, 50
Bates, B., 196
Battiscombe, G., 59
Becquerel, Alfred, 263
Bedell, M., 69, 70
Beers, Clifford
  Whittingham, 228
Behr, A. L., 97
Bell, Alexander Graham, 31, 40, 73–75, 82, 90, 92, 99, 100–106, 109–111, 113–117, 120, 137, 144, 168, 177
Bell, Alexander Melville, 31, 104, 263
Bell, L. V., 154
Bender, Lauretta, 253, 255
Bender, Ruth, x, 7, 11, 25, 28–32, 34, 37, 40, 71, 107, 108
Ben Khader, A. B. A., 9–10
Bennett, F. C., 296
Bentzen, F., 271
Berens, C., 123
Berkeley, George, 44, 125
Berkowitz, P. H., 255
Bernoulli, Jacob, 43
Bernstein, Charles, 180
Berry, C., 187
Berry, M. F., 262, 263, 265

Best, H., 115, 128, 129
Bettelheim, Bruno, 211, 251, 253, 280
Biklen, D., 187
Binet, Alfred, 153, 171, 174, 176, 183, 243
Bingham, D., 266
Blacklock, Thomas, 126, 140
Blanton, Smiley, 247
Blatt, Burton, ix, 71, 72, 88, 155, 289, 298, 300
Blee, K. M., 78, 79
Blinderman, A., 64
Blizzard, R. M., 205
Bloom, Benjamin S., 296
Blum, J. S., 177
Boake, C., 268
Boas, G., 68
Boatner, M. T., 34, 92, 93, 95, 108, 110, 111, 113, 115
Boccacio, 21–22
Bogdan, Robert, ix, 3, 155
Bolling, J. William, 107
Bonaterre, Abbé Pierre-Joseph, 51
Bonet, Juan Martin Pablo, 30, 32, 33, 36–38, 40
Boorstin, D. J., 56, 58, 63
Borenzweig, H., 211
Boring, E. G., 7, 26, 167, 172, 175, 176, 225, 259, 260
Bost, Jean, 159–160
Boswell, J., 5, 13–16, 18, 23, 190
Bower, E. M., 252
Bowlby, John, 205, 206
Boyd, W., 168
Brace, Charles Loring, 61
Braidwood, John, 93, 94, 107–108

327

Braidwood, Thomas, 32, 94, 107
Braille, Louis, 39–40, 43–44, 139–140, 258
Brasel, J. A., 205
Braudel, F., 18–19
Braunstein, P., 22
Braverman, S., 43
Breasted, J. H., 22
Breines, E. B., 215
Bremner, R. H., 207, 252
Brendtro, Larry K., 250
Brennan, W. K., 293
Brenzel, B., 238, 239–240
Breunig, H. L., 101, 113
Brewster, Mary, 203, 209
Brickman, W. W., 64
Bridgman, Laura Dewey, 62, 72, 103, 127, 135–137
Brigham, Amariah, 195, 228
Brill, R. G., 105
Broca, Pierre Paul, 267–268
Brown, Christy, 194
Brown, George, 161
Brown, Katherine Wood, 161
Browning, Elizabeth Barrett, 59, 225
Bruce, R. V., 100, 103
Bullock, H. D., 292
Bulwer, John, 31
Burlingame, Dorothy, 249
Burt, Cyril, 178–179, 241–242
Butler, Amos W., 1

Caddey, J. W., 241, 253
Campbell, J. K., 81
Cardano, Girolamo, 24, 29, 32
Carlebach, J., 234–236
Carpenter, Mary, 234–235
Carrier, J. G., 292
Caswell, Oliver, 136–137
Cattell, James McKeen, 175, 259–260
Cattell, R. B., 179
Chall, J. S., 273
Channing, William Ellery, 69, 181
Chapin, H. D., 205
Charcot, Jean Martin, 8, 47, 191
Charles I, king of France, 24
Chevigny, H., 43
Chiarugi, Vincenzo, 48–49
Christensen, E., 215
Cicerelli, V. G., 296
Clark, G. R., 75
Clarke, John, 104

Clerc, Laurent, 29, 31, 32, 35–36, 40–42, 71–72, 92, 94–98, 112–113, 134
Cleugh, J., 21–22
Clifford, D. P., 135
Cogswell, Alice, 90, 92–94
Cogswell, Mason Fitch, 92–94
Cohen, R. S., 255
Coleman, R. W., 205
Comenius, Johann Amos, 28, 66
Condillac, Etienne Bonnet de, 27, 28, 37, 52, 53, 172
Connor, F. P., 75, 76
Connor, L. P., 74, 111, 112
Constantine I, 12, 16–17
Corbin, A., 47, 224, 227
Cornett, Orin, 103, 104, 109–110
Coss, Claire, 208, 209
Costin, L. B., 58, 61
Cranston, M., 27
Cremin, L. A., 75, 78, 80, 81, 84, 209, 221, 287
Cronbach, L. J., 175
Crouch, B. A., 97–101, 114, 115, 211
Cruickshank, William M., 188, 193, 194, 271
Cubberly, E. P., 78, 86, 217
Curti, M., 59, 84, 229
Cushing, Harvey, 268
Cutler, R. L., 255
Cutsforth, Thomas D., 131, 136, 148, 149

Dalgarno, George, 31–33
Daltheus, Archbishop of Milan, 12
Dalzell, R. F., Jr., 58, 226
Darwin, Charles, 82, 83
De Carlo, L. M., 29
Decroly, Ovide, 185–186
Decroly, S., 186
Deloria, P. J., 123
deMause, L., 15
Demetz, Frederic Auguste, 238–239
Demos, J., 55, 56, 190
Demosthenes, 11
Descourdes, Alice, 186
Desloges, Pierre, 37
Despert, J. L., 1, 11, 14, 17, 56, 223

Deutsch, A., 56–58, 226, 228, 243, 249–250
Devereux, Georges, 15, 25, 254
Dewey, John, 73, 80, 81, 83–85, 210, 260, 288
Dickens, Charles, 136, 140, 189–190, 233, 234, 236, 238
Diderot, D., 25, 36, 44, 45, 124, 300
Digby, Sir Kenelm, 30–31
Divoky, D., 284
Dix, Dorothea, 47, 57, 69, 74–75, 128, 129, 135, 136, 156, 163, 226, 252
Doll, Edgar A., 176, 211, 243
Donald, D., 133–134, 226
Doren, G. A., 161
Doris, J., 76, 154, 166, 175, 177, 185, 191, 211, 245, 258–259
Dorris, M., 201, 227
Down, Jonathan Langdon Haydon, 159, 166, 170, 171, 258
Downs, R. B., 66
Drake, C., 273
Du Bellay, Joachim, 25
Dubos, J., 195, 196, 198
Dubos, R., 195, 196, 198
Duby, G., 18
Duchan, J. F., 187
Duck, Lavinia, 209
Dudley, Lewis, 103, 104
Dugdale, Richard L., 258
Duncan, P., 169, 180
Dunn, L. M., 184, 291
Dunsdon, M. I., 193
Dunton, W. R., 215
Durant, W., 3, 5
Dwyer, E., 227
Dye, H. B., 296

Eagle, C. T., 249
Eberle, L., 204
Edgerton, R. B., 155
Eliot, Charles W., 85
El Mudo (Juan Fernandez Ximenes de Navarette), 24
Emerson, Ralph Waldo, 70
Emminghaus, Hermann, 223
Epée, Charles Michel, l'abbé de l', 33, 34, 36, 38–40, 42, 44, 71, 72, 91, 118, 119, 128, 160

Erikson, E. H., 247
Erin, J., 152
Esquirol, Jean Etienne
  Dominique, 9, 24, 48,
  157, 168, 169, 223, 227,
  252
Estabrook, Arthur H., 259
Esten, R. A., 181
Evans, J. W., 296
Eysenck, H. J., 179

Fagan, T. K., 217, 218,
  242–244, 262
Farber, B., 290
Farel, A. M., 222
Farrell, Elizabeth K., 76,
  181–184, 185, 216, 217,
  245, 246
Farrell, G., 124, 129, 133,
  140, 141, 144, 145, 151
Faulk, M., 266
Fay, Edward Allen, 104, 116
Felt, J. P., 59, 237–239
Fennimore, J. K., 250
Ferguson, D. L., 299
Ferguson, P. M., 299
Fernald, Grace M., 274
Fernald, Walter E., 160, 161,
  163, 167–168, 180, 183
Fink, A. H., 255
Flexer, C., 120, 121
Forness, S. R., 16–17, 269
Foucault, M., 3, 43, 48, 49,
  164, 195, 224, 237–239
Frampton, M. E., 90, 146,
  148, 197
Franklin, Benjamin, 4, 49–
  50, 123
Frazier, T., 60
Freeman, B. J., 281, 283
Freitag, G., 277
French, J. L., 243
French, R. S., 4–6, 17, 19,
  45, 46, 173–174
Freud, Anna, 206, 211,
  249, 251
Freud, Sigmund, 228, 247–
  248, 251
Freund, E. D., 124, 130
Friedlander, Julius, 129–130
Froebel, Friedich, 67, 73,
  75, 81
Frostig, Marianne, 276
Fuchs, D., 150, 294
Fuchs, L. S., 150, 294
Fuller, Sarah, 101, 104
Furman, R. A., 248

Galen, Claudius, 7–9, 17,
  23, 223, 224
Gall, Franz Joseph, 166, 258
Gall, James, 141
Gallagher, J. J., 291
Gallaudet, Edward Miner,
  34, 42, 63, 71–72, 74, 93–
  95, 99, 101, 107–111,
  113, 115, 117, 118, 137
Gallaudet, Thomas
  Hopkins, 42, 61–62, 90,
  92–95, 108–109
Galton, Francis, 82, 85,
  114, 153, 175, 178, 259
Gannon, J. R., 113
Gardiner, R. A., 270
Gardner, Howard, 275
Garrett, Henry E., 178
Garrison, S. Olin, 182
Gay, Peter, 56, 227, 248
George, M. P., 256
George, N. L., 256
George, William Reuben, 250
Gérando, Joseph-Marie de,
  29, 41, 97
Gesell, Arnold, 73, 80–81,
  83, 187, 201, 216–218,
  260, 261, 295
Gesell, B., 83, 216, 218
Gindis, B., 269
Goddard, Henry H., 76, 82,
  153–154, 168, 176–178,
  182–184, 217, 244, 259,
  262
Goffman, E., 250
Goldstein, H. M., 185
Goldstein, Joseph, 249
Goldstein, Kurt, 268
Gottlieb, B. W., 278
Gottlieb, J., 278
Gould, S. J., 154, 167, 177
Graden, J., 292
Grandin, T., 282
Graves, R., 189, 248, 264
Gray, W. S., 273
Greanleaf, B. K., 1, 2, 22, 56
Green, Francis, 93, 107
Greenberg, J., 127, 142
Greer, C., 87
Griscom, John, 237
Grob, G. N., 225
Groce, N. E., 115, 164
Grosenick, J. K., 256
Guggenbuhl, Johann Jacob,
  158–159, 171
Guralnick, M., 296
Gutierrez, G., 283

Hagan, H. R., 253
Hale, N. G., 157, 224, 229,
  247, 248
Hall, Frank H., 114, 136,
  142, 151
Hall, G. Stanley, 68–69, 73,
  80, 83–86, 218, 242–244,
  248, 259–260, 265
Hall, W. C., 244
Hamaide, A., 186
Hammill, D. D., 276
Handlin, M. F., 56, 239
Handlin, O., 56, 239
Haring, Norris G., 271
Harris, William, T., 84–85
Harrison, C., 67, 73
Haskell, R. H., 177
Haüy, Valentin, 25, 38, 41,
  43–46, 122–124, 126,
  135, 138–140, 148, 258
Hawes, J. M., 238
Hawke, D., 50
Healy, William, 244–246
Hearnshaw, L. S., 179
Heinicke, Samuel, 33–34,
  103, 106
Heller, K. A., 292
Henig, R. M., 189
Hensley, G., 288
Heraclitus, 6
Herbart, J. F., 84–85
Hershey, M., 88
Hewes, D. W., 67, 68
Hewett, Frank M., 16–17,
  269, 271
Hilbert, C., 22
Hildreth, G. H., 243–244
Hill, Moritz, 34, 103
Hill, Patty Smith, 75–76
Hinshelwood, J., 274
Hippocrates, 6–8, 17, 23,
  25, 198, 262
Hobbes, Thomas, 26
Hobbs, Nicholas, 47, 88,
  250, 254
Hodge, A., 189, 248, 264
Holder, William, 32
Holl, J. M., 250
Hollingworth, Leta S., 86–87
Holmes, Oliver Wendell,
  134, 168
Holowinsky, I. Z., 77, 269
Holt, L. E., 201
Holtzman, W. H., 292
Homer, 25, 125
Horn, J. L., 86
Horne, D., 276

Howe, Irving, 79, 203, 209
Howe, Julia Ward, 78
Howe, M., 114, 136
Howe, Samuel Gridley, 56,
57, 60–62, 72, 74, 75,
92–93, 98, 99, 102–103,
106, 111, 115, 127–129,
131–137, 140, 143–149,
152, 155–156, 158, 160–
162, 164–165, 168–169,
187, 195, 227, 241, 258,
298
Hubbard, Mabel, 90, 102,
103–104, 111, 113, 134
Hudson, A. F., 104
Hughes, R., 233, 235–238
Hume, David, 26
Humphries, T., 90, 96,
117–119
Hunt, J. M., 296
Hurt, James, 263
Huysman, Roelof, 24
Hymes, James, 295

Innocent VIII, Pope, 19
Ireland, William W., 160,
164, 169–171, 191
Irvine, P., 186
Irwin, Robert B., 142, 143,
148, 151–152
Ishii, R., 159
Isserlin, Max, 268
Itard, Jean-Marc-Gaspard,
x, 3, 28, 30, 41, 48, 50–
54, 72, 157, 168, 171,
172, 258, 259, 260

Jackson, John H., 191, 192,
268
James, William, 81, 83,
228, 259–260
James I, king of England, 20
Jefferson, Thomas, 64
Jensen, Arthur, 179
Jeremiah, 9
Jerome, 13
Jesus, 8, 10, 11, 22, 223
Johnstone, E. R., 158, 182
Jones, K., 224, 245
Jordan, D. S., 116
Jordan, I., 120
Jung, C. G., 159
Justinian, 7, 13
Juul, K. D., 254

Kaestle, C. F., 66
Kahn, H. A., 123
Kamin, L. J., 179

Kanner, L., 10, 24, 26,
158–160, 180, 223, 280
Kaplan, F., 190, 236
Karchmer, M., 120
Katan, A., 248
Katz, M. B., 80, 87, 144, 239
Kaufman, J., 254, 256
Kazin, Alfred, 264–265
Keller, Helen, 56, 71, 73,
116, 127, 135, 136–138,
143, 211, 297, 300
Kelley, Florence, 209, 287
Kendall, Amos, 109
Kenney, Elizabeth, 199
Kephart, Newell C., 54,
270, 275–276
Kerlin, Isaac Newton, 158,
161–163, 167, 170, 174
Kerney, E., 146, 148
Kester, D. G., 265, 266
Kevles, D. J., 82
Kingsley, Charles, 263
Kingsley, Jason, 300
Kinniburgh, Robert, 94, 108
Kirk, Samuel A., 261, 274,
296
Kirk, W. D., 274
Kivitz, M. S., 75
Klein, Johann Wilhelm, 124
Klein, Melanie, 206, 248–249
Klencke, Philipp Friedrich
Herman, 263
Knight, Henry M., 161
Koestler, F., 151, 211
Koppitz, Elizabeth M., 272
Korgesaar, J., 269
Kozol, J., 88
Kraepelin, Emil, 223
Kramer, R., 72, 73
Kugelmass, J. A., 139
Kuhlman, Frederick, 176–177

Lamson, Mary Swift, 103,
136
Landini, Francesco, 25
Lane, Harlan, x, 28–29, 31,
32, 34–42, 51, 54, 61, 71,
90–92, 95–98, 100, 117–
119, 121, 134, 147, 291
Lapin, C., 281
Lapin, H., 281
La Ronciére, C., 15, 16, 21
Lash, J., 56, 71, 116, 127,
133, 136–138
Lathom, W. B., 249
Lazerson, M., 87
Leakey, T. A., 291
Lehtinen, Laura E., 270–272

Leseuer, François, 45, 46,
55, 122
Letchworth, W. P., 112,
142, 161, 196, 203–204
Letchworth, William Pryor, 57
Levitz, Mitchell, 300
Lewis, D. L., 287, 291
Lewis, N. D. C., 49, 228
Light, S., 215
Lincoln, Abraham, 109
Lincoln, D., 76
Linton, T. E., 254
Lipkowski, O., 269
Lippmann, Walter, 177–
178, 288
Lipson, M. Y., 274
Little, W. J., 159, 192, 258
Litwack, L. F., 292
Locke, John, 26–27, 44, 48,
52, 125
Lockhart, J. G., 199
Lombroso, Cesare, 167, 258
Lonergan, A., 123
Long, N. J., 250
Louis XIV, king of France, 26
Louis XV, king of France, 35
Louis XVI, king of France, 46
Lowenfeld, Berthold, x, 5,
17, 25, 45, 46, 124, 126,
143, 145–149
Luecking, E. M., 85
Lycurgus, 4

Mackenzie, C., 99, 100,
102, 114, 115
Macy, Anne Sullivan. *See*
Sullivan, Anne
Maennel, B., 180, 219
Mallory, B., 299
Mann, Horace, 34, 64–68,
74, 75, 78, 81, 102–103,
110, 128, 131, 134, 156,
162, 195, 226, 236
Mann, L., 276
Mann, Mary, 68
Mann, Thomas, 197
Marfo, K., 286
Marland, S., 86
Martens, Elise H., 169,
184–186, 297–298
Martin-Fugier, A., 157,
227, 233, 239, 248
Massie, Robert, 206
Massie, Suzanne, 206
Massieu, Jean, 41–42, 71,
94, 98, 122
Matson, Virginia F., 277–278
Mayer, Morris "Fritz," 250

McCarthy, J. J., 60, 274
McCullers, C., 90–91
McDowell, Mary, 210
McGee, P., 293, 298
McIntosh, R., 201
McNally, J., 298
McPherson, M., 261
Mead, Margaret, 1
Medici, Lorenzo de Piero
de' (Lorenzo the
Magnificent), 22
Meltzer, M., 129
Melville, Alexander, 100–
101
Mercer, C., 273, 278
Mercer, J., 291
Mercurialis, Jerome, 262
Mercurius, Franciscus,
Baron van Helmont, 31
Merrill, Maud, 176
Mesmer, Friedrich Anton,
46–47
Messick, S., 292
Meyer, Adolph, 228–229
Meyer, Mary Brook, 229
Michel, G. F., 273
Millard, W., 169, 180
Miller, J., 123
Miller, W. E., 58, 63
Milton, John, 25, 125
Monroe, Marian, 273, 274
Montaigne, M. de, 20, 21
Montessori, Maria, 53, 72–
74, 172, 173, 174, 185,
206, 211
Moore, M., 290
Moore, P., 265, 266
Moores, D., 120
Moorhead, H. B., 123
More, Thomas, 20
Morrison, T., 210
Morrison, W. D., 241
Morse, Samuel, 109
Morse, William C., 251–
252, 255–256
Moses, 10
Mulholland, M. E., 123
Murray, M. A., 20
Myklebust, Helmer R., 119,
267
Myrdal, Gunnar, 292

Nabakov, P., 123
Napoleon Bonaparte, 46,
166, 191
Naremore, R. C., 121
Neill, A. S., 248
New, R., 299

Nightingale, Florence, 212–
213
Nobel, Alfred, 191

Oberlin, Johann Friedrich,
55, 237
Oden, M., 87
Oestler, Richard, 59–60
Ogilvy, John and Jane, 159
Ohry, A., 202
Ohry-Kassay, K., 202
Oppenheim, A. L., 10
Orton, Samuel T., 274
O'Shea, William J., 289
Osler, William, 202
Ovrut, M., 273
Ozolins, A., 153, 298

Padden, C., 90, 96, 117–119
Paracelsus, 21, 23, 47
Paré, Ambroise, 23
Parkhurst, Helen, 221
Parrish, Joseph, 163
Paul, J. R., 198, 199
Peabody, Elizabeth, 67, 68,
212
Pearson, G. H. J., 247
Pearson, Karl, 82, 178
Pereire, Eugene, 157
Pereire, Giacobbo (Jacob)
Rodriguez, 33, 35–39, 71,
90, 95, 96, 106, 155,
157, 160, 172
Pereire, Isaac, 157
Perrot, M., 157, 227, 233,
239, 248
Pershing, John J., 215
Pestalozzi, Johann Heinrich,
28, 34, 66, 81, 103, 162,
171, 237
Peyser, N., 185
Phayre, Thomas, 23
Phelps, Winthrop M., 191
Philip II, king of Spain, 24
Philip IV, king of Spain, 30
Phillips, E. L., 271
Piaget, Jean, 218
Piers, Maria W., 2, 4, 12,
21, 27, 247
Pinel, Philippe, 47, 48, 50,
51, 168
Plank, Emma, 206
Plato, 4, 6, 82
Platter, Felix, 20, 23–24
Platter, Thomas, 23–24
Platz, Frederick, 160
Platz, Theresa, 160
Plutarch, 10

Polsky, H. N., 252
Polster, G. E., 58, 78, 79,
230, 247
Ponce de León, Pedro, 29,
30, 32, 96, 97
Poole, Ernest, 196
Porter, K. A., 225
Potts, W. A., 161
Powell, G. F., 205
Powell, H. G., 90, 197
Powell, T. H., 3
Pratte, R., 64, 78, 79, 208
Preston, J. A., 74, 75
Prichard, James Cowles, 227
Pritchard, D. G., 125–126,
131, 139, 140, 143
Provence, S., 205

Quimby, Phineas P., 224–225

Ramirez de Carrión,
Emmanuel, 30
Raphael, George, 33
Ratzeberg, F., 271
Reagan, T., 117, 120
Redl, Fritz, 250, 251
Reed, Andrew, 159, 162
Régnier-Bohler, D., 14
Reid, J. H., 167m 253
Reinemann, J. O., 237, 238
Reynolds, M. C., 293
Rhodes, William C., 256
Richards, J. B., 162
Richards, Laura E., 98,
111, 129, 134, 135, 143–
145, 147, 155, 156, 236
Richey, L., 292
Riis, Jacob A., 196
Rimland, Bernard, 281
Ritvo, E. R., 281
Roach, E. G., 276
Roberts, F. K., 124, 144
Robson, B., 67
Rodenberg, L. W., 43, 140–
142
Roe, F. W., 59
Rogers, Harriet Burbank,
103, 104
Rollin, Charles, 27, 172
Romulus and Remus, 5
Ronsard, Pierre de, 24–25
Rosen, G., 224
Rosen, M., 75, 135, 159–
162, 168, 268
Rosenberg, C. E., 190, 212
Rosenfeld, Hannah and
Isaac, 111
Ross, D., 83

Ross, I., 135, 136, 145
Roth, H., 263
Rothman, D., 57, 145, 229
Rothman, E. P., 255
Rousseau, Jean-Jacques, 27–28, 52, 66, 173
Rowling, M., 17
Rury, J. L., 74
Rush, Benjamin, 49–50, 97, 201
Russ, John D., 129
Russell, Bertrand, 82, 248
Russell, R. W., 279

Saboureux de Fontenay, 35–37, 71
Sacks, Oliver, 37, 41, 118, 119, 280, 282
Saegert, Carl Wilhelm, 160
St. Augustine, 12
St. Louis, 17
St. Lymnaeus, 17
Saint-Simon, Henri de, 157
Salmon, Thomas W., 243
Sanborn, Frank, 103, 138
Sapinsley, B., 228
Sapon-Shevin, M., 88
Sarason, Seymour B., vii–viii, 76, 154, 166, 175, 177, 185, 191, 211, 245, 258–259, 261, 270
Sargeant, John, 237
Scariano, M. M., 282
Schama, S., 39–41, 45
Scheerenberger, Richard C., x, 3, 12, 17, 48, 51, 71, 157, 158, 163, 165, 169, 170, 179, 180, 186–187, 191
Schenck, John, 20–21
Schiefelbusch, Richard L., 267
Schiff, Jacob, 209, 253
Schiller, J. S., 296
Schmidt, S. N., 289
Scholl, G. T., 123, 139, 145
Schrag, P., 284
Schurz, Margarethe Meyer, 75
Schwartz, Harold, 98, 129, 132–134, 137, 144, 147
Schwartz, K. B., 215
Scot, Reginald, 20
Scott, A. F., 200
Scott, R. A., 300
Scripture, Edward Wheeler, 265
Scripture, May Kirk, 265

Seguin, Edouard Onesimus, 27, 32–35, 38, 53–55, 68, 71, 72, 75, 90, 95, 110, 128, 155–158, 160–163, 166, 168–174, 185, 217, 259, 300
Selesnick, S. T., 223, 248
Semel, S. F., 221
Seneca, 5
Seymer, L. R., 212
Shahar, S., 2, 4, 9, 12–19, 21, 22
Shannon, D. A., 75
Shaw, Bernard, 100, 264
Sheed, W., 199
Sheldon, Edward, 75
Shorter, E., 224
Shuttleworth, G. E., 161, 180
Sicard, Roch-Ambroise Cucurron, 40–42, 46, 51, 54, 71, 108, 128, 155, 172
Silberman, C. E., 88
Silverman, L. K., 88
Simon, Theophile, 171, 176
Simons, M., 74
Skeels, H. M., 296
Skinner, B. F., 260
Skrtc, T. M., 293
Skultans, V., 49
Sleeter, C. E., 278
Slima, H., 9–10
Small, E., 251–252
Smalley, S., 283
Smith, M., 283
Smylie, M. A., 3
Snedden, D. S., 237, 238
Socrates, 191
Solnit, Albert J., 249
Sontag, Susan, 188, 194–195, 222
Soranus of Ephesus, 8, 47
Soren, D., 9–10
Spencer, Herbert, 24, 66
Spitz, René, 205
Spree, Frederick von, 20–21
Spring, J. H., 87, 150
Spurzheim, J. K., 166–167
Starr, Ellen Gates, 209
Starr, Floyd, 250–251
Starr, Moses Alan, 191
Steel, R., 178
Stern, William, 176
Stevens, G. D., 290
Stewart, Dugald, 108
Stewart, I. M., 212, 213
Stickney, W., 109

Stokoe, W. C., 119
Strauss, Alfred A., 194, 270–272
Sullivan, Anne, 56, 57, 71, 73, 127, 129, 136–138, 229, 297
Sumner, Charles, 34, 103, 110, 128, 136, 147, 156
Sumner, George, 162
Sumption, M. R., 85
Sylvester, E., 251
Szasz, Thomas S., 254

Talbot, M. E., 157, 168, 172, 174
Tanguay, P., 283
Tanner, D., 63, 80, 82
Tanner, L., 63, 80, 82
Tannhauser, M. A., 271
Tappan, P., 233
Taussig, E., 266
Taylor, Graham, 210
Taylor, H., 105
Taylor, I. W., 77, 97, 124, 127, 150, 193, 197, 200, 207, 208, 269
Taylor, S., 155, 299
Taylor, W. W., 77, 97, 124, 127, 150, 193, 197, 200, 207, 208, 269
Teeters, N. K., 233, 237, 238, 240
Teller, M. E., 197
Temkin, O., 8, 9
Terman, Lewis M., 87, 167–168, 176, 178, 218
Thomas, D. H., 123, 196
Thomas, M. G., 126
Thoreau, Henry David, 70
Thorndike, Edward Lee, 84, 85, 177, 178, 259–260
Thurer, S., 188
Thurston, H., 57, 202
Tims, M., 210–211
Tjossem, T., 201
Todd, L. P., 59
Townsend, M. E., 75
Townshend, John, 32
Tracy, M. L., 256
Trader, Georgia and Florence, 151
Traphagen, V., 223
Trent, S. C., 292
Trieschman, A. E., 250
Trotzkey, E. L., 202
Trumbull, Henry Clay, 109
Tsujimura, Y., 150, 159, 198

Tucker, R. K., 79
Tuke, Daniel Hack, 49
Tuke, Samuel, 48, 49
Tuke, William, 49
Turnbull, A. P., 289, 298
Turnbull, H. R., 289, 298
Tyler, Joseph D., 98, 113
Tyor, P. L., 154

Ulrich of Cluny, 13–14

Vallambert, Simon de, 23
Van Cleve, J., 97–101, 114,
  115, 211
Van Gogh, Vincent, 191
Van Hattum, R., 266
Victor (wild boy of
  Aveyron), x, 3, 28, 30,
  48, 50–54, 55
Villey, Pierre, 148
Vincent de Paul, 16, 47, 51,
  158, 203
Violas, P., 153
Vives, Juan Luis, 21
Voisin, Felix, 169
Voltaire, 27, 225
von Paradis, Maria
  Theresia, 44, 45, 124
Vygotsky, L. S., 269

Wait, William, 142
Waite, H. E., 102–104, 258
Walberg, H., 293
Wald, Lillian, 181, 197,
  203, 208–209, 216, 287
Walker, Alice, 10

Wallin, John Edward
  Wallace, 76, 123, 153,
  158, 181, 184–186, 201,
  216, 217, 243, 261, 288,
  289
Wallis, John, 31–33, 96, 107
Wang, M., 293
Ward, Lester F., 81–82, 85
Ward, Mary, 208
Ware, Henry, 70
Warner, M. L., 183
Watson, J. B., 260
Watson, James, 107
Watson, Joseph, 93, 107
Watson, Thomas James, 107
Webb, Beatrice and Sydney,
  210
Weber, L., 63, 75
Wehr, G., 159
Weiderholt, L., 276
Weise, Johann Traugott, 179
Wells, H. G., 20
Werner, Heinz, 270
Wernicke, Carl, 268
West, R. W., 265
Weyer, Johann, 20, 47
White, R., 123
White, W. D., 153
Whitney, E. A., 166
Whittaker, J. K., 250
Wickman, E., 243–244
Wiederholt, J. L., 267, 268
Wiggins, Kate Douglas, 63
Wilbur, C. T., 161
Wilbur, Hervey Backus,
  156, 160–161, 169–171

Wile, Ira, 202
Will, Madeline, 293
Williams, Donna, 281–282
Wilson, D. C., 136, 226
Wilson, Woodrow, 83
Wineman, David, 251
Wishner, J., 278
Wishy, B. W., 56, 60, 61,
  63, 68
Witkin, M. J., 254
Witmer, Lightner, 73, 76,
  83, 242, 243, 244, 259,
  261
Wixson, K. K., 274
Wolfensberger, W., 153
Wolff, P. H., 273
Wood, E. J., 3
Wood, M. M., 250
Woodward, J., 117
Woodward, Samuel Bayer,
  168
Wundt, Wilhelm, 259, 265

Yale, Caroline Ardelia, 104–
  105
Yates, J. V. N., 56–57
Yerkes, Robert M., 177
Young-Bruehl, E., 206,
  249, 251
Ysseldyke, J., 181, 245, 292

Zald, M. N., 249
Zigler, E. F., 187, 259, 296
Zilboorg, G., 2, 6, 9, 19,
  20
Zimmerman, D. P., 253

SUBJECTS

Abandonment, 4–5, 13–16, 190
Abuse, 16, 203
Academy for the Deaf and Dumb
  (England), 107
Academy of Sciences (France), 26, 39, 45, 47
Accidents, 14, 202–203
Adolescence, x, 1
African Americans, 60, 87, 128, 287, 292
  blindness and, 123, 146
  intelligence tests and, 178, 179
Aftereffects of Brain Injuries in War
  (Goldstein), 268
Age of Reason, 16, 164
Aggressive Child, The (Redl and Wineman),
  251
AIDS, 189, 222
Alcohol use, 201, 222, 227

Allied health professions, 211–215
Almshouses, 57, 91, 123, 129, 190, 237, 252
American Association of Instructors of the
  Blind, 142
American Association on Mental
  Deficiency (Mental Retardation), 181
American Association to Promote the
  Teaching of Speech to the Deaf, 113
American Association to Promote the
  Teaching of Speech to the Deaf
  (AAPTSD), 104, 105, 113–114
American Asylum for the Deaf and Dumb,
  108, 156
American Breeders Association, 191
American Foundation for the Blind, 137,
  143, 151
American Humane Association, 59, 203

American Notes and Pictures from Italy (Dickens), 136
American Orthopsychiatric Association (AOA), 246
American Physical Therapy Association (APTA), 213
American Printing House for the Blind, 140–141, 142
American Psychiatric Association, 49, 228, 247, 283–284
American Psychological Association (APA), 83, 244, 254
American School for the Deaf (Connecticut), 92–95, 99, 106
American Sign Language (ASL), 41, 92, 118, 119, 143, 258
American Speech-Language-Hearing Association (ASHA), 265–266
Americans with Disabilities Act of 1990 (ADA), 118, 221, 286
American Women's Physical Therapeutic Association, 214
Aphasia, 266–267
Army Alpha Test, 177
Articulation training, 112
Association for Persons with Severe Handicaps (TASH), 294–295
Association for the Care of Children's Health (ACCH), 206
Association for the Improved Instruction of Deaf Mutes, 111
Association for the Oral Instruction of the Deaf and Dumb, 108
Associationism, 26
Association of Medical Officers of American Institutions for Idiotic and Feeble-minded Persons, 158, 161
Asylum for the Education of Deaf and Dumb Persons, 112
Asylum for the Indigent Blind (England), 125–126
Asylums, 3, 12, 68, 110–111, 133, 145–147
for mental illness, 48–50, 128
for orphans, 229–232
Attachment, 4, 15
Attention Deficit/Hyperactivity Disorder (ADHD), 222, 270, 272, 279–280, 283–285, 298
Australia, 199, 236
Austria, 180, 251, 268
Autism, 252, 266, 279–283, 298, 300
Auxiliary Schools, 179–180, 181, 219

Belgium, 47, 127, 160, 180, 220
Bellevue Psychiatric Hospital (New York), 253, 255
Bell's Standard Elocutionist (Bell), 100

Bender Visual-Motor Gestalt Test, 272
Bethlehem Hospital (Bedl'm; London), 3, 49
Beyond the Best Interests of the Child (Solnit), 249
Bicetre (Paris), 9, 48, 157–159, 252
Binet-Simon scale, 217
Biological determinism, 153–154
Biological risk, 201–202
Birth, 201–202
Birth defects, 23, 222, 227
Black Death, 18–19, 21–22, 28
Blind education, 43–46, 62–63
day classes in, 143–152
in Europe, 124–127, 150–151, 269
Howe and, 132–137
literacy achievement in, 138–143
residential schools in, 124–137, 143, 148
state institutions in, 130–132
teacher preparation for, 124, 126, 140
in the United States, 127–132
Blind in School and Society, The (Cutsforth), 148
Blindness, x, 122–152
experiences of children with, 122–124
giftedness and, 25, 44
as hereditary defect, 116, 123
in the Middle Ages, 17
Boke on Children, The (Phayre), 23
Boston Line Type, 140
Boston Outdoor School, 197, 207
Braille, 139–143, 151, 152
Brain
ancient views of, 5–6, 7
language impairment and, 267–268
phrenology and, 166–167
Strauss syndrome, 270–271, 272, 284
Brown v. Board of Education, 292
Buck v. Bell, 168

Canada, 197
Central New York Institution for Deaf Mutes, 112
Cerebral palsy, 8, 192–195, 214, 220, 266, 271
Charity Organization Societies, 68
Child care manuals, 23
Childhood
approach to education in, 55
attitudes toward children, 65–66
changing status of children, 21–24
children as pawns in, 13–16
concept of, 1–2
conditional nurture in, 2, 289
"cult of childhood," 59, 68–69
family metaphor and, 57–59, 144–150, 227–229, 239
periods of, 14, 15

poverty in, 56–59
responsibilities of and for children, 55–57
uniqueness of, 235
Child labor, 2, 15, 59–60, 238
Child psychiatry, 247
Child Psychiatry (Kanner), 223
Children's Aid Society, 60, 219
Children's Bureau, 200–201, 209
Children's Century, 286–287
Children's Crusade, 16, 223
Children with Learning Disabilities Act
(P.L. 91-230), 262
Children with Learning Disability Act of
1969 (P.L. 94-142), 215, 220, 266,
277–279, 290, 292, 293, 294, 297, 299
Child study movement, 83–85
Child Welfare League of America, 200,
202, 230
*Chirologia, or The Natural Language of the
Hand* (Bulwer), 31
Citizens (Schama), 40–41
Civil rights movement, 291
Civil War, 78, 212, 231, 292
Clarke Institution, 101, 102, 105
Clarke School, 104, 111
Clinical method, 242–245
Clinical psychology, 261, 269–270
Clinical teaching approach, 255
Cloak of Competence (Edgerton), 155
Code of Hammurabi, 8, 10
Color vision, 123, 171–172, 217
Columbia Lodge (Scotland), 159
Combined Method, 110, 112
Common schools, 75, 77–81, 150, 154,
195, 239
Commonwealth Fund, 243
Communication disorders, 262–267
Conceptual Models Project, 256
Conference on Charities and Correction, 1
Confessions (St. Augustine), 12
Congenital moral imbecility, 167–168
Connecticut School for Imbeciles, 161
Conquest of Deafness, The (Bender), 29
Constructivism, 299
Convulsions, 8–9
Cottage Six (Polsky), 252
Council for Exceptional Children (CEC),
216, 246
*Course of Instruction for a Congenitally Deaf
Person* (Sicard), 42
Crack, 189
Cretinism, 23–24, 72–74, 158, 166
Cued Speech method, 110
Cystic fibrosis, 202

Dactylology, 31, 33, 36–37
Dalton Plan, 221

*Dangerous Classes of New York, and Twenty
Years' Work Among Them, The* (Brace),
61
Deaf culture, 35–36, 40–42, 96, 99–100,
117–119
Deaf education, 28–42, 65, 71–72, 269
American School for the Deaf
(Connecticut), 92–95, 99, 106
in Britain, 30–33, 93–94, 107
deaf authors and, 24–25, 36–38
in Germany, 33–34, 102–103, 110, 134,
160
in Italy, 97, 102–103, 105
manual alphabets, 30, 31, 34, 36–37,
137
in North America, 35–36, 291–292
oralism versus manualism in, 75, 92–95,
100–106, 110–112, 119–121
professionalization of, 74
residential schools in, 97–99, 102
sign language in, 35–42, 92, 118, 119,
143, 258
Spanish-French school, 29–30, 35–42,
96, 105
speech in communication and, 28–35
teacher preparation for, 104–105, 107,
112–113
Visible Speech in, 31, 100, 102, 112
Deafness, x
in ancient societies, 7
experiences of children with, 90–91
giftedness and, 24–25, 36–38
as hereditary defect, 114–117
infirmity model of, 91, 114–115
war and, 211
Decameron (Boccacio), 21–22
Defectology, 77, 269
De Formando Studio (Spencer), 24
Delaware, 129
Delinquency. *See* Juvenile delinquents
Demonology, 2, 19–21, 160
Denmark, 97, 150, 180, 203, 208
Dependency, x, 188
Depression, 223
Descent of Man, The (Darwin), 83
Description of the Retreat (Tuke), 49
Developmental diagnosis, 218
Developmental lines, 249
Developmental Test of Visual Perception, 276
Discovery of Witchcraft (Scot), 20
Disontogenesis, 269
Down syndrome, 3, 166, 266, 300
Dubnoff Center for Child Development
and Educational Therapy (California),
277
Dwarfism, 3–4, 11
Dynamic Sociology (Ward), 82

Earlswood Asylum, 192, 258
Ecriture Nocturne (Night Writing), 139
Edinburgh School for Blind Children, 141
Educational Psychology (Thorndike), 260
Educational Treatment Center for the
　Exceptional Child (Illinois), 277–278
Education of All Handicapped Children
　Act of 1975, 89
Education of Defectives in the Public Schools
　(Anderson), 186
Education of Handicapped Children, The
　(Wallin), 216
Education of Mentally Defective Children,
　The (Descourdes), 186
Education of the Congenitally Deaf, The
　(Gérando), 97
Education of the Imbecile and the
　Improvement of Invalid Youth, The
　(Brodies), 159
Education on the Dalton Plan (Parkhurst), 221
Egypt, ancient, 6, 8, 22
Elementary Education (Blind and Deaf
　Children) Act of 1893, 150
Elitism, 87
Elwyn Institute (Pennsylvania), 76, 162,
　163, 167, 170, 171, 174
Emile (Rousseau), 27, 173
England, 3–4, 19, 20, 23, 25, 26, 77
　blind education in, 125–126
　brideswells in, 234, 252
　deaf education in, 30–33, 93–94
　juvenile delinquency in, 233–236, 238,
　　244, 245
　mental retardation education in, 159,
　　180–181, 258
　physical disabilities in, 190, 193, 197,
　　203, 221
Enlightenment, 25, 44, 46–47, 65
Environmental risk, 203
Environmental tradition, 218
Epilepsy (convulsive disorder), 5–6, 8–9,
　165, 167, 191–192, 217, 219
Equipotentiality, 272
Essais, Les (Montaigne), 21
Essay Concerning Human Understanding, An
　(Locke), 26, 44
Essay Toward a New Theory of Vision
　(Berkeley), 44
Eugenics movement, 4, 82, 99, 115–117,
　153, 165, 177, 247, 259
Euthanasia, 165
Exceptional children
　abandonment of, 4–5, 13–16, 190
　conditional nurture of, 2, 289
　exploitation of, 3–4
　giftedness and. *See* Gifted persons
　medical treatment of, 5–9

moral treatment of, x, 3–4, 8, 43, 47–50,
　173–174
　and original sin, 12–13
　as pawns, 13–16
　poverty and, 18–19
　religion and, 9–12
　risk of, 3–4, 201–203
　and spiritual visitation, 10
　survival of, 4–5
　as wards of institutions, 12, 16–17
Exorcism, 7–8, 9

Failure to thrive, 205
Family metaphor, 57–59, 144–150, 227–
　229, 239
Family therapy, 254
Feral children, 50–54
Fetal Alcohol Syndrome/Fetal Alcohol
　Effect (FAS/FAE), 222, 227
Fingerspelling, 120, 135
Finland, 97, 150, 193, 208
Foster care, 60
Foundling homes, 12, 16–17, 205
Fragile X (Martin-Bell) syndrome, 283
France, 19, 20, 21, 22, 23, 24–26, 216
　deaf education in, 29–30, 35, 105
　juvenile delinquency in, 238
　mental illness in, 227
　mental retardation education in, 159–
　　160, 180
　physical disabilities in, 200
Free Appropriate Public Education
　(FAPE), 277–278, 290, 293, 294
Freeville Junior Republic, 250
Fresh Air Fund, 250
Friends Asylum, 49
Full Inclusion, 88, 150

Gallaudet College, 109, 113
Gallaudet University, ix, 98, 99, 109, 120
General Psychology (Goddard), 178
Genetic Studies of Genius, The (Terman),
　176
Genius, 85
German measles (rubella), 91
Germany, 24, 28, 86, 216, 219, 268
　deaf education in, 33–34, 102–103, 110,
　　134, 160
　juvenile delinquency in, 238
　mental illness in, 223–224
　mental retardation education in, 158–
　　159, 179–180
　physical disabilities in, 197
Germinal (Zola), 2
Gesell Institute of Human Development,
　218
Gestalt school, 270

Gifted persons
  with disabilities, 24–25, 36–38, 44, 124, 125, 191
  school programs for, 85–88
Glossolalia, 11
Great Expectations (Dickens), 234
Greece, 4–7, 200
Guild for Crippled Children of the Poor of New York, 219

Hallucinations, 20, 223
Handicapped Children's Early Education Program (HCEEP), 296–297
Head Start, 296
Healthy Personality for Every Child, A, 247
Hebrews, ancient, 6, 8
Hemophilia, 202, 206
Henry Street Settlement (New York), 208–209
Hereditary Genius (Galton), 82, 153
Hilfsschules (Auxiliary Schools), 179–180, 181, 219
Histories of American Schools for the Deaf (Fay), 116
Holt's Diseases of Infancy and Childhood (Holt), 205
"Home schools," 70
Horace Mann School for the Deaf (Boston), 102, 104
Hospitalism, 205–207
Hull House (Chicago), 209–211
Hydrocephaly, 5–6
Hypnosis, 47
Hysteria, 8, 47, 191, 223

Ideographic language, 119
Idiocy, 23, 168–170, 173, 177, 191
Idiocy and Its Treatment by the Physiological Method (Seguin), 172
Illinois, 131, 142, 244, 274, 277–278
Illinois Juvenile Research Institute, 244
Illinois School for the Blind, 142
Illinois Test of Psycholinguistic Abilities (ITPA), 274
Imbeciles, 23, 177
Immediate command, 174
Immigration
  education and, 87, 150, 264
  restrictions on, 78–79, 153, 196
  speech teachers and, 213
Impetigo, 202
Indiana, 131
Individualized Education Programs (IEPs), 215, 221, 279, 293, 294
Individuals with Disabilities Education Act, 89, 284, 286
Industrial Rehabilitation Act, 215

Infancy, 14
Infanticide, 2, 3, 5, 12, 13, 16
Infantile Autism (Rimland), 281
Infant mortality, 18, 56, 203, 205
Infant School movement, 62, 67, 68
Influenza pandemic, 189
Inquisition, 19–20
Institutional confinement, 47–48
Institution for Deaf-Mutes (Germany), 160
Institution for the Blind and Deaf and Dumb (England), 126–127
Institution Nationale des Jeunes Aveugles, 38, 45, 139
Institution Nationale des Sourdes-Muets, 38
Institution of Blind Workers, 46
Instruction of the Deaf and Dumb (Watson), 107
Intelligence and Experience (Hunt), 296
Intelligence quotient (IQ), 176–179
Interpretivism, 299
Introduction to the Theory of Mental and Social Measurement (Thorndike), 260
IQ studies, 87, 153, 176–179, 246, 278, 296, 298
Ireland, 159
Italy, 20, 21–22, 25, 180
  deaf education in, 97, 102–103, 105
  Montessori and, 72–74
  physical disabilities in, 197

Japan, 150, 159, 198
Joint Commission on Mental Health of Children (JCMHC), 246–247, 254–255
Junior high, 80
Juvenile delinquents, 232–246
  cottage living and, 238–242
  dispersion of, 236–237
  English reformatories for, 233–236
  guidance centers, 242–245
  houses of refuge for, 237–238, 239
  psychoeducational clinics, 242–245
  ungraded classes for, 245–246

Kendall School, 109
Kenney Institute (Minnesota), 199
Kentucky, 131
Kindergarten, 62–63, 75, 76, 104, 218
  in blind education, 145–146, 148
  and physical disability, 67–68
Kuhlman-Anderson Intelligence Test, 177
Ku Klux Klan, 78–79

Laggards in Our Schools (Ayres), 287–288
Language impairment, 267–277
Laura Bridgman (Howe and Hall), 136
Learning disabilities. *See* Specific learning disabilities

Least Restrictive Environment (LRE), 88,
  215, 279, 290, 294, 297
*Letter on the Blind for the Use of Those Who
  See* (Diderot), 25, 44, 300
Lexington School for the Deaf (New York
  City), 102, 111–112
Liaison teachers, 255
Life Space Intervention (Wood and Long), 250
Lipreading, 101, 104
Literacy, 138–143, 273–274
Logopedagogy (education for deaf-mutes), 269
London Asylum for the Deaf, 107
London Society for Teaching the Blind to
  Read, 126, 140

Madness and Morals (Skultans), 49
Magdalen Hospital (England), 159
Magic Mountain, The (Mann), 197
Making of Blind Men, The (Scott), 300
Malleus Maleficarum (The Witches'
  Hammer), 19–20
Manual alphabets, 30, 31, 34, 36–37, 137
Marasmus (failure to thrive), 205
Marriage and Morals (Russell), 82
Marriage of the Deaf in America (Fay), 116
Maryland, 129
Massachusetts, 85, 128, 156, 163, 225–228
Massachusetts Asylum for the Blind, 128
Massachusetts School for Idiotic and
  Feeble-minded Youth, 156, 163
Maturationist tradition, 218
*Medical Inquiries and Observations Upon the
  Diseases of the Mind* (Rush), 50
Meningitis, 201
Menninger Foundation, 253
Mental age, 176
Mental alienation, 20, 23–24, 164
Mental Health of the School Child, The
  (Wallin), 184
Mental hygiene movement, 228, 230, 243, 246
Mental illness, 223–229, 246–256
  asylums in treatment of, 48–50, 128
  categories of, 50
  feral children, 50–54
  as hereditary defect, 117
  mind cure and, 224–225
  moral management of, 225–229
  poverty and, 223–224
  psychoanalysis and, 247–249
  residential treatment for, 252–255
  therapeutic milieux for, 249–252
Mental modes of attention, 81
Mental retardation, 65, 153–187, 241, 282
  biological bases of, 153–154, 164–165
  cretinism, 23–24, 72–74, 158, 166
  day classes and, 179–187
  differentiation, 168–170

education and, 155–163, 168–174, 179–
  187, 258, 262, 289–290
in Europe, 158–160, 179–181
experiences of children with, 154–155
heredity and, 117, 153–154
idiocy, 168–170, 173, 177, 191
intelligence measures and, 153, 167,
  175–179
male dominance in teachers, 74–75
morons, 177
as pedagogical problem, 72–74
phrenology and, 166–167
in the United States, 160–163, 181–184
war and, 211
Mental tests, 86, 153, 167, 175–179, 217,
  243, 245, 259, 274, 276, 287–288
*Method of Scientific Pedagogy as Applied to
  Infant Education and the Children's
  Houses, The* (Montessori), 72–73
Michigan School for the Blind, 146
Middle Ages, 3, 9, 12, 15–17, 22, 23, 223
Milieutherapy, 250
Mills v. Board of Education, 290
Mind That Found Itself, A (Beers), 228
Minimal brain function, 272
Monasteries
  deaf education in, 29–30
  oblation and, 13–14, 15
Monstres et Prodiges (Paré), 23
Montgomery County (Maryland) Project,
  271–272
Moon Type, 140, 141
Moral education, 172
Moral treatment, x, 3–4, 8, 43, 47–50,
  173–174
Morons, 177
Muscular dystrophy, 202
Music, 125–126, 139
Music therapy, 249
My Left Foot (Brown), 194

National Association of State Boards of
  Education, 294
National Association of the Deaf, 100
National Commission on the Role of the
  School and the Community in
  Improving Adolescent Health, 1
National Institute for the Blind, 140
National Society for Crippled Children,
  220
Native Americans, 153
  blindness and, 123
  tuberculosis among, 196
Nativism, 27–28
Necrophagia, 9
Neglect, 203
Netherlands, 24, 97, 159, 160, 180, 214

Newborn
  abandonment of, 5
  infant mortality, 18, 56, 203, 205
  vision problems of, 123
New England Asylum for the Blind. *See*
  Perkins Institution
New England Institute for the Blind, 108
New Jersey, 85, 129
New York Association for Improving the
  Conditions of the Poor, 197
New York Asylum for Idiots, 161
New York Board of Regents, 76
New York Children's Hospital and Home
  for Idiots, 165
New York City Board of Education, 184,
  197, 203, 204, 207, 208, 219
New York House of Refuge, 162
New York Institution for the Blind, 128, 142
New York Institution for the Deaf and
  Dumb, 112
New York Orthopedic Hospital, 204
New York Point, 141, 142–143
New York School for the Blind, 148
New York Society for the Relief of the
  Ruptured and Crippled, 203–204
Nicholas and Alexandra (Massie and
  Massie), 206
Nobody Nowhere (Williams), 281
Normalization, 149, 159
Normal schools, 68, 74, 75, 77, 217
Norway, 97, 150, 180
Nouveau Christianisme (Saint-Simon), 157
Novum Organum (Bacon), 26
Nursery classes, 220, 295–297

Oblation, 13–14, 15
Occupational therapy, 214–215
Of Such Small Differences (Greenberg), 127,
  142
Ohio Asylum for Idiotic and Imbecilic
  Youth, 161
Ohio Department of Education, 106, 112,
  130, 151–152, 219, 272
Ohio Institution for the Instruction of the
  Blind, 62, 131
Ohio Plan, 220
Only Yesterday (Allen), 79
Opthalmia, 129
Orient State Institute (Ohio), 161–162
Origin of Species (Darwin), 83
Orphans, 68, 159, 229–232, 252
Orthogenetic theory, 270
Orthogenics, 242–245
Orthopedic impairments, 80, 198–200
Orthophrenic treatment, 169
Oswego Normal School (New York), 183
Otitis media, 25, 121

Parapsychology, 225
*PARC et al. v. Commonwealth of
  Pennsylvania*, 290
Parentectomy, 254
Parkhurst Prison for Boys, 234
Pennsylvania, 253
Pennsylvania Institution for the Instruction
  of the Blind, 128
Pennsylvania Training School for
  Feebleminded Children. *See* Elwyn
  Institute
People Will Always Be Kind (Sheed), 199
Perceptual-motor training, 274–277
Periere Society, 104
Perkins Institution, 114, 128, 130, 135,
  138, 140, 142–146, 148, 151
Philanthropy, 26, 58, 60–63, 124, 189
*Philocophus, or The Deafe and Dumbe Man's
  Friend* (Bulwer), 31
Phonoautograph, 101
Phrenology, 166–167
Physical and health impairments, 188–
  222
  causes of, 201–203
  cerebral palsy, 8, 192–195, 214, 220,
    266, 271
  and children in hospitals, 202, 204–207
  cultural imagery concerning, 188–189
  day classes for, 191–192, 219–222
  education and, 204, 207
  epilepsy (convulsive disorder), 5–6, 8–9,
    165, 167, 191–192, 217, 219
  experiences of children with, 189–191
  and hospitals for children, 203–204
  nursing and, 208–209, 212–213
  occupational therapy for, 214–215
  physical therapy for, 193, 213–215
  poliomyelitis, 198–200, 221
  and school health services, 216–218
  settlement houses and, 207–211
  social policy concerning, 200–201
  tuberculosis, 164–165, 191, 195–198,
    201, 202, 221
  war and, 211, 215
Physical modes of expression, 81
Physical therapy, 193, 213–215
Physiological method, 157, 172, 174
Play therapy, 248–249
Plessy v. Ferguson, 292
Poland, 77, 269
Poliomyelitis, 198–200, 221
Politics (Aristotle), 4
Poor Laws (England), 19, 61, 164,
  229
Portugal, 193
Positive Peer Culture (Trieschman,
  Whittaker and Brendtro), 250

Postlingual deafness, 91
Poverty, 18–19, 56–59, 122–123
  almshouses, 57, 91, 123, 129, 190, 237, 252
  and mental illness, 223–224
  and mental retardation, 155
  and physical disorders, 190, 207–211,
    222
Presbycusis, 39, 104
Principles of Psychology (James), 259
Progressivism, 81–82, 84–85, 88–89, 214–
  215, 221, 248
Project Re-ED, 255
Prussia, 180
Psychic Disturbances of Children
  (Emminghaus), 223
Psychoanalysis, 211, 230, 247–249
Psychological family, 249
Psychometric technology, 86, 153, 167,
  175–179, 217, 243, 245, 259, 274,
  276, 287–288
"Pull-out" programs, 88
Purdue Perceptual-Motor Survey, 276
Puritans, 56
Pygmalion (Shaw), 100, 264

Quakers, 49, 58, 64, 68, 123, 128, 163,
  170, 225, 237

Reading problems, 273–274
Reeducation, 254–255
Reformation, 19, 20, 125
Reformation of Schools, A (Comenius), 28
Regular Education Initiative (REI), 293
Rehabilitation Act of 1973, 284
Rehabilitation Act of 1977, 221
Religion
  exceptional children and, 9–12
  protectionism in schooling and, 78–79
Renaissance, 12, 14, 16, 18, 19–22, 24,
  25, 125
Republic, The (Plato), 4
Residential School, The (Frampton and
  Kerney), 148
Rheumatic fever, 219
Rhode Island, 253
Rochester Method, 120
Romanticism, 59, 195
Roman type, 140, 141
Rome, ancient, 3, 5, 7–8, 232
Royal Blind School of Edinburgh, 141
Royal Earlswood Asylum (England), 159
Rubella (German measles), 91

St. Joseph's Institution for the Improved
  Instruction of Deaf Mutes, 112
St. Mary's Hospital (New York), 204
Salpêtrière (Paris), 48, 158
Scarlet fever, 91, 102, 136–137, 201

Schizophrenia, 252
Schooling, 63–89
  for the blind. *See* Blind education
  child study movement, 83–85
  common schools, 75, 77–81, 150, 154,
    195, 239
  compulsory attendance, 63–65, 219, 288
  for the deaf. *See* Deaf education
  eugenics movement in, 82
  exclusion policies, 288–290
  for gifted students, 85–88
  homogenization of students versus
    diverse programs in, 77–81
  Infant schools, 62, 67, 68
  junior high, 80
  kindergarten. *See* Kindergarten
  and learning disabilities. *See* Specific
    learning disabilities
  and mental retardation. *See* Mental
    retardation
  Montessori and, 72–74
  normal schools, 68, 74, 75, 77, 217
  pedagogical innovation in, 66–68
  and physical impairments. *See* Physical
    and health impairments
  professionalization of teaching, 68, 74–77
  progressivism in, 81–82, 84–85, 88–89,
    214–215, 221, 248
  rote instruction in, 65–66
  school health services and, 216–218
  special education, 70–74, 75, 253–256,
    257–262, 266, 292–293
  universal, 63–65
  vocational training, 80
Scotland, 159, 193, 197
Sea Breeze Hospital (New York), 196–197
Seizure disorders, 8–9
Sensorimotor schemata, 275
Sensorium commune, 6–7
Servant of Humanity (Richards), 134
Service coordination, 297
Settlement houses, 207–211
Sexual abuse, 203
Shriners' Hospitals, 204
Sickle cell disease, 202
Sign language, 41, 92, 109–111, 118–121,
  143, 258
Sisters of Charity, 75, 203, 212
Smith College, 244
Social Contract, The (Rousseau), 27
Social Security Act of 1935, 221, 231
Social Security Amendments of 1965, 246
Society for Crippled Children, 193
Somebody Somewhere (Williams), 281–282
Sonia Shankman Orthogenic School, 251, 253
Spain, 23, 24
  deaf education in, 29–30, 35, 96
Spastics, 193

Specific learning disabilities, 3, 257–285
Attention Deficit Disorder/Attention
Deficit Hyperactivity Disorder (ADD/
ADHA), 222, 270, 272, 279–280,
283–285, 298
autism, 252, 266, 279–283, 298, 300
communication disorders, 262–267
fragile X (Martin-Bell) syndrome, 283
language impairment, 267–277
parent advocacy and, 277–280
special education and, 257–262
tuberous sclerosis, 283
Speech-language pathology, 267
Speechreading, 104
Speech therapy, 33
*Stability and Change in Human
Characteristics* (Bloom), 296
Stanford Revision of the Binet Scale, 176, 177
Starr Commonwealth (Michigan), 250–251
State Industrial School for Girls, 239–240
Stepmothers, 14
Sterilization, 168
Stewart Institution (Ireland), 159
Strauss syndrome, 270–271, 272, 284
Strephosymbolia, 274
Stuttering, 262–263
Stuttering and Lisping (Scripture), 265
Sunbeam Circle, 219–220
Superintendents of the American Institutions
for the Improvement of Idiots and Feeble
Minded Children, 160
Surdopedagogy (education for the deaf), 269
Surdus Loquens (Amman), 33
Sweden, 75, 97, 127, 180, 216
Switzerland, 23–24, 27, 159, 166, 180, 208
Syphilis, 164–165

Talks to Teachers (James), 260
Taylor Arithmetic Frame, 126
Teacher-counselors, 250, 255
*Teacher's Manual for the Education of the
Blind* (Klein), 124
Telecommunication Devices for the Deaf
(TDDs), 101
Telephone, 113
Teletypewriter (TTY), 101
Temperaments, 7
Temple of My Familiar, The (Walker), 10
Temple School (Boston), 69–70
Tennessee, 131
Texas School for the Deaf, 120
Token economies, 173, 271–272
Total Communication (TC), 95, 120
Trachoma, 123, 138, 202
Tracking, 86, 178
Transcendalists, 70
Transdisciplinary-team approach, 297–298
Treatise of Human Nature, A (Hume), 26

Treatise on Disease of Ear and Hearing
(Itard), 54
Treatise on Insanity, A (Pinel), 48
Trephination, 5–6, 8, 9
Tuberculosis, 164–165, 191, 195–198,
201, 202, 221
Tuberous sclerosis, 283
Tuke's Retreat, 108, 228
Twenty Years at Hull House (Addams),
209–210
Typholopedagogy (education for the
blind), 269

Ungraded classes, 182, 245–246, 289
United Cerebral Palsy Association
(UCPA), 193, 220
United States
asylums in, 49–50
blind education, 127–132
deaf education, 35–36, 291–292
mental retardation, 160–163, 181–184
social policy for children in, 55–59
U.S. Department of Education (USDOE), 293
U.S. Department of the Interior, Office of
Handicapped Children, 180
Utopia (More), 20

Vineland Training School for
Feebleminded Girls and Boys, 153–
154, 182, 216, 243, 244
Visible Speech, 31, 100, 102, 112
Visual efficiency, 152
Vocational training, 80

Wales, 77
Walker in the City, A (Kazin), 264
Wars
brain injuries following, 267, 268–270
children as victims of, 211, 215
Washington Research Project, 288–289
Wayward Youth (Aichhorn), 251
Wet-nurses, 5, 14–15, 21
When the Mind Hears (Clerc), 96–97
When the Mind Hears (Lane), 29
White House Conferences on Children and
Youth, 57, 200, 219, 247, 286, 290
Whole-language instruction, 53
Wisconsin, 266, 288
Witch-Cult in Western Europe (Murray), 20
Worcester Asylum for the Insane, 108
Worcester College for the Blind, 126
Worcester State Hospital (Massachusetts),
225–228
Working with Children in Hospitals (Plank), 206
World Health Organization, 206
World War II, 215, 267, 269

Yugoslavia, 77

About the Authors

Philip L. Safford, Ph.D., is Professor of Special Education at Kent State University. His publications include three books on special education, and he is co-author of a new text, *Human Diversity in Education: An Integrative Approach*. He is editor of *Early Childhood Special Education*, Volume 5 of the Yearbook of Early Childhood Education (Teachers College Press, 1993).

Elizabeth J. Safford has a Master of Library Science degree and also a Master of Arts degree in History, with emphasis in Historical Editing. Her background has included research librarian experience, editorial assistant positions with *The New England Quarterly* and *World Almanac*, and development work for the Eye Research Institute and Boston University. She is currently on the editorial staff of *The Journal of Orthopaedic Research*.